The Spiritual Wisdom of the Gospels for Christian Preachers and Teachers

Year A

On Earth as It Is in Heaven

John Shea

LITURGICAL PRESS

Collegeville, Minnesota

www.litpress.org

Cover design by Joachim Rhoades, O.S.B.

1   2   3   4   5   6   7   8

Library of Congress Cataloging-in-Publication Data

Shea, John, 1941–
    The spiritual wisdom of the Gospels for Christian preachers and teachers
/ John Shea.
        p. cm.
    Includes bibliographical references and index.
    ISBN 0-8146-2913-X (Year A : pbk. : alk. paper)
        1. Bible. N.T. Gospels—Criticism, interpretation, etc.   2. Bible.
N.T. Gospels—Homiletical use. 3. Lectionary preaching. I. Title.

BS2555.52.S54 2004
251'.6—dc22   2003025635

Contents

Acknowledgments

This four-volume set, *The Spiritual Wisdom of the Gospels for Christian Preachers and Teachers*, has been a long time in the making. Along the way, there have been many collaborators, people whose critical comments and ongoing support have kept me thinking, meditating, and writing about Gospel texts. Although it is impossible to mention every student or workshop participant who asked a question or volunteered a comment that improved my understanding and articulation, I am thankful to all of them.

In particular, there have been some key organizations, congregations, and people who have told me, "This is useful," "Keep doing it," "Stay here," "Talk to us," "What do you need," and "When are you ever going to put this stuff in print." This is what writers yearn to hear, so I am grateful:

To Lilly Endowment, Inc., especially to Fred Hofheinz, who saw the contribution a spiritual-literary interpretation of Gospel texts would make to Christian preachers and teachers and graciously and generously funded this project.

To Rev. Jack Wall, Roger Hughes, Al Hellwig, Bob Kolatorwicz, and the staff and community of Old St. Patrick's Church who pioneered Awakenings, an early morning group of Gospel lovers, and became the home base for this project.

To the ecumenical advisory group: Rev. Wayne Priest of Queen of All Saints Basilica, Rev. Dean Francis of First United Methodist Church of Evanston, Rev. Paul Koch of Ebenezer Lutheran Church, Canon Linda Bartholomew of Christ Church Cathedral, and Rev. Carol Allen of Fourth Presbyterian Church. These creative Christian preachers and teachers from the Catholic, Methodist, Lutheran, Episcopalian, and Presbyterian traditions took their time and focused their talent on reading and evaluating the Sunday-by-Sunday spiritual commentaries and teachings.

To Rev. Andrew Greeley, John Cusick, Edward Beck and many others who offered insights I eagerly received.

To Robert Demke, who gave much-needed computer advice and administrative assistance.

To Grace Lutheran Congregation and School, for their gracious hospitality.

To Peter Dwyer, director, Mark Twomey, Rev. Cyril Gorman, O.S.B., Rev. Linda Maloney, Colleen Stiller, and all the staff at the Liturgical Press for their interest in this project and their expertise in helping to implement it.

Finally, to Anne, companion, lover, wife, friend of the Spirit.

Unless otherwise noted, Scripture quotations are from the New Revised Standard Version Bible: Catholic Edition. Copyright © 1989, 1993, Division of Christian Education of the National Council of the Churches of Christ in the United States of America. Used by license of the copyright holder. All rights reserved.

Where noted, Scripture texts in this work are taken from the *New American Bible with Revised New Testament and Revised Psalms.* Copyright © 1991, 1986, 1970 Confraternity of Christian Doctrine, Washington, D.C., and are used by permission of the copyright owner. All rights reserved. No part of the *New American Bible* may be reproduced in any form without permission in writing from the copyright owner.

Where noted, Scripture texts in this work are taken from the King James Version of the Bible, available on the Internet at http://www.bibles.net/ (accessed March 5, 2004).

Introductory words that are added to the Gospel pericopes are based on what is found in *Lectionary for Worship*, Ritual Edition, (Minneapolis: Augsburg Fortress, 1996), a presentation of the *Revised Common Lectionary.* Copyright © 1992 by the Consultation on Common Texts (CCT), 1522 K Street NW, Suite 1000, Washington, D.C. 20005-1202. All rights reserved.

Pages 12, 126, 211, 236, and 317: Excerpts from the Gospel of Thomas trans. Stephen Patterson and Marvin Meyer in *The Complete Gospels: Annotated Scholars Version,* ed. Robert J. Miller, rev. ed., Sonoma, Calif.: Polebridge Press, 1994. Reprinted with permission.

Page 40: Excerpt of "What Am I Leaving Out?" from *Tales of a Magic Monastery* by Theophane the Monk. Copyright © 1981 by Crossroad. All rights reserved. Reprinted with permission.

Page 41: Excerpt from *A Little Book on the Human Shadow* by Robert Bly; edited by William Booth (San Francisco: Harper & Row). Reprinted with permission from HarperCollins Publishers, Inc. Copyright © 1988 by Robert Bly.

Page 71: Fourth stanza of "Vacillation" reprinted for sale in the U.S.A. with the permission of Scribner, an imprint of Simon & Schuster Adult Publishing Group, from *The Collected Works of W. B. Yeats,* vol. 1, *The Poems, Revised,* edited by Richard J. Finneran. Copyright © 1933 by The MacMillan Company; copyright renewed © 1961 by Bertha Georgie Yeats. Reprinted for sale outside of the U.S.A. with the permission of AP Watt Ltd. on behalf of Michael B. Yeats.

Pages 95–96: "Tickets for a Prayer Wheel" reprinted from *Tickets for a Prayer Wheel* by Annie Dillard, by permission of the University of Missouri Press. Copyright © 1974 by Annie Dillard.

Page 117: *Rumi—Fragments, Ecstasies,* translated by Daniel Liebert, Omega Publications (N.Y.), 1999. All rights reserved. Reprinted with permission.

Page 224: Selected lines of "The Swan" from *Selected Poems of Rainer Maria Rilke,* edited and translated by Robert Bly. Copyright © 1981 by Robert Bly. Reprinted with permission from HarperCollins Publishers, Inc.

Page 224: Selected lines of "Pax" by D. H. Lawrence from *The Complete Poems of D. H. Lawrence,* by D. H. Lawrence, edited by V. de Sola Pinto and F. W. Roberts, copyright © 1964, 1971 by Angelo Ravagli and C. M. Weekley, Executors of the Estate of Frieda Lawrence Ravagli. Used by permission of Viking Penguin, a division of Penguin Group (U.S.A.) Inc. In the United Kingdom, copyright © Laurence Pollinger, Ltd., London. Reprinted with permission.

Page 299: Excerpts from the English translation of *Rite of Baptism for Children* copyright © 1969, International Committee on English in the Liturgy, Inc. All rights reserved.

Pages 308–9: Story and excerpt from *How Can I Help?: Stories and Reflections on Service* by Ram Dass and Paul Gorman; New York: Alfred A. Knopf, 1987. Copyright © 1985 by Ram Dass and Paul Gorman. Reprinted with permission.

Preface

Writing this Resource

The Spiritual Wisdom of the Gospels for Christian Preachers and Teachers is a set of four books based on the Sunday Gospel readings in *The Revised Common Lectionary* and The Roman Missal's *Lectionary for Mass*. There will be one volume for each of the liturgical cycles: A, B, and C. The fourth volume will explore the Gospel texts that are suggested for feasts, funerals, and weddings.

These books have a triple audience. The primary audience is Christian preachers and teachers who use the Gospel texts of the Lectionary cycle in their preaching and teaching. The secondary audience is all Christians who consult and meditate on the Gospels as a guide for their lives. The third audience is spiritual seekers of all faiths and no faiths who are drawn to the realistic spiritual wisdom of the Gospels. I hope that the books of this series will be a help to all three audiences.

Preachers and Teachers

Over ten years ago, Rev. Wayne Prist of the Center for Development in Ministry thought Lectionary based preachers and teachers should gather before Advent, Lent, and a section of Ordinary Time to review the Sunday readings. Although many excellent Scripture scholars were available to facilitate and resource this project, Rev. Prist wanted something different than scholarly exegesis. "I think we should focus on the personal, preachable, and teachable meanings of the texts." He asked if I wanted to give it a try. I said, "Why not?"

But I also said I would have to limit myself to the Gospel texts. I knew this would result in a lopsided approach, the type both Scripture and liturgical scholars lament. However, this was not because I preferred the Gospels to the other books of the Bible the Lectionary uses. Nor was I subtly advocating for fewer scriptural readings for Sunday liturgies. The reason for the Gospel restriction was both personal and practical.

Personally, I had meditated on Gospel texts for years and, quite simply, I felt that I had more to say about them than other texts. Practically, the days were scheduled from 9:00 a.m. to 3:00 p.m. If we were going to cover six to nine Sundays, we had to set limits. So we began a series of three days each year, one each for Advent/Christmas, Lent, and Ordinary Time. The title of the series was "Gospel Food for Hungry People."

The days were well attended and are still going on. There have also been many spin-offs. I have given weeklong and weekend retreats on Gospel stories. I developed a course, Gospel Narratives and Spiritual Development, that I taught at Loyola University of Chicago, Assumption University of Windsor, and Retreats International at Notre Dame. I have also given workshops on using Gospel stories in preaching and teaching to Lutheran, Methodist, Episcopalian, Mennonite, Presbyterian, and Catholic clergy. It is out of these experiences of talking and listening that I gradually became clearer about what I was doing and what would be helpful.

Cards on the Table—Face up

At one of the workshops on learning to listen and tell Gospel stories, a participant asked, "What are your basic assumptions when you come to the Gospels?" Seeing my own assumptions accurately was no easy task. I am usually too busy acting out of them to notice them. But I tried to articulate some of the "pre-understandings" I brought to the texts. I concluded with, "There, the cards are on the table." He responded, "Yes, but they are face down."

I want to try to turn a few of the cards face up.

I am a storyteller, and I have always gravitated toward the literary forms that are present in the Gospels, in particular the narrative structure of the whole Gospel and the narrative structures of the specific stories within the Gospels. So I tried to give the stories a close reading, paying careful attention to the interplay of plot and character. I saw that Gospels stories had particular characteristics that encouraged reading them in a particular way. I outlined these characteristics and gave interpretations of specific stories in *Gospel Light: Jesus Stories for Spiritual Consciousness* (New York: Crossroad, 1998).

But my ultimate interest and the interest of the preachers and teachers were not literary. We were interested in theological and spiritual meanings that could connect with contemporary life. Attending to the literary form had to be a means to that end. I found that if I focused on the mindsets of the characters and how Jesus complimented, critiqued, praised, and excoriated those mindsets in the light of his own mindset, I could uncover the raw material of spiritual development.

This raw material was the images, ideas, attitudes, and actions that either opened or closed the mind to the Divine Spirit and either facilitated or blocked the flow of spirit into creative speech and action. Therefore, the shorthand name for this endeavor is a "literary-spiritual interpretation." I have developed this approach at length in the introductory essay to this resource book, "Preaching and Teaching the Gospels as Spiritual Wisdom." I encourage all who would consult the Sunday-by-Sunday pieces to take the time to read this essay. That essay puts all the cards on the table—face up.

In the Marketplace

I knew that eventually I wanted to write resource books for preachers and teachers using this approach. However, when I looked at the market, I found there was no shortage of Lectionary-based resources. Some rehearsed the latest academic positions on scriptural texts, providing updated historical, philological, and theological information. Often they geared this information toward "themes" that would be appropriate for preaching and teaching. Some were very process oriented, helping the preacher or teacher attend to the text through carefully worded questions and imaginative exercises. Some developed theological themes that integrated the three readings, and then positioned the three readings within the larger liturgical season. Some strove to integrate the scriptural text into the liturgical movement as a whole. Some enumerated homily hints and teaching aids that would make the text "come alive." Some supplied stories, individual examples, and cultural analyses that could be used in preaching and teaching. Some went beyond the role of a resource and created a homily or teaching that the preacher or teacher could read to congregations or students. These resources addressed different concerns depending on what they considered important and helpful to the preacher and teacher.

Although the type of resource I envisioned did not fit any of these categories, I learned a great deal from consulting them. They did many things remarkably well, and that meant I did not have to "reinvent the wheel" and do the same material. I envisioned preachers, teachers, and spiritually interested people having a number of Lectionary-based resources on their book shelves. I wanted to provide one more book that would complement but not compete with the type of resources that were already out there. The intended audiences would correlate what they needed with what each resource had to give. The ultimate goal was to be helpful.

A Middle Ground Resource

I wrote a proposal to the Lilly Endowment to fund the writing of a Lectionary-based resource that focused on the spiritual wisdom of the Gospels. This resource would be written in consultation with an ecumenical advisory board (Catholic, Lutheran, Presbyterian, Methodist, and Episcopalian). They generously funded the proposal, and I began writing a resource that I characterized as a middle ground.

On the one hand, I do not enter into the scholarly debates on the meaning of texts. I am not a Scripture scholar, but I am a voracious reader of Scripture scholarship. So scholarship has always been consulted, but it stays offstage. It is deep background for the close reading of the text. Nor do I provide instructions in hermeneutics. I do not try to coach preachers and teachers in the art of literary-spiritual interpretation. As important as this skill is, it is beyond the definite and limited help this resource offers.

On the other hand, I do not give explicit instructions on *how* to use the spiritual wisdom of these Gospel texts in preaching and teaching. This resource book starts a process without ending it. It stays a considerable distance from concrete acts of preaching and teaching. It does not seek to structure stories and thoughts in ways that make for effective preaching and teaching. As important as this concern with the actual delivery of the spiritual wisdom of the Gospel is, it is beyond the limited and definite help this resource offers.

Therefore, the middle ground was between remote exegesis and actual delivery. What I wanted to create was substantive pieces of Gospel spiritual wisdom. These pieces would flow from the specific Sunday Gospels, develop spiritual perspectives, and address contemporary situations. The wager was: if these pieces were sufficiently intelligent and relevant, preachers and teachers would find a way to use them.

Writing the Middle Ground

However, as I wrote this middle ground between scholarship and actual preaching and teaching, it proved to be bumpy territory. I quickly decided that each Sunday piece should have two parts. The first part would be a commentary that gives a close reading of the Gospel text from a literary-spiritual perspective. I wanted a firm grounding in the Word. The second part would be a teaching that develops a spiritual insight that had surfaced in the reading of the text. The Gospels initiate spiritual wisdom, but they seldom fully flesh it out. This part would try to bring the spiritual wisdom of the Gospels into dialogue with contemporary life. However, as I actually began writing, both parts underwent development.

Commentaries have been around a long time and are plentiful. They also have a reputation for being repetitive. I knew I did not want to rehearse the standard material, but I found myself re-saying things that had been said many times before. Nor did I want to be pulled into scholarly debates and take sides. Yet the urge to join the discussion was great.

The very richness of the Gospel stories and texts also became a temptation. Every symbol cried out for elaboration; every image begged for reflection; every single-sentence idea yearned to mature into a paragraph. I had caught the writer's disease: "This is too interesting not to include." The commentary section became scattered and unwieldy and, as a result, unhelpful.

So I was forced to discipline myself and choose a consistent path through the text. I could not consider everything. I had to make a choice for one reading and unfold it in a brief but insightful way. However, discipline has never been easy for me. Although I have tried to be lean, there are some Sundays when the commentary bulges. This is especially true for those Sundays with long Gospel readings, especially the Johannine stories of the woman at the well, the man born blind, and Lazarus on the third, fourth, and fifth Sundays of Cycle A. But, in general, the rich overflow of the text was left on the cutting room floor.

The second part is a teaching that develops a spiritual theme from the Gospel and connects it to contemporary life. At first, I tried to be consistent from Sunday to Sunday. This teaching part would always have the same elements—an experience told in story form, a reflection on the experience, a connection to some doctrinal or ethical piece of Christian faith, and, where possible, a tie-in to a specific Christian denominational tradition. But I soon realized this was not a helpful harness but a straight jacket. It did not allow the movement of the mind or inspiration of the will.

So the form of the teachings became very diverse. The forms differ from Sunday to Sunday. Some Sundays I elaborate a spiritual teaching in the form of ideas. On other Sundays stories and poems predominantly carry the teaching. Sometimes there is cultural commentary that uncovers commonly held assumptions that either contradict or support the spiritual wisdom of the Gospels. Sometimes I have inserted a personal note that I hope is not so idiosyncratic that others cannot appreciate it. Although the teaching stayed rooted in the Gospel, it grew in many different ways.

So this middle ground resource became smoother terrain by tightening the commentary and loosening the teaching. This combination seemed to work. The ecumenical advisory group commented: "It got the ball rolling," "It gave me the idea I needed," "It showed me something I didn't see," "It made me think more deeply," and "It made me read the Gospel differently." These resource pieces were doing something without doing everything.

Logistics

There are some practical issues about the layout of this book. The audience for this resource is ecumenical. Therefore, the Sunday Gospel readings are taken from both *The Revised Common Lectionary (RCL)* and the *Lectionary for Mass* of the Roman Missal *(LM)*. For most of the Sundays the readings in both these lectionaries are the same. In that case, the spiritual commentary and teaching is the same. On some Sundays there is more text recommended either by the *RCL* or *LM*. For example, on the Thirtieth Sunday in Ordinary Time the *LM* has Matthew 22:34-40 and the *RCL* for Proper 25, the same Sunday, has Matthew 22:34-46. In that case and all the others cases like it, the extended text is included and receives commentary. But the teaching section reflects only the text that is shared by both lectionaries.

There are some specific situations that need comment: (1) In the *RCL* the same text, Matthew 7:21-29, is recommended for both the Ninth Sunday after Epiphany and Proper 4. It can be found under the Ninth Sunday after Epiphany. (2) The Transfiguration story (Matt 17:1-9) is the reading for Transfiguration Sunday in the *RCL* and the Second Sunday of Lent in the *LM*. It can be found under Transfiguration Sunday. (3) On the Fifth Sunday in Ordinary Time, *LM* has Matthew 5:13-16 and the *RCL*, for the Fifth Sunday after Epiphany, has Matthew 5:13-20. But verses 17-20 are included in the *LM* Sunday reading for the Sixth Sunday in Ordinary Time. Therefore, verses 17-20 are commented on in the text for the Sixth Sunday in Ordinary Time. (4) On the Twelfth Sunday in Ordinary Time the *RCL* has Matthew 10:26-33 and the *RCL* for Proper 7, the same Sunday, has Matthew 10:24-39. Therefore, the text for the Twelfth Sunday of Ordinary Time and Proper 7 begins with verse 24 and ends with verse 33. Verses 10:37-39 are included in the text for the Thirteenth Sunday of Ordinary Time and Proper 8. (5) The Sunday text for Proper 13 includes Matthew 13:31-33, but those verses have already been included in the commentary for the Sixteenth Sunday in Ordinary Time.

As mentioned above, the full scope of this set, *The Spiritual Wisdom of the Gospels for Christian Preachers and Teachers,* will not only include volumes on Cycles A, B, and C. It also includes a fourth volume on feasts, funerals, and weddings. This volume works with the Gospel texts suggested for these liturgies. Therefore, Christmas and the Sundays to the feast of the Epiphany, all of Holy Week, from Palm Sunday to Easter Sunday, Pentecost, Holy Trinity Sunday, and the Marian feasts will be in the fourth volume. The Gospels for those feasts are not included in this volume on Cycle A.

Circling the Hat

There is a spiritual exercise entitled: circling the hat. A hat is placed in the center of a circle of people. Each person is asked to describe the hat from the vantage point of their place in the circle. As the circle moves, people see the same hat but from a different perspective. When the hat has been completely circumnavigated, there is a full and well-rounded appreciation of the hat. In one way people have been looking at the same hat, but in another way they have been seeing it just a little differently.

In working with the Gospel texts of Cycle A, I had a "circling the hat" feeling. St. Matthew has some themes that figure regularly in what he has to say. He revisits them throughout his Gospel. For example, he stresses the need for personal initiative in appropriating the teachings of Jesus. He says it forthrightly in the images of storm, rock, and sand on the Ninth Sunday in Ordinary Time; he intimates it with the symbol of a wedding garment on the Sunday of Proper 23; he returns to it with lamps and oil on the Thirty-Second Sunday in Ordinary Time; and it is not far from Peter's failed attempt to walk on the waves in the story for the Sunday of Proper 14. It is the same theme, but each text gives it a distinctive treatment.

The same is true with the readings from St. John on the Sundays after Easter. They circle around how Jesus' death and resurrection affect his relationship with the Father and with his disciples. They explore it on the Second Sunday of Easter with the resurrection narratives of the appearances of Jesus to the disciples and to Thomas, on the Fourth Sunday of Easter with images of sheep and sheepfold, and on the Fifth and Sixth Sundays of Easter with direct spiritual teaching about the stronger-than-death communion of the Father, the Son, and the disciples. Each Sunday we circle the hat, each Sunday seeing a nuance we had not previously appreciated.

This circle-the-hat approach has strong backing in spiritual traditions. In Jewish spiritual teaching there is the story of the Rabbi who began to tell a story in a sermon. A man stood up and said, "We've heard that one." The Rabbi responded, "Did you pray today?" The man answered, "Yes." The Rabbi said, "Did you pray yesterday?" The man again answered, "Yes." Then the Rabbi said, "If you prayed yesterday, why did you pray today?" Sacred texts and their insights are not about conveying information or even communicating knowledge. They are more like prayer. Each time we ponder them they bring us into the presence of God. It is salutary to circle significant spiritual themes, appreciating them from many angles.

Jelaluddin Rumi, the Sufi mystic and poet, had a different reason for returning to sacred texts and themes. He compared sacred stories to bath water. Both were meant to mediate fire to the person. The bath water brought physical fire to the skin; the stories brought spiritual fire to soul. So Rumi thought we should enjoy sacred stories and themes because they cleanse us "with a secret we sometimes see—and then not."

Spiritual wisdom is a sometimes thing. It is not our conventional way of thinking, and so it appears to us as a secret. When our eyes are cleansed by a teaching, they are not completely opened. They close again. We see the secret—and then not. So we have to return and grasp it again. When we meet sacred texts and themes for a second or third time, we welcome them as old friends who will converse with us and bring us their ancient wisdom in a new way.

Occasionally, in the teachings that accompany the Sunday texts, I found myself circling the hat. Although the majority of the teachings work with a different idea or theme each Sunday, there is some overlap. For example, I circled the hat of calling Jesus both brother and Lord on the feast of the Baptism of the Lord and the Thirty-Second Sunday in Ordinary Time, Proper 27. On both the Second Sunday and Fifth Sunday of Easter the mystery of our communion with the departed is unfolded. How we move from being a "hearer of the Word" to a "doer of the Word" is tracked on the Ninth Sunday, the Twenty-Eighth Sunday, and Thirty-Second Sunday of Ordinary Time, Propers 4, 23, and 27. There are other examples of overlapping themes. But they are not repetitious. Each treatment sees the idea or theme from a different perspective, from another stopping place on the circle.

On Earth as It Is in Heaven

There is no way to summarize the spiritual wisdom in the Gospel readings for Cycle A. It ranges widely, touching in original ways on many concerns. Also, it is profound. It demands pondering, luring the ones contemplating these texts far beyond conventional ways of thinking.

But there is a key idea, an underlying perspective that is important to comprehend. This perspective is captured in the phrase that I have used as the title for this volume of spiritual commentary and teaching, *On Earth as It Is in Heaven.*

As every Christian knows, this phrase appears in the Lord's Prayer. But not every Christian realizes how startling and foundational it is. In the context of the Gospel, the Lord's Prayer is both Jesus' personal way of praying and the prayer he teaches to his disciples. Therefore, it is the way he transmits his interior consciousness to his followers. If a large part of the portrait of the disciples in the Gospels is that they lack understanding, much of it can be traced to their inability to "get into" this prayer. The mind of Christ is available in the prayer, but it is not easy to put on that mind. The structure of Jesus' awareness is offered to all, but it is a strange offering.

The ordinary way we think is that we are earthlings. We are a bundle of needs on every level. We scramble for food, clothing, and shelter. We seek out social security and position. We need to be affirmed on a regular basis and told we have dignity and worth. A successful life is one where needs are successfully met. The spiritual wisdom of Jesus acknowledges these multiple hungers and thirsts and then proceeds to go in another direction, "stepping over" these blatant, screaming facts.

Jesus does not begin on earth. His prayer begins with the consciousness of his communion with God and all creation. He is aware of his solidarity with all there is (Our), and that he and everything else are receiving life from a loving Ultimate Source (Father), a Source that transcends creation (in heaven) even as it intimately sustains it. In short, his awareness is structured by a sense that he is the Son of God.

When he tells the disciples to pray in this way, he is encouraging them to begin in the same place, as sons and daughters of a loving transcendent reality.

If we can cultivate this heaven consciousness, it will drive us down to earth with the agenda of the Father. We will stay in touch with his name, be energized by his will, and pursue his kingdom. We are not earthlings praying to heaven for our needs. We are heaven's children with the clay of earth in our hands, molding it into the world God envisions. The more disciples pray this prayer, the more they enter into this Christic identity of incarnating Spirit into the affairs of earth.

Therefore, to say "on earth as it is in heaven" presupposes we have a heaven consciousness. But this transcendent awareness is not easily attained or sustained. So the spiritual wisdom of Cycle A often takes the form of reminding people who they really are, telling them how not to get caught in lesser identities, warning them about the need to personally work at this, and showing them how metanoia (a change of mind) is the only doorway into the kingdom of heaven.

This heaven consciousness unfolds into earthly actions. But what actions are the ones that carry the divine will and the divine intentions for the new organization of human life onto the earth? So the spiritual wisdom often takes the form of telling people to resist certain types of behaviors, telling them how to redefine family and neighbor relations, teaching them how to relate to the demands of the state and the pieties of religious traditions, and reminding them what is at stake in how they live their lives.

On Earth as It Is in Heaven symbolizes the good news project of Jesus, and of anyone who would ponder the spiritual wisdom of the Cycle A readings. All—Christian preachers and teachers, Christians who want to enter more deeply into the spiritual wisdom of the Gospels, and spiritual seekers of all faiths and no faiths—are welcomed.

Introduction

Preaching and Teaching the Gospels
as Spiritual Wisdom

Summary: Preaching and teaching the Gospels as spiritual wisdom is a wager. It presupposes Christian congregations and individual believers are ready to listen and learn. They are interested in developing themselves spiritually, but they are not quite sure what it entails or how to go about it. This combination of interest and ignorance opens them to the vision of spiritual transformation in the Gospels. A key feature of this vision is spiritual wisdom. Spiritual wisdom is the catalytic agent. It churns the mind and begins the process of change. When preachers and teachers present the Gospels as spiritual wisdom, they facilitate and resource a process of spiritual transformation.

Therefore, this introduction has three sections.

    I. The Spiritually Interested Yet Spiritually Illiterate Culture
    II. The Vision of Spiritual Transformation in the Gospels
    III. How Gospel Texts Work As Spiritual Wisdom

These sections provide the background for the major focus of this resource book, a spiritual commentary and teaching on each Sunday Gospel for Cycle A of the *Lectionary for Mass* of the Roman Missal and *The Revised Common Lectionary*.

I. The Spiritually Interested Yet Spiritually Illiterate Culture

"It's the only chance we have."

The uncle of a young man who was just ordained a priest made this remark. He was introduced to the professor of homiletics at the reception after the ordination. The introduction was a simple, "Fr. Peterson teaches preaching at the seminary."

And the uncle said, without pausing, "It's the only chance we have."

"What is?" asked Fr. Peterson.

"You know, liturgies, preaching, that kind of stuff."

"Chance for what?"

"You know, God, sacred, Spirit, that kind of stuff."

1

Many people would disagree with this uncle's novice foray into liturgy and theology. They would point out that "God, sacred, Spirit, that kind of stuff" is not confined to liturgies and preaching. The spiritual dimension of the human person and its grounding in God can come into awareness through any human experience. People experience their souls and the Divine Source of their souls through the experiences of love, protest, parenting, play, work, communion with nature, the passionate pursuit of truth, suffering, moral ambiguity, etc. This man is putting too much pressure on liturgy, particularly on preaching. He should wake up to wider possibilities.

However, the uncle, directly but inarticulately, is pointing to an expectation. He is spiritually interested, but he does not get many chances to explore that interest. He expects his church-going experience to acknowledge and develop this part of him that is not the explicit focus of his work and personal life. I do not want to make too much of this brief and flimsy conversational exchange, but I do not think the uncle is alone. Many churchgoers are spiritually interested but spiritually uninformed, and they are looking for wisdom and guidance to spiritually develop.

There is always a need to characterize both the people to whom Christian faith is being preached and taught and Christian faith itself. The point of the characterization is to find a common ground where people and faith meet. Of course, this characterization will always be partial. The people and the faith will always be more than their portrayals. The characterization only provides a working model. But a working model is necessary if preaching and teaching are to be clearly focused and if people are to be consistently addressed. The wisdom about using characterizations is to value them for what they can provide but to hold them lightly and not become overly attached to them.

A potentially useful characterization of contemporary people begins with the wager that they are spiritually interested. Many cultural commentators talk about a widespread hunger for the spiritual. This hunger is found in an intense way within religious traditions, but it is not confined to churches, synagogues, mosques, and temples. Organized religion may be the home of the spiritual, but it is not its exclusive dwelling place. Interest in the spiritual is emerging in the corporate world, in the athletic sphere, in areas of social justice, in the struggles of community organizing, in particular movements (e.g., ecological, feminist, elder), and in health care. This interest also spans generations. It is present among the elderly, the baby boomers, Generation X, and even children.

This across-the-board interest suggests the image of America may be shifting from a secular culture to a spiritually interested culture.

Why is there an expanding interest in the spiritual?

Some commentators point to positive influences: contact with Eastern religions and spiritual philosophies, an increase in scientific knowledge that leads into mystery rather than away from it, a mind-boggling awareness of the reach of the cosmos, a deepened sense of our symbiotic relationship to the earth, a commitment to social justice and the well-being of all people, etc. Most people could add to this list both personal experiences and other cultural developments that stimulate interest in the spiritual.

Other cultural observers see the interest in the spiritual as a response to negative experiences. People are reaching for the spiritual as a way to reclaim dignity and purpose in the midst of fears, moral failures, and a general sense that "things are out of control." According to these observers, the underlying energy of contemporary spiritual interest is the ambiguous and destructive events of our times: the ongoing horrors of wars that have demonstrated an increased capacity for violence, runaway technology that dehumanizes people even as it claims to advance their causes, economic uncertainty, terrorism, viral epidemics, increasing disparity between the rich and the poor, rampant and illegal greed in the business community, moral laxity among the leaders of the world, pervasive narcissism and restlessness, the frantic pace of life, the debunking of the myth of progress, etc. Most people could add to this list both personal experiences and other cultural developments that profoundly worry them, that make them pause and consider the possibility of the spiritual.

Traditionally, both positive and negative experiences have awakened people to the spiritual. Thus, in any given individual, the interest in the spiritual may emerge both as a recoiling response to certain negative experiences and as an inclination to pursue certain positive experiences. Positive and negative experiences work together to stimulate interest in the spiritual.

This contemporary interest does not signal one more period of "religious revival." It is not an "idea whose time has come—again." This interest, at least in some of its manifestations, is not in the spiritual life in itself, especially if this life is played off against physical, mental, and social life. Rather it is in the spiritual transformation of life as a whole. When the spiritual is understood and integrated into one individual consciousness or the consciousness of a community, it changes the quality of physical, mental, and social life. In this way, the spiritual is not a competitive interest. It complements and reenergizes the so-called "worldly interests," and the hope is that it will transform them in a way that will be beneficial to the next stage of human evolution.

This extensive interest in the spiritual has spurred some commentators to understand the spiritual as a permanent dimension of the human. It is a birthright, a raw potential that is hardwired into each person. It can be ignored and dismissed, but it cannot be erased. As with every given of the human condition, we must accept it as part of ourselves and develop its abilities. In the past this effort of spiritual development was pursued by only a few or restricted to the elite of organized religions. Today more are interested—even if they are interested only on their own terms.

However, this interest is not necessarily well informed. It is an open-ended sense that life has a deeper meaning and purpose than its physical, psychological, and social aspects promise. This intuitional sense of the spiritual turns people into searchers and shoppers, and the marketplace is glutted with products and services. Although "casting about" is a legitimate way to pursue the interest, some of the services and products come with *caveat emptor* labels. There is a great deal of false advertisement about what the spiritual is and how it can be developed. In particular, there are many half-baked spiritual ideas that cause confusion and, if people take them to heart, contribute to serious mental and social suffering. This is a time of both spiritual interest and spiritual illiteracy.

At its best, this spiritual illiteracy simply indicates innocence and unfamiliarity. It signals the spiritual is unexplored territory for most people, and this is to be expected. The forerunner of the current spiritual interest was secularity. Secular consciousness was a sustained focus on the fascinating adventures and urgent problems in the physical, social, and mental realms. However, theologians always pointed out that this focus was a severe restriction of consciousness. It pushed the spiritual dimension to the periphery or completely off the screen of consciousness. Secular awareness was another example of what G. K. Chesterton said about George Bernard Shaw: "He is like the Venus de Milo. What there is of him is perfect." What there was of secular consciousness was fine. The problem was that the spiritual was missing. So when the missing spiritual enters awareness, it arrives as the new kid on the secular block. From the point of view of religious traditions, it is the oldest kid on the block. But from the point of view of an awakened secularity, it is an interesting but unknown quantity.

To characterize people as spiritually illiterate may sound harsh. But it is not meant as a criticism or a negative judgment on what concerns people pursue. Rather it is a recognition of a condition that keeps spiritually interested people open and learning. In fact, spiritual illiteracy is not merely the condition of the beginner. It is also the condition of the adept. No one ever masters the ways of the Spirit. Acknowledging that "we do not know" is crucial to spiritual growth. So when initial spiritual illiteracy becomes spiritually literate, it still must bow its head in ignorance and so, paradoxically, become wiser.

This combination of spiritual interest and illiteracy is a cultural mood. It is present both outside and inside organized religions. Within Christian churches it has a distinctive face. Many Christians profess their faith on a regular basis through prayer, participation in worship, ethical behavior, etc. However, according to the classic formulation, faith always seeks understanding (cf. e.g., St. Anselm). This understanding is more than the rational coherence of Christian revelation or the alignment of the truths of faith with other truths of history, biology, physics, politics, etc. Understanding entails the interior realization of faith perceptions and the integration of these perceptions into all aspects of life. It is precisely in this endeavor that there is both interest and illiteracy. Christians want this, but they are not sure how to make it happen.

This is the point of connection between people characterized as "spiritually interested yet illiterate" and the Christian faith. The Christian faith is a storehouse of spiritual wisdom that meets the spiritual interests of today's Christians. If people have an "awakened desire" for the spiritual, Christian faith knows how to sustain this desire. If people have sketchy ideas about spiritual reality, Christian faith can evaluate those ideas and suggest adjustments and alternatives. If people wonder how spiritual reality is contacted and integrated, Christian faith knows both the intellectual and practical aspects of spiritual development. Christian faith may not be able to completely feed the contemporary hunger for the spiritual, but it can put food on the table.

In particular, the vision of spiritual transformation in the Gospels is appropriate. It correlates closely with the contemporary interest in the spiritual. When people open to the spiritual influence of the Kingdom of God in the Gospels, their bodies, minds, intimate relationships, and social commitments are healed. The spiritual is not reduced to these effects, but the advent of the spiritual affects the whole of human life. In addition, the Gospels leave no doubt that this is not an easy process.

Falling away is at least as prevalent as pushing ahead. In short, the Gospels can be read as a demanding invitation into an untapped human potential. This is an enticement for spiritually interested yet spiritually ignorant seekers.

II. The Vision of Spiritual Transformation in the Gospels

Antonio Machado, the Spanish poet, once said of Christ,

All his words were
one word: wake up!

He might have added some other forceful imperatives. "Waking up" belongs to a family of images in the Gospels. Christ also enjoins people to "see, hear, rise, and find themselves." These images are the positive side of a paired process. People are asleep and they have to wake up, lost and they have to be found, blind and they have to see, deaf and they have to hear, dead and they have to rise to life.

These images, taken from physical life, point to the changes of consciousness and action that are necessary to respond to Jesus and his preaching. When both John the Baptist and Jesus cry out, in essence "Change your mind *(metanoeite)*, the Kingdom of God is near" (translation mine; cf. Matt 3:2) they stress the need for a different level of perception in order to respond to the spiritual dimension of life characterized as God's Kingdom. This different level of consciousness unfolds into different ways of speech and action. The basic spiritual maxim is: "If you know these things, you are blessed if you do them" (John 13:17). Spiritual transformation is comprised of understanding and action.

Therefore, we will explore the surface state of consciousness and action known in the Gospels as being asleep, blind, deaf, dead, and lost. Then we will portray the depth state of consciousness and action known as awake, seeing, hearing, rising, and being found. Of course, the next step will be to investigate the perils and possibilities of moving from the surface state of consciousness and action to the depth state of consciousness and action through hearing the Word.

Asleep, Blind, Deaf, Lost, and Dead

"As [Jesus] walked along," St. John writes, "he saw a man blind from birth" (John 9:1). This is the human condition. This is not a man or woman who has lost sight through accident. It is what has been present from the beginning. Human birth equals spiritual blindness. The Johannine Jesus makes the same point with Nicodemus (John 3:1-21). He tells him he must be born not only of water (physical birth), but also of Spirit. "What is born of the flesh is flesh, what is born of the Spirit is Spirit." This instruction to Nicodemus is meant to help him "see the Kingdom of God." However, all he can reply is, "How can these things be?" He remains blind to the spiritual. Spiritual consciousness is a human potential, but it is not easy to actualize.

This condition of being asleep, blind, deaf, lost, and dead refers to spiritual ignorance. At its most basic, spiritual ignorance means the spiritual dimension of life simply does not enter into consciousness. In Luke's Gospel, the people who fail to take into account the spiritual are called foolish. There is the barn builder (Luke 12:16-21) who talks to his soul as if it was a physical reality, "Soul . . . relax, eat, drink, be merry" only to find out it belongs to the spiritual realm as God directly addresses him, "You fool! This very night your life is being demanded of you." When the disciples on the road to Emmaus interpret Jesus' life and death only in sociopolitical terms, the risen, incognito Christ says in frustration, "Oh, how foolish you are . . . !" (Luke 24:25). At this point, it is not a matter of a muddled understanding of God, self, neighbor, and creation. It is simply lack of attention to the spiritual as a whole.

In St. Matthew's Gospel Jesus comments directly on this spiritual obtuseness. Between the parable of the sower, seed, and soils and the interpretation of the parable, Jesus quotes Isaiah and says these words have been fulfilled:

> You shall indeed listen, but never understand,
>   and you shall indeed look, but never perceive.
> For this people's heart has grown dull,
>   and their ears are hard of hearing,
>   and they have shut their eyes;
>   so that they might not look with their eyes,
>   and listen with their ears,
> and understand with their heart and turn—
>   and I would heal them. (Matt 13:14-15)

Although Jesus will tell them parables that will express and communicate the spiritual dimension, they will not be able to grasp their meaning. Their physical senses are fine; they see and hear. But their ability to understand with their heart, the spiritual center of their being, is underdeveloped. The result is that they will not turn for healing. They will not be made whole by the inclusion of the spiritual into their self-understanding.

Physically Preoccupied

One reason for this spiritual density is preoccupation with the physical. In St. Matthew's Gospel, Jesus advises, "[D]o not worry about your life, what you are to eat or what you will drink or about your body, what you will wear" (Matt 6:25). This is not an attack on the legitimate concerns of physical life. Rather it is pointing out how physical life monopolizes awareness and causes anxiety. Later in the passage, Jesus will make the same observation in shrill, almost hysterical, tones. "Therefore, do not worry, saying, 'What will we eat?' or 'What will we drink?' or 'What will we wear?'" We all know the panic and terror that instinctively arises when our food and shelter are threatened. Is there any alternative?

Jesus suggests there is a bigger picture to take into account. This bigger picture can enter awareness by focusing on the present experience of birds and flowers. When we attend to the birds and the flowers, we can appreciate the gift dimension of our life. Life is not only strenuous and often anxious effort; it is also an act of receiving sustenance from the source of life. This change of consciousness can transform how we relate to our basic needs. "But strive first for the kingdom of God and his righteousness and all these things will be *given* to you as well" (Matt 6:33). However, when we identify with the anxiety over the precariousness of our physical life, it dominates awareness, and we are asleep to this spiritual possibility.

The way the physical restricts consciousness is also the background for the Markan Jesus' painfully plodding gastrointestinal teaching on defilement. The context of this teaching is the question of what foods are clean and unclean. The assumption is that people can contaminate themselves spiritually by eating certain foods. Jesus refutes this assumption: "there is nothing outside a person that by going in can defile, but the things which come out are what defile" (Mark 7:14). Jesus moves awareness from physical exteriority to spiritual interiority.

The ability to receive this new teaching entails breaking the stranglehold the physical has on human awareness. This is not an easy task. Later, the disciples ask for an explanation of his teaching. A frustrated

Jesus begins, "Then do you also fail to understand? Do you not see . . ." (Mark 7:18) and then he goes on to explain how food goes into the stomach and is eliminated. He contrasts this with the heart out of which come evil thoughts, the true source of defilement. However, monitoring different foods is easier than scrutinizing the conniving heart. Strict allegiance to physical laws takes consciousness down a path that makes it difficult to appreciate the subtleties of spiritual realities. Often the spiritual is not perceived because the eyes and ears are mesmerized by the physical.

The Gospel of John also highlights how the physical can block our appreciation of the spiritual. Jesus' healings and miracles are signs, manifestations in the outer world of the inner spiritual reality that animates all things. However, what people immediately come into contact with are these physical sights and sounds, and many cannot get beyond them. They do not trace the physical to its spiritual source.

One of the most flagrant examples of this is the feeding of the five thousand with the five barley loaves and two fish (John 6:1-14). After the people had eaten, Jesus perceived that they would come and make him king by force. This is an indication that they have remained on the physical and social level. They have not seen the sign for a sign. Its gross reality is what engrosses them. Jesus avoids them by withdrawing into the hills, a place where spirit is nurtured in prayer and solitude.

Later, Jesus will say to them directly, "'Very truly, I tell you, you are looking for me, not because you saw signs, but because you ate your fill of the loaves" (John 6:26). Then Jesus tries to move their consciousness to the spiritual dimension. "Do not work for the food that perishes, but for the food that endures for eternal life, which the Son of Man will give you." This is the constant struggle of people who hear and see Jesus in John's Gospel. Can they move from the physical sights and sounds to the spiritual truth of his identity, and through that identity, to the eternal life he desires to give? More often than not, the physical captures consciousness so thoroughly that it blocks out the spiritual.

Socially Preoccupied

Preoccupation with the social also blocks out the spiritual. In Luke's story of the wedding feast, those invited politely excuse themselves because of other commitments:

> But they all alike began to make excuses. The first said to him, "I have bought a piece of land, and I must go out and see it; please accept my

regrets." Another said, "I have bought five yoke of oxen, and I am going to try them out; please accept my regrets." Another said, "I have just been married, and therefore I cannot come." (Luke 14:18-20)

People who are spiritually asleep, blind, deaf, lost, and dead people do not look that way. They appear to be engaged, energetic, and even entrepreneurial. They are making deals and marrying spouses. In another passage, Luke compares them to the people of Noah's time: "They were eating and drinking, and marrying and being given in marriage, until the day Noah entered the ark, and the flood came and destroyed all of them" (Luke 17:27). These people know everything except what St. Luke considers the one thing necessary (see Luke 10:42).

St. Matthew's Gospel continually harps on the human drive to look good before others. The religious acts of prayer, almsgiving, and fasting are vitiated because people engage in them "in order to be seen" (Matt 6:1-18). This outer emphasis keeps people from the interior contact with their "Father who sees in secret." This same conviction is expressed in the question, "What does it profit [persons] if they gain the whole world, but lose or forfeit themselves?" (Luke 9:25). Vigorous efforts in the social world for advancement and gain preempt spiritual inquiry and development. And, of course, some of the Pharisees are consistently badgered because they love the outer world of salutations in the marketplace, being called teacher, long tassels and widened phylacteries on their clothing, and the outside of the cup (cf. Matt 23:1-8, 25). All these "loves" keep their consciousness outside, busy with everything except what counts. Therefore, they are blind guides leading the blind (see Matt 15:15). Spiritual sight is denied them.

Social preoccupation takes a particularly dark turn when it becomes addicted to maintaining present unequal economic arrangements. The Gospels often present the people on top as vigilant about their position and willing to do anything to keep it. Gentile leaders are criticized because they "lord it over" those whom they are supposed to help (Matt 20:25). The rich man who wears fine clothes and feasts can ignore the naked beggar who starves at his gate (Luke 16:19-31). Religious leadership can put heavy burdens on others and "not lift a finger" to help them (Matt 23:4). The healthy can push the sick to the edge of the crowd (Mark 10:48 and parallels). Men can plan to stone a woman in order to trap a prophet (John 8:3-6). Righteous and sinner never share a meal. When people are obsessed with the rules and regulations that govern the relationships between Jews and Gentiles, men and women, rich and poor, leadership and led, the spiritual dimension is crowded out. Quite simply, defending social and financial dominance takes time and energy. It also produces people who are asleep, blind, deaf, lost, and dead to the spiritual.

A Dangerous Misperception

A misperception that often thrives in spiritual circles is that the physical and social realms in themselves are hindrances to spiritual development. This is not true. They are essential dimensions of the good creation, and full spiritual development entails transforming our relationship to them in the light of spiritual reality. However, in order to do this, consciousness must learn to disengage from these dimensions and welcome the more elusive spiritual. At first, this appears to be a simple calculus. We can only get so much into our head at one time; and when the head is full, we refuse access to whatever knocks for entry. We think and dwell on the physical and social too much. We should open the door to the spiritual.

However, it is more than a "shared time" arrangement. The Gospels think exclusive preoccupation with the physical and social results in negative mental states. We are filled with worry, anxiety, nitpicking attitudes, defensiveness, violent thoughts, narcissism, boredom, and fear. We are so turned in on ourselves that we do not take pleasure in the physical or feel secure in the social. It is only when the spiritual is allowed in that we inhabit the physical and social with grace and pleasure. Without the spiritual, we are only partly living. We go through the motions—eat, drink, dress, sex, talk, listen, buy, sell, save, spend— but something is missing. Therefore, breaking the hold of the physical and social on our consciousness and attending to the spiritual is for the ultimate purpose of returning to the physical and social with the pleasure, meaning, and passion that the spiritual bestows.

Awake, Seeing, Hearing, Living, and Found

If people who are asleep, blind, deaf, dead, and lost are not conscious of the spiritual because they are preoccupied with the physical and social, what do a people look like who *are* awake, seeing, hearing, living, and found? People who are awake, seeing, hearing, living, and found are aware of the spiritual depth of their own beings and how that depth opens to God and receives energy from God. From this starting point, they realize a communion with both creation and neighbor and a call to incarnate this consciousness in personal behavior and social policy.

Consciousness of Self and God

In the opening scene of the Sermon on the Mount (Matt 6–7) Jesus sees the crowds and goes up on a mountain. The mountain gives Jesus a higher perspective, and he speaks what he sees from this higher point of view. People are a blessedness that manifests itself in circumstances as varied as mourning, peacemaking, mercy, and persecution. Furthermore, people are the salt of the earth and the light of the world. They bring both zest and illumination into creation.

Of course, this truth about people is in danger. Salt can lose its savor; light can be snuffed out by a basket. In other words, people are something they might not be aware of and, therefore, something they might not enact. Jesus' words are an effort to awaken them, to make them seeing, hearing, and living. He is finding the lost, and that is why Antonio Machado also has written that Christ said:

> Find the you that is not you
> and never can be.

Jesus came "to seek out and to save the lost" (Luke 19:10). This does not mean particular people but the spiritual dimension of all people "the you that is not you and never can be."

Finding this "you" takes the form of spiritual self-knowledge. The Lukan Jesus suggests this approach when he corrects the Pharisees' outer-centeredness with, "the kingdom of God is within you" (Luke 17:21; NRSV alternative trans.). The Gospel of Thomas carries it further.

> If your leaders say to you, "Look, the (Father's) kingdom is in the sky," then the birds of the sky will precede you. If they say to you, "It is in the sea," then the fish will precede you. Rather, the (Father's) kingdom is within you and it is outside you.

> When you know yourselves, then you will be known, and you will understand that you are children of the living Father. But if you do not know yourselves, then you live in poverty, and you are the poverty. (GT 3)

The initial step on the path of awakening is knowledge of ourselves as more than physical, psychological, and social organisms.

However, this self-knowing is simultaneously a knowing of God. When we see the truth about ourselves, we see that we are God's children: "to all who received him, who believed in his name, he gave power to become children of God, who were born, not of blood or of the will of the flesh or of the will of man, but of God" (John 1:12-13). St. Augustine knew this connection. "A person must first be restored to himself/herself, that making of himself/herself as it were a stepping stone, he/she might rise thence to God." At a later moment of Christian history, Bossuet emphasized the same path. "Wisdom lies in knowing God and knowing oneself. From knowledge of self we rise to knowledge of God." This interior movement of knowing oneself in such a way that one knows God is characterized as "going in and going up."

More precisely, "going in and going up" is the distinction between introspective interiority and transcendent interiority. In introspective interiority we "go within" and witness the activity of the mind body organism. In doing so, we become intimate with ourselves and understand our bodily messages, our personality, our motivation, and the myriad "tapes" our minds carry and play. In this process, we can gradually shift awareness from what we see about ourselves to ourselves as the seer.

This begins the process of "going up." We realize we are transcendent to the processes we are observing. We also realize we are capable of this transcendence because we are rooted in a larger transcendence. We are grounded in God, and our initial awareness of this reality is that it sustains us by its own life. When this happens, we have a vibrant realization of what it means to be a creature whose life is ultimately not its own. We have, as it were, found the soul and through the soul found the God who loves us. Many consider this the essential realization in spiritual development, the key to becoming awake, seeing, hearing, living, and found.

Consciousness of Creation and Neighbor

Waking up, seeing, hearing, living, and finding yourself entails more than self-knowledge and knowledge of God. St. John begins his Gospel by connecting the Word with God, with creation, and with the spiritual illumination of people. "In the beginning was the Word, and the Word was with God, and the Word was God . . . . All things came into being through [the Word] . . . What has come into being in [the Word] was life, and the life was the light of all people" (John 1:1-4). In other words, all things are sustained by divine life. When this divine life enters into the human world, it becomes a light in the mind. The light in the human mind allows people to see the life that is everywhere. When people wake up to the fact they are children of God, always sustained by divine life, they also notice everything else is also sustained by divine life. They are not separate, isolated individuals but common citizens of creation. They are brothers and sisters of the universe.

In particular, they are brothers and sisters of one another. Jesus' double commandment to love makes this connection. If we love God with all our heart, soul, and mind, we will uncover ourselves as God's creation. This self-knowledge becomes the lens through which we see others and realize they are sustained in the same way. This allows us to love our neighbor as ourselves. Although we respect all the differences along physical, social, and mental lines, we also acknowledge we are spiritually in intimate communion with one another.

Consciousness and Action

Therefore, awakening, seeing, hearing, living, and being found means a breakthrough in understanding ourselves, God, creation, and neighbor. But according to the spiritual maxim, "If you know these things, you are blessed if you do them" (John 13:17), the new understanding must be translated into action. In St. John's story of the footwashing and footdrying, we are given a glimpse of spiritual consciousness in action. "Jesus, knowing that the Father had given all things into his hands, and that he had come from God and was going to God . . ." (John 13:3). This is the child of God consciousness, an awareness of his communion with God who is imaged as a Father who has trusted him with all things. He knows his origin and his destiny and the potential of the present moment to reveal the Father, the generative source of love. God consciousness drives Jesus into action, pushes him along the path of incarnation. He becomes lovingly involved with feet, the symbol of our journeying on the earth. The essence of the Word, as Word, is to become flesh.

St. John paints a detailed picture of how this Word becomes flesh. "Jesus . . . got up from the table, took off his outer robe, and tied a towel around himself. Then he poured water into a basin and began to wash the disciples' feet and to wipe them with the towel that was tied around him" (John 13:3-5). Jesus' knowing unfolds into a doing, and the doing, because it comes from a spiritual consciousness, carries the spiritual care of this higher order. The excellence of this care derives from the sustained focus on each aspect of what is needed to deliver the care. He is no place else but in the towel, basin, water, and feet. His spiritual consciousness translates into the painstaking process of loving the physical.

St. Matthew also stresses the need for consciousness to unfold into action. The Sermon on the Mount ends with Jesus warning his listeners that only hearing his words will not protect them from the storms of life (see Matt 7:24-27). They must put his words into action to become a house built on rock. Also crying "Lord, Lord" will not be enough. They must *do* the will of the Father (Matt 7:21). In a similar way, people may accept the invitation to the wedding feast, but they will have to have a wedding garment to remain inside (Matt 22:13-14). The wedding garment symbolizes a willingness to be married, to seriously engage the work of the kingdom. In another parable (Matt 25:1-13), all ten virgins have lamps, the illumination provided by Christian faith. But only five have oil for their lamps, the symbol that they know how to make the lamp come alive through good works. The spiritually awake, hearing, seeing, living, and found are those whose minds and wills are engaged, who both understand and act.

Awake and Asleep, Seeing and Blind, Hearing and Deaf, Living and Dead, Found and Lost

Individually and collectively, we are a people in the making. Our consciousness is a moveable feast. We participate in darkness and light, in remembering and forgetting, in sleep and wakefulness, in seeing and blindness, in hearing and deafness, in dead and risen life, in conditions of being lost and in the homecoming joy of being found. In the Gospels the words and deeds of Jesus have the power to move people along the path of illumination and action, toward the positive sides of these pairs. Hearing the Word becomes the catalyst of metanoia, the change of mind and behavior that indicates we are responding to the kingdom of God.

However, there is a realistic assessment of the success of Jesus' preaching and teaching. Crowds vacillate; individual seekers both embrace his words and turn away; disciples do and do not get it, sometimes in the space of a few lines; religious leaders are consistently hard hearted, refusing to be moved. Jesus is a word that needs pondering in order to be received, and that pondering often leads to costly change. Many are not capable of this pondering or willing to pay the price of change. Others hear and respond, and so they begin the arduous process of spiritual development.

The parable of the sower, the seed, and the soils (Mark 13:3-8) shows the variations on this struggle to wake up through encountering the words and deeds of Jesus. It is so central a parable that St. Mark comments, "Do you not understand this parable? Then how will you understand all the parables?" (Mark 4:13). The tendency is to think each soil—side of the road, rocky, thorny, and good—represents a different type of person. But a more inclusive approach interprets each soil as each person under different circumstances.

This is certainly how it has played out in my life. I have stonewalled some seeds so successfully that they were exposed to the birds of the air; I have received some seeds with joy, but I did not take them into my heart and ponder them and so they withered; I have allowed the thorns of my cares, pleasures, and finances to choke the growth of the seed rather than allow the seeds to transform the thorns into flowers; and I have "gotten it together" and produced fruit. These intimate and intricate dynamics of seed and soil spell out the struggle to move from sleep to wakefulness, blindness to sight, deafness to hearing, from being dead to being alive, and from being lost to being found.

Attention

The seed that falls by the side of the road and is devoured by the birds means we do not have the time or inclination to entertain the teachings of Jesus. The side of the road is not the middle of the road, the place where we normally walk. If we would consider the seeds, we would have to alter our routine, step outside the way we work. But this does not happen because the devouring birds do not allow it.

The devouring birds are symbols of our inattention to the seed, our failure to heed and consider what we have heard. The seed of the word is given no chance. As soon as it lands, it is taken away. The Gospel interpretation is that these birds are like the devil. The devil, *diabolus*, does what his name signifies. He breaks things apart. When we are this first soil, there is brief contact with the Word, but no real coming together at all. The seed and the soil are quickly separated. The seed may be a wake-up call, but we turn away and go back to sleep.

Understanding

The seeds that fall on rocky ground meet thin soil, but they manage
to quickly spring up. The soil is receptive, but it is not deep enough.
Without root, the fledging growth cannot bear the heat of the day, and
it withers. This symbolizes situations where we hear the word and receive it with joy but do not work on realizing its truth into our lives.
The word is incompletely understood, and so it cannot withstand
counterarguments and violent attacks.

The importance of understanding the Word is distinguished from
amazement. In the Gospels people are often amazed at Jesus' teachings
or healings. Sometimes this amazement is a first step toward understanding. When the amazement of people causes them to praise God,
they are beginning to understand the nature of God and become spiritually seeing. Amazement is a draw that leads to further exploration.

However, amazement can also be a block to understanding. When
Jesus is trying to bring Nicodemus into spiritual consciousness, he tells
him, "Do not be amazed that I told you, you must be born anew" (see
John 3:7). He is afraid amazement will addle the mind and keep Nicodemus from following his teaching. When the women enter the tomb and
see the young man in white on the right side of where they laid him,
Mark tells us the women are "utterly amazed." But the man in white cautions them, "Do not be amazed!" (Mark 16:5-6; NAB). He wants them to
understand, not just to be stupefied. At the birth of Jesus, when the shepherds tell what they have seen (see Luke 2:15-19), all who hear it are
amazed. But Mary, both mother and disciple, ponders the events in her
heart. Comprehension is more valued than astonishment.

Understanding is also distinguished from love. The most poignant
relationship in the Gospels is between Jesus and Peter. Peter generously and impetuously receives Jesus and his teaching. But he doesn't
always get it. He intuits that Jesus is "the Messiah, the Son of the living God" (Matt 16:16), but he cannot grasp that suffering is part of that
identity. He wants to be able to walk on the sea of danger as Jesus does
and he asks for the ability, "command me come to you on the water"
(Matt 14:28). But he sinks, and Jesus places the problem squarely on his
"little faith" (v. 32; emphasis mine), that is, his failure to understand
and grow into *great* faith.

It is in the footwashing and footdrying episode (John 13:1-11) that
Peter's rocky ground condition is most clearly seen. Peter fiercely re-
sists Jesus' act of service. Jesus interprets this resistance as a lack of
understanding. "You do not know now what I am doing, but later you

will understand" (v. 7). Then Jesus warns Peter that the refusal to be washed means they will have to separate. Peter cannot bear this possibility, so he enthusiastically moves from a footwashing to a bath. "Lord, not my feet only but also my hands and my head!" (v. 9). However, Jesus is not talking about a physical washing but about the spiritual ability to receive love from God. Jesus and Peter are experiencing, what people today call, a "disconnect." Peter may be fiercely attached to Jesus, but he cannot quite fathom him.

Jesus says that Peter will move from attachment to understanding "later," afterwards. This means after his denial. Peter boastfully tells Jesus he will lay down his life for him. In his own mind, this is a sign of his love for Jesus. But Jesus responds, "Will you lay down your life for me? Very truly, I tell you, before the cock crows, you will have denied me three times" (John 13:38). The morning of Peter's enlightenment will only follow the night of his ego failure. He will understand the need to allow God to enter him as a source of strength and renewal only after his reliance on himself has failed. His attachment and allegiance to Jesus does not substitute for understanding.

When we call Peter the rock, we may mean that he is a firm foundation for the Church. But if we consider Peter the second soil of rocky ground, we may learn a great truth about the Church as the following of Christ. At one time or another, most Christians have been amazed at the teachings of Jesus and have felt great love for the one who spoke and lived them. At the same time, the teachings remain a permanent puzzlement, and Jesus himself is a larger-than-life figure always ahead of us on the road. This second soil condition is a real place to be: amazed at the Word, lovingly attached to the Word Made Flesh, and yet not being on a path of understanding either the teaching or the Teacher. This second soil is a definite advance on the first, but it points to work that still needs to be done.

Integration

The seed that falls on the third soil finds itself among thorns. If it is to grow, it must deal with this competitive environment. Like the rocky soil, the thorns pose a threat to the growth of the seed. But it is a different kind of threat. There is nothing wrong with the soil. In fact, the soil is highly productive. The question is: how will the seed deal with everything else that is growing? If the second soil needs understanding to be more hospitable to the seed, the third soil needs to learn to integrate the seed with the thorns. This is not an easy task.

The seed symbolizes the spiritual teaching of Jesus and the thorns symbolize "the cares of the world, and the lure of wealth, and the desire for other things" (Mark 4:19). Of course, humanity is a combination of spirit and world. Ideally, the spiritual is folded into and transformative of physical, social, and psychological life. Spirit and world are brought together. However, these two aspects have often been characterized as rivals, and so one must dominate over the other. In this situation the parable thinks the world often wins and chokes the seed. This predicted success of the thorns is often what happens. The spiritual is not integrated; it is eliminated.

The Lessons Learned

The fourth soil to receive the seed, the good earth, is the soil that has learned the lessons of the first three failed attempts of the seed and the soils to produce fruit. St. Luke characterizes the people of this soil as those who "hold ['the word God'] fast" (8.11, 15). They do not let the birds of the air take it from them and devour it (8·4) They have learned how to keep the word close. They do not let their minds wander into other affairs and forget the teachings they have heard. The teachings become their life companions; they develop strategies on how to attend to them.

These people of the fourth soil hold this word fast "with a generous and good heart" (Luke 8·15; NAB; see NRSV). This means they have pursued a deeper understanding of the word. The heart is the spiritual center of the person. It connects the person to God, the only Good One and the source of all goodness, and it is the place from which creative action in the world springs. When the heart is good, it is because it has learned to open to God and receive divine goodness. When it is generous, it has learned to mediate this goodness into the world. St. Matthew reflects this deeper understanding of the heart as good and generous when he encourages the hearers of the word to let their light shine before people. These people will see their "good works and give glory to [their] Father in heaven" (Matt 5:16). Human goodness will be a manifestation of divine goodness. The heart now understands its communion with God and neighbor. It is fluid, receiving from God and giving to others. It is no longer the non-understanding rocky soil.

Those of the fourth soil who hold the Word fast "with a generous and good heart" (Luke 8:15; NAB) have to "bear fruit with patient endurance" (8:15). This is what is necessary for the integration of the spiritual into the physical, social, and mental realms. Spiritual integration is not easy or fast. It is a painstaking process, and we can become impatient and abandon it. Perseverance is prescribed. If all these things are in place, fruit flows naturally, new action emerges from the new consciousness.

Therefore, the Gospels present a picture of spiritual transformation as a movement from preoccupation with physical need, social standing, and financial security to a realization of a deeper self who is in communion with the divine source, in solidarity with other people and creation, and who mediates Spirit into the physical, social, and mental realms. The catalyst of this transformation is hearing the Word and the consequent activities of attending, understanding, and integrating this Word into the full range of the human project.

III. How Gospel Texts Work As Spiritual Wisdom

Therefore, the Gospels as a whole, all of the many words of the many texts, can be approached as *the* Word; and the Word can be characterized as spiritual wisdom that is meant to trigger spiritual transformation. However, in order to preach and teach the Gospels in this way, there is a need to have some theory of how spiritual wisdom works, what its strategies are, and how it evaluates success and failure.

Spiritual wisdom is a form of artful language that targets the mind in order to open the person to the Spirit. Therefore, the goal of spiritual wisdom is to open the person to receive Spirit from God and to release that Spirit in the world. However, in order to do this, spiritual wisdom focuses on the mind. The mind is the gatekeeper of both the soul's access to God and the soul's capacity for creative action in the world. Spiritual wisdom addresses the mind, the way it opens and closes to God and the way it blocks and facilitates action. It acts on the mind to increase attention to the spiritual, develop understanding of the spiritual, and integrate the spiritual with physical, social, and mental life.

It does this skillfully with language used for maximum effect. Spiritual wisdom employs clever and endlessly inventive ways to dismantle forms of consciousness that contribute to sleep, blindness, deafness, and being dead and lost, and it constructs forms of consciousness that contribute to wakefulness, seeing, hearing, living, and being found. In the service of this process, it is shameless in the strategies it employs.

Spiritual wisdom may conform to its stereotype and take the shape of inspirational and lofty thoughts—but only if they work. Jesus may rhapsodize:

> I thank you, Father, Lord of heaven and earth, because you have hidden these things from the wise and the intelligent and have revealed them to infants; yes, Father, for such was your gracious will. All things have been handed over to me by my Father; and no one knows the Son except the Father, and no one knows the Father except the Son and anyone to whom the Son chooses to reveal him.
>
> Come to me, all you that are weary and are carrying heavy burdens, and I will give you rest. Take my yoke upon you, and learn from me; for I am gentle and humble in heart, and you will find rest for your souls. For my yoke is easy, and my burden is light. (Matt 11:25-30)

But does it work? Does the mind turn toward Spirit or world in a new way? Spiritual wisdom does whatever it takes to make this happen.

Sometimes spiritual wisdom criticizes how the mind clings to positions even when experience refutes them: "Even after you saw" that "tax collectors and prostitutes believed [John]," "you did not change your minds and believe him" (Matt 21:32).

Sometimes spiritual wisdom plants a new idea: "You have heard that it was said, 'An eye for an eye and a tooth for a tooth.' But I say to you, Do not resist evil . . ." (Matt 5:38-39).

Sometimes spiritual wisdom argues the implications of a wrong response: "whenever you enter a town and they do not welcome you, go into its streets and say, 'Even the dust of your town that clings to our feet, we wipe off in protest against you. Yet, know this: the kingdom of God has come near'" (Luke 10:10).

Sometimes spiritual wisdom exposes false logic:

> Every kingdom divided against itself becomes a desert, and house falls on house. If Satan also is divided against himself, how will his kingdom stand?—for you say that I cast out the demons by Beelzebul. Now if I cast out the demons by Beelzebul, by whom do your exorcists cast them out? Therefore they will be your judges. But if it is by the finger of God that I cast out the demons, then the kingdom of God has come to you. (Luke 11:17-20)

Sometimes spiritual wisdom explores the implications of a significant experience:

The seventy returned with joy, saying, "Lord, in your name even the demons submit to us!" He said to them, "I watched Satan fall from heaven like a flash of lightning. See, I have given you authority to tread on snakes and scorpions, and over all the power of the enemy; and nothing will hurt you. Nevertheless, do not rejoice at this, that the spirits submit to you, but rejoice that your names are written in heaven." (Luke 10:17-20)

Sometimes spiritual wisdom confronts wrong actions: "Let her alone; why do you trouble her? She has performed a good service for me" (Mark 14:6).

Sometimes spiritual wisdom spars with metaphors: "[Jesus] answered, 'It is not fair to take the children's food and throw it to the dogs.' She said, 'Yes, Lord, yet even the dogs eat the crumbs that fall from their masters' table'" (Matt 15:26-27).

Sometimes spiritual wisdom sings of the world that is possible:

Woman, believe me, the hour is coming when you will worship the Father neither on this mountain nor in Jerusalem . . . But the hour is coming, and is now here, when the true worshipers will worship the Father in spirit and truth, for the Father seeks such as these to worship him. (John 4:21, 23)

Sometimes spiritual wisdom weeps over the world that is: "How often have I desired to gather your children together as a hen gathers her brood under her wings, and you were not willing!" (Matt 23:37).

Sometimes spiritual wisdom blows on the ashes of the heart till they flare to flame: "Were not our hearts burning within us while he was talking to us on the road, while he was opening the scriptures to us?" (Luke 24:32).

Sometimes spiritual wisdom dances on the line between possibility and impossibility: "Truly I tell you, it will be hard for a rich person to enter the kingdom of heaven. Again I tell you, it is easier for a camel to go through the eye of a needle than for someone who is rich to enter the kingdom of God" (Matt 19:23-24).

These are just some of the concrete strategies of spiritual wisdom. But whatever the particular strategy, the general intent is to honor, scold, cajole, threaten, compliment, bully, confront, and caress the workings of the mind until it "understands and does" these things. Therefore, spiritual wisdom is not always pretty, and it is not always effective. But it is a strenuous effort to massage the mind in such a way that it can open and receive Spirit from God and release that Spirit into the world.

Conclusion

Preaching and teaching the Gospels as spiritual wisdom begins with recognizing the spiritual interest and spiritual illiteracy of people and the way the Gospels can speak to their situation. The Gospels provide a model of spiritual transformation that is triggered by hearing the Word and pondering it as spiritual wisdom. When we learn to attend, understand, and integrate the spiritual wisdom of Gospel texts, we move in starts and stops from being asleep to being awake, from blindness to sight, from deafness to hearing, from being dead to being alive, and from being lost to being found. It is a journey of consciousness and action. And it is never finished.

First Sunday of Advent

Matthew 24:36-44

⟡

Staying Awake in Everyday Life

A Spiritual Commentary

[Jesus said to the disciples:] "But about that day and hour no one knows, neither the angels of heaven nor the Son, but only the Father.

God, the mysterious and transcendent Father, is the only reality who knows when the event called "the coming of the Son of Man" will happen. So we on earth cannot plan for it in the normal way. Since we do not know when it will arrive, we cannot schedule our preparation. We do not know when we should stop doing "business as usual," focus our attention and energy on the upcoming event, and start getting ready. The way we prepare for the "coming of the Son of Man" will have to be different.

For as the days of Noah were, so will be the coming of the Son of Man. For as in those days before the flood they were eating and drinking, marrying and giving in marriage, until the day Noah entered the ark, and they knew nothing until the flood came and swept them all away, so too will be the coming of the Son of Man.

Although we do not know *when* it will come, we do know something about *how* it will come. It will be like it was in the days of Noah. Although the people in the "days before the flood" were usually considered evildoers, this is not what St. Matthew's Jesus stresses. He characterizes them as caught up in the everyday affairs of life—eating and drinking, marrying and giving in marriage. There is nothing wrong with these activities except that they are all consuming. They keep them from "knowing" something deeper, something of vital importance for their well-being. They are ill prepared, and so the flood carries them away. "[T]he coming of the Son of Man" has an element of danger in it if you are inattentive. Therefore, the preparation project for the "coming of the Son of Man" is not to be caught unaware.

Then two will be in the field; one will be taken and one will be left. Two women will be grinding meal together; one will be taken and one will be left.

These two images continue the themes of everyday life and danger. Preparation for the day of the Lord does not mean stopping everyday life. Both men, the one "taken" into the kingdom and the one left behind, are out in the field. Both women, the one "taken" into the kingdom and the one left behind, are grinding at the mill. It is not that one is out in the field and the other is praying, or that one is grinding at the mill and the other is in the temple. So the encouragement of the text is not the strategy of traditional piety—to quit the tasks of everyday life and engage in religious activity, especially when you know a major religious moment is about to occur.

So where is the difference between these two men and women? If both are doing the same things, why is one taken and one left?

The text does not explicitly consider this question. But the context suggests that inner vigilance and awareness make the difference. On the visible, outer level both men and both women are the same. Therefore, the difference must be interior. It must be on the level of awareness. Attentiveness seems to be the lesson to draw from the comparison of the "days of Noah" and the day of "the coming of the Son of Man." And, in the next line, the storyteller makes it explicit in a bold injunction:

Keep awake therefore, for you do not know on what day your Lord is coming. But understand this: if the owner of the house had known in what part of the night the thief was coming, he would have stayed awake and would not have let his house be broken into. Therefore you also must be ready, for the Son of Man is coming at an unexpected hour.

The event called "the coming of the Son of Man" is now also properly called "the day of the Lord." Although we do not know when it will come, its importance for the well-being of people is strongly stressed. The negative images of being swept away in a flood and left behind in the field or at the mill are complemented by the image of having your house broken into. Not to be ready for this day is to suffer severe consequences.

However, everything hinges on how "the coming of the Son of Man" and "the day of the Lord" is understood. A literal approach sees it as the cosmic coming of an end-time figure in an outer, visible way to judge the living and dead. There will come a day when Jesus will return and those who have fallen asleep, who have not faithfully practiced his teachings, will be judged negatively. We cannot prepare for this judgment at the last minute for we do not know when the last minute will be. Therefore, enlightened self-interest would dictate ongoing, scrupulous observance.

The difficulty of this approach is connecting fidelity to Jesus' teachings with a coming but not-yet-arrived cosmic event. When the second coming does not come, it is difficult to stay poised and waiting. Even when we are assured that second coming delayed is not second coming denied, vigilant awareness devolves into "hoping to hear in time." When a questioner asked Pope John XXIII what he would advise people in the Vatican to do if he heard Christ was coming a second time, he responded, "Look busy." This great comic line depicts the ordinary way we think. The thunderous command to "stay awake" is reduced to "wake me when he's near." And if he is never near or if people have cried "wolf" too often and said he was near but he was not, the rationale for fidelity and attentiveness is undercut.

But "the coming of the Son of Man" and "the day of the Lord" can be understood in a different way. They can be interpreted as symbolic code for God's invitation into the fullness of human life through Christ. The Lord is eternally present to human life, creating, judging, redeeming, and calling it to fullness. However, we are often not aware of this permeating divine activity. When, through the teachings of Jesus, God's redeeming presence enters human consciousness, it is "the day of the Lord" and the "Son of Man" has arrived. We never know when this will happen. So we must "stay awake through the night." This breakthrough can happen at any time. When it does and our attentiveness receives its gracious communication, we are dry in Noah's ark, taken into the Kingdom, and safe in our own house. "[Y]ou know what time it is . . . it is now the moment for you to wake from sleep" (Rom 13:11).

Teaching

There is a story entitled, "What is the World Like?":

> God and a man are walking down the road. The man asks God, "What is the world like?"
>
> God replies, "I cannot talk when I am thirsty. If you could get me a drink of cool water, we could discuss what the world is like. There is a village nearby. Go and get me a drink."

The man goes into the village and knocks at the door of the first house. A comely young woman opens the door. His jaw drops, but he manages to say, "I need a glass of cool water."

"Of course," she says, smiling, "but it is midday. Would you care to stay for some food?"

"I *am* hungry," he says, looking over his shoulder. "And your offer of food is a great kindness."

He goes in and the door closes behind him.

Thirty years go by. The man who wanted to know what the world was like and the woman who offered him food have married and raised five children. He is a respected merchant and she is an honored member of the community. One day a terrible storm comes in off the ocean and threatens their life. The merchant cries out, "Help me, God."

A voice from the midst of the storm says, "Where is my cup of cold water?"

Spiritual traditions always warn people about becoming lost in the world. (They also warn about being lost in God, but that's another issue.) The demands of everyday life are merciless. There is always more to do and not enough time to do it. A friend of mine wants inscribed on her tomb the saying, "It's always something." At times this constant activity may be boring; at other times it may be exciting. But from the point of view of the story it breeds lack of attention to the demands of God.

What is the world like? The answer of the story is that it is a place of forgetfulness. Or, in the metaphor of Matthew's text, it is a place where we fall asleep. We do not stay attentive to the spiritual dimension of life. Eating and drinking, marrying and giving in marriage, working in the field, and grinding at the mill take all our time and, more importantly, take all our mind. When this happens, we find ourselves lacking passion, purpose, and pleasure. As one perplexed person put it, "How can I be so busy and yet so empty?"

This dominance of everyday activity is particularly true in the Christmas season. Already busy people become busier. They have to prepare for the season, which often means more shopping and more work. Unfortunately, this frantic preparation often puts people to sleep spiritually. People begin to long not for the birth of the Christmas Christ, but for the lazy, doldrums days of January. The rush of the season works against the message of the season.

Almost everyone has experienced his or her spirits being depleted and even defeated. However, often the alarm does not go off. We tolerate what T.S. Eliot called, "living and partly living." We wrongly treat spirit as a luxury. If our bodies are hurting, we will pay attention to them and work hard to recover our physical health. If our financial security or social status is under attack, we will struggle and fight ceaselessly for our money and position. But we will allow our spirit to languish and even atrophy. This tendency to neglect spirit may be the underlying insight of Matthew into the people of Noah's time. They valued everything but the Spirit that ultimately sustained them.

How are we to keep spiritually aware in the midst of everyday activity? How are we to keep awake while working in the field and grinding at the mill? This is not easy. We may have the desire, but we may lack the know-how. And to shout the command, "stay awake!" (v. 42; NAB) as St. Matthew's Jesus does, may strengthen commitment, but it does not show a way forward. We need to complement desire with strategies.

Some friends of mine, long-time victims of the stress of everyday activities, suggest smuggling spiritual exercises into the world of work. A Jewish doctor says a Hebrew prayer of purification every time she washes her hands. She explains that the prayer is not meant to purify but to remind her that the person she is treating is more than their disease. In other words, she stays awake to the spiritual dimension of people while she attends to their bodily distress.

A man pauses before a Christmas tree in the building where he works. He brings to mind the connection between heaven and earth and ponders the theological truth that creation is grounded in God. He says that as long as he holds onto this truth, his day goes better. "I notice more. I see the deeper sides of people. And I'm more patient, and respectful." The awareness of Spirit brings pleasure, passion, and purpose.

Spiritual exercises help us "stay awake through the night." These exercises may be the rituals and prayers of a faith tradition that we engage in with other people. But they may also be home grown practices. Personal "things" we have learned to cultivate in order to stay focused on the deeper dimension of life. These practices become the path to the Gospel value of constant, vigilant awareness. And constant, vigilant awareness is the precondition in order to know and respond to the "coming of the Son of Man" and the arrival of the "day of the Lord."

Second Sunday of Advent

Matthew 3:1-12

Leading the Heart

A Spiritual Commentary

In those days John the Baptist appeared in the wilderness of Judea, proclaiming, "Repent, for the kingdom of heaven has come near."

This suggestive opening gives the impression John simply materialized in the desert of Judea. He appeared "out of nowhere." We are not told how he got there. We are just told he is there, and that is how to picture him—suddenly there, with all the disruptive impact that implies. "Suddenly appearing" moves the mind to mystery. His presence is not an arbitrary happenstance. Something is afoot; the hidden energies of history are at work. A mystery is unfolding.

The very place of his appearance is an opening into that mystery. The desert is outside the circle of the village and the gates of the town, far from the supports of civilization. It is a place where spiritual seekers go to confront the inner demons and beasts, to strip off the accretions, to purify the mind, to return to essentials. As Lawrence of Arabia put it, "The desert is clean."

This purification climate of the desert complements John's activity, an activity so central to him it becomes part of his name. He baptizes people, washes off the toll of living, returns them to freshness. He pushes them beneath the water and pulls them out, ready and eager for the sky. As the prophet predicts, "Therefore, I will now allure her, and bring her into the wilderness, and speak tenderly to her" (Hos 2:14; cf. 2:16 NAB: "So I will allure her; / I will lead her into the desert / and speak to her heart"). That is John's vocation. His work is to lead the heart to the place where God will speak.

This "heart-leading" is called *metanoia* (repentance). This term carries the double connotation of changing your mind and your behavior. It signals a need to go beyond your present mindset and allow a new mindset to drive new actions. If this repentance is engaged in correctly, people will be open to the "kingdom of heaven." This reality—the king-

30

dom of heaven—is at hand but only the repentant will see it and reach for it.

> **This is the one of whom the prophet Isaiah spoke when he said, "The voice of one crying out in the wilderness: 'Prepare the way of the Lord, make his paths straight.'"**

John's voice emerges out of his desert purification, and it is a cry from John's heart to all hearts. It is not a small voice or a muffled desire. It is an all-out cry, an impassioned combination of invitation and announcement. It is fired by the perception that there is a promise at the center of repentance.

Repentance is not an end in itself. It is the first step in a process of fulfillment. The letting go is for the purpose of receiving. The stripping away is preparation for new clothing. The arduous task of clearing a path is for the arrival of what is deeply desired. John the Baptist knows that the way to the garden of human flourishing is through the desert of self-confrontation, and this insight is the energy of his passionate preaching.

> **Now John wore clothing of camel's hair with a leather belt around his waist, and his food was locusts and wild honey.**

John wears symbolic clothes and eats symbolic food. Both the clothes and the food allude to people and processes in Israel's history, people and processes that explore the dynamics of repentance.

His clothing recalls Elijah, in particular one chilling episode (1 Kgs 1:1-18). Ahaziah, the king of Israel, had fallen through some latticework and was seriously injured. So he sent messengers, "Go, inquire of Baal-zebub, the god of Ekron, whether I shall recover from this injury" (v. 2). But Elijah, having been informed of this situation by an angel, waylays the messengers and tells them to return to Ahaziah with this message, "'Is it because there is no God in Israel that you are going to inquire of Baal-zebub, the god of Ekron?' Now therefore thus says the LORD, 'You shall not leave the bed to which you have gone, but you shall surely die'" (vv. 3-4). When the messengers tell Ahaziah, he asks them what the man who said these things looked like. They answered, "A hairy man, with a leather belt around his waist." Ahaziah simply says, "It is Elijah the Tishbite" (v. 8).

Elijah harassed kings who did not remain faithful to YHWH and the covenant. John is the latest to wear Elijah's mantle. He confronts Herod with his adulterous behavior, a behavior that shows a break with the God of Israel. In fact, John's path is to expose all false kings, all those possessions and positions to which we give ultimate allegiance. John the Baptist does not allow deception. He is searingly honest. This unflinching honesty is a core component of repentance.

John's diet is a combination of inedible locusts and untamed honey. Locusts were one of the plagues that God, through Moses, brought upon Egypt. The purpose of the plagues was to soften the heart of Pharaoh so he would let God's people go. The locusts symbolized divine judgment, a judgment that was not arbitrary or vindictive but was always geared to bring about change. John swallows down divine judgment.

The wild honey recalls the God-given food of Ezekiel. God shows Ezekiel a scroll, written on back and front with words of "lamentation and mourning and woe" (Ezek 2:10). One might say it was a scroll of locusts. Then God says, "O mortal [NAB: 'Son of man'], eat what is offered to you; eat this scroll, and go, speak to the house of Israel" (3:1). When Ezekiel eats the scroll, it becomes as sweet as honey in his mouth. The harshness of divine judgment becomes the sweetness of human fulfillment. John can hold together locusts and honey. He is the embodiment of the saying, "You are what you eat."

Then the people of Jerusalem and all Judea were going out to him, and all the region along the Jordan, and they were baptized by him in the river Jordan, confessing their sins.

The experience John offers is very attractive. People are drawn to the invitation that there is a promise of fulfillment in repentance. At first glance it may seem like a forbidding message, but it is a forceful expression of a truth that every heart knows. So people leave their usual locales and journey to the Jordan where they acknowledge all that blocks them from God and neighbor. This acknowledgment is key to repentance and mind change. They are moving from a mind that was ignorant of its deceptions to a mind that acknowledges them.

But when he saw many Pharisees and Sadducees coming for baptism, he said to them, "You brood of vipers! Who warned you to flee from the wrath to come?

Some of these people belong to established religious parties. Whatever else Pharisees and Sadducees are, they are characterized here as vipers. Vipers lurk along footpaths and spring out at travelers from beneath rocks. If a path is going to be cleared, it must be freed of vipers. Their poison stops progress.

The nature of their poison is externalism. They are afraid of divine punishment. So they will undergo John's baptism as an insurance policy against divine wrath. They will comply ritually, but their hearts will remain untouched. The Gospels often attack the mind set of "polishing the outside of the cup" (cf. Matt 23:25), of loving ceremony and show but neglecting the hard work of inner change. Therefore, John's injunction will be, "Get serious. This is about real change."

Bear fruit worthy of repentance.

John's strategy for "outside" people is to stay focused on the outside and demand that it change. They must modify their behavior. This new behavior will be proof that there has been a change of heart. If they say their hearts are changed without a corresponding change of behavior, you can be assured no real inner change has occurred. John is in a long line of prophets who insist the "proof is in the pudding."

Do not presume to say to yourselves, 'We have Abraham as our ancestor'; for I tell you, God is able from these stones to raise up children to Abraham.

They may not hear this demand of John to produce fruit because they have a louder inner voice that drowns it out. This inner voice speaks a presumption that will inhibit their efforts to change, a presumption so deep they say it to themselves in the secret recesses of the heart. They are children of Abraham and that is enough. They might be able to "flee from the wrath to come" simply because they have Abraham's blood. There is no need for inner repentance for they can claim physical descent. They are part of the chosen people and this fact of their birth takes precedence over inner change and moral living.

John's response to this presumption is brutal. The Pharisees and Sadducees may prize and cling to their physical descent from Abraham. But this means nothing to God. What is special to them is nothing special to God. Children of Abraham are "no sweat" for God. He can raise them up from stones. It is not important in God's sight and so presenting it to God as a safeguard for salvation is completely wrongheaded.

Even now the ax is lying at the root of the trees; every tree therefore that does not bear good fruit is cut down and thrown into the fire.

The way they are thinking deludes them. They must understand the imperative of the desert. Do not delay decision. The time is now. Either produce or perish. Anything that contributes to vacillation or resistance must be eliminated. Do not play games and try to comply on the outside while remaining unchanged on the inside. Do not cling to automatic privileges like the prestige of your family or ethnic group or religion as a safeguard against divine command to change. None of these things will clear the path; none of them will open you for the coming Kingdom.

I baptize you with water for repentance, but one who is more powerful than I is coming after me; I am not worthy to carry his sandals. He will baptize you with the Holy Spirit and fire. His winnowing fork is in his hand, and he will clear his threshing floor and will gather his wheat into the granary; but the chaff he will burn with unquenchable fire."

John works with water for repentance; Jesus works with fire for Spirit. Both are needed, but one is greater. The goal is always superior to the means. Water cleans and waits. Fire enlightens and inspires. In a poem, "The Man Who Was a Lamp," I had John say:

I can denounce a king
But I cannot enthrone one.
I can strip an idol of its power,
But I cannot reveal the true God.
I can wash the soul in sand,
But I cannot dress it in white.
I devour locusts and turn them into honey,
But I cannot lace his sandal.
I can condemn the sin,
But I cannot bear it away.

John is not Jesus, but the way to Jesus.

However, there is one dynamic they share. How you respond to who they are and what they say is crucial to your well-being. John lays an ax to the root of the tree. Jesus pounds the threshing floor with a winnowing fan. The result in both cases is a division. The productive tree stands and the unproductive tree falls. The wheat is gathered into barns and the chaff is confined to fire. John and Jesus are both offers that can be refused.

Teaching

So I will allure her;
  I will lead her into the desert
  and speak to her heart. (Hos 2:16; NAB)

I have translated this, "The desert will lead you to your heart where I shall speak." The heart is the material pump of the body, the physical muscle that keeps blood flowing and the body alive. In biblical theology it becomes a metaphor for the spiritual center of the person. The "heart" is a space of consciousness where the person is both open to God and ready to act on that openness. It keeps spiritual life flowing and the spiritual person alive. To say, "the heart is hard," is to imply the person is not in conscious contact with God and consequently does not act out of that awareness. There is no flow. To say, "the heart is on fire," is to imply the person is in conscious contact with God and is acting out of that awareness. There is flow. It is the heart where the deepest contact with both God and the world is made.

But how do we get to the heart? How do we allow consciousness to rest in the spiritual center of our being?

The desert will lead us there. In particular, the person who lives in the desert will lead us there. But be warned. His tactics are rigorous. The heart is camouflaged by self deceptions, and we are skilled in not looking at these most comforting delusions. But the voice crying in the wilderness is determined to make us look. There is something infinitely better than our present way of deception. But we will not be open to it until we acknowledge and let go of the avoiding strategies of the mind. Repentance is the path.

Repentance begins by entering the desert. The desert means "off on our own," far from the madding crowd. Until we enter into solitude and do some inner work, we are always a one-sided creation of other people. We are living a life we have not investigated and claimed. It may be a safe life, a well-respected life, and a well-rewarded life, but it is not our life. We need to purify and simplify, to come back to what is essential, and to rethink where we have been and where we are going. We need to uncover the core desires that drive us and evaluate them.

A first step on the path to the heart is: "Who taught us to flee from the wrath that is to come?" Who taught us to act only as a reaction to the possibility of injury? Why do we only do things to protect ourselves? In fact, we may have come to the desert in this half-hearted position. We are not seeking authentic living, but only some external compliance that may keep us from harm. But heart action is not reactive behavior to the dangers of life. Heart action is the overflow of inner fullness. But we will not reach the heart until we realize how blindly we are attached to the reactive ego.

The path to the heart continues with the injunction, "Do not presume to say to yourselves, 'There is something special about us that God loves and this exempts us from this painful process of honest appraisal.'" In other words, we deceive ourselves. We identify with some aspect of "who we are" that we think will spare us. Then we market that delusion to ourselves and to others. The hard word of the heart leader insists that what God loves is this painful process. For it is through this process of "dis-identifying" with our "self-righteousness" that we open to the heart. The open heart receives God's life and conveys it into the world.

When we arrive at the heart, we will know the truth of loving both God and neighbor. Until we arrive there, we are deluded. We live in what Reb Menahem Nendle of Korzk, known as the Kotzker, called a world of phantoms—false perceptions we treat as real. The story is told of the Kotzker:

> One day he and Reb Hirsh of Tomashov came to bridge where several women began throwing stones at them.
> "Have no fear," said the Kotzker. "They are not real women, or are their stones real. They are mere phantoms."
> Reb Hirsh was silent for a moment, then asked, "Might we not be phantoms too?"
> "No," came the Kotzker's answer, "as long as we have at some time had the genuine urge to repent." (Abraham Joshua Heschel, *A Passion for Truth* [New York: Farrar, Straus and Giroux, 1973])

The "genuine urge to repent" is an expression of our desire to be real, to be conscious of our ultimate grounding and live out of that grounding.

Why did the people come to John and submit to his harsh words and tactics? Why do we continue to journey to his desert? We sense the promise in repentance, the promise to move beyond half-heartedness and delusion, the promise to be real, the promise that will lead us to our heart.

Third Sunday of Advent

Matthew 11:2-12

Opening to Wholeness

A Spiritual Commentary

When John heard in prison what the Messiah [the Christ] was doing, he sent word by his disciples and said to him, "Are you the one who is to come, or are we to wait for another?"

St. Matthew, the storyteller, cleverly disassociates himself from John's question. He tells us John has heard about the "works of *Christ*." Therefore, Jesus is the *Christ*, the Messiah, the one who is to come. The question is answered for St. Matthew, but not for John.

What John has heard about Jesus has raised a question. John's vision of what was to come emphasized judgment, punishment, and vindication. What he is hearing about Jesus does not fit these expectations. So he wants Jesus to declare himself and clarify the issue.

The phrasing of the question—"Are you the one who is to come, or are we to wait for another?"—sets the tone for the whole passage. The Baptist and his disciples are looking for someone. But what exactly are they looking for, what are the deepest desires of their hearts? If they can bring to consciousness the deepest desires of their hearts, they might be able to answer their own question.

Jesus answered them, "Go and tell John what you hear and see: the blind receive their sight, the lame walk, the lepers are cleansed, the deaf hear, the dead are raised, and the poor have good news brought to them. And blessed is anyone who takes no offense at me."

Jesus does not answer the question directly. Instead he points to his works. He is applying one of John's stinging criteria to himself—"You will know them by their fruits" (Matt 7:16). John's disciples are to tell John what they see and hear. The implication is that each person must come to their own conclusion about whether Jesus is the one for whom they are waiting. It is more important to grasp the meaning of the works of Jesus than for him to claim a title. Titles, as the Gospels make

37

abundantly clear, are open to misunderstanding. Works are definitive statements.

Jesus' works are imaginative examples of restoration. Something that was missing is found; something that was wounded is healed. Sight, mobility, cleanliness, hearing, life, and dignity are returned to people who did not have them. In the mythology of Gospel times, Jesus is restoring creation, undoing the effects of Adam's fall. He is reconnecting people with God and the symbolic result is a whole human person.

This activity may not be what John is looking for. It does not have the edge of judgment that John's preaching pushed. Jesus may be an offense to the fierce apocalyptic mindset. But the one who is blessed by God does not take offence at this restoration activity. In fact, that one will recognize it as both God's creative activity and the desires of his or her own heart.

As they went away, Jesus began to speak to the crowds about John: "What did you go out into the wilderness to look at?

The audience changes from John's disciples to the crowds. In this instance, the crowds symbolize common humanity, the ordinary run of women and men.

Jesus probes their hearts by questioning them about why they were attracted to John. When they went into the desert of self-examination where John lived, what drove them? What were they looking for? This question, which will be repeated three times, is the strategy of a spiritual teacher trying to uncover the deepest desires of the heart. Only if they understand their deepest desires will they be able to respond to Jesus.

A reed shaken by the wind?

Were they looking for someone who was the plaything of every influence, at the whim of swirling outer forces? The supposed answer is no.

What then did you go out to see?

Jesus launches a second probe into their desires. If it wasn't a reed swayed by the wind, then what was it? Looking into the heart to see what drives us is not an easy task. Finding the root desire is a journey of discovery. A guide is helpful and, in this text, Jesus is the guide. One of the duties of the guide is to push the question and not allow us to settle for surface answers.

Someone dressed in soft robes? Look, those who wear soft robes are in royal palaces.

Did you go into the desert for pomp, circumstances, and glitz? Are you a royal watcher? If you are, you are in the wrong place.

What then did you go out to see?

This is third probe and, honoring the law of threes, it is the one that reaches its target. Jesus is about to deliver the "thrust home," the uncovering of the heart.

A prophet? Yes, I tell you,

The real longing is to connect with a prophet, a God-grounded man who cannot be pushed around and confronts the abuses of people who live in palaces. This is a prophet who speaks the word of God. This word of God may be a word of repentance, but there is a promise in the repentance, a promise that rings the human heart like a bell.

and more than a prophet. This is the one about whom it is written, 'See, I am sending my messenger ahead of you, who will prepare your way before you.'

They wanted a prophet who could not only criticize sin but could point to redemption. In other words, John points to Jesus. Jesus is the promise at the heart of prophetic repentance, and so Jesus is the ultimate reason they went into the desert. They may not have known it, but what Jesus does is what they want. They wanted their sight restored, their legs moving, their skin clean, their ears open, their life flowing, their poverty enriched. In other words, they want wholeness and renewal. To the question, "Are you the One Who Is to Come or shall we look for another?" Jesus answers, "Well, here is what I do. But what are you looking for? If you uncover the deepest desires of your heart, you will answer your own question and you will know I am the One."

Truly I tell you, among those born of women no one has arisen greater than John the Baptist; yet the least in the kingdom of heaven is greater than he."

Two levels are assumed. One is "born of women" and John is the foremost development of that level. Standard Christian interpretation has seen this level as the human struggle to hear and obey God's call. Yet a second level, "the kingdom of heaven," is vastly different. To touch this level, even in the least way, raises you above the Baptist. Standard Christian interpretation has seen this level as grace, God's loving presence flooding into the open soul.

The deepest desire of the heart is to be connected to God, the source and parent. People have strayed from this relationship and, consequently, live in exile from their true selves. But they search for what they have lost. Therefore, what they went out to see was the possibility of reconnecting, of restoring what they had lost, of reinhabiting the garden in the fierceness of the desert. What they found was John as the path to Jesus. Jesus is the New Adam or, in another image, the bridegroom. John is the friend of the bridegroom and rejoices at the sound of his voice (see John 3:29). John clears the path, but Jesus walks on it.

Teaching

In *Tales of a Magic Monastery* (New York: Crossroad, 1981) 22–23, Theophane the Monk tells this story. He is in the House of God and late at night he hears a voice.

> "What are you leaving out?"
> I looked around. I heard it again,
> "WHAT ARE YOU LEAVING OUT?"
> Was it my imagination? Soon it was all around me, whispering, roaring, "What are you leaving out? What are you leaving out?"
> Was I cracking up? I managed to get to my feet and head for the door. I wanted the comfort of a human face or a human voice. Nearby was the corridor where some of the monks live. I knocked on one cell.
> "What do you want?" came a sleepy voice.
> "What am I leaving out?"
> "Me," he answered.
> I went to the next door.
> "What do you want?"
> "What am I leaving out?"
> "Me."
> A third cell, a fourth, all the same.
> I thought, "They're all stuck on themselves." I left the building in disgust. Just then the sun was coming up. I had never spoken to the sun before, but I heard myself pleading, "What am I leaving out?"
> The sun too answered, "Me." That finished me.
> I threw myself flat on the ground. And the earth said, "ME."

"What are you leaving out?" is not a question we often associate with the spiritual life. But it is a question that is presupposed in Jesus' vision of restoring the human. He is going to bring back sight, hearing, movement, vitality, and dignity. Obviously, these have been lost, and the heart's desire is to reclaim them.

However, we do not randomly lose "parts" of ourselves. We cut them off, pushing them out of awareness. One psychological interpretation of this process is in terms of persona and shadow. The persona is an idealized self-image we have created. It is through this persona that we present ourselves to the outer world. However, this self-image has been built up by a process of denying certain aspects of ourselves. As the T-shirt says, "Denial is not a river in Egypt." These neglected aspects are the shadow, the parts of ourselves that we do not allow into the light of consciousness. The result is we hold in our consciousness only a fragment of our totality. In this way, we create a very tight shoe that does not allow all of who we are to dance.

Robert Bly personally describes this phenomenon of shadow as a "long bag we drag behind us."

> When we were one or two years old we had what we might call a 360-degree personality . . . but one day we noticed that our parents didn't like certain parts . . . They said things like: "Can't you be still?" Or "It isn't nice to try and kill your brother." Behind us we have an invisible bag, and the part of us our parents don't like, we, to keep our parents' love, put in the bag. By the time we go to school our bag is quite large. Then our teachers have their say: "Good children don't get angry over such little things." So we take our anger and put it in the bag. By the time my brother and I were twelve in Madison, Minnesota, we were known as "the nice Bly boys." Our bags were already a mile long. (*A Little Book on the Human Shadow*, ed. William Booth [San Francisco: Harper and Row, 1988, 17])

Of course, these repressed negative and positive aspects do not stay in the bag. At a later point in our life, they reappear and ask to be integrated in a different way.

What are some of the common deselected "parts" of the human?

We may screen out our body and with it the swings of pain and pleasure. As James Joyce quipped, "Mr. Duffy lived a short distance from his body." Or we may screen out our emotions. We have no highs or lows. We live numbed, permanently on anesthesia. Or we may exclude our mortality. We think pondering death is morbid, and so we refuse to deal with our finitude and its consequences for how we live. Or we may push away those aspects of ourselves that we think would offend our family or friends or the ideals of society. We are not living our lives. We are playing a part others have chosen.

Therefore, restoring the human means the return of the repressed. In theological language, it means recognizing the essential goodness of creation, being in harmony with our complete finitude. The first creation story of Genesis says, "God saw *everything* that he had made, and indeed, it was very good" (Gen 1:31). First God sees all; then God sees it is good. In the sight of God all are good. Therefore, essential aspects of creation do not have to be rejected.

But how does God see?

> My father, of blessed memory, once said to me, on the verse in Genesis: "And He saw all that He had made and behold it was good" —my father once said that the seeing of God is not like the seeing of man. Man sees only between the blinks of his eyes. He does not know what the world is like during the blinks. He sees the world in pieces, in fragments. But the master of the universe sees the world whole, unbroken. That world is good. Our seeing is broken, Asher Lev. Can we make it like the seeing of God? Is it possible? (Chaim Potak, *The Gift of Asher Lev* [New York: Alfred A. Knopf, 1990])

When Jesus answers the question, "Are you the one who is to come, or are we to wait for another?" by pointing to the blind seeing, this is one interpretation of what he means. His work is to move people beyond pieces and fragments. He is going to give them the ability to see without blinking. He is going to open the heart to the wholeness of creation for this is what the heart always wants. This is what the crowds went into the desert to see, and it is Jesus who knows how to see in this way and knows how to teach others to see in this way. The One Who Is To Come has arrived.

Fourth Sunday of Advent

Matthew 1:18-24

Making a Home for Spirit

A Spiritual Commentary

Now the birth of Jesus the Messiah took place in this way.

In St. Matthew's story the birth narrative naturally appears at the beginning, but it was crafted after the life, death, and resurrection of Jesus. Therefore, it is more in the nature of a theological reflection on the meaning of Jesus than a factual account of his birth. In general, birth narratives follow the acorn-oak pattern. The larger dynamics that will shape his life (the oak) are present in embryonic form at his birth (the acorn). In another image, the birth narrative is the overture. It sounds themes that will be developed in the symphony of his life.

When his mother Mary had been engaged to Joseph, but before they lived together, she was found to be with child from the Holy Spirit.

In one line the storyteller sets the tension. Mary is officially betrothed to Joseph, but they have not had sexual relations. However, she is found to be pregnant. This is a scandal. Either she was raped or she had illicit sexual relations with someone else. However, the theologically constrained storyteller does not pursue these lurid and down-to-earth possibilities. Instead, he tells the readers that the child in Mary's womb is the work of the Holy Spirit.

The basic theme is stated. The work of the Holy Spirit emerges in human life as a scandal. During his life Jesus will be considered a scandal. He will challenge the prevailing understanding of the law, eat with tax collectors and sinners, and make claims that sound like blasphemy. However what looks like a scandal on one level is really the work of God on a deeper level. Even as an embryo Jesus caused scandal. What can you expect when he grows up?

Her husband Joseph, being a righteous man and unwilling to expose her to public disgrace, planned to dismiss her quietly.

Joseph is permitted to hold a public inquiry to determine how Mary got pregnant. But no matter what the finding of this public inquiry is, rape or consensual sex, Mary's situation is worsened. Her shame is exposed in a public way. Joseph decides not to claim this right of the injured husband. He decides to break the marriage in as quiet a way as possible.

In the storyteller mind, this decision of Joseph makes him righteous. He is sensitively applying the law. He is not demanding public, legal exposure and punishment. In fact, he is trying to save as much of Mary's honor as possible. He is not holding Mary in her shame; he is trying to mitigate it. Joseph understands and acts on the distinction between the person and the person's perceived sin. He is trying to respect the person and yet not undercut the purposes of the law.

Of course, this struggle will be an ongoing tension of Jesus' ministry. He will declare the center of the law is love of God and love of neighbor (Matt 22:37-39). That center should flow through and interpret every particular law and how it is applied. But this is creative activity and difficult work. In the Christian tradition, Joseph is a carpenter. In spiritual teaching, carpentry is the way we pull together the pieces of life, fashioning a home for our truth. Joseph the carpenter is at work here, trying to build a response of love in a world of law. This man is an appropriate legal father for the child who will grow up and say the law should be fulfilled (see Matt 5:17-18), and with almost the same breath say, "unless your righteousness exceeds that of the scribes and Pharisees, you will never enter the kingdom of heaven" (Matt 5:20). The paradox is established: to fulfill the law you have to go beyond it.

> **But just when he had resolved to do this, an angel of the Lord appeared to him in a dream and said, "Joseph, son of David, do not be afraid to take Mary as your wife, for the child conceived in her is from the Holy Spirit. She will bear a son, and you are to name him Jesus, for he will save his people from their sins."**

However, Joseph never gets to carry out his righteous plan of "quiet divorce." Instead, he is introduced to a new plan. He experiences a divine communication in a dream. In St. Matthew's birth story, Herod the king has to consult Scripture and priests to find out what God is doing. Joseph need only go to sleep, to move beyond ordinary waking consciousness and into deeper regions of awareness open to him. In other words, Joseph has direct, personal experience of divine intentions and activity.

This fact establishes a tension between tradition and experience. What tradition labels scandal, Joseph is told to call Spirit. Tradition says to divorce her; the dream experience says to take her into his home. Of course, this foreshadows the tension of all who will hear and be drawn to Jesus. Is he a scandal to be rejected or manifestation of Spirit to be welcomed?

The essence of the angelic communication is that a deeper divine plan is at work and Joseph is part of it. His role is to shelter Mary and name the child "Jesus, for he will save his people from their sins." This naming is appropriate activity for Joseph, not only because he is of the house of David and therefore establishes Jesus as a son of David, but also because he is no stranger to the inner struggles of sin and forgiveness. His righteous intention with regard to Mary can be read as a creative attempt to bring love into the world of law, to extend forgiveness to what looked like sin. He should name the child Jesus for the very presence of the child is a catalyst for clarifying his own deeper instincts, affirming the path he was going to take, and encouraging him on the path that now lies before him.

All this took place to fulfill what had been spoken by the Lord through the prophet: "Look, the virgin shall conceive and bear a son, and they shall name him Emmanuel," which means, "God is with us."

St. Matthew tells his readers that this is all part of a plan. Through the prophet the Lord said this would happen and, behold, it is happening. The natural inclination to be "in on a secret" is heightened. St. Matthew is letting us in on God's secret, the hidden divine plan. If the readers have religious instincts and want to tie themselves to what is ultimate, this connection of past prophesy to present fulfillment will win them over.

St. Matthew also supplies for us the deeper reason why Jesus will save his people from their sins. He is "Emmanuel—God with us." Forgiveness of sins is the effect of God's presence. Therefore, the people who will call him Emmanuel (*"they* will name [call] him . . .") are those who through him have been liberated from the bondage of sin. In St. Matthew's vision these people will be members of many nations. Through Joseph's acceptance of Mary and his naming of the child, Jesus will be the inheritor of the promises of the house of David. However, in the name "Emmanuel" is the indication that Jesus belongs to all people, to all people grounded in God. Salvation may come through the Jews (John 4:22) but it is meant for all.

The "God with us" at the beginning of Matthew's Gospel is matched at the end of the Gospel by the mountaintop Jesus saying, "I am with you always, to the end of the age" (Matt 28:20). The deepest truth about Jesus is that he is the presence of God that does not depart even when he is no longer physically present. That is why Jesus is portrayed in this story as not having a biological father. The truth about him that must be recognized and acknowledged is his spiritual parentage. Any reduction of who he is—and what he is about—to physical and social causes will miss the essence of the revelation. This is the truth on which Jesus will insist. In a different context he will exhort both the crowds and his disciples: "call no one your father on earth, for you have one Father—the one in heaven" (Matt 23:9).

When Joseph awoke from sleep, he did as the angel of the Lord commanded him; he took her as his wife.

The essence of biblical anthropology is "hear and obey." First people must discern the voice of God amid the cacophony of human noise. Then they must obey that voice, enact it in time and history. They struggle to make immanent what they perceived in a moment of transcendence. If they do this, in spiritual traditions they are characterized as being awake.

Joseph wakes up. This means more than he arises from physical sleep. It means he now perceives the divine dimension of what is happening. Mary's condition is not scandal but Spirit, and so he takes her into his home. He embraces the truth of what is occurring and unites himself to it.

This is the path of a righteous Jew becoming a follower of Jesus. They have to move from the perception of scandal to the perception of Spirit, from the perception that what is happening is against the God of Israel to the insight that what is happening is the activity of the God of Israel. If this is difficult when the happening is Mary's pregnancy, imagine the difficulty when the happening is Jesus' execution, approved by both Jewish and Roman authorities.

Teaching

Christian imagination has never been satisfied with the Gospels. The stories are often theologically succinct and, if meditated on, spiritually rich; but they are seldom humanly abundant. As one teenager told me, "They leave out too much good stuff." Of course, Christians have felt obliged to fill in the gaps.

One storyline has Joseph and Jesus working in their Nazareth carpentry shop. As Joseph teaches the secrets of the hammer, the plane, and the saw to the boy who "grows in age, wisdom, and grace" (Luke 2:52; trans. mine), he also confides in him his life "learnings." As with all parents, Joseph talks too much. But the boy is an exceptional listener to the one speaking:

> Remember, Jesus, whatever we're making, along with it we're always making a home for Spirit. Your mother thinks a home for Spirit is like an empty cup. But I favor a spacious room with a large window for sun—and a door that is hard to find.
>
> The best way to begin is to clear a space, and the best way to clear a space is to stop the mind from judging. Whenever things seem simple and obvious and the mind is feasting on its certainty and outrage, go slow. There is more than you think, only it hasn't appeared yet. Judgment stops the appearance of more. It cuts down people and situations to the little you know. It closes possibilities.
>
> Also when you do not judge, you often avoid disgracing another. The law is our measure. It is a tool of judgment, but someone always wields it. Do not use it as a hammer to hit or a saw to cut. Our tools are to fashion a table, not to brutalize the wood. The law is a tool to fashion a people of love, but it can break people and lose its sense of purpose. It always fears life will get out of control. So it wants to make examples of people who break it. It feeds and grows strong on transgression. It smacks its lips over scandal. But scandal is not the same as real offense. Scandal can be the irruption of God's love that our feeble minds have yet to understand. So find a way to honor the law and honor the person who, in our limited understanding, has broken it. This is not easy.
>
> It requires making law work for love. Love is the sun; law its furthest and often weakest ray. If you hold onto love, you will see how the law can reflect it. If you lose love, law will not substitute for it. It will only be something you use to promote yourself and punish others. When you love the person through the law, you shape the law to the reality that is always more than you know. This gives life a chance to breathe and people a chance to change. And the deepest change will not be in other people, but in yourself. Love takes the beam out of your own eye. It does not focus on the splinters in the eyes of others.
>
> Once something happened and I was tempted to judge and punish. But I held back and waited, and a deeper door opened—the door that is hard to find. I was led into a room of sun, a home for Spirit. Your mother and you were there—and a presence of light who talked to my fear. I

sensed all distances had been traversed, all separations connected. It was a dream, but it was not sleep. The dream awakened me. It took the beam out of my eye. I saw that making a home for Spirit is an endless adventure—like you growing up, my son.

So see everything twice, Jesus. See it once with the physical eye and then see it again with the eye of the heart. At first glance, you often see an uneven and unusable piece of wood. You may be about to throw it away. But do not be fooled by surface appearances. Look deeper. On second glance, you may see a lovely arm of a chair hidden in its unaccustomed shape. When you see the loveliness, Jesus, embrace it. Take it into your home. Do not hesitate and do not ask questions. Argue with everything, Jesus, but be obedient to love.

The boy listened.

The Baptism of the Lord
Matthew 3:13-17

Awakening to Love

A Spiritual Commentary

Jesus came from Galilee to John at the Jordan, to be baptized by him.

Jesus does not stumble upon John. He deliberately travels to John at the Jordan in order to be baptized. This is the beginning of Matthew's insistence that Jesus is directing events. Even when it seems like Jesus is a victim of either caprice or overriding social forces, the storyteller will portray him as covertly in charge or being obedient to a God-guided drama of which he is fully aware. This literary device is at the service of a theological conviction. Jesus' life is part of a pre-ordained divine plan to bring people to salvation.

John would have prevented him, saying, "I need to be baptized by you, and do you come to me?"

But Jesus answered him, "Let it be so now; for it is proper for us in this way to fulfill all righteousness."

Then he consented.

This is an enigmatic exchange between Jesus and John. Scholars speculate that the baptism of Jesus by John was an embarrassment for Christians. John's baptism was for the repentance of sins, and so it could be concluded that Jesus had sinned. Also, the one who baptizes is greater than the one who is baptized, and so it could be concluded that John was superior to Jesus. This dialogue between John and Jesus forestalls these false conclusions. John admits Jesus' superiority, and Jesus gives a reason other than forgiveness of sins for the baptism—the fulfillment of all righteousness.

This conversation may also be read as a spiritual exchange between two men aware of their complementary roles in a larger drama. John's acknowledgment that he needs Jesus' baptism is more than simply admitting Jesus' superiority. It is recognition of the proper order of things. John baptizes with water for the forgiveness of sins. This baptism is not an end in itself, but an opening for Spirit. It is Jesus who baptizes with Spirit. John is well aware of what he is able to do. He is now looking for the next step, for the fulfillment of his baptizing activity. "I need to be baptized by you," reflects John's hunger to go beyond repentance to the experience of Spirit.

However, John will not have his way. The storyteller wants to communicate a different teaching. "All righteousness" must be fulfilled, and so John is to allow the baptism of Jesus. This phrase "all righteousness" may refer to fulfilling past prophecies. Jesus is careful to follow the path prescribed for him, and that path entails continuity with the prophetic tradition of which John, the new Elijah, is the supreme exemplar. "[A]mong those born of women no one has arisen greater than John the Baptist" (Matt 11:11). The revelation of Jesus goes beyond the prophetic tradition, but it does not bypass it.

But also "all righteousness" may refer to the need for a complete conversion process. Jesus' baptism with Spirit does not substitute for John's baptism with water. Both are needed. The revelation of Jesus includes the revelation of John even while it transcends it. John is the forerunner and essential preparation for Jesus. John clears a path. Without this cleared path Jesus will not arrive. There must be both repentance and the coming of the Spirit, a disidentification with sin and an identification with the Spirit-infused Child of God. This carefully structured exchange reflects this nuanced position: the ultimate goal of John's baptizing activity is Jesus, but the advent of Jesus does not make obsolete the work of John. John and Jesus are fundamentally linked, and they symbolize the essential relationship between the forgiveness of sins and new life in the Spirit.

> **And when Jesus had been baptized, just as he came up from the water, suddenly [or *behold*] the heavens were opened to [or *for*] him and he saw the Spirit of God descending like a dove and alighting on him. And a voice from heaven said, "This is my Son, the Beloved, with whom I am well pleased." (alternatives mine)**

However, despite the essential connection between John and Jesus, the emphasis is not on John's baptism. There is no description of Jesus going into and going under the water. All the action happens after the baptism, when Jesus comes up from the water. The storyteller inserts the word "behold" to alert us to the upcoming revelation. This is a personal experience for Jesus. The heavens are being opened *for him* and *he saw* the Spirit of God. In contemporary language, Jesus' consciousness is awakened to the divine source of his life, a source that gives itself to him in love.

This source experience is expressed in symbols that resonate throughout the Hebrew Scriptures. The prophet Isaiah is longing for God to come and be among his people. He cries out, "O that you would tear open the heavens and come down" (Isa 64:1; cf. 63:19 in NAB)! The opened heavens symbolize the possibility of the presence of God. When the heavens are closed, God is unavailable to human experience. When the heavens open, perhaps something will come through that opening, come down from above. Torn heavens are the first step in the availability of God.

The Holy Spirit, the immanent presence of the transcendent God, comes down through the ripped sky as Jesus rises up out of the water. The Holy Spirit descends like a dove. In Hellenistic cultures a lover might convey his feelings to a beloved by giving him or her a dove. So the dove may symbolize love and prepare the way for the announcement, "This is my Son, the Beloved, with whom I am well pleased." The words of the heavenly voice interpret the meaning of the descending heavenly gift.

However, Jesus' coming out of the waters and the descending of the dove may also allude to the Noah story. In that story the dove symbolized the first messenger of a new beginning, a renewal for the earth. After the flood that destroyed the sinfulness of the earth (cf. John's baptism), Noah's ark, with its cargo of living things, floated on the waters (Gen 8). To find out if the waters were receding and a renewed earth emerging, Noah sent out a dove. The first time he did this, the dove returned because it "found no place to set its foot" (v. 9). The second time the dove returned with an olive branch in its beak. Land was somewhere. The third time the dove did not return, and Noah knew that earth had emerged and the dove had found a place to nest. This return of the earth meant a new covenant between God and humankind. After the removal of sin, a new possibility of life had arrived.

The story of Noah extends the meaning of the Holy Spirit coming upon Jesus as a dove. Jesus is the messenger of a new covenant. Through him the earth will emerge out of the waters of sin just as he has emerged out of the waters of the Jordan. After all, an angel told Joseph in a dream to name him Jesus because he will save his people from their sins.

But what is life like after sin? When the Holy Spirit comes upon you, what does it accomplish? What is its communication?

The meaning of the dove-Spirit is expressed by the voice from the heavens. "This is my Son, the Beloved, with whom I am well pleased." Although the story has stressed that this is a personal experience of Jesus, the voice from heaven does not speak to him personally. It does not say, *"You* are my Son, the Beloved," as it does in Mark (1:11) and Luke (3:22). Instead it proclaims to everyone, "This is my beloved Son" (Matt 3:17; NAB) This announcement style means that others are supposed to hear this voice. It is not an intimate small whisper in the heart of Jesus. Although it is a personal experience, the identity of Jesus is not a personal privilege. The Spirit-infused Jesus embodies the news of the new covenant, a possibility for all people. When you repent and leave your sins in the waters of the Jordan, God's love awaits you, making you daughters and sons of divine pleasure.

Teaching

There has always been a creative tension in the way Christians relate to Jesus Christ. On the one hand, Jesus is the unique Son of God, irreplaceable and beyond imitation. On the other hand, Christians participate in the identity of Jesus Christ, continuing his presence on earth and imitating his way of life. Therefore, Christians are "sons and daughters in the Son." The descending dove and the speaking sky that combine to communicate love and mission to Jesus are passed along through Jesus to all his followers. The ultimate communication of the story of Jesus is for his followers to see and hear what he saw and heard as he came up out of the waters of the Jordan.

Jesus is the firstborn. As Paul says, God calls people "to be conformed to the image of his Son, in order that he might be the firstborn within a large family" (Rom 8:29). In another image taken from the letter to the Hebrews, Jesus is a "pioneer" (Heb 12:2). He has blazed a trail for others to follow. In yet another image, Jesus can be called first awakened from sleep (cf. Eph 5:14 and Col 1:18) Jesus' baptism has awakened him to his ultimate identity as the beloved one. Now his mission is to awaken others to their ultimate identity as beloved ones.

One astute observer of Gospel stories suggested that Zacchaeus came to see and love in himself what Jesus saw and loved in him. By extension, it could be said that Peter came to see and love in himself what Jesus saw and loved in him, and Magdalene came to see and love in herself what Jesus saw and loved in her. Jesus sees the "child of God" (see John 1:12 and 1 John 3:1) in people with such clarity and persistence that they begin to see it in themselves. But, in order for him to see the "child of God" in others, he must first know it in himself. In this sense, Jesus' baptism by water and Spirit is the precondition for the baptism by water and Spirit of all Christians. The one who would awaken others to love must first himself be awakened.

Therefore, awakening to love is essentially an interpersonal chain. The awakened Jesus awakens others, and then those awaken still others. In this way, communities are built up, traditions developed, and the revelation of Jesus is passed from generation to generation. This might be one of the meanings of the word "evangelization." Evangelization happens when awakened people awaken others to their "child of God" identity.

However, this awakening to love is neither a quick nor romantic process. It is a long haul endeavor that demands rigorous self-examination, persistence, and not a little courage. First, it must be understood that coming into a "child of God" identity is not chasing an ideal. It is not trying to become something that at the moment people are not. People *are* beloved children of God. There is no need to make them children of God. The task is for them to realize this truth of their identity. Therefore, Jesus awakens people to what they already are. He facilitates awareness; he does not bring to them something that had been previously absent. This perception is captured in the saying, "Jesus stands by the river selling river water."

Second, it must never be forgotten that people are more than just children of God. They are also children of Ralph and Anna, Marlene and Bob, Roxanne and Pete. They are bodies with inherited tendencies toward sickness and health, conditioned personalities built up out of experiences and internalizations, roles and responsibilities that go so deep they often practically define who they are. The "son and daughter of God" identity is not another identity, existing alongside or above this complex human make-up. The "child of God" identity exists within the flux and flow of the total reality of people. Therefore, awakening to the "child of God" identity initially means discerning it in the midst of other elements and noticing how it is expressed and repressed in the dynamics of body, mind, and social relationships. In other words, the "child of God" identity entails dealing with both finitude and sin.

Therefore, as some aspects of the Christian tradition have always maintained, the human person is a combination of essential communion and existential alienation, an original blessing and a profound curse. The way through the alienation to the communion and through the curse to the blessing is a difficult path. In the Gospels Jesus has walked this path and helps others walk it. He is not a blind guide leading the blind. He is a seeing guide leading the blurred. He is patiently persistent in his efforts to awaken people to love. All that he says and does— his exchanges with people, his stories, his teachings, his deeds of power, and his instructions to his disciples—are in the service of this awakening. They are the strategies of a spiritual teacher more than they are the pronouncements of a theologian.

For me, this emphasis on the way people come to their "child of God" identity is the ultimate reason why John must baptize Jesus. As the embodiment of divine love, Jesus must know the whole process of awakening. Realizing the "child of God" identity is not only welcoming the Spirit and hearing the voice. It also entails "dis-identifying" with all that is not love. This is what John's desert and his cleansing baptism are all about. Jesus himself continues John's baptism in his preaching and teaching about the forgiveness of sins. What he learned at the Jordan was: only if you ascend out of the waters of repentance can you see the dove descend and hear the voice speak.

In St. Matthew's story the dove makes a direct descent, and the "beloved child of God" identity is instantly bestowed in the revelatory moment of the accompanying heavenly voice. But I like the three-stage foray of Noah's dove. First, it goes out and can find no land. So it returns to the ark, its only refuge from the destructive waters. Our first attempts to understand and make our own a "child of God" identity are often unsuccessful, and we scurry back to safety. Next, the dove returns with an olive branch. We begin to see signs of a new possibility, but we are not there yet. Finally, we do not return for we have found a place to stand. Once again, as in the act of creation, God has created land out of the chaotic waters, and we have a place to stand against the destructive sea. The place we are standing is called, "the beloved child of God."

Second Sunday in Ordinary Time
Second Sunday after Epiphany
John 1:29-42

Tracking Testimony

A Spiritual Commentary

[John the Baptist] saw Jesus coming toward him and said, "Behold, the Lamb of God, who takes away the sin of the world." (John 1:29; NAB)

When John sees Jesus, it is not merely a physical sighting. He sees into the mission of Jesus. His seeing is a revelation, and so it begins with the word that triggers revelation, "Behold."

The content of the revelation is that Jesus takes away the sin of the world. "Sin" does not refer to the many individual transgressions of the human race. Rather it points to the fundamental alienation of God from creation. Jesus bridges this basic separation. Therefore, he is the way to God, the door leading to life.

In the prologue of the Gospel of John (1:1-18) the Word (*logos*) is the original way God and creation are in communion. The Word is both with God from the beginning and is God. Also "all things are made through that one [*logos*]. There was nothing that was made that was not made through that one" (John 1:3; trans. mine). Therefore, the Word is the connective channel between God and creation.

However, this primordial condition has been compromised by human sinfulness. In theological language, creation has become "the world" (e.g., 1 John 2). World is creation in its alienated state, creation that does not acknowledge or open to its Divine Source. The connection with God has been broken or lost sight of or obscured. Now the "*logos* Made Flesh" (Jesus) is coming into the world to reverse the estrangement and to reestablish communion with God. In this sense, he takes away the sin of the world. Therefore, Jesus coming to John should be read as "The true light, which enlightens everyone . . . coming into the world" (John 1:9). John the Baptist sees it, i.e., knows its deep meaning. John the Baptist "saw Jesus coming toward him."

This mission of Jesus, the Word Made Flesh, is expressed in the title, "Lamb of God." This title could connect with many other references to "lamb" in the Scriptures. One of these is the lamb that was sacrificed in the temple as a sin offering. This ritual lamb reestablished the relationship to God after it had been broken (see, e.g., Lev 4:32-35; NAB, "lamb"; NRSV, "sheep"). The sacrificed lamb was a liturgical process humans constructed to overcome sin and to reunite with God.

However, Jesus is not a lamb of sinful humans. Jesus is the "Lamb of God." The chasm between God and the world is overcome by divine initiative. In John's Gospel Jesus frees the temple animals (John 2:13-22). They are no longer needed. Temple sacrifice is no longer the way sin is overcome. God and the world are permanently united in the person of Jesus, and so entering into communion with Jesus, remaining with him, is entering into union with God.

> **This is he of whom I said, 'After me comes a man who ranks ahead of me because he was before me.' I myself did not know him; but I came baptizing with water for this reason, that he might be revealed to Israel."**

John's further testimony is a blend of insight and ignorance. He cleverly uses the world of time to suggest the world of eternity. Usually the one who comes *before* ranks *ahead* of those who come *after*. But, in this case, Jesus who comes *after* ranks *ahead* of John because he existed *before* John. "In the beginning was the Word, and the Word was with God, and the Word was God" (John 1:1). John is sent from God in time; Jesus is with God from eternity. "He existed *before* me" (John 1:30; NAB; emphasis mine). Throughout the Gospel Jesus' identity will be expressed as "I am." This signifies the eternal presence of God within time. John perceives this truth.

However, John did not always perceive this truth. He did not always know the essential meaning of Jesus. This lack of knowledge is especially ironic because he came baptizing precisely so that "this one" would be recognized in Israel. How could Jesus be acknowledged in Israel if he was unknown to the one who was supposed to introduce him to Israel? The underlying problem seems to be: exactly what was John looking for? What were his expectations? Whatever they were, they blinded him rather than gave him sight. John admits to an ignorance that somehow gave way to insight.

So how did the insight arrive? How did John come to know the identity and mission of Jesus?

And John testified, "I saw the Spirit descending from heaven like a dove, and it remained on him. I myself did not know him, but the one who sent me to baptize with water said to me, 'He on whom you see the Spirit descend and remain is the one who baptizes with the Holy Spirit.' And I myself have seen and have testified that this is the Son of God."

John participated in Jesus' post-baptismal experience. He saw the Spirit come down like a dove from heaven and remain upon him. (See the commentary for the Baptism of the Lord.) The description of the Spirit remaining upon Jesus signals this is more than a momentary experience or a divine gift for a special task. The Spirit and Jesus are permanently connected. There is an important implication to this "remaining" together of Jesus and the Spirit. But it seems this implication is initially hidden from John.

Once again John testifies that he did not know him. Although he saw the experience, he could not interpret it correctly. He did not know all that it meant. This ignorance is resolved by listening to the voice of the one who sent him. "There was a man sent from God, whose name was John" (John 1:6). So John hears the voice of God. In the Synoptic Gospels the descending Spirit and dove are accompanied by a divine voice from the opened heavens declaring Jesus the Beloved Son. In the Gospel of John this divine voice acclaiming Jesus is missing. Instead, a divine voice, the originating source of the Baptist's mission, speaks to John about the full meaning of his experience of Jesus. It is God's voice that ultimately prompts the testimony of John, a testimony that bears witness to the truth about Jesus. It is not a voice from heaven, but a voice through John. Human witnessing has replaced direct revelation.

The voice tells John how to interpret what he saw, how to understand the dove remaining on Jesus. This means that Jesus is the giver of the Spirit. He is the one who will baptize with the Spirit. It is through him that the divine Spirit enters the world and brings life. But the sending of the Spirit is the work of God. If Jesus now sends the Spirit, that must mean that Jesus is the Son of God. The divine voice aids John's understanding, and he is ready to join all Christians who "speak of what we know and testify to what we have seen" (John 3:11). So John ends his inner journey of discernment with, "I myself have seen and have testified that this is the Son of God."

However, John's testimony is situated within a double, interpersonal context. He is both witnessing to the truth of Jesus and at the same time talking to whomever will listen. The purpose of John's testimony is to attract others to Jesus. He says this about himself, "I came baptizing with water for this reason, that he might *be revealed to Israel*" (emphasis mine) and the Gospel states this as his ultimate goal: "He came as a witness to testify to the light, so that all might believe through him" (John 1:7). The text may reflect John's path of coming to see the truth of Jesus, but it does not want us to dwell on John. John will later say, "He [Jesus] must increase, but I must decrease."

> **The next day John again was standing with two of his disciples, and as he watched Jesus walk by, he exclaimed, "Look, here is the Lamb of God!" The two disciples heard him say this, and they followed Jesus.**

Now we will see John's verbal testimony unfold into action. In the presence of two of his disciples he sees into the truth of Jesus as he walks by and expresses this truth in the image of a lamb. As a lamb sacrificed in the temple atones for the people's sins and reunites them to God, so the one John encourages his disciples to behold overcomes alienation and unites people to God. The disciples are attracted to this possibility of communion, and their following of Jesus begins.

> **When Jesus turned and saw them following, he said to them, "What are you looking for?"**
>
> **They said to him, "Rabbi" (which translated means Teacher), "where are you staying?"**
>
> **He said to them, "Come and see."**
>
> **They came and saw where he was staying, and they remained with him that day. It was about four o'clock in the afternoon.**

People may begin to walk after Jesus at the behest of others. But Jesus quickly turns and engages them in a personal way. The Teacher is always eager to teach. He asks about their desires. What they are looking for is exactly what Jesus wants to teach them. They want to know "where he lives" or "where he is staying." This is symbolic code for what drives him. What is the structure of his selfhood? What is he all about? This is the right thing to be looking for.

Now Jesus turns their following into a calling, "Come and see." He invites them into a personal knowledge of himself. They accept the invitation. They "see and remain." This means they come into his revelation and receive it into the depths of their being. The timing of this experience coincides with the time of temple worship, four o'clock in the afternoon. Jesus is the new "lamb" of God who replaces the need for the animal sacrifices of the temple. Through interpersonal conversation and not through ritual, Jesus overcomes their alienation and unites them to the Father.

> **One of the two who heard John speak and followed him was Andrew, Simon Peter's brother. He first found his brother Simon and said to him, "We have found the Messiah" (which is translated Anointed). He brought Simon to Jesus, who looked at him and said, "You are Simon son of John. You are to be called Cephas" (which is translated Peter).**

The evangelization pattern is established. John sees the theological truth of Jesus, witnesses to it, and two disciples follow his lead. These two disciples experience the theological truth of Jesus, and one of them, Andrew, witnesses to it, and brings his brother to Jesus. Jesus sees into his brother, into an essence unobservable to others, and renames him. People have to find out for themselves the truth about Jesus, but others who have already discovered that truth show them the way.

Teaching

I was teaching a course on Christology. Halfway through the semester, a student approached me after class. "Can I ask you a question," he said.

"I'm a teacher and you're a student, ask away."

"Do you have a personal relationship to Jesus?"

I looked at him. This was not a witch-hunt. He was genuinely interested. I was being offered an opportunity to testify. And the offer was specifically Christian. He was not asking about the activity of God in my life or my spiritual journey or how I understood a specific belief. He wanted to know about my relationship to Jesus.

I was silent. Finally, I said to him, "I don't want to respond predictably or flippantly. I'd like to think about it and get back to you."

In the past I had responded both ways—predictably and flippantly. In the Catholic world in which I grew up, the question was not about a personal relationship with Jesus but the more intellectual, "What think ye of the Christ?" I knew the Chalcedonian answer, and I spat it out with more conviction than understanding, "one divine person in two natures." But I knew the student wanted more than this predictable, Catholic, orthodox testimony. He wasn't looking for my commitment to the Church's conciliar degrees.

I had also offered flippant testimony. Years ago, I was lying on the North Avenue beach in Chicago in the late afternoon. The sun was beating down on me when all of a sudden a shadow blocked the light. For a moment I thought it was a passing cloud, but then I opened my eyes and there were two young people standing over me.

They were well washed and groomed. He had on a white shirt and tie, and she wore a blouse and a skirt. They were carrying their shoes, and they each had a Bible in hand.

They looked down at me and asked, "Do you know the Lord Jesus as your personal savior?"

I looked up and answered without missing a beat, "Unfortunately, yes."

I have always had a hard time with the Jesus of the Gospels. I do not completely understand much of what Jesus says and does. Needless to say, what I do understand I have great trouble living out. Yet there is this attraction. I keep returning—studying, praying, and trying to find through Jesus a passion and direction for my life. Combined with this, I projected onto the two questioners at the beach that sunny faith that feels it completely owns grace and insists everyone share its syrup. So I put together "unfortunately" and "yes." It was an attempt to be both honest to myself and disconcerting to them. It was not my best moment.

Now there was another chance to "bear witness to Jesus." As I pondered the student's question, I ran into the trickiness of testimony.

I had to distinguish where I was personally with Jesus from the plethora of images and ideas in the Christian tradition. Testimony was neither about adequacy to the Scriptures and tradition nor about what other people have said Jesus has meant for them. Testimony is searingly individual. There can be no hiding in the rhetoric or faith of others.

Nor is a one-word answer appropriate. To the pointed question, "Do you have a personal relationship with Jesus," it is not enough to say "Yes" or "No." And certainly it is high evasion to utter an offended, "Of course." The point is not to state "where you are at" but to unfold the path, to tell the story of how you got to where you are at. When John the Baptist testifies, he tells of "not knowing" Jesus and how he came to recognize him. Of course, this is done in succinct, symbolic code, but it is still bearing witness to a process. Testimony should not rush to the conclusion. It should articulate the adventure.

Therefore, a presupposition for testimony is the ability to be congruent with inner perceptions and feelings and to be able to retrieve how they have changed and developed. This scrutiny has to be undertaken with uncompromising honesty. Sidestepping difficulties or shrugging off nagging doubts as part of the "struggle of faith" short circuits the full current of testimony. The first step of bearing witness is honest self-examination.

In my experience, honest self-examination leads to complexity. Recently, I came across a story about three people who arrived at the door of a spiritual teacher. He asked them all the same question: "Did you come to me because of others or because of yourself?" The first answered that he had been sent by others. He was dismissed. The second answered that he came on his accord. He also was dismissed. The third stammered that he had heard of him from others and yet he also thought he came on his own—partially out of curiosity, partially out of frustration, partially because he was addicted to searching, and probably out of a host of other motives of which he was not aware. The spiritual teacher said, "You'll do." The multilayered mind was accepted.

We do not know all the reasons that drive us. And certainly I do not know all the reasons I am drawn to Jesus and struggle to follow him. I am complex and this complexity cannot be reduced to single-pointed clarity. One benefit of complexity is: if taken seriously, it inevitably brings humility. In relation to Jesus, there develops a "not knowing" that honors the mystery of attraction. I like to fantasize that part of John the Baptist's "not knowing" of Jesus was the sheer complexity of the reasons he was attracted to him.

So in my own mind, hallmarks of testimony began to develop— honest self-examination, sufficient complexity, and true humility. But what about the other side of testimony? Testimony is supposed to attract others to Jesus. Would my testimony, although true to myself, be too weak and vacillating and convoluted? Honest complexity to me might be muddle to someone else. Would my witness turn people away from Christ rather than draw them close? Would I turn into a negative witness? After hearing me, would they look elsewhere?

Slowly, I came to see this worry should not occupy too much thought and time. The more I thought about "reception" the more it hooked my ego and turned my testimony toward performance. I was rehearsing what I was going to say, editing for audience effect. I was compromising the struggle to be faithful to what I was thinking and feeling. So I stopped thinking about how to package my relationship to Jesus. (This is a difficult discipline for a teacher and writer.) It would have to be enough to speak the only truth I knew.

About a week after the student asked me the question, I asked him to walk me back to my office after class. I told him the type of scrutiny his question had triggered in me, and then I launched into my relationship with Jesus. To my surprise, I found myself saying that the Gospel stories about Jesus continue to connect my spirit to the Spirit. Jesus effectively baptizes me with the Spirit. Although I was in line with John the Baptist, I did not know if I wanted to say this is the only way to encounter the Spirit of God. But one thing for sure, it had been my way.

I looked at the student. He had gotten more than he had bargained for. He seemed embarrassed. Was he more attracted to Jesus? Or was he in the same place he was before I testified? Or was he repelled? I couldn't tell, and he didn't say. Ah, the continuing trickiness of testimony.

Third Sunday in Ordinary Time
Third Sunday after Epiphany
Matthew 4:12-23

—⚜—

Following Fascination

A Spiritual Commentary

Now when Jesus heard that John had been arrested, he withdrew to Galilee. He left Nazareth and made his home in Capernaum by the sea, in the territory of Zebulun and Naphtali, so that what had been spoken through the prophet Isaiah might be fulfilled: "Land of Zebulun, land of Naphtali, on the road by the sea, across the Jordan, Galilee of the Gentiles—the people who sat in darkness have seen a great light, and for those who sat in the region and shadow of death light has dawned."

Events take a turn for the worst. Herod arrests John. The restricted dungeon replaces the open desert. The voice crying out in the wilderness must thunder in prison. Authorities are doing what authorities do best—attempting to silence what threatens them.

Jesus' response is immediate. He moves into Galilee, the territory ruled by Herod Antipas who arrested John. As an infant Jesus ran from one Herod, as an adult he no longer runs. He walks steadily into the teeth of resistance. He is intent on treading on the snake and the scorpion, not walking around them. This is a dangerous move, taking a message of light into a land of darkness, a message of life into the land of the dead. Jesus could suffer the same fate as John.

But everything is happening within a larger plan. Underneath the machinations of the human actors, divine prophecies are unfolding. Isaiah has predicted this path. Jesus is not foolhardily playing into the hands of the wicked. He is playing out the divine drama, moving according to God's ancient plan, proclaiming a message that cannot be imprisoned.

From that time Jesus began to proclaim, "Repent, for the kingdom of heaven has come near."

The torch that fell from the hand of the Baptist is caught and raised by Jesus. The voice in the desert now has become another voice in the villages and countryside. The everlasting message goes on. The kingdom of heaven is at hand but people do not know how to reach for it. If people would learn to change their minds (repent of the way they think and act), the spiritual energy of heaven would flow into them. The problem is not the timing of the arrival of the kingdom of heaven. The problem is with sitting "in darkness" and being "overshadowed by death" [Matt 4:16; NAB; cf. Isa 8:23]. People must become aware (the remedy for darkness) of the presence of God and open to its enlivening energy (the remedy for death). The kingdom of heaven is now, but people are not.

But Jesus needs more than himself to help people see this hidden heaven. He needs to gather disciples for this work.

> **As he walked by the Sea of Galilee, he saw two brothers, Simon, who is called Peter, and Andrew his brother, casting a net into the sea—for they were fishermen.**

> **And he said to them, "Follow me, and I will make you fish for people." Immediately they left their nets and followed him.**

> **As he went from there, he saw two other brothers, James son of Zebedee and his brother John, in the boat with their father Zebedee, mending their nets, and he called them. Immediately they left the boat and their father, and followed him.**

If people will fish for people, first they must be fish caught by Jesus. Jesus invites four particular individuals, two sets of brothers, to come after him. They are to enter Jesus' consciousness and learn the change of mind and will that is necessary to receive spiritual energies. This discipleship will unfold into the mission of teaching others what they have learned from Jesus.

One condition of following Jesus is leaving their work (nets and boats) and family (their father). Jesus is the "kingdom in himself," and so opening to him entails a "repentance," a turning away from present preoccupations to entertain a more adventuresome possibility. These brothers are being called to become conscious of a deeper dimension of life, the spiritual sea in which all people swim. This is a different level of consciousness and activity, but it can be compared to what they know best. As they now gather fish, so eventually they will gather people.

However, there is a great deal of difference between fishing for fish and fishing for people. Fish can be caught against their will and violently pulled from the sea. People are caught by uncovering the deep desires of their hearts. These two sets of brothers already know this "heart" level. When they heard Jesus' command, they were moved to "immediately" follow him. Argument would come later. Vacillation would come later. Abandonment would come later. For now they found themselves walking behind a home more primordial than sea and family. The desire of their heart had been uncovered and called forth. Jesus catches these future catchers of men.

> **Jesus went throughout Galilee, teaching in their synagogues and proclaiming the good news of the kingdom and curing every disease and every sickness among the people.**

Jesus is not hiding from Herod. He is intensifying his activity— teaching, proclaiming, and healing throughout all of Galilee. He is a single-minded man on a mission. John's imprisonment is not going to stop him, and people are fascinated by him.

Teaching

I have seen a mother lean down to correct a child and say words so perfect, say sentences of such loving discipline, that, if the truth of what is happening is to be known, God must be praised. I have seen a man face death in such a way that it had no sting, and my fascination made me mute. I have listened to a woman forgive a system that had badly violated her and forgive the men and women in that system who were unwilling accomplices. She forgave them not because she was too weak to retaliate but because forgiveness was the only way life could be served, both in her and in those who had hurt her.

These are fascinating responses. In fact, every day people are leaning into life and either coaxing or muscling it toward redemption. In creative ways that are difficult to predict, they are making things better. If we catch them at it and find ourselves attracted, we may want to know more.

We follow fascination, especially fascination that has our "name" on it. When we see someone thinking, feeling, or acting in a way which, at the present moment, we are not capable of but which we wish we were capable of, that way of thinking, feeling, or acting has our "name" on it. We see it as a liberating next step for ourselves and we apprentice ourselves to it. It draws us into discipleship. A disciple is merely a fascinated person who desires to know and do what they see in another.

Our lives are ~~inescapably~~ interpersonal. We are always noticing others, what they think, say, and do. Toward many we are either indifferent or envious. Toward others we gravitate and learn. Sometimes this is a secret apprenticeship. These people do not know we are secretly taking clues from how they go about things. In biblical terms, we are watching them lace and unlace their sandals.

If we reflect on our lives, we will most likely discover a pattern of serial discipleship. We have watched our parents, friends, teachers, coworkers, bosses, spouses, siblings, and pass-through people "lace and unlace their sandals." While we may never literally leave our nets, boats, and families, we take our attention from everyday preoccupations long enough to follow the adventure of human possibility.

In the Gospel, Jesus is portrayed as a fascinating person. He does not back away from Galilee where Herod Antipas has imprisoned John. Rather he goes about "all of Galilee" (Matt 4:23; NAB). He does not wait for people to come to him and ask to be his disciple. He assertively chooses them. This directness honors them, and they leave what they are doing to follow him. Jesus is a forthright energy, and this energy fascinates because it is the polar opposite of the universal human trait of timidity. We want to know more about where this man is coming from. We suspect it would remedy ennui and listlessness. As Martin Luther asked, "What drives Christ?" Christ is only too willing to tell us, and so we continue to go back to his story to learn from him, to make our own the Spirit that drives him.

I heard about a woman who was the director of a drug rehabilitation center. One day a tall, strong man with a baseball bat entered the reception area. He was shouting obscenities and began banging the bat on the desks of the secretaries and admitting personnel. They jumped back and tried to get as far away from him as possible. One ran into the back room and called the police.

The woman who directed the center came out and walked right up to the screaming man waving the bat. She ducked under his reach and wrapped his arms around his chest. In a heartfelt voice she repeated over and over again, "Oh, you poor man! Oh, you poor man!" They stood together in that strange embrace for a while, and then the man began to sob. The woman led him to a chair. He slumped into it and waited for the police. He never let go of the baseball bat.

I want to know how that woman laces and unlaces her shoes. I find her fascinating. And I suspect she knows what drives Christ.

Fourth Sunday in Ordinary Time
Fourth Sunday after Epiphany
Matthew 5:1-12

Uncovering Blessedness

A Spiritual Commentary

When Jesus saw the crowds, he went up the mountain; and after he sat down, his disciples came to him. Then he began to speak, and taught them, saying:

What does Jesus see when he sees the crowds?

Seeing is a physical act insofar as it notices outward appearances, those aspects of people that are available to the senses. So the crowds may be composed of men and women, tall and short, skinny and fat, smelly and fragrant, bearded and unbearded, well dressed and disheveled, etc. But seeing is also a mental act insofar as it evaluates people in terms of categories the mind uses. Most often the mind uses social categories. So the crowds may be rich and poor, Jews and non-Jews, Pharisees and Sadducees, free and slave, tax collectors and taxed, etc. But seeing is also a spiritual act insofar as it is aware of the spiritual nature of people. The eye of the soul sees people in relationship to the Divine Source and in communion with all of creation.

Jesus sees with all three eyes. He perceives the physical, social, and spiritual reality of people. But in this passage special emphasis is given to the spiritual. Jesus goes up on a mountain to be closer to God and to see people from this higher perspective. However, this higher, spiritual seeing will exist side by side with a physical and especially with a social seeing. The spiritual truth of who they are interacts with their social conditions and will eventually judge and overcome their oppressiveness.

This way in which Jesus sees—holding together social and spiritual reality—is what the disciples must learn to do. Therefore, they come close so they can put on the eyes of Jesus. Jesus sits, the traditional posture of the teacher, in order to instruct them in his wisdom.

"Blessed are the poor in spirit, for theirs is the kingdom of heaven.

Blessed are those who mourn, for they will be comforted.

Blessed are the meek, for they will inherit the earth.

Blessed are those who hunger and thirst for righteousness, for they will be filled.

Jesus sees the negative circumstances that surround and pervade people—the poverty that goes so deep it crushes the spirit and reduces people to a constant state of mourning. In this situation they are meek, not becoming violent and vengeful but hungering and thirsting for more equitable treatment, more just allocation of resources. These are people caught in an unjust system and being ground up by it. They are also trying to find a way to respond. Jesus sees this social reality clearly, the terrible toll it is taking, and the eagerness to change it.

However, he also spies a blessedness existing at the center of their struggle. This blessedness is given by God and so, by definition, is more powerful than the social-political system that overwhelms them. This blessedness is already present for "theirs *is* the kingdom of heaven." Yet it is a blessedness that is working its way toward a fuller, future manifestation. It is moving mourning toward comfort, meekness toward inheritance, and hunger and thirst toward satisfaction. It is giving notice to the present situation that it is not ultimate and will not last.

The first beatitude most trenchantly symbolizes Jesus' double vision. The effect of social poverty has penetrated so deeply that it has depleted and defeated people's spirit. They are not only poor in food, clothing, shelter, and social standing, they have lost spirit—zest, passion, pleasure, purpose. Human evil has done its worse to them. Yet it is precisely at this most destructive moment that the kingdom of heaven is still present. Human evil, even at its most devastating, cannot destroy God's gift. The presupposition is that people are in touch with their oppression and pain, and they fear its powerful and extensive reach. But they are out of touch with their blessedness. Jesus' teaching makes them aware of the source of hope already present but not yet fully manifested.

Blessed are the merciful, for they will receive mercy.

Blessed are the pure in heart, for they will see God.

Blessed are the peacemakers, for they will be called children of God.

Blessed are those who are persecuted for righteousness' sake, for theirs is the kingdom of heaven.

The blessedness not only survives and overcomes negative situations. It shines forth positively, bringing its energies to the tasks of bettering life.

When blessedness flows as mercy, it participates in the law of spiritual abundance. The giving of mercy makes mercy more available, not only to those to whom it is shown but to the givers themselves. Mercy grows and expands in the giving. It becomes an atmosphere that all are invited to breathe.

When the blessedness generates a clean heart, a heart that has purified itself of false attachments and realizes its essential dependence on God, it is capable of seeing the God-groundedness of all things. What people know in themselves, they are able to see in others. They have opened the inner eye and see the God-groundedness of all things. As the poet said of Jesus, "Ah! There was a heart right! / There was single eye!" (Gerard Manley Hopkins, "The Wreck of the Deutschland," stanza 29). This seeing heart moves them to respect and compassion. Their ethical behavior is the result of their spiritual vision.

When the blessedness flows out as peacemaking, it is an overflow of the peace that the children of God know. It has been said that God is a power that moves everything there is toward everything else that is. The advent of God's peace is the restoration of relationships—between God and people, between people, and between people and the earth. Those who facilitate the renewal of peace in these relationships are God's children, for they bear forth God's work.

When the blessedness leads to a righteous life, a life in communion with God and neighbor, and this new way of being so threatens the existing social systems of domination that they persecute these people of the new way, then look no further—in this combined moment of righteousness and persecution the kingdom of heaven is manifest. In fact, this is the supreme revelation because in this tension of the kingdom of heaven and the alienated earth the transforming power of God is clearly seen.

So . . .

Blessed are you when people revile you and persecute you and utter all kinds of evil against you falsely on my account. Rejoice and be glad, for your reward is great in heaven, for in the same way they persecuted the prophets who were before you."

The unfolding goodness of the blessed naturally attracts evil. Evil knows that its day is over, and so spins out of control in a frenzy of persecution, "and utter[s] all kinds of evil." It is thrashing about doing what it can to kill the kingdom of heaven. Of course, all the accusations of the wicked are false, spewed forth because they fear the power that Jesus has unleashed. Their rantings and ravings are their death throes. So it is time to rejoice and be glad, for heaven is unfolding on earth. The prayer of Jesus is coming to realization—"on earth as it is in heaven" (Matt 6:10). Of course, violent response is to be expected. It has always been this way—the greater God's presence the greater the resistance. Prophets are always persecuted.

Teaching

There are many dramatic moments in the Gospels, moments that have attracted poets, playwrights, novelists, and filmmakers. There is the Lukan Jesus sitting silently after reading Isaiah with the eyes of the whole synagogue on him; the Johannine Jesus as a prisoner instructing the procurator on the true meaning of kingship (John 18:33-37); the Markan Jesus caught in a boat with dense disciples asking his heart's most persistent question, "Do you not yet understand?" (Mark 8:21). The stories of the Gospels may not be long and involved, but there is bare-bones theater at the core of many of them.

In my imagination this opening, soaring rhetoric of the Sermon on the Mount is stunning drama. There is Jesus, an inner circle of disciples, and an outer circle of crowds. His words embrace both circles. But with his mountain sight what will he say?

Perhaps he will talk about a lost covenant. Once Israel walked closely with God, now sin has separated them. We must reclaim our heritage, return to the glory of the past. Many have adopted this type of religious rhetoric.

Or perhaps he will follow the emphasis of John the Baptist. Something is coming from the future, something with a winnowing fork in one hand (see Matt 3:12; Luke 3:17) and an ax in the other. Repent now or face the fire. The rhetoric of punishment always has an audience.

But neither past glory nor future fear is Jesus' voice. His focus is on the deepest truth of the present, a truth that contradicts the surface of what is happening and that will eventually win out. It is a rhetoric of direct engagement. The repeated "blessed"—hammering home the single, foundational truth and the many manifestations of this blessedness, from mourning through mercy and peace to persecution—shows its force and creativity. Everything about the structure of this speech is meant to persuade the listener and the reader of a deeper way to see what is happening.

And when I read it, and then speak it out loud, and then, with feeble skill, reach inside and "say it with feeling," it touches a place in me that is seldom reached. It is so clear eyed and yet so daring, so sure of itself as it contradicts so-called "common sense," so confident in the victory of its unconventional perceptions. I am swept along. By the end I see, however dimly, what Jesus sees when he looks at me, one among the crowds, pushing toward the circle of disciples.

I am reminded of what David Whyte said about poetry:

> [It is the] art of overhearing ourselves say things from which it is impossible to retreat. A true line acts like a lightning rod in a storm. All our doubts about the reality of the experience disappear in a flash as the accumulated charge contained in the electric ripeness of the moment runs to earth. Just before we are struck, we even feel, as in a true lightning storm, the hair rising on the back of the neck, as we realize "it" is being said. (*The Heart Aroused: Poetry and the Preservation of the Soul in Corporate America* [New York: Currency Doubleday 1994] 287)

For me this is the impact of Jesus' rhetoric. In its grip it becomes impossible to retreat and I know a moment of "electric ripeness" is arriving. Then I am struck. "It" is being said and "it" is carrying me away.

I am also reminded of a stanza of Yeats' poem, fittingly called "Vacillation":

> My fiftieth year had come and gone,
> I sat, a solitary man,
> In a crowded London shop,
> An open book and empty cup
> On the marble table top.
> While on the shop and street I gazed
> My body of a sudden blazed;
> And twenty minutes more or less
> It seemed, so great my happiness,
> That I was blessed and could bless.

(stanza 4; in *The Winding Stair and Other Poems* [London: Macmillan, 1933])

Yeats realizes for "twenty minutes more or less" a truth similar to the one that Jesus' rhetoric conveys. He is blessed and can bless. To know this for as long as twenty minutes is itself a blessing.

But what happens after the twenty minutes? What happens after the crowds disperse? What happens after the rhetoric fades?

It is easy to be cynical. We can quickly point out that the view from the mountain is temporary. We always return to flat land, back down to earth with a thud. Poverty crushes all the way through, mourning has no comfort, persecution is victory for the persecutors, mercy is limited, peacemaking impossible, and meekness inherits nothing but its own refusal to fight back. Jesus had us breathing rare air for a moment, but now we choke on human pollution.

But we can also be thankful. With Jesus' rhetoric we broke through to a truth that ordinary language cannot communicate. That we cannot sustain the realization of this truth or that we do not know how to enact it only means there is more work to be done. Rhetoric is the seed; action is the fruit. Without the seed there is no fruit. The memory of "twenty minutes more or less" can change a person. We must follow the electricity. We must allow the electric ripeness to run to earth.

The beatitudes are the beginning of the massive teaching of Jesus known as the Sermon on the Mount. The ending of Sermon is a contrast between wisdom and foolishness. The foolish person is one who hears the words of Jesus and *does not* put them into action. The wise person is one who hears the words of Jesus and *does* put them into action (Matt 7:24). Both hear the words, but one dismisses them and one perseveres in them. One hears the words as a truth "from which it is impossible to retreat." The injunction is clear: act out of blessedness and the rhetoric will not be a transient lightning bolt of truth but an abiding light that the darkness cannot overcome.

Fifth Sunday in Ordinary Time
Fifth Sunday after Epiphany

Matthew 5:13-16 *LM* • **Matthew 5:13-20** *RCL*

(Users of the *Revised Common Lectionary:* see the following Sunday for further commentary.)

━━━❧

Becoming Salt

A Spiritual Commentary

[Jesus said:] "You are the salt of the earth; but if salt has lost its taste, how can its saltiness be restored? It is no longer good for anything, but is thrown out and trampled under foot.

This is a statement of the essential spiritual dilemma. We are something we may not realize. We are a potential that may not be actualized, a gift that may not be developed, a high calling that may not be heeded. When this happens, people lose their flavor. The strong conclusion is: what is most valuable for the earth is now least valuable. It is not savored but trampled under foot.

The direct address, *"You* are the salt of the earth," is designed to be convincing and to bring awareness. It is meant to cut through lesser evaluations ("You are a sinner" or "no good" or "mediocre" or "a loser") and establish this truth in the minds and hearts of those who are addressed. Hot on the heels of this high compliment is a warning. Stating these negative consequences is meant to galvanize our freedom into the commitment to become the salt that we are. This is the function of negative predictions in spiritual teaching. They are meant to entice freedom into action.

Our salt identity is for the benefit of the earth. Our lives are a mission to bring zest and meaning to the earth. What is wasteful is to lose this ultimate purpose and passion, to forget this high calling and be reduced to a shriveled identity. This can happen. Cynics would say it inevitably happens.

You are the light of the world. A city built on a hill cannot be hid. No one after lighting a lamp puts it under the bushel basket, but on the lampstand, and it gives light to all in the house. In the same way, let your light shine before others, so that they may see your good works and give glory to your Father in heaven."

73

Once again, the direct address, "You," is meant to be convincing. The truth that people are the light of the world is as clear and unavoidable as a city on a mountain. As the sun is to the physical world, we are to the human world. Perhaps this is evident to Jesus, the one saying these words. But for most of us this is a stretch, an over-evaluation of the two-legged, stand-up humans. Those who see themselves scrambling for food, shelter, and social position may not be persuaded by these words.

The statement on salt asked a question with the suggestion of a failed response, a loss of flavor, and a wasting of the commodity. The fate of human beings as the light of the world is more positively drawn. It is assumed that light is meant to give light and not to be suffocated by a basket. So, as the song says, "let your light shine" (Matt 5:16). This means perform good works. These good works will attract people who will see in them not the goodness of the human actors but the reflection of the divine source. People who are light draw others to the Light.

The deeper identity of people is now fully revealed. We are salt and light because God, whose children we are, is committed to making the earth and world something new. When we become who we are, we also become transparent to the One who makes us who we are. "Glorifying the heavenly Father" is the recognition of this truth.

Teaching

When I heard that this pastor died, I said aloud to myself, "The world is now a less interesting place."

I did not say the world was less just or good or merciful. This would be a more edifying remark. But from my limited perspective this man was an endless experiment. He was a shot of zest, salting every bland situation.

The parish decided to put up a basketball court in the parking lot. Everyone agreed it would be a good thing and give the teenagers a place to play and congregate. The pastor suggested they put three basketballs in a net and tie the net around the base of the stand that supported the backboard and basket. This way if people were just wandering by and wanted to shoot a few baskets, a ball would be available.

The parish council said that was ill advised. The kids would steal the balls. They wouldn't last a day.

The pastor said he had thought about that and had a solution. He was not going to buy three cheap basketballs. He was going to buy three expensive basketballs. When people saw that these were top-of-the-line balls, they wouldn't take them.

Needless to say, the parish council didn't buy this reasoning. But this was a Catholic parish and the pastor does what the pastor wants. Three expensive basketballs were placed in the net.

The first one disappeared in a week. The second one was gone in a month. But it was five months before the third one vanished.

The parish council admitted the balls lasted longer than they thought. But still they gloated, men and women of the world teaching the idealistic pastor a thing or two.

The pastor brought three new expensive basketballs. He stated his principle clearly, "Good basketballs for good people."

Something is lost when the spiritual identity of "salt" and "light" is translated into the activity of doing good works. We often harbor a pedestrian notion of goodness. Doing "good" is a wooden application of principle to unruly situations. We seldom think of it as entailing creative engagement with the wily world. Yet the people of salt and light are called upon to envision and execute experiments. When the experiments fail, it is not time to retreat to old ways but to try new experiments. "Good basketballs for good people."

When we realize our identities as salt and light, we begin to have faith in the world as a corollary of faith in God. God's energies are directed to the betterment of the world. So God's people are driven by the same purpose. The world for all its recalcitrance is in the process of becoming the good creation. We are the flavor and fire of this development. Think big. Think new. Think creative.

Teilhard de Chardin, mystic and scientist, was afraid people would lose their zest and passion for the development of the world. So he tried to uncover this zest and passion as the deep desire of their hearts. He wrote that the "only worthwhile joy is that of co-operating as one individual atom in the final establishment of a world." When his friends said they did not feel this drive in them, he said to them, "You are not searching to the full depth of your heart and mind. And that, moreover, is why the cosmic sense and faith in the world is dormant in you." Jesus' words that we are the salt of the earth and the light of the world are meant to awaken our cosmic sense and our faith in the world. The awakened sense unfolds into experiments on every level, even with basketballs.

Sixth Sunday in Ordinary Time
Sixth Sunday after Epiphany

Proper 1

Matthew 5:17-37 *LM* • Matthew 5:21-37 *RCL*

Working on Yourself

A Spiritual Commentary

[Jesus said to the disciples:]

This first Scripture quotation (from the NRSV translation) and its commentary are given for users of the *Lectionary for Mass:*

> **"Do not think that I have come to abolish the law or the prophets; I have come not to abolish but to fulfill. For truly I tell you, until heaven and earth pass away, not one letter, not one stroke of a letter, will pass from the law until all is accomplished. Therefore, whoever breaks one of the least of these commandments, and teaches others to do the same, will be called least in the kingdom of heaven; but whoever does them and teaches them will be called great in the kingdom of heaven. For I tell you, unless your righteousness exceeds that of the scribes and Pharisees, you will never enter the kingdom of heaven.**

Jesus' intention is not to do away with the law and the prophets. In fact, he is the fulfillment of their many promises. The law and prophets structure the relationship between God (heaven) and people (earth) and contain promises about the shape of salvation history. Therefore, as long as heaven and earth are connected and influencing one another and as long as promises remain unfulfilled, the law and the prophets are in effect. Facile rejection of these Scriptures is an uninformed response. Only the least in the kingdom do not see continuity between Jesus and the law and prophets. The great in the kingdom of heaven can connect the dots from Adam to Christ and honor all facets of God's purposes in history.

However, Jesus' revelation does take precedence. It fulfills the law and prophets, transcending them in a movement of higher righteousness. This transcending movement includes and uplifts certain aspects of the law and the prophets and allows other aspects to fall away. Those aspects of the law and the prophets that are at the heart of the tradition are affirmed and deepened, e.g., the prohibition against murder and adultery will be strengthened and interiorized. Those aspects that are more peripheral, clearly irrelevant to present problems, and prone to distortion are dismissed, e.g., the elaborate procedures around swearing an oath. Within the overall attitude of fulfilling the law and the prophets, Jesus affirms some aspects and purges others

In particular, Jesus' call to higher righteousness is critical of the type of righteousness practiced by the scribes and Pharisees. These religious leaders are fixated on externals. Whatever they do, they do to be "seen by others" (Matt 6:5). They pray on street corners, sound trumpets before they give alms, and look dismal when they fast (see Matt 6:1-5). All this calls attention to themselves, and they gain a reputation for righteousness. This ego-centered, outer-directed focus makes them oblivious to the real needs of people. Instead, they tinker with trifles, obsessing with the letter of the law and losing sight of the inner Spirit of their faith. The higher righteousness of Jesus reclaims this inner Spirit and its innate connection with justice, love, and compassion.

For users of the *Revised Common Lectionary* and the *Lectionary for Mass:*

> **You have heard that it was said to those of ancient times, 'You shall not murder'; and 'whoever murders shall be liable to judgment.' But I say to you that if you are angry with a brother or sister, you will be liable to judgment; and if you insult a brother or sister, you will be liable to the council; and if you say, 'You fool,' you will be liable to the hell of fire.**

Murder is an act of aggression. But it exists on a continuum of inside to outside dynamics. Inside the murderer there is anger and contempt. This anger and contempt overflow into abusive speech, and the abusive speech eventuates in vicious murder. Past commandments have focused on the final act, the culmination of the process. This teaching of Jesus focuses on the origin and growth of the thought, what the ancient rabbis called "evil imaginings." Murderous acts will only be stopped when the violent seeds in the heart are either extirpated or not allowed to grow.

> **So when you are offering your gift at the altar, if you remember that your brother or sister has something against you, leave**

> your gift there before the altar and go; first be reconciled to
> your brother or sister, and then come and offer your gift. Come
> to terms quickly with your accuser while you are on the way to
> court with him, or your accuser may hand you over to the
> judge, and the judge to the guard, and you will be thrown into
> prison. Truly I tell you, you will never get out until you have
> paid the last penny.

Liturgy is not a substitution for dealing directly with the person you
have wronged—but most of us wish it were so. Bringing a gift to the altar
to atone for your sins and be forgiven by God is easier than seeking out
the one you offended and engaging in a difficult process of reconciliation.
The human tendency is to avoid this type of face-to-face confrontation. In
fact, we are so inventive in avoidance that St. Matthew's Jesus has to use
the threat of harsh consequences to encourage the offender to pursue this
course of action. "Why can't I just leave a gift at the altar and tell God I'm
sorry?" Because even now your opponent has engaged a lawyer who has
never lost a case and your court date has been set in the court of a hang-
ing judge. Move.

> You have heard that it was said, 'You shall not commit adultery.'
> But I say to you that everyone who looks at a woman with lust
> has already committed adultery with her in his heart. If your
> right eye causes you to sin, tear it out and throw it away; it is
> better for you to lose one of your members than for your whole
> body to be thrown into hell. And if your right hand causes you
> to sin, cut it off and throw it away; it is better for you to lose one
> of your members than for your whole body to go into hell.

One of the most famous adulteries in the Bible (2 Sam 11) starts, "It
happened, late one afternoon, when David rose from his couch and was
walking about on the roof of the king's house, that he saw from the roof
a woman bathing; the woman was very beautiful . . . So David sent
messengers to get her, and she came to him, and he lay with her." This
is not a love story. David's lust unfolds into coercive rape: "get her . . .
lay with her." It also begins a course of action that will lead to further
deceit and eventually a murder and an elaborate cover-up. But it all begins with lust of the eyes on a palace roof. "Can fire be carried in the
bosom without burning one's clothes?" (Prov 6:27).

Once again, what can short-circuit these evil imaginings that unfold
in powerful negative ways?

St. Matthew's Jesus suggests a "whatever it takes" attitude and uses strong, symbolic rhetoric to impact the listener. If it is the right eye or right hand that is causing trouble, then they must go. Why? Enlightened self-interest. They are only a part; and if those parts are bringing the whole into destruction, they must be sacrificed. Once again, dire consequences are spelled out as a motivation to moral behavior. Gehenna awaits those who have not learned to amputate their problems.

This radical rhetoric encourages us to engage in the difficult inner work that is needed. If males are going to understand their lustful, oppressive attitudes toward women, they must explore their thoughts. The right hand and the right eye are scapegoats, mere servants of strangely twisted mental and emotional processes. However, they function as symbols of how a part of us, sexual desire, can dominate the whole and bring it to ruin. If we do not learn about and integrate our sexual drives into our larger life values and goals, we will be undercut by this lack of attention.

> **It was also said, 'Whoever divorces his wife, let him give her a certificate of divorce.' But I say to you that anyone who divorces his wife, except on the ground of unchastity, causes her to commit adultery; and whoever marries a divorced woman commits adultery.**

When a husband can divorce his wife for almost any reason, there is no need to explore and evaluate what is weakening his commitment. He is simply getting rid of what no longer pleases him. (The case of "unchastity" might mean adultery on the part of the woman, or it might mean consanguinity—NAB, "unless the marriage is unlawful" (v. 32)—where the husband and wife are related by blood.) In the culture of first-century Palestine a woman who had been cut loose had to quickly find another man in order to survive. Therefore, the male-initiated divorce caused the woman to commit adultery. This begins a process of adulterous contacts, for the man who marries her likewise commits adultery.

> **Again, you have heard that it was said to those of ancient times, 'You shall not swear falsely, but carry out the vows you have made to the Lord.' But I say to you, Do not swear at all, either by heaven, for it is the throne of God, or by the earth, for it is his footstool, or by Jerusalem, for it is the city of the great King. And do not swear by your head, for you cannot make one hair**

white or black. Let your word be 'Yes, Yes' or 'No, No'; anything more than this comes from the evil one."

Swearing an oath is supposed to guarantee truthfulness. However, when a person swears before God or by heaven, earth, or Jerusalem that are closely connected to God, they are overstepping their bounds. They are trying to bring God in as a reliable witness for their pledges. But God does not do the bidding of presumptuous people. These people cannot even control the color of their hair. Why do they think they can co-opt the maker of heaven and earth?

Also, oaths backfire. The more people swear "on the Bible," the more suspicious is their testimony. The only way they can tell the truth is if they have invoked a higher power that will punish them if they do not carry out what they have promised. "With God as my witness . . ." or "If I do not do this, may God . . ." is the bloated speech of people who have no intention of doing what they say.

Oath taking should be replaced by integral speech. The words of a person's mouth should match the thoughts of the heart. In honest communication, the type of communication that sustains community life, yes and no is all that is needed.

Teaching

One of the oldest spiritual injunctions is, "Know yourself." It is meant to push people down a path of self-discovery. Although this search may begin with social ambitions and intimate relationships, eventually it will turn inward. The ones who want to know themselves will set up a watching and listening post in the center of their being. They will begin the arduous task of observing the machinations of the mind and the flutterings of the heart.

This inner work is sometimes divided into transcendent interiority and introspective interiority. Transcendent interiority is the discovery of the deeper self or the higher self; the witness. Ken Wilber describes this witness:

> You needn't try to see your transcendent self, which is not possible anyway. Can your eye see itself? You need only begin by persistently dropping your false identifications with your memories, mind, body, emotions, and thoughts. And this dropping entails nothing by way of super-human effort or theoretical comprehension. All that is required, primarily, is but one understanding: *whatever you can see cannot be the*

Seer. Everything you know about yourself is precisely not your Self, the Knower, the inner I-ness that can neither be perceived, defined, or made an *object* of any sort. Bondage is nothing but the mis-identification of the Seer with all these things which can be *seen*. And liberation begins with the simple reversal of this mistake. (*No Boundary: Eastern and Western Approaches to Personal Growth* [Los Angeles: Center Publications, 1979] 137)

This is quite a discovery—an ultimate non-observable self.

Introspective interiority points to everything the Seer sees. In particular, the Seer gradually accumulates knowledge about how the mind works in general and how his or her mind works in particular. When this knowledge is received nonjudgmentally and responded to with love, it becomes the malleable material of transformation. We come into reflective awareness of the deeper drivers of our moods, motivations, and behaviors. We are ripe for inner change that will manifest itself in new, outer behavior.

This powerful Gospel text from the Sermon on the Mount suggests we search the mind and come to self-knowledge around a few crucial issues. We should know how anger rises in us, comes to expression, and then subsides. We should watch lust and note how it grips us and rushes us along paths we may not choose. We should also come to understand how we want shortcuts to forgiveness, how we hesitate and sometimes completely stall when it comes to initiating reconciling conversations. Why are the drives to anger and lust so powerful and the drive to reconciliation so weak? Coming to this knowledge is the work we must do on ourselves if the Sermon on the Mount is to be heeded.

And, of course, the origins of false speech must be appreciated. Self-knowledge involves becoming truthful about lying. Why do we think the lie is so necessary? A lie that is known as a lie is truly a failure. Is it partially because there is no congruence between our consciousness and our thoughts and feelings? We say things that are untrue because we do not do what is true. Some say, "Silence is the mother of integrity." Only when we are quiet can we touch the depth of our feelings and thoughts and bring them forward adequately. When this happens, we delight in wholeheartedness. We are integral; the inside and the outside are in communion. But this is a rare experience. We are not expert in the skills of silence, and so most of the time our speech is fragmented and inevitably incomplete. The more we know about ourselves, the more the blocks to higher righteousness become evident.

As I was writing this reflection, the phone rang. I picked it up and a friend of mine asked me what I was doing. I said I was meditating on the Sermon on the Mount. "Oh," he said, "that's just a list of things you can't do."

That may be forever true. But if we are to move toward its wisdom even a little, we must begin the difficult but loving work of self-knowledge.

Seventh Sunday in Ordinary Time
Seventh Sunday after Epiphany

Proper 2

Matthew 5:38-48

Cultivating Cleverness

A Spiritual Commentary

[Jesus said to the disciples:] "You have heard that it was said, 'An eye for an eye and a tooth for a tooth.'

This commandment, which is about to be superceded by Jesus's commandment, was itself a major step toward controlling violence. Previously, the law of Lamech prevailed. "I have killed a man for wounding me, a young man for striking me" (Gen 4:23). There was no equality in inflicted damage. A slap brought down upon itself the full revenge of murder. But under the dictum of an "eye for an eye," retribution was carefully measured.

But I say to you, Do not resist an evildoer. But if anyone strikes you on the right cheek, turn the other also; and if anyone wants to sue you and take your coat, give your cloak as well; and if anyone forces you to go one mile, go also the second mile.

"Do not resist an evildoer" does not mean becoming a doormat to violent people. It does not encourage us to acquiesce in our own humiliation and pain. Rather it discourages repaying evil with evil. Higher righteousness does not contribute to the spiral of violence. So this is not a passive stance. It is a proactive, highly-engaged alternative to retribution in kind.

But what are the alternatives? How does it go beyond "an eye for an eye and a tooth for a tooth"?

Jesus gives three brief examples that embody creative strategies geared to the social violence against the lower classes in first-century Palestine. These clever actions are meant to change the balance of power from the violent ones to the nonviolent ones. A great deal of historical knowledge is needed to grasp how ingenious these alternative responses are, but Walter Wink provides a provocative summary:

> Turn your cheek, thus indicating to the one who backhands you that his attempts to shame you into servility have failed. Strip naked and parade out of court, thus taking the momentum of the law and the whole debt economy and flipping them, jujitsu-like, in a burlesque of legality. Walk a second mile, surprising the occupation troops with a sudden challenge to their control. (*Engaging the Powers: Discernment and Resistance in a World of Domination* [Minneapolis: Fortress Press, 1992], 185)

Discipleship is more than a bland refusal to participate in violence. It is a new, creative, and courageous way of acting. It sees into the hidden dynamics of imposed violence, exposes them, and opens up other possibilities.

Give to everyone who begs from you, and do not refuse anyone who wants to borrow from you.

Once again, Jesus is providing an alternate strategy. Every society has an unjust stratified economic structure that keeps the beggar begging and the borrower in debt. As an academic economist told me, "Need is not an economic category." But it is a human category. Jesus' strategy is to recognize it and act on it. Instead of protecting your own wealth at all costs, acknowledge mutual need as the foundation of community living. Of course, that is easier said than done.

You have heard that it was said, 'You shall love your neighbor and hate your enemy.' But I say to you, Love your enemies and pray for those who persecute you, so that you may be children of your Father in heaven; for he makes his sun rise on the evil and on the good, and sends rain on the righteous and on the unrighteous. For if you love those who love you, what reward do you have? Do not even the tax collectors do the same? And if you greet only your brothers and sisters, what more are you doing than others? Do not even the Gentiles do the same? Be perfect, therefore, as your heavenly Father is perfect."

This teaching charts a movement from selective love to universal love. In order for this to happen, love has to overcome the great divide between friends and enemies. Loving those who love you and hating those who hate you is predictable and unremarkable. Everybody does that, even people who are unscrupulous, like tax collectors. The alternative of universal love is in imitation of the heavenly Father. His sun impartially shines upon the good and bad; his rains impartially fall upon the just and the unjust. This is the perfection of the Father, and the children are to embody it.

Teaching

Christians have been terrified of this teaching on nonretaliation and universal love. They too quickly interpret it as passive and idealistic advice that will make them vulnerable in a hostile and aggressive world. They are not about to turn the other cheek or give the enemy an edge. So they interpret the teaching in ways that are true but inadequate. They take the adventure out of it.

Some point out that these actions of nonretaliation and universal love are in imitation of God. So humans as humans will obviously not be capable of them. They can only be attempted under the influence of grace. If Christians try to do this, they will be thrown back again and again on the need for divine grace. This teaching makes this powerful theological point.

Yes, but . . . This observation may be true, but its train of thought has to be pursued. The question now becomes: how do we open to grace so that we can persevere in living a nonretaliatory and universal way of love.

Others take these imperatives as a spiritual ideal. Only fully-realized and integrated disciples are capable of such heroism. Different stages of spiritual development must be taken into account. There are preliminary stages that have to be successfully completed before disciples can embody universal love and nonretaliation.

The story of the snake is instructive. The snake hears the stunning teaching of Jesus from a wandering preacher and immediately refuses all violence. He will bite no one. When the local children realize he won't bite, they begin to beat him with sticks everyday. The snake is near death when the preacher returns and asks about his health. The snake tells him of his heroic actions expecting to be praised. But the preacher says, "I told you not to bite. I didn't tell you not to hiss."

Too quick a move from retaliation to nonretaliation, from selective to universal love can be hazardous. A gradual approach is the only realistic one. People should move from active retaliation (bite) to only threatening retaliation (hiss), from loving only their own family to loving others in the village, etc. Jesus' teaching is the full expression of spiritual maturity. We are on the path, but we are walking baby step by baby step.

Yes, but . . . This misses the strenuous proactive atmosphere of what Jesus teaches. Each injunction presumes that the disciples are waging love in the world. They are waging this love with all the danger, sacrifice, and cost that it takes to wage war. But most of all they are waging love through cleverness. They are marshalling every bit of their ingenuity to find ways that nonretaliation and universal love can be integrated into the violent and preferential situations of their society. They may fail, but in order to fail they have to try.

Years ago, as part of a larger conference, I attended a breakout session on prison reform. I knew nothing about it, but I had heard that prisons were places where very few reformed and many hardened. The main presenter had spent a good deal of his life advocating for a better prison system. His opening line was, "I'm here to tell you it can get better." He began to talk, and it became obvious he was trying to point a way beyond retaliation, for both inmates and society.

Although he was not a great speaker, his presence was captivating. Even though I knew I would never be involved in prison reforms, I felt a flutter of hope; an alternate way was possible. He was holding fast the vision of a nonretaliatory prison system, as strange as that sounds, and pushing it at the existing structures of punishment. His proactive strength was quiet but unrelenting. Even if he failed, there was a way in which he wouldn't fail.

Vaclav Havel, the former president of the Czech Republic and a political prisoner for many years, said that hopeful causes are not necessarily those that have a promise of early success. They are those that are good in themselves and therefore worth working for. In Christian language, they are rooted in the goodness of God, and the people who advocate for them share that goodness.

The key is to hold the value of nonretaliation and universal love first and look at what is happening in social situations second.

A large faith-based school system, engaged in an extensive process to determine their values, sought interviews with alumni, teachers, administrators, staff, and students. During the process, once the values were determined, they were printed on everything from letterheads to bookmarks. Now the concerns were how to live them, how to integrate them into every policy and pedagogy.

At a later meeting the president of the system honestly remarked, "We were working on this dismissal policy. I looked up, and there on the wall were these values. I said to myself, 'What in the world do those values have to do with what we are doing?'" People laughed.

This is precisely the wrong way to go about it. The Gospel teaching intimates: hold the value first and then frame the policy. If you frame the policy out of existing instincts, the dominant ways of retaliation and preference will appear and not be noticed. But if you start with nonretaliation and universal love, creative energies will be released.

We have praised heroic Christians who are willing to lay down their lives for their faith. We need to praise clever Christians who are able to see ways to integrate nonretaliation and universal love into stubborn systems. These women and men hold steady these values with an inner strength and combine them with their extensive and intricate knowledge of legal, educational, medical, political, and business systems. An alternate path opens, and we lift our faces into the rain and sun of the one God.

Eighth Sunday in Ordinary Time
Eighth Sunday after Epiphany

Proper 3

Matthew 6:24-34

܀

Beholding Birds and Flowers

A Spiritual Commentary

[Jesus said to the disciples:] "No one can serve two masters; for a slave will either hate the one and love the other, or be devoted to the one and despise the other. You cannot serve God and wealth.

Masters always make servants. What dominates our consciousness and dictates our actions is what we ultimately value and is that with which we identify ourselves. It masters us. We attend to it so completely that when other concerns seek our attention, we push them away. This is especially true when our ultimate options are either God or money. If we feverishly seek money as the foundation of our security, we will have no time for the type of security God provides. God will seem vague and illusive next to the soothing social value of cash. On the other hand, if we seek God, the anxious quest for physical security will not be as all-important at it once was. Although the text presents God and money as an either-or proposition, God and money can be integrated into the life of an individual. But only if God is the master.

Therefore I tell you, do not worry about your life, what you will eat or what you will drink, or about your body, what you will wear.

This is a teaching about how to move from the money-master to the God-master. The first part is a bold injunction that both recognizes the power of inner anxiety over physical survival and, at the same time, asks us to let go of it. This anxiety about the future, what we *shall* eat, *shall* drink, *shall* wear, is so pervasive that it seems natural, something that comes with the territory of the vulnerable body. So telling us not to worry seems to go against a built-in part of the human condition.

Is not life more than food, and the body more than clothing?

The first step toward calming this anxiety is to raise our thoughts a little higher. Life is more than food; it is about love, companionship, work, etc. The body cannot be reduced to clothing. It is about sexuality, delighting in the sensuous appreciation of nature, etc. The teaching tries to paint a bigger picture for our consciousness to consider. It is prying consciousness away from its fixation on food and shelter.

Look at the birds of the air; they neither sow nor reap nor gather into barns, and yet your heavenly Father feeds them. Are you not of more value than they?

The teaching now wants us to behold the birds, to see into them and learn something essential from them that also is true of human life. The birds do not strain after food, yet a loving transcendent reality sustains them. If this is true of the birds, how much more is it true of the higher human level of creation?

This picture may not be as effective as the teaching wants it to be. Birds scavenge for food just as every animal does and, if no food is found, they die. But the teaching is not concerned with realistic appraisals of animal life. It wants to change human consciousness so it can see another possibility. Life is more than an anxious project of survival. It can be appreciated as a gift from God.

And can any of you by worrying add a single hour to your span of life?

This is a direct question and the assumed answer is: no. The teaching wants us to see through the ineffectiveness of anxious inner states. They are nonproductive. In themselves they cannot significantly change the physical-social world. This is another reason not to worry. Worry in itself accomplishes nothing.

And why do you worry about clothing? Consider the lilies of the field, how they grow; they neither toil nor spin, yet I tell you, even Solomon in all his glory was not clothed like one of these. But if God so clothes the grass of the field, which is alive today and tomorrow is thrown into the oven, will he not much more clothe you—you of little faith?

The teaching has shown that chronic anxiety over food is misplaced. Now it considers the worry about clothing. We are asked to behold the lilies and how they grow. They do not put out any effort. They grow out of an inner, beautiful unfolding. Solomon, on the other hand, strove all his life through violent conquest to acquire the beautiful treasures of the world. Yet his glory is nothing compared to the lilies.

Now if the quickly perishable lilies are so favored by God, how much more will God clothe the higher human level, especially those who are listening to the teacher's words? But, of course, we are people of little faith. We cannot sustain this consciousness of our free, God-given beauty because we are constantly fretting about clothing. If we could clock how much inner time is spent on anxiety over survival and how much inner time is spent on contemplating the giftedness of life, anxiety would win, going away. Little faith translates into little contemplation.

> **Therefore do not worry, saying, "What will we eat?" or "What will we drink?" or "What will we wear?" For it is the Gentiles who strive for all these things; and indeed your heavenly Father knows that you need all these things. But strive first for the kingdom of God and his righteousness, and all these things will be given to you as well.**

The teaching thinks it has made its point. So now it mocks the anxiety by portraying it in shrill direct discourse. This shrill, frantic worry is for the Gentiles who do not yet know the revelation of Jesus. Those who know this revelation know the transcendent source of love is aware of everything we need. Therefore, our inner life is freed from preoccupation with physical survival and open for another possibility. We can seek first the kingdom and its righteousness, a way of life grounded in God and in creative service to our brothers, sisters, and neighbors. If we dedicate ourselves in this way, what we need for physical survival will be available to us. But it will not be there as a result of frantic effort. It will be given as the support of kingdom activity, added on to the primary mission of transforming life.

> **So do not worry about tomorrow, for tomorrow will bring worries of its own. Today's trouble is enough for today."**

The teaching returns to its future emphasis with a twinkle of dark humor. "Tomorrow thinking" and the anxiety it brings is needless overkill. You do not have to worry about tomorrow. When tomorrow comes, it will come with its own worries—and it will be called today. Instead, focus on the present which, by the way, is not without trouble. Take it, as they say, a day at a time.

Teaching

"I don't do anything unless there's a buck in it."

The man who said this had a no-nonsense look in his eyes and a slight, smug smile that suggested he was on to something that was undeniable. What was undeniable is that life is an anxious project of survival. Of course, it is not mere survival; it is survival in style. We have a certain lifestyle, and it has to be maintained at all costs. Therefore, as another man told me, "I'm constantly chasing dollars."

If these men could be characterized as servants, who is the master?

A financial planner once looked at me across the table and spoke this piece of loaded motivation, "Don't outlive your money." She went on to explain that people are living longer and spending all their money, mostly on healthcare costs. This is not a desirable future forecast. She wanted to galvanize me into making more money. That meant putting money concerns high in the internal hierarchy of my mind. If it occupies the thoughts, then the Buddha's warning is apropos: "You are what you think."

Now I know the limits of money. It cannot secure you against death and by no means does it automatically bring happiness. But it does keep one type of wolf from the door. Food and shelter cease to be a concern. In one of Robinson Davies' novels, a character suggests that Jesus was really a wealthy oriental who had "made his bundle" and then went into religion. Once the basic needs are taken care of, you can lift your thoughts higher. Basic physical needs dominate everyone. But if you got them out of the way, you can put your time and energy into more noble projects.

This way may seem eminently sensible. But the spiritual teaching of this text goes in another direction. I think St. Matthew's Jesus would point out that even though you have "made a bundle," you may feel you never have enough money. Even though your physical needs are met, you will continue to strive after treasure that rusts and can be eaten by moths. After all, you have gotten good at it.

Once money is the master, it does not let go easily. Our pursuit of it can become insatiable, a ceaseless striving that leaves us unfulfilled. Theologians call this condition concupiscence. Concupiscence tries to fill the God-space in us with something other than God. Nothing else satisfies, but we continue to look for substitutes. When money is the substitute, there is never enough even though it promises ultimate security with "just a little more."

So how should we grapple with this spiritual teaching about anxious survival and money versus birds and flowers and God?

Although there have been and are many Christians who believe that if your primary concern is the kingdom and its righteousness God will provide for your physical needs, I cannot wholeheartedly go there. If this is faith, then I fall in with the crowd that Jesus characterizes as "you of little faith." Physical needs are provided for by human effort working in conjunction with the God-given basics of creation. But God does not miraculously supply food and shelter, even if we are completely kingdom driven. This was Satan's temptation to Jesus in the desert, and he refused it (e.g., Matt 4:1-11).

I think the teaching initiates a process of integration. It presents us with two alternatives. Either (1) understand and inhabit your life as an anxious project for future physical survival or (2) understand and inhabit your life as a present gift sustained by God prior to any human activity to secure it. The teaching assumes the first state of anxiety consciousness is "where most people are at" and advocates for the second state of gift-consciousness. The rhetoric of the text is meant to help us attain, in a fleeting way, "gift-consciousness."

If we have more and more experiences of gift-consciousness, we will learn to appreciate ourselves from this perspective. Then we will put this sensibility into dialogue with anxiety-consciousness. In an ideal picture of transformation, this conversation will gradually loosen the stranglehold of anxiety-consciousness. Eventually, our anxieties will be integrated into gift-consciousness, and there will be one master, God. The ones who serve this master will know how to use the powerful tool of money and how to deal with the mental spasms of worry.

Ninth Sunday in Ordinary Time
Ninth Sunday after Epiphany

Proper 4

Matthew 7:21-29

Withstanding Storms

A Spiritual Commentary

[Jesus said to the disciples:] "Not everyone who says to me, 'Lord, Lord,' will enter the kingdom of heaven, but only the one who does the will of my Father in heaven.

The kingdom of heaven is a state of consciousness and action that the teachings of Jesus invite people to consider. However, this does not mean people rely on Jesus and beg him for acceptance and mercy. People must learn how to do the will of the Father for themselves. Jesus may provide the teaching, but he does not substitute for personal engagement. Crying "Lord, Lord" does not replace individual responsibility.

On that day many will say to me, 'Lord, Lord, did we not prophesy in your name, and cast out demons in your name, and do many deeds of power in your name?' Then I will declare to them, 'I never knew you; go away from me, you evildoers.'

This personal engagement and transformation takes priority over every other form of following Jesus. People who do "kingdom things"— prophecy, exorcisms, and miracles—in Jesus' name and leave it at that will be met with a devastating proclamation, "I never knew you." The followers of Jesus must learn to do things in their name, in their own awakened authority of God's kingdom. Dependency on Jesus may look like loyalty, but Jesus sees it as betrayal. In fact, he goes so far as to see it as a form of doing evil. If you think clinging to Jesus will save you, the text warns that the one you are clinging to will not recognize you. If rhetoric can wake up people, this strenuous rejection should do it.

Everyone then who hears these words of mine and acts on them will be like a wise man who built his house on rock. The rain

fell, the floods came, and the winds blew and beat on that house, but it did not fall, because it had been founded on rock. And everyone who hears these words of mine and does not act on them will be like a foolish man who built his house on sand. The rain fell, and the floods came, and the winds blew and beat against that house, and it fell—and great was its fall!"

If you are only a hearer of the Word and not a doer of the Word, what is at stake? When the storms of life come, you will collapse because you have not built on a firm foundation. But if you have built on a firm foundation, you will withstand the storms. Once again, St. Matthew's Jesus uses future consequences as a spur to undertake the journey of personal transformation through understanding and enacting the words of Jesus. Will you become "stormproof" or "storm vulnerable"?

Now when Jesus had finished saying these things, the crowds were astounded at his teaching, for he taught them as one having authority, and not as their scribes.

Jesus did not speak *about* God and spiritual transformation like a scribal scholar, distanced and removed. He spoke *from* God and from his own spiritual transformation. If people speak with an interior awareness of the realities they are talking about, their words carry authority. They are able to awaken life in those who hear them. This is how Jesus spoke and, therefore, his teachings astonished people. But if they listened closely, they would know that astonishment is only an understandable first response. It must lead beyond itself to the hard work of understanding and integration.

Teaching

How do you go about "stormproofing" yourself? How does one move from being a hearer of the Word to being a doer of the Word?

St. Matthew predicts dire consequences if this does not happen. But the Epistle of James explores this process more substantively.

But be doers of the word, and not merely hearers who deceive themselves. For if any are hearers of the word and not doers, they are like those who look at themselves in a mirror; for they look at themselves and, on going away, immediately forget what they were like. But those who look into the perfect law, the law of liberty, and persevere, being not hearers who forget but doers who act—they will be blessed in their doing. (Jas 1:22-25)

If you hear the word and do nothing else, you deceive yourself. The point of hearing is not hearing. The point of hearing is doing.

There are two aspects to doing the word. The first is to see yourself in the mirror and not forget what you see. The mirror is the teaching of Christ. At the beginning of the Sermon on the Mount, Jesus called people blessed, light, and salt. The reason is that they are connected to God and meant to bring God's love and reconciliation into the world. Blessedness, salt, and light are the real faces of the followers of Jesus.

But we have other names, names that are true but partial. We are named according to our body—tall, short, bald, hairy, ugly, beautiful, fat, skinny, etc. We are named according to our role—son, daughter, husband, wife, carpenter, tax collector, etc. We are named according to our gender and ethnic group—male, female, Jew, Greek, Ethiopian, etc. We are named according to our personality— shy, assertive, extrovert, introvert, etc. We have many names, and the names that designate our physical, social, and psychological characteristics are reinforced by our everyday activities. The transcendent face of blessedness, salt, and light that we saw in the mirror of Christ is easily forgotten. But doers of the Word remember it.

The second aspect is our ability to look into the perfect law of liberty. Our transcendent self cannot be coerced by circumstances. It is not reactive to whatever is happening, reducible to stimulus and response. It is capable of responding "out of kind." It can do good when good is not done to it; it can love when it is hated; it can extend peace when it is under attack. This law of liberty is not easily engaged. So if it would be the defining way we are in the world, we must persevere. But if we do, blessedness flows. This blessedness—the actions of the transcendent self—withstands storms.

So doing the Word entails being grounded in divine love and acting out of that awareness. But how does that make us "stormproof"? Life is storm. We are buffeted from within by our endemic mortality that eventually wins. We are slashed from without by persecution and the violent attacks of violent men. How does the transcendent self looking into the perfect law of liberty withstand those blowing winds?

In "Tickets for a Prayer Wheel," Annie Dillard writes:

I think that the dying
pray at the last

> not "please"
> but "thank you"
> as a guest thanks his host at the door.
> Falling from mountains
> the people are crying
> thank you,
> thank you,
> all down the air;
> and the cold carriages
> draw up for them on the rocks.

> ([Columbia: University of Missouri, 1974], 127)

We withstand because we cannot be reduced to the storm. We are capable of gratitude in the very act of dying. The transcendent self is always more than its circumstances. And if we court it and integrate it into all our frailties, we are "doing the Word" that makes us known by Jesus. "I do not know you" (Matt 25:12) changes to "enter into the joy of your master" (Matt 25:21, 23) and "inherit the kingdom prepared for you from the foundation of the world" (Matt 25:34).

Huston Smith, a philosopher of the spiritual, talked about his daughter's death in a way that suggests "withstanding storms." He acknowledged that during the eight and a half months of her sickness with cancer, he was tossed on the "emotional waves of ups and downs that are the human lot." So withstanding storms does not mean suppressing emotions:

> But I want to spell out how she and her immediate family rose to the showdown . . . Even when her condition had her at the breaking point, her farewells to us, her parents, in our last two visits were "I have no complaints" and "I am at peace." Her last words to her husband and children were "I see the sea. I smell the sea. It is because it is so near." She always loved the sea. I think it symbolized life for her.

Huston Smith commented further, "Her life had had its normal joys and defeats, but the spiritual work that she accomplished in those thirty weeks of dying was more than enough for a lifetime" (*The Way Things Are: Conversations with Huston Smith on the Spiritual Life*, ed. Phil Cousineau [Berkeley: University of California Press, 2003]). Storm-proofing means spiritual work has moved us from being hearers of the Word to being doers of the Word.

So the full truth is: we withstand storms by realizing our transcendent face and communicating love even while we sink.

Transfiguration Sunday

Matthew 17:1-9

Visiting the Mountain

A Spiritual Commentary

Jesus took with him Peter and James and his brother John and led them up a high mountain, by themselves.

Jesus has selected three of his disciples and led them up a high mountain. These three are an inner circle, and they are going to have access to the inner truth about Jesus. Although at the center of this story will be a transfigured Jesus, it is more a story about what it means to be a disciple than it is a statement about Jesus' identity.

The high mountain symbolizes the human ascent to God. If a cloud descends while one is on a high mountain, the divine and the human connect. At this point in the story, the human ascent has happened. The divine descent is still to come.

And he was transfigured before them, and his face shone like the sun, and his clothes became dazzling white.

The inner reality of Jesus, his relationship to God as his Father, permeates his entire being. His invisible spiritual relationship to God becomes visible. His body becomes radiant. In particular, his face, that part of his body that the disciples can see, shines. Also his clothes, symbolizing everything and everyone that comes into contact with him, become transparent to his inner reality. God may dwell in unapproachable light, but this light becomes approachable in Jesus.

Suddenly there appeared to them Moses and Elijah, talking with him.

Moses and Elijah are also mountain men. In the course of their law making and prophetic careers they return to the mountain to find both illumination and inspiration. They ascend the mountain to find direction for the affairs of the plains. The conversation is on the mountain, but what is discussed is the mission on the earth.

The disciples see Jesus talking with Moses and Elijah. This vision confirms for them that he is in continuity with the law and the prophets, an agent of God's purposes within history. This is a good thing for them to know and Peter, speaking for the group, says so.

> **Then Peter said to Jesus, "Lord, it is good for us to be here; if you wish, I will make three dwellings here, one for you, one for Moses, and one for Elijah."**

Peter responds to what he sees by addressing Jesus as Lord and opening himself to Jesus' command, "If you wish . . ." Seeing the transfigured Jesus has made Peter, James, and John more insightful and more compliant. They see the truth about Jesus and open themselves to his will.

Peter surmises that Jesus may want them to make three tents, presumably so that Jesus, Moses, and Elijah can settle in and continue the conversation. However, Peter's suggestion is about to be interrupted. A voice from a cloud has another agenda.

> **While he was still speaking, suddenly a bright cloud overshadowed them, and from the cloud a voice said, "This is my Son, the Beloved; with him I am well pleased; listen to him!"**

Contact. The ascending mountain meets the descending cloud. The voice repeats the words it said at the baptism. "This is my Son, the Beloved; with him I am well pleased." However, it adds a crucial command: "listen to him." The point for the disciples is not to overhear the conversation among these three key players of salvation history. The point is for them to listen to Jesus. Jesus is more than a lawgiver and a prophet. He is the Beloved Son. Their openness to what Jesus wants is the right path, but they must open even further.

> **When the disciples heard this, they fell to the ground and were overcome by fear. But Jesus came and touched them, saying, "Get up and do not be afraid." And when they looked up, they saw no one except Jesus himself alone.**

It is not what the voice says that prostrates the disciples with fear. It is the very fact of the voice. The transcendence of God always creates fear in the creature. The "infinite qualitative difference" between God and creation makes humans quake. No one can see God and live. The disciples do not want to look up.

However, Jesus has another response. The formal transcendence of God is balanced by the nature of God. The communication of the voice, a communication that must be heard, is love. The human is not crushed by the divine but elevated by it. So Jesus touches them and issues the commands they must listen to: rise and do not be afraid. Although they cannot face the transcendent reality of God, they can lift their eyes and look at the immanent presence of God in Jesus. Moses and Elijah have disappeared. Only Jesus is left to teach them what they must know. He is the guide beyond fear and into love.

> **As they were coming down the mountain, Jesus ordered them, "Tell no one about the vision until after the Son of Man has been raised from the dead."**

Now Jesus and the disciples descend, and Jesus issues an enigmatic command. Usually when people go to the mountain and experience a vision, a communication from God, they return to tell the people. Going to the mountain is followed by proclaiming on the earth. However, Jesus commands the disciples to be silent. The voice from the cloud instructed the disciples to listen to Jesus. Now they must listen, and listening to Jesus is not an easy task. What he has to say is often difficult to fathom and, when fathomed, difficult to swallow. In particular, the disciples have not been able to grasp his predictions about his upcoming suffering, death, and resurrection. They have not listened. Now Jesus enjoins them again to listen.

It seems the reason they were given the vision is to overcome their resistance to what Jesus is teaching. They have balked at the future Jesus has insisted on. In response to this opposition, Jesus had told Peter "you are setting your mind not on divine things but on human things" (Matt 16:23). This limited way of thinking will only change if they learn to listen to Jesus, who thinks "the things of God."

Therefore, the privilege of witnessing Jesus' transfiguration was for the purpose of confirming him as someone to whom they must listen. They must open themselves to what he is saying about his suffering, death, and resurrection. The disciples have seen his glory so they might understand and persevere with him on his path. The real action is not on the mountain but in the upcoming events of death and resurrection in Jerusalem. It is through these events that the revelation of God and truth of Jesus will be most clearly seen. These events are more important than the transfiguration, but the transfiguration encourages them in their struggle to allow Jesus to show them the way.

Teaching

I believe a factor in the phenomenal success of Scott Peck's *The Road Less Traveled* was the opening line, "Life is difficult."

That is how life often hits us, how it feels "from the inside." It does not mean we do not laugh or celebrate or rest or play. Life is not impossible or joyless or meaningless. But it is one thing after another, each one demanding we get out of our favorite chair. It is increased taxes, or a son who isn't learning at school, or a daughter who is learning too much outside of school, or the threat of downsizing, or the reality of downsizing, or a drop in the market, or the wrong numbers on the blood profile, or the need to plan more in order to get what you want, or the need to replan after you don't get what you want. What makes life difficult is that we continually face physical, mental, and social challenges.

What "difficult" seems to imply is that an intentional effort is needed, and this intentional effort involves a continual investment of energy. I was talking to a fourth-year high school student in his last semester. I said, "Will the last semester be a piece of cake?" He replied, "I'm afraid it is going to be difficult." When I asked why, he told me that a new French teacher had taken over. She was a woman with a Ph.D. "And they just don't give those things away," he said. "Hard times ahead." As he said this, I could see he was gearing up, getting ready for the challenge. He was not giving up, but he was preparing to engage on a higher level. A corollary of "Life is difficult" is "Life is a test."

Gearing up is needed, for the sad fact is that human situations fall apart unless they are constantly built up. The law of "wind down" applies. Unless we wind things up, they devolve into less than they should be. Without continual intentional effort, relationships become routinized and predictable and, in many cases, dissolve. Without continual intentional effort, personal goals remain unrealized dreams. Without continual intentional effort, enterprises flounder. Weeds grow around mansions; sagebrush rolls through ghost towns. Even in paradise, humans had to tend the garden. Human life is difficult because cosmic life is unfinished.

It can get tougher. Human life becomes more difficult when the circumstances we face interact with a moral agenda we carry. When we are committed to compassion and we face situations of suffering, we must struggle not to dismiss or ignore them. When we are committed to peace and we face situations of division and hostility, we must find a way to engage them without worsening the conflict. When we value honesty and we face situations of cover-up, it is difficult to find and walk the path of truth. Life is difficult when we try to bring to it what is best in us. It takes continual creative effort to suffuse situations with compassion, peace, and honesty. Virtue is hard work.

Spiritual traditions have an approach to the difficulties of life, in particular the moral difficulty. They make a distinction between effort that is expended before illumination and effort that is expended after illumination. Effort expended before illumination is a result of the grunt of the human will. It is sheer will power, generated by determination. Illumination means people consciously connect to the Divine Source and allow divine energies to flow through them. Therefore, the effort expended after illumination is a joint enterprise, a cooperative effort with grace. Human will rides the divine wind. However, in order to realize human effort as a cooperative response to divine grace, it is necessary to visit the mountain.

The disciples do not understand Jesus' insistence on suffering, death, and resurrection. This path of sustained effort severely contradicts their expectations. Jesus takes them to the mountain to reveal to them the divine origins of this path. Once they comprehend the divine origins, they will "rise without fear" and "listen to him." The wind will no longer be in their face, but at their back. They will learn to open to God's will and be able to engage the difficulty of Jesus' way. Peter is correct. The mountain vision of the disciples is good for them and, by extension, special spiritual experiences are good for us.

But what exactly is the good they do?

Special spiritual experiences are resources and encouragements to stay committed to the Christian struggle. If life in general is difficult, Jesus' way of moral transformation is even more difficult. Over the years I have listened to many recitals of spiritual experiences, times when people felt connected to God, times when they realized the Love that "moves the sun and the stars," times when they saw clearly the spiritual foundation of the universe. Since these experiences are always demarcated, having a beginning and an end, I would ask these people about the aftermath. Many would say they seek other experiences like it, or they have stored it in memory, or they have committed it to writing and carry it with them. Although these responses seem normal, they smack of tent building on the mountain.

The point is not to hold special experiences, but to listen to them. The extraordinary vision is not valuable in itself. It is a "good" that recommits us to the challenges of goodness. We need to experience higher truths for engaging the "long-haul" difficulties of moral living. We need to visit the mountain, but not stay there. Say not, "I've been to the mountain." Say, "I've returned to the earth and am walking toward Jerusalem."

First Sunday of Lent

Matthew 4:1-11

~~~

Knowing Who You Are

A Spiritual Commentary

Jesus was led up by the Spirit into the wilderness to be tempted by the devil.

Jesus has just been baptized and has heard the voice from heaven, "This is my Son, the Beloved, with whom I am well pleased" (Matt 3:17). But what does it mean to be the Beloved Son in whom God is well pleased? The devil will have some suggestions. But in this story the devil is not like the lion: "Like a roaring lion your adversary the devil prowls around, looking for someone to devour" (1 Pet 5:8). The Spirit is leading Jesus into this encounter with the devil. The testing by the devil will serve the Spirit's agenda. It will deepen Jesus' understanding and commitment.

He fasted forty days and forty nights, and afterwards he was famished.

Jesus' fasting "for forty days and forty nights" is a symbolic way of saying he withdrew from the physical sphere and fed himself from the domain of Spirit. His food was the words that the voice from heaven spoke. Then he returned to the physical realm: "afterwards he was famished." The temptations can now begin. How will the spiritual truth of Jesus' identity hold up in the physical, religious, and social realms?

The tempter came and said to him, "If you are the Son of God, command these stones to become loaves of bread."

But he [Jesus] answered, "It is written, 'One does not live by bread alone, but by every word that comes from the mouth of God.'"

This exchange alludes to Israel's exodus experiences in the desert, in particular their problems with hunger and the conclusions they quickly drew when their stomachs were empty. If they were hungry, they pleaded with Moses for food and intimated that God was not with them. Had God taken them out into the desert because there were not enough "graves in Egypt" (Exod 14:11)? They only knew they were loved if their stomachs were full (see Exod 16 and 17).

The tester suggests the same condition on Jesus' identity as the Son of God. Jesus' beloved status means that he will always be full. This fullness will be supplied by supernatural means, taking the inedible and turning it into food. The laws of planting and harvesting will be suspended. Jesus rejects this connection between being physically filled and being spiritually loved. The word from the mouth of God was that Jesus is the Beloved Son. He may be full and he may be hungry. But the word remains true in both situations. Negatively stated, Jesus will be empty, but he will still be the Beloved Son.

> **Then the devil took him to the holy city and placed him on the pinnacle of the temple, saying to him, "If you are the Son of God, throw yourself down; for it is written, 'He will command his angels concerning you,' and 'On their hands they will bear you up, so that you will not dash your foot against a stone.'"**

> **Jesus said to him, "Again it is written, 'Do not put the Lord your God to the test.'"**

Engraved on the pinnacle of the temple are the wings of eagles. As the wings of a mother eagle catch its young when they flutter in their fledging attempts at flight, so the wings of God will lift up his beloved whenever he falls. Therefore, as the Son of God, Jesus will always be safe. Like the physical fullness, this safety will be supplied by supernatural intervention. God's angels will hover around him, and he will not injure even his foot. The laws of gravity will be suspended.

The devil bolsters this faulty theology by citing Scripture. Jesus has quoted Scripture, and now the devil returns the volley. But Scripture alone will not decide the outcome of this duel of wits. It is Jesus' personal experience of divine love and its implications that allows him to choose and interpret the proper text and not misuse texts for suspicious purposes. The devil wants Jesus to presume on divine love and play the privileged Son toying with danger. But Jesus thinks this whole way of construing God's loving care is wrongheaded. You do not put yourself in danger so God can protect you and show others that you are truly God's Son. In the course of Jesus' life he will not be safe, and yet he will not waver from the conviction that God loves him. Negatively stated, Jesus will be hurt, but he will still be the Beloved Son.

> **Again, the devil took him to a very high mountain and showed him all the kingdoms of the world and their splendor; and he said to him, "All these I will give you, if you will fall down and worship me."**

> **Jesus said to him, "Away with you, Satan! for it is written, 'Worship the Lord your God, and serve only him.'"**

The third temptation has to do with political conquest and power. The assumption is that the kingdoms of the world belong to the devil. If Jesus worships the devil and adopts his ways, he will receive control over these kingdoms. There is a splendor to these kingdoms and so they are powerfully seductive. They are a real temptation, fittingly placed at the end as the final enticement to Jesus' freedom.

But Jesus is a Jew of the first commandment. He only worships "the Lord your God." He has no other gods, and so Satan's attempt to substitute himself for the true God is rejected with vehemence—"Away with you . . ." Jesus' refusal to worship Satan means he will not have political power and influence in the kingdoms of the world. Negatively stated, Jesus will be politically powerless, but he will still be the Beloved Son.

> **Then the devil left him, and suddenly angels came and waited on him.**

The devil had tried to seduce Jesus into thinking that what it means to be God's Son is to be physically full, physically safe, and politically powerful. Jesus refused that interpretation. God agreed with Jesus, for the angels, who would not have helped him float down from the pinnacle of the temple, come to minister to him after he has successfully resisted these temptations.

Teaching

The great advantage of temptations is that they lie in wait. They are there before we are, and they get to make the first move. In this story of Jesus' temptations the devil initiates contact, decides the subject matter, and suggests paths of action. This puts Jesus on the defensive from the beginning. The devil is so much in charge that he gets to "take" Jesus to the pinnacle of the temple and to the top of the mountain. The Spirit led him into the desert, but after that the devil chose the settings. Only after the third temptation does Jesus muster the muscle to banish him, "Away with you, Satan!" He is finally in charge.

This is how it is. In the midst of temptation we often feel we are being pulled along too quickly. We do not have enough time to think it through, to consult, and to see all the implications. This is because speed and pressure are essential features of the temptation. The temptation conveys, "You have to do this now, and if you don't, the consequences will be serious." When we look back, we say we have been led astray, and that is accurate. We went along because we could not apply the brake. We were no longer in control. The temptation had the upper hand. "How did I get into this, anyway?"

In general, a temptation is a suggested course of thinking and action that is not in our best interests or in the best interests of others. In the face of it we are forced to decide. It is as if we are standing on the edge of a cliff. We either fall or step backward.

Of course, there are different levels of temptations. Looking up and finding the dessert cart has returned to your table is not in the same category as your boss in the accounting firm suggesting you cook the books or be fired for incompetence. We can laugh about the extra chocolate mousse, but the stakes are higher in terms of personal integrity and consequences when the temptations are legally criminal. However, there is a way in which all temptations, minor and major, include the question of identity, the sense of who we are.

Jesus' temptations are directly on the level of spiritual identity. The devil begins two of the three temptations with, "If you are the Son of God." Then Satan spells out actions that are appropriate to this "Son of God" status. So the temptations may be actions in the world, but they are based on a false understanding of who Jesus is. This level of identity, of "who we think we are," is the hidden dimension on which the temptations play. When we do not know who we are, we enter into the temptation. When we do know who we are, we can reach for the resources to resist it.

However, knowing who you are and remembering it is not an easy feat. In a movie I saw so long ago that I have forgotten the title, a young man is leaving Greenwich Village to make his fortune in Hollywood. As he is walking away from his two-flat home with luggage in each hand, his mother opens the window and yells to him this parting advice, "Remember, your grandmother snuck over the Russian border in a hay wagon." She is afraid that in the foreign territory of Hollywood he will forget who he is and succumb to temptation. She thinks this memory of his grandmother will keep him on the straight and narrow. Who knows?

What Jesus remembers is "every word that came forth from the mouth of God." In particular, he remembers the word he heard when he emerged from the waters of John's baptism, "This is my Son, the Beloved, with whom I am well pleased" (Matt 3:17). He has meditated on this word for a sacred time of forty days and forty nights. In the process he has come to conclusions about what it means. The strength of these conclusions is what he is in touch with. Therefore, he can push back. He can say, "No!" Knowing who you are is the flip side of saying who you are not.

Jesus may be conscious of his true identity in a clear and immediate way, but for most of us it is a more labored and reflective effort. We do not always remember our spiritual identity. So temptations appear to us as options, possibilities that have to be weighed rather than demonic invitations that have to be dismissed. In particular, temptations are attractive because they appeal to our fantasy selves, those aspects of ourselves that want to be above it all. And this is the opportunity, our good fortune to have what we always wanted—a life that is always satiated, without injury, and rippling with splendiferous power. How can we remember who we are when we are offered this tantalizing possibility of who we might become?

So my suggestion in the face of all questionable offerings is to slow things down. Think about it by ourselves and talk about it with friends. But this thinking and talking has to be more than a strategy session. It must be a process of theological reflection, a consideration of who we are as sons and daughters of God—and what understandings and actions are appropriate to this truth about us. So pick friends for this conversation who know the difference between temptation and option. If they are swayed by fantasy, they can become unwitting allies of the temptation.

And do not decide until you know *who* is deciding. The best way to say no is to be in touch with a stronger yes.

Second Sunday of Lent

(*Revised Common Lectionary*; users of *Lectionary for Mass*
see Transfiguration Sunday, pp. 97–102)

John 3:1-17

Serving Spirit through Theology

A Spiritual Commentary

**Now there was a Pharisee named Nicodemus, a leader of the
Jews. He came to Jesus by night and said to him, "Rabbi, we
know that you are a teacher who has come from God; for no
one can do these signs that you do apart from the presence of
God."**

This is a story about a Pharisee who happens to be called Nicodemus.
Nicodemus symbolizes the Pharisaic mindset. This mindset is attached to externals. It relishes first places at table, long robes with wide
phylacteries, polished cups, and salutations in the marketplace (see
Matt 23:1-25; Luke 20:45-46). This fascination with the outside hinders
this mindset from recognizing hidden, inner truths. Therefore, there is
a large segment of reality that is not available to this benighted perspective. He comes by night, which means he is unable to see (understand) and, at least in this episode, he remains in darkness.

His ignorance is not his alone, for he is a ruler of Jews. His limita-
tions are those of the religious elite of Jerusalem and he speaks for them
when he says, "we know." They have seen the signs and acknowledge
that Jesus is a teacher sent from God. This seems to be an appropriate
conclusion and the first step on the road to faith. However, seeing the
signs is the domain of physical sight, for the signs are manifestations on
the physical level of truths available on the spiritual level. It is the
physical, the outside, that has attracted Nicodemus.

A man of the Pharisees would be expected to notice the spectacular
surface. But he asks to go further. In calling Jesus "Rabbi" and acknowledging him as a teacher sent from God he is implicitly asking for
a teaching from the spiritual realm, from the kingdom of God. However, there is a precondition for understanding this type of teaching. It
is this precondition that this Pharisee will not be able to fathom.

Jesus answered him, "Very truly, I tell you, no one can see the kingdom of God without being born from above."

Nicodemus said to him, "How can anyone be born after having grown old? Can one enter a second time into the mother's womb and be born?"

Jesus tells him in a very solemn and direct way that only those who have been "born anew" can understand the kingdom of God. This type of birth awakens people to the spiritual realm. But Nicodemus takes "born from above" to mean "born again," and he interprets it in the most gross physical way. He does not awaken to the spiritual, but becomes mired in the physical. He entertains an impossible vision. An old man is returning to his mother's womb for a second try at the birth process. This is a laughable image, but it is one that shows how flat-minded Nicodemus is. He is stuck at the level of blood, and the prologue of John's Gospel has stated that "to all who received him [Jesus the Word of God], who believed in his name, he gave power to become children of God, who were born, not of blood . . ." (1:12). Jesus is not talking about blood, but Nicodemus cannot get beyond it.

Jesus answered, "Very truly, I tell you, no one can enter the kingdom of God without being born of water and Spirit. What is born of the flesh is flesh, and what is born of the Spirit is spirit. Do not be astonished that I said to you, "You must be born from above." The wind blows where it chooses, and you hear the sound of it, but you do not know where it comes from or where it goes. So it is with everyone who is born of the Spirit."

Nicodemus said to him, "How can these things be?"

Jesus tries to move Nicodemus beyond the physical level—unsuccessfully. He begins again with solemn and direct speech. This is speech designed to have an impact. He acknowledges physical birth, "born of water," and adds another dimension, "Spirit." To see the kingdom of God, to understand a spiritual teaching, one needs both. It is important to acknowledge that one has to be both flesh and spirit to receive a spiritual teaching on earth. It is not enough to be merely spiritual or merely physical. But since Nicodemus has tried to understand Jesus' words on the physical level and has misinterpreted them, he must be told that the merely physical cannot understand the spiritual. Flesh can understand flesh, but only spirit can understand Spirit.

Having stated this truth, Jesus enjoins Nicodemus not to marvel at the saying, "You must be born from above." His first response—return to his mother's womb—was an act of marveling. Marveling is the opposite of understanding. Marveling interprets symbolic language in a literal way and then gapes and gawks at the ridiculous thought. In place of marveling, Nicodemus will be asked to follow an image into the spiritual truth Jesus is trying to communicate.

The wind is able to be experienced ("you hear the sound of it"), but it cannot be controlled ("it blows where it chooses") or fully comprehended ("you do not know where it comes from or where it goes"). To be born of God is to experience God's being sustaining your own being. At the same time you realize you cannot control this life, and its origin and destiny remain a mystery. This self-understanding is a prerequisite for understanding a more developed teaching about Spirit, a teaching Nicodemus has requested but one that he is not yet ready to receive. In order to receive a spiritual teaching, one must be born of the Spirit. Spiritual communication is for spiritual people. God only talks to God's children. The One who has come down from above converses with those who are "born from above." But, for the present, Nicodemus is definitely "from below."

He remains puzzled. "How can these things come about?"

Jesus answered him, "Are you a teacher of Israel, and yet you do not understand these things? Very truly, I tell you, we speak of what we know and testify to what we have seen; yet you do not receive our testimony. If I have told you about earthly things and you do not believe, how can you believe if I tell you about heavenly things?

Jesus thinks Nicodemus should know "these things." Nicodemus is a teacher himself, a teacher in Israel, and yet this basic truth about the spiritual identity of the human person has eluded him. Nicodemus' ignorance is contrasted with the personal knowledge of the Christians. As Nicodemus spoke in the plural for "all Pharisees and leaders," Jesus now speaks in the plural for Christians who are more enlightened in spiritual matters than the official teachers. But the official teachers will not listen to them. In fact, in further episodes, they will proclaim their darkness to be light, their ignorance to be knowledge.

Nicodemus' quest for a spiritual teaching does not match his ability to hear it. Jesus has told him "earthly things"—the spiritual connection of the person with what is ultimately free and mysterious. He has not understood this. What if Jesus were to tell him "heavenly things"—truths about the Divine Being Itself and its fullness of love? If he cannot understand the lower, how will he understand the higher?

Although Nicodemus is unresponsive, the readers are not. In fact, we, as readers, have been prepared for the teaching that Jesus is about to unfold. Watching Nicodemus stall has allowed us to open. We know we are more than complex material beings. We are also children of God, and we are eager for a teaching from the Divine Parent.

No one has ascended into heaven except the one who descended from heaven, the Son of Man.

Before the teaching is elaborated, the credentials of the teacher are established. Jesus is the only one who can give a true teaching. Others claim they ascend into heaven through prayer or trance, talk to God, and bring a teaching back to earth. Usually the teaching they bring back is about judgment. What are the criteria by which God will judge people?

But the Son of Man is the one on earth on whom angels descend and then ascend back to heaven. "Very truly, I tell you, you will see heaven opened and the angels of God ascending and descending upon the Son of Man" (John 1:51). He is the true connection between heaven and earth. In another image, the Son of Man comes down from above (see John 6:62). Therefore, his first move is descent. His path is not a precarious climb to heaven. Rather he graciously descends to earth. Therefore, the revelation of the Son of Man is authentic. What he will say about judgment is the truth.

And just as Moses lifted up the serpent in the wilderness, so must the Son of Man be lifted up, that whoever believes in him may have eternal life.

After the Israelites escaped Egypt, they wandered in the desert and complained bitterly to God. God sent serpents into their camp. The serpents bit people and they died. God told Moses to make a bronze serpent, put it on a stick, and hold it high. The people who looked on it were cured of their snake bite. It is a form of homeopathic medicine. What brings the disease in one form cures the disease in another form.

Humans are bitten by death. The Son of Man, the one who comes down from above, becomes death, death on a cross. He is lifted up so the people can see him. If they see him and believe, eternal life will flow into them. What are they to believe? They are to comprehend how divine life has entered into human life precisely at that point where human life is failing (death). At that point divine life sustains the human person through the loss of temporal life. Eternal life both suffuses and transcends temporal life, and this truth is realized by looking on the crucified one. In one form death brings a loss of life; in another form—the crucifixion of the Son of Man—death brings a fullness of life.

> **For God so loved the world that he gave his only Son, so that everyone who believes in him may not perish but may have eternal life. Indeed, God did not send the Son into the world to condemn the world, but in order that the world might be saved through him.**

This is the inner truth, the truth at the center. Or, in another image, this is the highest truth, the truth above all other truths. Or in another image, this is the revelation of the hidden actor behind it all. The revelations involved in this episode are progressive. It begins with what may be a stretch but what is definitely within our reach. We are beings who are grounded and sustained by an ultimate Mystery, but we do not control or completely comprehend this Mystery. Then we are gradually led to a spiritual knowing that blows our mind. The dynamite revelation is that the essence of that Mystery is a self-giving love completely dedicated to human fulfillment. This is what drives everything.

The Son of Man was sent into the world by divine love. Divine Love could not tolerate the sight of human perishing. Divine Love wants to fill people with a life that does not end. Even if the people in the world have strayed from their grounding in God and oppressed one another, God does not seek condemnation. The divine desire is for salvation. The judgment of God is love and life.

However, the judgment of humans may be otherwise.

Teaching

I have taught theology for over thirty years. During that time I have been told theology is (1) abstract, (2) irrelevant, (3) the private preserve of eggheads, (4) second best to the rote recitation of scriptural texts, and (5) something to be left behind when you have learned to think for yourself.

However, I have also been a spiritual director for people and fancy myself on a spiritual path. In directing people and observing myself, I have found that theologies continually pop up. Even if people think they are free of them, or if they have sworn off them, or if they have declared them irrelevant, theological ideas hang on and, given any attention at all, multiply. Many people carry scraps of ultimate ideas about God, sin, salvation, and themselves. These ideas may be buried, but they are definitely not dead. They exert influence, and often that influence is very restrictive. The Buddha suggested that people are what they think. Given some of the theologies people have in the carrying case of their mind, this is a scary observation.

The reason theological ideas are important is that they inhabit the mind as gatekeepers. In vertical imagery, the mind is positioned between the soul above and the body and the world below. The mind must learn to open to the flow of Spirit from the soul and convey it to the body and through the body into the world. In order for the mind to do this, it must be given instructions. If the instructions to the mind close it down rather than open it up, the mind is isolated from the flow of Spirit. Some theological ideas have a tendency to cut the mind off from the soul. They close the gate rather than open it. These ideas then work against the ultimate spiritual well-being of the person.

When people attend to their spiritual development, they often bump into some residual theological ideas. When they begin to pray and meditate on a regular basis and read authentic spiritual teachings, they begin to notice their theologies and evaluate how they are functioning. Often in order to mature spiritually, they have to change theologically. The Gospels are famous for citing "hardness of heart" (e.g., Luke 8:12) as the reason many people could not positively respond to Jesus' teaching. This has nothing to do with the pump in the left-middle of the chest. The arteriosclerosis is in the mind. The apertures are too small, clogged by narrow theological ideas that do not know they are meant to serve Spirit.

The Nicodemus story revolves around some theological ideas that hinder the flow of Spirit. Nicodemus gravitates towards physical signs, but he sees them more as spiritual fireworks than as pointers to another dimension. He is stuck on what he can see with his physical eyes. This predicament is the perennial human condition. Addicted to the "lust of the eyes" [see Ezek 6:6; NAB] we are continually on the hunt for spectacular divine activity in the midst of visible human life. We overinterpret events, not taking into account physical, psychological, and social factors.

This fever for physical seeing keeps us from subtler interior movements. Nicodemus could feel himself as a body, but he could not feel himself as living by the wind of the Spirit. Part of this block was a theological understanding of divine activity as interruption in the outer world. He judges the spiritual only by its disruptive impact on the physical. This idea makes Nicodemus squint. Jesus' language is a strenuous effort to change this theological blinder so that he might see more.

However, the showcase theological idea of the story is one that Nicodemus never gets to hear. Since he has not comprehended the "earthly things," he is not treated to the "heavenly things." But we are. We are told that God is love, and that the entire divine intention is to give eternal life to human creation. Even if this human creation is in rebellion against God, God does not seek its condemnation but rather continues to work for its salvation. To this end, God has sent the Son, Son of God and Son of Mary, to enter into human death and to bear people beyond it. This startling act of self-giving will have the power to enlighten even darkened minds and awaken them to the true nature of the Spirit in whom "we live and move and have our being" (Acts 17:28).

The power of this cluster of theological ideas is only seen when the theological ideas it seeks to replace are spelled out. God is not a distant reality who only communicates with creation through a chain of lesser intermediaries. The divine Son, who is one with the Father, is God's connection to the world. God does not hold back. The divine nature is intimately involved with creation.

Also, God is not a force for condemnation. God has no interest in punishing wrongdoers. By implication, God's primary posture is not a call for humans to be good and an evaluation of their performance. The human enterprise is not a scramble for self-salvation, and the law court is not the primary imagery for divine judgment.

The Divine does not seek its own glory. God is not a self-obsessed reality always looking for recognition and obeisance. Therefore, the people of this God are not to see themselves as begrudging servants of a divine will that is always demanding inhuman efforts from them. They are not slaves of God, sacrificing themselves for divine glory.

Rather God is an infinite self-giving into creation. The Divine glory is to communicate life to creation. Grace is the essence of God. God is the food people must learn to eat, and the light people must learn to see by. The first and perennial posture of the human toward the Divine is openness. What the Son of Man brought down from heaven was a theological revelation that challenged the dominant way we think about God, a way of thinking that blocks us from the flow of Spirit.

We can hear this Johannine thunderclap and sense its liberating effects on our mind and, through our mind, on our entire being. But it is hard to make this new theology our own. It is difficult to allow it to occupy a significant space in our mental life. The theology of the judging God and God's punishing ways is deeply ingrained. When Jesus tries to wash Peter's feet, a symbol of the self-giving love of God, Peter replies, "You will never wash my feet" (John 13:8). The old theology does not give way easily. Our mental tapes and social experience support and give credence to the evaluating God of rewards and punishment. But if we can hold the idea of divine love steady, even for a short period of time, it will open the mind to Spirit. Once we drink from Spirit, we will know the truth of John's theology: "We declare to you what was from the beginning, what we have heard, what we have seen with our eyes" (1 John 1:1).

Third Sunday of Lent

John 4:5-42

Disappearing into the Fullness of Joy

A Spiritual Commentary

SCENE ONE

[Jesus] came to a Samaritan city called Sychar, near the plot of ground that Jacob had given to his son Joseph.

Jesus was traveling from Judea to Galilee, and so it is geographically necessary to pass through Samaria. However, more than geography is implied. At the end of this story, the Samaritans will acknowledge Jesus as Savior of the world. He is not only a Jewish messiah, but a universal liberator. Therefore, he has to go everywhere. He has to pass through Chicago and Timbuktu. The "had to" is a theological imperative more than it is a travel itinerary.

The mention of Jacob and Jacob's well alludes to a story in Genesis (29:1-14) that prefigures a major theme of the woman at the well story. Jacob comes into a field with a well in the middle of it. The well is covered by a huge stone. There are three flocks of sheep in the field with accompanying shepherds. While Jacob is talking with the shepherds about his kinsman, Laban, Rachel, Laban's daughter, arrives with her sheep. Jacob tells the shepherds they should roll back the rock from the mouth of the well so that Rachel's sheep could drink. The shepherds refuse, saying, "We cannot until all the flocks are gathered together" (v. 8). But Jacob goes to the well and moves back the huge stone so that Rachel's sheep can drink now. For one who can roll back the stone from the mouth of the well, the water is available now.

The woman at the well is a story about opening the well of eternal life now. There is no need to wait until the end of time when all "the flocks" will drink together. The one who is Living Water provides divine life now. The time of waiting is over.

Jacob's well was there, and Jesus, tired out by his journey, was sitting by the well. It was about noon.

Jesus may be physically weary because it is a long walk from Jerusalem to Sychar. But he is theologically weary because he has just come

116 of the text

from Nicodemus who was not able to successfully dialogue with him. Jesus was not able to communicate divine life to him. It is this failure to communicate life that makes Jesus weary.

Jesus is the fullness of life roaming the world. He is trying to find people to whom to give this life. When people receive life from him, he grows strong. He does not feel depleted but fulfilled. When spiritual life is given and received, it grows; and all, giver and receiver, are invigorated.

Jesus is weary because he has found no one to believe in him, to enter into him and receive his fullness of life. But things are about to change. Nicodemus came at night, symbolizing his ignorance. It is now noon, the fullness of day, symbolizing illumination. Who will arrive with the brightness of the sun? Anyone familiar with patriarchal literature could guess that if a man is sitting at a well, a woman will soon appear.

> **A Samaritan woman came to draw water, and Jesus said to her, "Give me a drink." (His disciples had gone to the city to buy food.)**
>
> **The Samaritan woman said to him, "How is it that you, a Jew, ask a drink of me, a woman of Samaria?" (Jews do not share things in common with Samaritans.)**

The woman's desire is to draw water and, by the time she has finished talking to Jesus, her thirst will be slaked. But it will be in a way she does not presently imagine. Jesus begins the conversation by abruptly asking for a drink. But the paradox is: Jesus gets a drink when people allow him to give them a drink. The wise Sufi elder Rumi said:

> Not only the thirsty seek water,
> the water as well seeks the thirsty.
>
> (*Rumi—Fragments, Ecstasies*, trans. Daniel Liebert
> [New Lebanon, N.Y.: Omega Publications, 1999])

Jesus is living water looking for someone who is thirsty. When the thirsty drink from the water Jesus offers, Jesus himself gets a drink. By the end of this exchange, Jesus will have his drink, for he is talking to a thirsty woman.

In this story the spiritual slowness of the disciples contrasts with the spiritual speed of the woman. "Going into town to buy food" is the knee jerk mechanism of those who are unaware of inner food and drink. The disciples are with the Living Water and the Bread Come Down from Heaven, but they have left him to seek food and drink elsewhere. Their imaginations have collapsed into the material level. They always have to "go and buy," thinking the only resources are outside themselves. The disciples are spiritually dense, and this denseness is the backdrop for the porous receptivity of the woman.

Jesus' request of the woman breaks the social rules. A Jewish man just talking to a Samaritan woman in public would be forbidden. But to say, "Give me a drink," could be interpreted as a sexual overture. Often men who consorted with women who were not their wives were reprimanded with, "Drink from your own well"—see Proverbs 5:15-18:

> Drink water from your own cistern,
> flowing water from your own well.
>
> . . . .
>
> Let your fountain be blessed,
> and rejoice in the wife of your youth.

This is strange behavior and the storyteller wants us to know it, for he interjects "Jews do not share things in common with Samaritans."

This woman might easily have walked away. But she is intrigued. She wants to know why he is breaking these social rules. At this stage she is primarily aware of his gender and ethnicity, a Jew and a man. But since he is not acting like a Jew and a man, she suspects something more may be afoot. Asking why he is asking for a drink is the opening Jesus needs. He just may get his drink.

Jesus answered her, "If you knew the gift of God, and who it is that is saying to you, 'Give me a drink,' you would have asked him, and he would have given you living water."

The tables are quickly turned, and from here on Jesus will direct the dialogue. The woman will follow it with exquisite sensitivity.

She has to know two things. The first is the gift of God and the second is who is saying to her, 'Give me a drink.' It is important to note that the storyteller does not just say "who is asking her for a drink," but "who it is that is saying to you, 'Give me a drink.'" There is a need for a direct quotation. She has to know who is putting his speech into her. At the end of this dialogue, Jesus will put another word into her, a word that will simultaneously give her the living water she seeks and Jesus the drink he wants. This is a win-win story.

Therefore, this statement of Jesus sets the content of the conversation. In the next three pieces of dialogue, she will come to know the gift of God and ask Jesus for a drink. In the following pieces of dialogue, she will come to know who is saying to her, "Give me a drink," and with that knowledge he will give her living water. But, at this point in the story, we are at the beginning of the spiritual quest, not at the end.

The woman said to him, "Sir, you have no bucket, and the well is deep. Where do you get that living water? Are you greater than our ancestor Jacob, who gave us the well, and with his sons and his flocks drank from it?"

She picks up on the last words Jesus said to her, "living waters." She mistakes this for an abundance of H_2O. This mistake leads her to make wrongheaded observations. She notices that he does not have a bucket. Since water is in the ground, deep in the ground, he has no way to get it. Besides that, is he making a claim that he has more water than is in Jacob's well? Centuries ago Jacob drank from this well and, since then, all his progeny and even the flocks have been able to find water in this well. There is a lot of H_2O in Jacob's well.

The first step toward spiritual maturity is becoming comfortable with spiritual symbolism. Paradoxically, this often happens by taking the symbolism literally, and then seeing that it could not possibly mean what it literally purports. The woman begins with a statement that poses a difficulty if Jesus' words are taken at face value. He has no bucket and the well is deep. But her next two sentences are questions, not statements. Her questioning suggests she is beginning to open to the possibility that this Jew may not be talking about H_2O.

Jesus said to her, "Everyone who drinks of this water will be thirsty again, but those who drink of the water that I will give them will never be thirsty. The water that I will give will become in them a spring of water gushing up to eternal life."

Jesus corrects her literalism and points her to the spiritual. The water in this well is H_2O. People need this water to survive physically, and they need it repeatedly. Physical life is characterized by recurrent states of hunger and thirst and is maintained by corresponding repetitive acts of eating and drinking.

By contrast, the water Jesus gives quenches spiritual thirst in such a way that this thirst never reoccurs. The reason it does not reoccur is the nature of the water that quenches it. This water is really eternal life, and eternal life "just keeps on giving." In the imagery of the story, the well becomes "a spring of water gushing up to eternal life." Therefore, spiritual thirst does not have a chance to reoccur because the spiritual water, of its nature, never stops: "he gives the Spirit without measure" (John 3:34).

> **The woman said to him, "Sir, give me this water, so that I may never be thirsty or have to keep coming here to draw water."**

She grasps what Jesus is saying and requests "this water" for two reasons. She does not want to thirst spiritually. This is the first intimation in the story that she is spiritually thirsty, but it will not be the last. Nor does she want to be restricted to the physical level of life where the only water she knows is water drawn from the ground of earth. Pulling H$_2$O out of the earth requires she come "here," to Jacob's well, to drink. She wants water she can carry with her. She wants water she can drink from at any time and at any place, a water in the ground of herself. Then she will not have to "come here to draw water."

This completes the first part of the conversation. She knows the gift of God, living water as eternal life, and she has asked for it.

> **Jesus said to her, "Go, call your husband, and come back."**
>
> **The woman answered him, "I have no husband."**
>
> **Jesus said to her, "You are right in saying, 'I have no husband'; for you have had five husbands, and the one you have now is not your husband. What you have said is true!"**

As Jesus initiated the first part of the conversation with "Give me a drink," he initiates the second part of the conversation with, "Go, call your husband." As water imagery was used to symbolize spiritual life in the first part of the conversation, marriage imagery will be used to symbolize spiritual life in the second part.

In the culture of Jesus' time, a true husband is one who makes his wife fruitful, i.e., makes her pregnant. She, in turn, brings children, the fruit of her pregnancy, to her husband. When this physical and social dynamic is used to illumine the spiritual dimension of life, it highlights the role of the true God and the role of the true believer. The true husband (God) puts life into his wife. She bears this life into the world (manifests Spirit in the flesh) and presents the children to her husband (acknowledges that God is the source of her fruitfulness).

To connect the water imagery to the marriage imagery, this woman is spiritually thirsty because she has never found a true husband who has put life into her. In this sense, she has no husband. Jesus compliments her for knowing this truth: "You are right in saying . . ." and

"What you have said is true!" Scholars tell us that the five "husbands who are not her husband" are the five gods the Samaritans brought back from the Babylonian exile, and the current "husband who is not her husband" is the truncated form of Judaism the Samaritans espoused. But what is important is that she has worshiped other gods and none of them has given her life. So they are "husbands who are not husbands." Therefore, she is still a woman looking for a true husband who will make her a true wife. What she has yet to discover is that her future true husband is talking to her.

The woman said to him, "Sir, I see that you are a prophet.

Jesus has pointed out how all her husbands have been unable to give her life, how all the gods she has worshiped have failed her. This is what a prophet does: unmasks the false promises of idols. She perceives this and moves from Jesus as a Jewish man to Jesus as a prophet. Her insight is deepening.

Our ancestors worshiped on this mountain, but you say that the place where people must worship is in Jerusalem."

If a prophet can denounce false gods, perhaps he knows how to contact the true God, the one who will give her life. She poses her search in terms of finding the right mountain—Gerizim or Zion—and in terms of two traditions of fathers—Samaritans and Jews. She put these geographical options to Jesus, but he does not play by the game she proposes.

Jesus said to her, "Woman, believe me, the hour is coming when you will worship the Father neither on this mountain nor in Jerusalem. You worship what you do not know; we worship what we know, for salvation is from the Jews.

The conversation is ripening, coming to a point where Jesus will give her the "living water." So Jesus' speech becomes assertive and urgent, "Woman, believe me." What she is to believe is that this past way of trying to find the right mountain on which God really lives is nearly over, "the hour is coming when." The Father will not be worshiped in the way our fathers have taught. Besides, the contrast between Samaritans and Jews is not a difference of mountains. It is a difference of knowledge. Knowing the true God is the key; worship follows from that. What the Jews know about God is the divine activity of salvation. This is the being and activity of the true God and so Jews "worship what we know, for salvation is *from* the Jews."

> **But the hour is coming, and is now here, when the true worshipers will worship the Father in spirit and truth, for the Father seeks such as these to worship him. God is spirit, and those who worship him must worship in spirit and truth."**

However, salvation may come from the Jews, but it does not belong to the Jews, for the time of a new revelation is "coming and is now." In this present time, true worshipers are those who know the intimate connection between God and worshipers. God is Spirit and Truth and, therefore, "those who worship [God] must worship in spirit and truth." The believer participates in the life of God and shares its qualities of Spirit and Truth. Spirit points to the invisible foundation of the world in God. Truth points to the revelation of that foundation, the consciousness that is needed to perceive it and respond to it. Worship begins when people become aware of the spiritual life that permeates all creation.

> **The woman said to him, "I know that Messiah is coming" (who is called Christ). "When he comes, he will proclaim all things to us."**

The woman picks up on the idea of truth as a consciousness of spiritual reality, as a "showing of all things." This reflects the fundamental truth of the prologue. "*All things* came into being through [the Word], and without [the Word] not one thing came into being" (John 1:3). The truth of the Messiah is the revelation of the spiritual foundation of all things, the origin and continual participation of creation in God. But this is precisely what Jesus has been doing. He has been leading her away from materialism and ethnocentrism to a realization of the universal presence of Spirit. She can be in communion with this presence if she follows the clues Jesus is providing. So the conclusion, a conclusion she does not draw, is that Jesus is the Messiah, the one the Samaritans have hoped for. The conversation has progressed from Jesus the Jewish man to Jesus the prophet to Jesus the Messiah. It is about to go further.

> **Jesus said to her, "I am he, the one who is speaking to you."**

Now she is ready. So Jesus reveals his deepest identity to her. He is the "I am." He participates in and communicates the very being of God. However, the truth about "I am" is that it is simultaneously a "that you may be." God's very being is self-communication. So when Jesus says, "the one who is speaking to you," he is tapping into his ultimate identity as the Word. As the Word of God speaking human words, he is putting God's being and love into her. She is sharing in the structure of his identity. She now knows who is saying to her, "Give me a drink," and he has given her living water. On one level, the conversation is over. On another level, it continues forever.

SCENE TWO

Just then his disciples came. They were astonished that he was speaking with a woman, but no one said, "What do you want?" or, "Why are you speaking with her?"

The disciples provide a vivid contrast to the woman. Instead of the questioning and give-and-take of real dialogue such as Jesus just had with the woman, the disciples marvel and keep silent. Marveling means they see something they do not understand. But instead of pursuing what they do not know until they know it, they simply do not say anything. This is not the way of spiritual development.

If they had asked Jesus, "What do you want?" he would have replied, "I want a drink." If they had asked Jesus, "Why are you speaking with her?" he would have replied, "She is giving me a drink." This is important knowledge about Jesus, but it is knowledge they will not get because they refuse to ask.

Then the woman left her water jar and went back to the city. She said to the people, "Come and see a man who told me everything I have ever done! He cannot be the Messiah, can he?" They left the city and were on their way to him.

She leaves the water jar (H$_2$O container) because the physical dimension of life no longer preoccupies her consciousness. Her participation in "living water" has widened her interests. Turning *away* from the chores of everyday life, she turns *toward* the city. She now has a new role to play—witness to the Christ.

She invites the people by proposing a possibility. She witnesses that this man told her all she ever did. This does not mean that Jesus had supernatural knowledge of all the little-known facts of her life. Rather he told her the energizing center of her activity, the source that drove her. He told her of her endless quest to find a true husband who would give her life, and then he became that true husband.

Although this is a powerful experience for her, she does not impose it on others. Rather her question concerning his identity as the Messiah is an invitation, an invitation the people accept. They leave the city and are coming to Jesus. She is bringing children to her true husband.

> **Meanwhile the disciples were urging him, "Rabbi, eat something."**
>
> **But he said to them, "I have food to eat that you do not know about."**
>
> **So the disciples said to one another, "Surely no one has brought him something to eat?"**

The disciples continue their wrongheaded approach. They went to town to buy food and now they offer it to Jesus. He tells them he has food of which they do not know. This remark of Jesus puzzles them as much as his talking to a woman. But once again they do not ask him what he means. Instead, they talk to one another, sharing their ignorance, and asking the ironic question about someone bringing him food. Of course, the woman has brought him food. When she accepted the food (eternal life) Jesus offered, Jesus' own hunger was fed.

> **Jesus said to them, "My food is to do the will of him who sent me and to complete his work. Do you not say, 'Four months more, then comes the harvest'? But I tell you, look around you, and see how the fields are ripe for harvesting.**

Jesus continues to tell them what refreshes and strengthens him. He feeds on God's will and work. God's will and work is for Jesus to give divine life to people. To feast on this food it is not necessary to wait for the harvest season. This food is available now. "[L]ook around you, and see how the fields are ripe for harvesting" (or "Lift up your eyes, and look on the fields; for they are white already to harvest"; KJV) may allude to the Samaritans who are coming to him dressed in white baptismal robes. In order for Jesus to complete his work people must come to him. They must find him in the company of the Church. Therefore, the role of the Church is to bring Jesus his food. The disciples have offered him physical food from town and told him, "Rabbi, eat!" Now Jesus has told them what nourishes him. Can they bring him this "people food," people who are eager and open to what he passionately wants to give?

Or is someone else already doing that?

> **The reaper is already receiving wages and is gathering fruit for eternal life, so that sower and reaper may rejoice together. For**

**here the saying holds true, 'One sows and another reaps.' I sent
you to reap that for which you did not labor. Others have labored, and you have entered into their labor."**

The harvest is now and the disciples are to gather it in. People are
coming to them to find eternal life in Christ, and they are to receive
these people. However, this reaping is a time for communal rejoicing,
a time to remember the sower and the reaper. The disciples are entering into the labor of others. The missionary woman has sowed the
seed; the male disciples are reaping the benefits. Ultimately, both are
providing food for Jesus; both are needed for Jesus to complete his
work. But there is a cautionary note in how this instruction is phrased.
In the excitement of harvest the disciples may forget the labor of the
sower. Jesus urges them to remember.

SCENE THREE

**Many Samaritans from that city believed in him because of the
woman's testimony, "He told me everything I have ever done."**

The woman's testimony concerned how Jesus revealed her to herself. He told her she had an unslaked thirst for God and was a woman
without a true husband to give her life. Then he gave her a drink and
made her fruitful. He disclosed an essential human hunger and then he
fed it. Her story of coming into life and love was powerful enough to
bring others to believe in Jesus. However, "believing in him" seems to
mean they are attracted to him and want to "see for themselves." Her
witness sowed the seed.

**So when the Samaritans came to him, they asked him to stay
with them; and he stayed there two days.**

The effect of the woman's testimony is not only that the Samaritans
come to Jesus. They also know what to ask him. They want him to remain with them. In other words, they want to commune with him, to
enter into the structure of his selfhood, to share in his living relationship with God. Through the woman's testimony they know what Jesus
does, and they ask him to do that for them. When the request is correct, Jesus cannot refuse. He remained with them two days. I do not
know what "two days" symbolizes. But obviously it is enough time for
communing with God in Jesus to happen.

And many more believed because of his word. They said to the woman, "It is no longer because of what you said that we believe, for we have heard for ourselves, and we know that this is truly the Savior of the world."

This personal, firsthand contact not only brings more people to God's life in Jesus. It also clarifies the role of the woman's testimony. Jesus is the ultimate evangelizer. All the sowing and reaping, of the woman and the disciples, are only to bring Jesus into direct contact with his food. What the Samaritans know through firsthand contact with Jesus builds upon but goes beyond the woman's individual testimony. In hearing for themselves, they have come to know that Jesus is the Savior of the world. What he did for the woman he did for them, and what he did for them he will do for everyone. He not only brings alienated individuals and ethnic groups back into communion with God. He offers divine life to the entire world.

Teaching

Spiritual teachers often invite people into "patterns of experience." A pattern of experience is expressed as a sequence of realizations. For example, the Gospel of Thomas outlines these steps.

> Those who seek should not stop seeking until they find. When they find, they will be disturbed. When they are disturbed, they will marvel, and will reign over all. (GT 2)

St. Paul proposes a sequence that begins with suffering, "knowing that suffering produces endurance, and endurance produces character, and character produces hope, and hope does not disappoint us, because God's love has been poured into our hearts through the Holy Spirit that has been given to us" (Rom 5:3-5). With a smile, Mother Teresa often handed out a "business card" with this information:

> The fruit of SILENCE is prayer.
> The fruit of PRAYER is faith.
> The fruit of FAITH is love.
> The fruit of LOVE is service.
> The fruit of SERVICE is peace.

If you can trace the spiritual logic that connects the unfolding states of consciousness in these three sequences, you will uncover their spiritual wisdom.

Sometimes these "patterns of experience" with their sequence of realizations can be easily grasped. When they are, their wisdom seems undeniable. In other words, the "pattern of experience" in the spiritual teaching matches the "pattern of experience" in the life of the seeker. At other times, the "pattern of experience" in the teaching is difficult to grasp and it challenges the "pattern of experience" in the life of the seeker. In other words, the seeker only partially "gets it" and cannot see how it is possible to put the wisdom into action.

In the story of the woman at the well there is a "pattern of experience" that could be called the fullness of joy. It is a pattern that is difficult to grasp and even more difficult to enact. If this pattern were put into deliberately enigmatic language, it might read:

> The one who hears the voice of the bridegroom rejoices greatly.
> Bringing the bridegroom children,
> that one disappears into the fullness of joy.

The one who hears the voice of the bridegroom rejoices greatly. The pattern begins with the joy at hearing the voice of the bridegroom. John the Baptist uses this imagery about his feelings for Jesus: "He who has the bride is the bridegroom. The friend of the bridegroom, who stands and hears him, rejoices greatly at the bridegroom's voice" (John 3:29). "[H]ears . . . the bridegroom's voice" means comprehending the truth of Jesus. In the story of the woman at the well, the woman moves from understanding Jesus as a Jew, to understanding him as a prophet, to understanding him as the Messiah, to receiving his revelation of himself as "I am." She hears his voice when he says, "I am he, the one who is speaking to you." When she grasps this "I am," she participates in this identity. She is filled with being and love, a being and love she has always been looking for. Her joy is great. She has heard the voice of the bridegroom.

Bringing the bridegroom children. In the social milieu of John's Gospel there were two joys associated with marriage and family. The first joy was the voice of the bridegroom, the wedding, and the wedding night. This first joy matured into a second joy, a fullness of joy. This happened when the marriage became fruitful and children were born. These two joys provide the imagery for the spiritual perceptions of Jesus, the woman, and the people of Samaria.

When she hears the voice of the bridegroom, she becomes the bride who rejoices greatly. This first joy becomes the impetus for mission. She goes forth attracting people to the voice she has heard. These people are symbolically her children. She is presenting them to her true husband, the one who has made her fruitful. This true husband will bless and embrace them, giving them the life that flows through him. She brings others to the one who bestows the gift of God, a gift she has already experienced. In doing this, she enters a second joy, a fullness of joy.

That one disappears into the fullness of joy. Now this "pattern of experience" moves into deep waters. An aspect of the fullness of joy is the disappearance of the one who first heard the voice of the bridegroom. Individual joy is part of a larger pattern, and that larger pattern seems to suggest messengers should not claim permanent status. In the story of the woman at the well, the people plainly tell her that although she was needed at one point, she is no longer needed. Now they have seen for themselves. Intermediaries are passé. The story does not tell us how the woman responded to becoming suddenly obsolete. But John the Baptist is in a similar position, and he takes it quite well.

The disciples of John the Baptist are upset as they tell John about Jesus: "[T]he one who was with you across the Jordan, to whom you testified, here he is baptizing, and all are going to him" (John 3:26). In the mind of the disciples, this is hardly how to return a favor. John lauds Jesus, and Jesus puts John out of business. John and his disciples have been left behind.

However, this is not how the Baptist sees it. From his point of view, this is all part of a larger plan. "No one can receive anything except what has been given from heaven" (John 3:27). Therefore, this is not an unfortunate turn of events. He said he was not the Messiah (Christ), but the one sent "ahead of him" (John 3:28). He rejoiced when he heard Jesus' voice (John 3:29) and now that others are going to him, John says, "my joy has been fulfilled. He must increase, but I must decrease" (John 3:30). John's decreasing is not a painful loss of position. It is the fulfillment of his mission and releases him into a fullness of joy.

"Decreasing" is usually not a positive experience. Many people decrease because they are no longer needed or useful, but they decrease into bitterness. They are pulled kicking and screaming from center stage. "After all, I got there first. Don't forget it." But John the Baptist and, by extension, the woman decrease into joy. Witnesses to Jesus work themselves out of a job and, at the same time, work themselves into the fullness of joy.

How can this be?

It is in realizing, and not forgetting, what the "gift of God" really is. Jesus told the Samaritan woman that it was crucial to "know" the gift of God. This "knowing" entails profoundly grasping the nature of Spirit. The gift of God is the free offer of living water. It can never be possessed and used for the promotion of who we are and what we are about. When we try to seize Spirit, it goes elsewhere. "Disappearing" means not claiming the "gift of God" as an ego asset and, therefore, continuing to drink from the inner fountain. This is what John the Baptist and the Samaritan woman know. This is what I only dimly see.

Fourth Sunday of Lent

John 9:1-41

~~~~~~

Completing Creation

A Spiritual Commentary

SCENE ONE

As [Jesus] walked along, he saw a man blind from birth.

This is not a random sighting of a man who is physically blind. In this one man Jesus sees the essential human condition he has been sent to alleviate. The fact that the man is "blind from birth" symbolizes that this blindness comes with the territory of the human. It is a "not seeing" that afflicts all, a characteristic of creation. Of course, not all people are born physically blind. So this one person's physical blindness is a symbol of a universal spiritual opaqueness.

At the beginning of the story the man will be quickly cured of his physical blindness. This cure will be a sign, a manifestation on the physical level of the spiritual need to move from darkness to light. The rest of the story will be a contrast between the formerly blind man and the Pharisees. The formerly blind man gradually will learn to follow the sign of his own physical healing into spiritual sight. The Pharisees will not allow the sign to lead them. They will do all in their power to discredit the sign. As the man who was formerly blind becomes illumined, the Pharisees become benighted.

> **His disciples asked him, "Rabbi, who sinned, this man or his parents, that he was born blind?"**
>
> **Jesus answered, "Neither this man nor his parents sinned; he was born blind so that God's works might be revealed in him. We must work the works of him who sent me while it is day; night is coming when no one can work. As long as I am in the world, I am the light of the world."**

The disciples assume this man's physical blindness is the result of sin. What they would like to nitpick is: whose sin? Jesus refuses this question and the theological quibbling it creates. He will not answer it as it is posed. This may be because he does not hold the underlying assumption that the result of sin is physical impairment. The idea of God visiting suffering on people for their transgressions or the transgressions of their ancestors (see Exod 20:5) is not how he thinks.

However, Jesus is also pointing the disciples to the larger symbolic level. The point is not to argue how this condition of blindness came to be. Rather the blindness is an occasion for the works of God to become manifest. Since the first day of creation to the present, the work of God is to bring light out of darkness. Jesus and the disciples have been sent to do just that—"The works that the Father has given me to complete, the very works that I am doing, testify on my behalf that the Father has sent me" (John 5:36; see 14:12). They have only so much time to accomplish this. Since this is Jesus' essence, "I am the light of the world" (John 8:12), he must be about "bringing light to the world." He has no choice. There is an urgency and eagerness for him to do this, so much so that . . .

> **When he had said this, he spat on the ground and made mud with the saliva and spread the mud on the man's eyes, saying to him, "Go, wash in the pool of Siloam" (which means Sent).**
>
> **Then he went and washed and came back able to see.**

In the beginning (Gen 2:4-7) God made "clay of the ground" (v. 7; NAB), breathed into it, and the human person became a living soul. Now Jesus spits, a symbolic gesture that conveys the bestowal of his inner reality, makes clay, and anoints the man's eyes. Jesus is not making a second human; he is not starting from scratch because the first effort was defective. Rather he is completing creation. Creation is a work in progress, and Jesus is activating the latent but underdeveloped spiritual sight of the human person. This is why one of the titles for Jesus in the early church was "eye salve."

The man born blind is sent to a pool called "Sent." The word resonates. Jesus has just done the work he was sent to do and that he will send his disciples to do—to complete creation by opening spiritual eyes to see and respond to the Divine Source. However, after the man has washed in the pool called "Sent," the man himself becomes "Sent." He becomes a witness not only to what happened to him on the physical level, but also he eventually witnesses to the spiritual truth that was manifested in his physical healing—a truth about the one who opened his eyes.

SCENE TWO

The neighbors and those who had seen him before as a beggar began to ask, "Is this not the man who used to sit and beg?"

Some were saying, "It is he."

Others were saying, "No, but it is someone like him."

He kept saying, "I am the man."

A new creation is not a different man, a different person. It is the same person with a different consciousness. When the man who was formerly blind admits, "I am the man" (in the Greek "*egō eimi*"), he affirms both his continuity and discontinuity with his previous existence. I am the man who used to sit and beg, but also now "I am." In other words, he participates in the essential structure of Jesus' selfhood, "I am." He is sharing the identity of the one who opened his eyes.

But they kept asking him, "Then how were your eyes opened?"

He answered, "The man called Jesus made mud, spread it on my eyes, and said to me, 'Go to Siloam and wash.' Then I went and washed and received my sight."

They said to him, "Where is he?"

He said, "I do not know."

The neighbors focus on the sign that is available in the sensory world and want to know how his physical eyes were opened. The man repeats what happened without any interpretation. The key player is simply designated "The man called Jesus." Then the neighbors and the man engage in a double meaning exchange. On one level the neighbors seek Jesus' physical location. Is he in the temple or by the pool called Siloam or in Bethany, etc? The man says he does not know his location.

On a deeper level, the query "Where is he?" means "Where does he come from?" which is code for "Who is he?" They are asking about the identity of Jesus. On this deeper level, the man also does not know. At this stage, all he knows about is "a man called Jesus." This is a very surface appreciation of the reality of Jesus.

SCENE THREE

They brought to the Pharisees the man who had formerly been blind. Now it was a sabbath day when Jesus made the mud and opened his eyes. Then the Pharisees also began to ask him how he had received his sight.

He said to them, "He put mud on my eyes. Then I washed, and now I see."

Some of the Pharisees said, "This man is not from God, for he does not observe the sabbath."

But others said, "How can a man who is a sinner perform such signs?"

And they were divided.

So they said again to the blind man, "What do you say about him? It was your eyes he opened."

He said, "He is a prophet."

At the beginning of this scene, the man who was formerly blind might be characterized as having the experience but missing the meaning. When questioned, he just gives the observable sequence of events: clay, washed, see. But the Pharisees continue to grill him, and their next question moves him beyond a surface rendition of what happened. He comes to understand that it is not just a man called Jesus but a prophet who has opened his eyes. He is following the visible sign into its invisible foundation. It is ironic that, as the Pharisees flounder in the darkness, they are unwittingly helping the man who was formerly blind move toward the light.

On the surface level the Pharisees are floundering over what is appropriate on the Sabbath. However, Sabbath questions are, at base, questions about the nature of God. For the storyteller, the fact that Jesus completes creation on the Sabbath is exactly right. The Sabbath is the day for God's work, and giving people physical and spiritual sight, bringing light out of darkness, is the quintessential work of God. What better way to honor the Sabbath than "to do the will of the one who sent me" (John 4:34; NAB).

However, for these Pharisees God is not a flow of life into people but the maker and enforcer of laws. Therefore if a law is broken, the person who broke it is a sinner, having transgressed a divine regulation.

One of God's laws is not to work on the Sabbath. Making clay falls into the category of work. This understanding of God means that they inevitably concentrate on questions of sin. To some degree the disciples of Jesus share this perspective. They automatically interpret the absent sight of the man born blind in terms of sin. When God is the maker and enforcer of laws, people are either righteous or sinners.

Therefore the division among the Pharisees is whether Jesus is righteous or a sinner. On the one hand, he looks like a sinner because he breaks God's law by working on the Sabbath. On the other hand, he looks like a righteous person because he does things that only someone associated with God could do. This causes cognitive dissonance among the Pharisees. Their inherited categories are not adequate to their contemporary experience. There is nothing wrong with cognitive dissonance. What is wrong is how they go about trying to regain cognitive harmony.

SCENE FOUR

The Jews did not believe that he had been blind and had received his sight until they called the parents of the man who had received his sight and asked them, "Is this your son, who you say was born blind? How then does he now see?"

His parents answered, "We know that this is our son, and that he was born blind; but we do not know how it is that now he sees, nor do we know who opened his eyes. Ask him; he is of age. He will speak for himself."

His parents said this because they were afraid of the Jews; for the Jews had already agreed that anyone who confessed Jesus to be the Messiah would be put out of the synagogue. Therefore his parents said, "He is of age; ask him."

The easiest way for the Pharisees to maintain their inherited theology is to discredit their contemporary experience. If he was *born* blind, the people who would know would be his parents. Perhaps he was not born blind. "Is this your son, *who you say* was born blind?"

However, this ploy does not work. The parents affirm the fact that he was born blind, but they claim ignorance about his present sight and who opened his eyes. They may be genuinely ignorant, but their motivation for dodging the question is fear. They do not want to be thrown out of the synagogue. They know what these Pharisees want.

They do not give it to them, but they do not stir their anger either. They will leave that to their son.

SCENE FIVE

So for the second time they called the man who had been blind, and they said to him, "Give glory to God! We know that this man is a sinner."

He answered, "I do not know whether he is a sinner. One thing I do know, that though I was blind, now I see."

The Pharisees here want the man to change his story. Their theology makes Jesus a sinner, and they want the man to acknowledge this fact. For them, this is the truth. If the man admits it, he will be praising God. But the man will travel another path to praising God, by acknowledging God's work of creation in him.

So the man will not play the Pharisaic game of divine laws and human lawbreakers. He will be loyal to his liberation, faithful to his experience. A hallmark of Christians in John's Gospel is that they speak of what they know. So that is what he does. He speaks of what he knows, and what he knows is that he was unable to see and now he sees.

They said to him, "What did he do to you? How did he open your eyes?"

The Pharisees persist in their questioning. This is more a police interrogation than a theological debate. They are trying to trip him up. If he tells them again, they may find a hole in his story. However, the man who once sat, begged, and kowtowed to everyone to get coins is about to get feisty.

He answered them, "I have told you already, and you would not listen. Why do you want to hear it again? Do you also want to become his disciples?"

Then they reviled him, saying, "You are his disciple, but we are disciples of Moses. We know that God has spoken to Moses, but as for this man, we do not know where he comes from."

He accuses them of not listening to what he has already said. Why do they want to hear it again? Perhaps it is because they are interested in becoming Jesus' disciples. This, of course, is the exact opposite of their motivation, and the suggestion releases their venom.

They revile him, saying that *he* is a disciple of Jesus. This may have been a revelation to the man who was formerly blind. More accurately, he is a disciple-in-the-making, and the more they question him the more like a disciple he becomes. They are disciples of Moses because they know that God spoke to Moses, the lawgiver. They do not know where Jesus comes from—what his credentials are. Just a short time ago, the man who was born blind told the neighbors he did not know where Jesus was. But things have changed, his eyes are more fully open, and he is about to tell the Pharisees where Jesus comes from.

> **The man answered, "Here is an astonishing thing! You do not know where he comes from, and yet he opened my eyes. We know that God does not listen to sinners, but he does listen to one who worships him and obeys his will. Never since the world began has it been heard that anyone opened the eyes of a person born blind. If this man were not from God, he could do nothing."**

What is a marvel is the Pharisees' refusal to see the obvious. They are using their minds to deny the truth. If you trace the sign, you will know that the man who performed it is from God. That is where he comes from. This is not the work of sin but the continuing work of creation—"Never since the world began." If they can appeal to Moses, this man will go back even farther—to the dawn of time. Therefore it is God's work, and the one who does it is one who does the will of God and to whom God listens. This is the only legitimate conclusion to be drawn from his experience of having his eyes opened by the man called Jesus who, upon reflection, has to be a prophet and a man from God.

> **They answered him, "You were born entirely in sins, and are you trying to teach us?"**
>
> **And they drove him out.**

The Pharisees do not engage the reasoning of the man who was formerly blind. Instead, they attack his origins. They sought to discredit Jesus by saying they did not know where he came from. Now they discredit this man by saying they do know where he comes from. His blindness was an indication he was born in utter sin. Therefore, to try to teach those who are righteous is utter gall. Their theology of the Sabbath has kept them from acknowledging the healing work of God in

Jesus. Their theology of sin now keeps them from listening to the truth the formerly blind man is telling them.

The standard authoritarian response to a person who persists in theological error is to cast him or her out. What his wily parents managed to avoid befalls the man who was formerly blind. He is cast out because he has read the sign of his transition from blindness to sight correctly and acknowledged Jesus as a man from God.

SCENE SIX

Jesus heard that they had driven him out, and when he found him, he said, "Do you believe in the Son of Man?"

At the beginning of the story Jesus saw the man and moved toward him. The man born blind did not cry out for mercy or in any other way try to attract attention. The initiative was entirely Jesus'. Now at the end of the story Jesus is seeking him out again. What Jesus began, he will finish.

Opening his physical eyes was a sign that, if followed, would lead to spiritual sight. He clung to the sign and followed it faithfully. Although his physical eyes opened immediately, his spiritual eyes only opened gradually through the rough-and-tumble relationship with his neighbors and the Pharisees. At first all he could see was "a man called Jesus." Then he came to greater clarity and saw this man was a "prophet." Finally, he realized this prophet was a "man who did God's will and to whom God listened." But there is one more step, a final penetration of the spiritual truth of his movement from blindness to sight. Jesus offers it to him in the symbolic statement, "Do you believe in the Son of Man?"

> **He answered, "And who is he, sir? Tell me, so that I may believe in him."**
>
> **Jesus said to him, "You have seen him, and the one speaking with you is he."**
>
> **He said, "Lord, I believe."**
>
> **And he worshiped him.**

The phrase "Son of Man" does not resonate with the man. He does not know to whom Jesus is referring and so requests information about this "Son of Man." He is ready to believe, but in order to do this he must have further understanding. He is about to receive it.

Jesus does not give him information about the Son of Man as a future end-time figure who will conduct a universal judgment. Instead, he says that he has already seen him and he is speaking to him now. Something has happened to him and is happening now in his conversation with Jesus that is appropriately called "Son of Man." The "Son of Man" may be someone the now seeing man is not conscious of, but it is not someone he has not experienced. In fact, the "Son of Man" is the depth of what he has experienced and what is happening to him now in the speech of Jesus. As Jesus opened his physical eyes at the beginning of the story, he now opens his spiritual eyes.

These words of Jesus shock him, shine into the last darkness, and bring him to full illumination. He sees clearly, and belief flows from him in words ("Lord, I believe") and actions ("he worshiped him"). Jesus has completed creation; the last of the clay has worked its transformation and the scales have fallen from his washed eyes. The human being who is spiritually blind from birth is now fully illumined.

But what did the man finally see in this enigmatic exchange with Jesus?

In John's Gospel, the "Son of Man" is the one on whom the angels of God descend and ascend. "Very truly, I tell you, you will see heaven opened and the angels of God ascending and descending upon the Son of Man" (John 1:51). What the man who was formerly blind realized was that Jesus is not just sent from God. He is the very being and love of God present in the world. Jesus holds together heaven and earth. Angels descend and ascend upon him, the Son of Man, and his words carry the power of the Eternal Word through whom all things were created (John 1:3).

As the consciousness of the man born blind gradually matured into the realization of this truth, he knew God's creative power was at the center of his being. The first day of creation was happening again. The first day is not a past happening, over and done with. The first day of creation is always happening. What God does on the first day is bring light out of darkness (Gen 1:1-5), and that is what God is doing every day, even today. When he came to that realization, he simply confessed it as belief in the Son of Man on whom the angels of God never cease to descend and never cease to ascend. The revelation of Jesus is that God is not separate from the world; God is at work within it bringing it to completion.

Jesus said, "I came into this world for judgment so that those who do not see may see, and those who do see may become blind."

Some of the Pharisees near him heard this and said to him, "Surely we are not blind, are we?"

Jesus said to them, "If you were blind, you would not have sin. But now that you say, 'We see,' your sin remains."

Son of Man is a title usually associated with judgment. Previously, Jesus has said he was "the light of the world" (John 9:5). Now a consequence of being the light is stressed. If people do not respond to the light, the light becomes judgment on their lack of response. Avoid Jesus as light: meet him as judge.

Jesus helps those who are spiritually blind see the God-given creation of which they are a part. He opens their eyes. However, for those who already think they know God's plan and purpose, Jesus' presence makes them blind. This blindness is caused by their refusal to follow the sign that Jesus presents into the truth of his identity and consequently to participate in that identity. Therefore Jesus invites decision. Some rise into light; others sink into darkness.

Some of the Pharisees catch the drift of this enigmatic saying, and so they question him. Is he talking about them and intimating that they are blind? This question gives Jesus a chance to correct Pharisaic theology just as he corrected similar theology with the question of the disciples at the beginning of the story, "Rabbi, who sinned, this man or his parents, that he was born blind?" What is the theological message of this complex story?

Physical blindness is not a matter of sin. Neither is spiritual blindness a sin. Blindness is not a positive and willful resistance to the divine invitation to life. It is just the raw, unfinished material of creation. It is the darkness God uses to bring forth light. It is what the work of God works on.

Sin, on the other hand, is a stubborn attachment to a darkened understanding of God, creation, and Jesus, and then calling this benighted consciousness light. Sin is calling blindness sight, mistaking ignorance for truth. When the Pharisees do not open to the sign but cling to their falsehoods and actively suppress the truth, their sin remains. They say they see, but they see not. They name underdeveloped creation as sin, yet it is not sin. They proclaim their darkness as light, yet it is not light. It is reminiscent of another Gospel saying, "If what should be light in you is darkness, then how great will the darkness be" (Matt 6:23).

Teaching

Over the years I have come to believe that divine reality is not separate from creation. In fact, divine reality interpenetrates creation and is the ultimate energy of its evolution. I believe this for a variety of reasons, not all of which I am aware of or can articulate. But some of the reasons are:

(1) I think it is present in the best of the biblical tradition.
(2) It is attested to by mystics of many faith traditions.
(3) It is coherent with other truths from different human sciences.
(4) It is a theological idea that makes me hopeful.

However, the story of the man born blind is asking for more than mental assent to a powerful theological thought. It is asking for us to become aware of the reality to which the idea points. It moves toward mystical recognition and suggestions like that of William Blake. "If the eyes of perception were cleansed, we would see things as they are—infinite." At the beginning of "Auguries of Innocence," Blake expands the suggestion in concrete imagery.

> To see a World in a Grain of Sand,
> And a Heaven in a Wild Flower,
> Hold Infinity in the palm of your hand,
> And Eternity in an hour.

The emphasis is on *seeing* the spiritual in and through the material, *perceiving* the infinite grounding of the finite world, *sensing* the Eternal Now in the flux of temporal unfolding. This is not belief in the God-world connection; it is consciousness of it. It is an awareness of heaven and earth as interpenetrating realities.

For me, the movement from belief to consciousness is a proper sequence. I come to believe something, then I try to personally experience it. In traditional language, faith seeks understanding. What I receive as an inheritance from the past and hold as a conviction urges me to explore it. In this way of thinking, faith is not an end. It is an invitation into understanding. Understanding is more than internal consistency and compatibility with other truths. Understanding entails awareness, consciousness of the God-world connection. Therefore faith, by its very nature, encourages us toward seeing, points us toward the task of spiritual development.

However, spiritual development is a difficult task, and I have never found spiritual seeing to be a steady form of sight. If spiritual sight completes creation by disclosing the Source that sustains and continually transforms it, then the best I can say about my spiritual eyes is that they are blurred. I have heard other people talk about experiencing the presence of God. They cite specific experiences—the birth of a baby, the death of a parent, a time in the mountains or by the ocean, falling in love, etc. Symbolically, they saw angels descending and ascending upon the Son of Man.

However, this language of illumination can lead us to look for "big bang" experiences. When we hear people tell of soaring into the seventh heaven, we feel more earthbound than ever. Special experiences are for special people. We resign ourselves to a faith that does not seek understanding, a blind faith. In fact, some people extol blind faith as an ideal. I think this praise for blindness is often fueled by a sense that spiritual sight is too far beyond us. We bump about in creation with a lot of energy. But seeing the Source in the tributaries is for monks and hermits.

David Steindl-Rast has some helpful observations on becoming aware of the divine-human communion. He says this awareness may come suddenly or gradually. He uses an image to explore this distinction. Some years spring comes suddenly. One day we notice spring has arrived. Other years we catch it in the act of arriving. We notice the first trees to bloom, the few shoots of grass that gradually become a lawn, the birds returning. Steindl-Rast's point is that sudden or gradual is not important: "And so all that matters is that you eventually become aware deep within you of ultimate communion."

When I read this, I liked the idea of one day waking up and it was spring. I have this very lazy idea about the movement from faith to consciousness. It does not entail rigorous asceticism and long-haul persistence in spiritual exercises. If you think enough about the belief, ponder it day after day, it will unobtrusively slide from the status of an idea to a more abiding realization. When the mind attends to an idea, it forms an eye to see the reality the idea represents. It is best not to evaluate if the eye is being formed—can you see the first leaves or hear a distant bird? Just cultivate the idea, and one day it will be spring. As I said, this is spiritual development for the lazy.

Fifth Sunday of Lent

John 11:1-45

⟶⟩⟩⟩

Causing and Consoling Grief

A Spiritual Commentary

Now a certain man was ill, Lazarus of Bethany, the village of Mary and her sister Martha. Mary was the one who anointed the Lord with perfume and wiped his feet with her hair; her brother Lazarus was ill.

This introduction foreshadows some of the themes of the story. Lazarus of Bethany is first designated a "certain man" [or one] who is ill. This means his story is not his alone, but the story of all who become ill. Lazarus means "God helps" and Bethany means "the house of the afflicted." Therefore, ultimately this is a story of how God helps those in the house of the afflicted—not just Lazarus but also his sisters Mary and Martha and, as it turns out, even some Jews from Jerusalem.

Mary is featured more prominently than her sister Martha. Although she will not actually anoint the Lord until later in the Gospel, she is designated as the one who has done this. Her anointing symbolically expressed the pouring out of Jesus' life that would bring life to others, and her position at his feet means she is the servant-disciple of his revelation. The storyteller wants us to know that Mary learns from Jesus and understands who he is and what his death is meant to do. When she appears later in this story, she will be a catalyst for Jesus' entry into the grief and death of his friends. This entry is what must happen for Jesus' identity and mission as the resurrection and the life to be effective for believers.

> **So the sisters sent a message to Jesus, "Lord, he whom you love is ill." But when Jesus heard it, he said, "This illness does not lead to death; rather it is for God's glory, so that the Son of God may be glorified through it."**
>
> **Accordingly, though Jesus loved Martha and her sister and Lazarus, after having heard that Lazarus was ill, he stayed two days longer in the place where he was.**

The message of the sisters is not that "Lazarus is ill" but that the one whom the Lord loves is ill. This establishes the tension of the story. It is not just a story of illness and death but a story of the illness and death of someone the Lord loves. How will the love of God in Jesus respond to the illness and death of one whom God loves?

The purpose of this illness is not death. This illness and death will become a sign that shows forth both the glory of God and the glorification of the Son of God. "Glory" is a difficult word. It usually implies a heightened sense of self-importance. To bestow glory is to raise someone beyond the ordinary and honor him or her in special ways. On this level, what is going to happen during the illness and death of Lazarus will focus human consciousness on God and God's Son and elicit human worship.

However, there is another level. The glory of God is not self-referential. The glory of God is to give God's own life to people. God's own life holds people through the losses of death and brings them to life in the far reaches of God. God's own life is communicated to people through the Son of God.

In particular, when the Son of God enters the world of death he brings God's own life to that place of complete human failing. In this way he is glorified because he brings God's glory to the experience of illness and death and transforms it into an existence beyond loss. What is going to happen during Lazarus' illness and death will be a sign of divine life sustaining human life through the disintegration of death.

The storyteller is compelled to tell us that Jesus loved everyone involved—Mary, Martha, and Lazarus. It is because of this love that he delays for two days. Of course, this seems strange. If he loved them, it would seem he would be anxious to be with them. And when he finally does arrive, Martha will imply he should have been there sooner. How is love expressed in delay?

In order for people to believe in the spiritual strength of love, it has to be manifested in the physical world. Lazarus must die, and God's love in Jesus must bring him back to temporal life. Of course, as it is often remarked, Lazarus will die again. Although eternal life suffuses temporal becoming, it is not temporal becoming. But Lazarus' resuscitation is a sign in the physical dimension that expresses a greater truth in the spiritual dimension. Comprehending this spiritual strength of love would console Martha and Mary. A hurried journey to Bethany to stop Lazarus from dying will not facilitate the spiritual realization of how love conquers death. The path of revelation demands the death of Lazarus.

Then after this he said to the disciples, "Let us go to Judea again."

The disciples said to him, "Rabbi, the Jews were just now trying to stone you, and are you going there again?"

Jesus answered, "Are there not twelve hours of daylight? Those who walk during the day do not stumble, because they see the light of this world. But those who walk at night stumble, because the light is not in them."

After the two days, Jesus sets his face toward Judea—again. The disciples think this is dangerous. The religious authorities in Judea just recently tried to stone Jesus. The last time was almost the last time. Why go again?

Jesus responds with an enigmatic maxim that speaks to his particular circumstances. The maxim works both practically and symbolically. There are always twelve hours to a day, and if people are out and about during that time they will not stumble, for they will see (physically) by the light of this world (the sun). However, if they go out at night, they will stumble because they have no light in themselves. By definition, there is no outer light at night. The only hope for not stumbling is inner light. Since they do not have this, they will stumble. This is a slightly odd rendition of not stumbling and stumbling, and it makes an obvious, if lapidary, point.

However, when these normal conditions are applied to Jesus they take on a quite different meaning. As there are twelve hours in a day, there is a certain amount of daylight time to Jesus' life. Daylight time is time when no harm will befall him. This time is fixed by God. So he does not have to worry about returning to Judea. His life is part of a divine plan and timetable. As John the Baptist attested, "No one can receive anything except what has been given from heaven" (John 3:27). Things are not being controlled by Jesus' decision or even by the plotting of the religious authorities. It is necessary to see a larger design. Since Jesus sees it, he is not fearful about Judea.

In this daylight time Jesus sees by the light of the world. But this does not mean sunshine guides him. Jesus is the light of the world (John 9:5). His inner illumination discloses the truth about human existence. He sees from the inside out, by his own interior radiance. This is why he does not stumble. Even when night comes and physical harm happens to him, he will not stumble (lose contact with God) because he has light inside himself.

This is why Jesus does not fear returning to Judea where they have just tried to stone him. God's plan will unfold in God's time. Even when that plan includes night, Jesus will not stumble because he will walk by his inner light. The disciples may think returning to Judea is poor judgment, but Jesus is guided by this larger vision.

> **After saying this, he told them, "Our friend Lazarus has fallen asleep, but I am going there to awaken him."**
>
> **The disciples said to him, "Lord, if he has fallen asleep, he will be all right."**
>
> **Jesus, however, had been speaking about his death, but they thought that he was referring merely to sleep.**
>
> **Then Jesus told them plainly, "Lazarus is dead. For your sake I am glad I was not there, so that you may believe. But let us go to him." Thomas, who was called the Twin, said to his fellow disciples, "Let us also go, that we may die with him."**

It is love that is driving Jesus to go to Judea. "No one has greater love than this, to lay down one's life for one's friends" (John 15:13). Jesus goes to awaken Lazarus, a friend to Jesus and the disciples. The disciples are still fearful of the return to Judea, and they argue with Jesus that he does not really need to go. If Lazarus is asleep, he will recover on his own. As usual, they cannot hear the symbolic language of Jesus. By saying Lazarus is asleep and will be awakened, Jesus is talking about the "non-finality" of death.

This failure of the disciples to follow the symbolic language moves Jesus to blunt talk. He tells them directly that Lazarus is dead, and that he is glad that he was not there. If he was there, he might have prevented Lazarus from dying. This would have stopped what was needed. The death and resuscitation of Lazarus will be a sign that will bring his disciples to belief. Therefore, it is important that they come with Jesus, for what will happen with Lazarus will be for their benefit. Therefore, "let *us* go to him."

Jesus has now explained why he is not afraid to go to Judea and why his disciples should accompany him. Has he successfully persuaded them? Thomas is on board, and he encourages the others. He is loyal to Jesus. But has he understood him? It is Jesus' death as the Son of God that will bring life. Thomas' role is not to die. He is a disciple and his role is to receive life from the crucified one.

**When Jesus arrived, he found that Lazarus had already been in
the tomb four days. Now Bethany was near Jerusalem, some
two miles away, and many of the Jews had come to Martha and
Mary to console them about their brother. When Martha heard
that Jesus was coming, she went and met him, while Mary
stayed at home.**

Jesus does not arrive in the "nick of time." His delay was successful. Lazarus is dead, four days in the tomb. This is important. If love is
stronger than death, it must overcome death, not merely deathlike
symptoms. The four days in the tomb establish the first condition for
the revelatory sign—a dead Lazarus. In the context of the whole
Gospel, Lazarus' resuscitation from death is made possible by Jesus
entering into death with the power of God's everlasting life and,
through his own death, companioning the death of all his friends.
Therefore we are told that "Bethany was near Jerusalem," the place of
Jesus' crucifixion.

Many of the Jews of Jerusalem had come to console Martha and
Mary. Their consolation will consist in sharing the tears of the two sisters. Jesus will also share in those tears, but he will take consolation a
step further. He will restore Lazarus to them. Some of the Jews will
learn from this and believe in the resurrection and the life; others will
be threatened and follow more fiercely the path of plotting Jesus'
death.

In the Gospel of Luke (10:38-42) Martha and Mary represent action
and contemplation. In that story action wants to take over contemplation, but Jesus does not allow it. Martha and Mary are sisters with distinct gifts, and they are meant to live together.

In John's Gospel Martha and Mary represent two levels of consciousness. Martha displays an open-ended trust in Jesus and recites
titular confessions that underline Jesus' importance. However, Martha,
by herself, may not fully understand all that she is saying. Mary represents a deeper consciousness, one that says less but understands
more. Her comprehension is profound because she hears and responds
to the voice of Jesus. Therefore, Martha and Mary may be held together
as sisters in terms of a lesser and greater consciousness of who Jesus is
and what he must do.

**Martha said to Jesus, "Lord, if you had been here, my brother
would not have died. But even now I know that God will give
you whatever you ask of him."**

Jesus said to her, "Your brother will rise again."

Martha said to him, "I know that he will rise again in the resurrection on the last day."

Martha believes and trusts in Jesus. She thinks that if Jesus had arrived earlier, Lazarus would not have died. In her mind Jesus has the ear of God. Whatever he asks for, he gets. So if he had been physically present before Lazarus' death, he would have asked God to keep Lazarus alive and God would have acceded to this request. Jesus would have prolonged Lazarus' earthly life. Even now there may be something he can do. But it is not specified what that might be. Martha is an open-ended believer.

However, these affirmations of Jesus stop short of fuller appreciations. Jesus is more than a healer, one who makes people well and delays their dying. Also, he is more than someone who has the ear of God. Later in the story he will pray to God, but primarily for the benefit of other people in order to reveal to them a union with the Father that goes beyond getting prayers answered. What Martha knows is considerable, but it is not the full revelation.

Jesus' simple response, "Your brother will rise," means he has not come too late. He has come too late to stop Lazarus from physically dying, but he has not come too late to raise him from death. Jesus has said that Lazarus' death was to show God's glory. This glory goes beyond healing people. It is shown most clearly by "raising them from the dead." This spiritual truth will be manifested in the sign of Lazarus' resuscitation.

Martha also knows about resurrection. It will happen on the last day. Once again this knowledge may preclude her from seeing more deeply into the present and who is talking to her. Jesus tries to refocus for her what resurrection means.

> **Jesus said to her, "I am the resurrection and the life. Those who believe in me, even though they die, will live, and everyone who lives and believes in me will never die. Do you believe this?"**
>
> **She said to him, "Yes, Lord, I believe that you are the Messiah, the Son of God, the one coming into the world."**

Resurrection is not only a future happening. It is present in Jesus right now. Those who participate in the structure of his identity with the Father enter into eternal life. If they have physically died, they will

continue to live in a transformed way. If they are living in this transformed way now, they will not spiritually die even when the physical
body dies. Therefore, resurrection and life are what happens to those
who are in union with Jesus. Martha knows that Jesus' presence can
delay death, that God always hears him, and that there will be a resurrection on the last day. But can she grasp this essential truth. What
Jesus asks her is, "Do you believe *this*?"

Martha responds, "Yes," and backs it up by restating what she has
always believed. She recites titles that point to Jesus' importance. It is
almost as if she is "ticking off" accepted communal confessions of belief. Since Jesus is the Messiah, the Son of God, the One who is "coming into the world" (John 1:9), whatever he says is worthy of belief.
This shows belief in the person of Jesus. It does not show understanding of the content of what has just been revealed. In fact, it avoids the
question by honoring the person.

> **When she had said this, she went back and called her sister
> Mary, and told her privately, "The Teacher is here and is calling
> for you."**
>
> **And when she heard it, she got up quickly and went to him.
> Now Jesus had not yet come to the village, but was still at the
> place where Martha had met him.**

Martha has said what she knows; she has gone as far as she can. To
go more deeply into Jesus' revelation of himself as the resurrection and
the life—and what resurrection and life mean—a deeper level of consciousness will have to be called forth. Martha hands over the conversation to Mary. The transition is secret, not available to others, because it
occurs in the hidden depths of the believer, symbolized by Mary sitting
in contemplation. The reason for Martha calling Mary is that the teaching of Jesus about resurrection and life calls for this level of appreciation.
Whenever Jesus calls someone, it is for the purpose of participating in
the fullness of his life. Martha went out to meet Jesus on her own. Mary
is called by name, the way a good shepherd calls his sheep.

Mary responds immediately and with energy. When she hears, she
rises, and follows the lead of the voice. She goes to him in the very place
where Martha had met him. She will take up where Martha left off.

> **The Jews who were with her in the house, consoling her, saw
> Mary get up quickly and go out. They followed her because**

they thought that she was going to the tomb to weep there. When Mary came where Jesus was and saw him, she knelt at his feet and said to him, "Lord, if you had been here, my brother would not have died."

The Jews, among whom there will be believers and unbelievers, follow Mary. Their style of consolation is to join in the grief and weep with the close relatives of the deceased. Sharing their grief means following the trail of their tears. When the loved ones who are left behind are filled with loss, they may run to the tomb to get as close to the dead body as possible. At the tomb the weeping can become intense and overwhelming. At the sight of the rock that seals the tomb the sense of separation is permanent and unbearable. Going to the tomb symbolizes entering more deeply into the power of death and weeping more deeply over the power of this negative lord.

But Mary is not going to the tomb. She is going to Jesus. The lure of his voice is more powerful than the pull of the tomb. When she *sees* Jesus, it is more than a physical sighting. She sees into him and grasps him in his essence, his life-giving relationship to the Father. With this realization she falls at his feet. This position is one of both worship and discipleship. She knows that he, in himself, is the presence of God and she is open to learning what he will teach her. It is not what she knows, it is what she has heard from him. Since she is taking up where Martha left off, the teaching she has heard concerns Jesus' identity as the resurrection and the life and what this means for those who believe in him. The question put to Martha has been passed on to Mary. "Do you believe *this*?"

Mary responds with the same words that Martha used to greet Jesus. But on Mary's level of consciousness the meaning is considerably different. The truth of spiritual statements is located in the consciousness of the one saying them. "Lord, if *you* . . ." points to what Jesus said he was, the resurrection and the life. "[H]ad been here" means in this place of death and grief. "[M]y brother" is the one whom the storyteller has emphasized that Jesus loves. "[W]ould not have died" means that he would not have lost contact with the living God whom Jesus mediates. Mary's words are not a complaint or the expression of a faith that has been disappointed. Instead, they express the truth of Jesus' own death, a truth expressed in the anointing with oil and wiping of Jesus' feet with her hair.

Unless the "I am the resurrection and the life" enters into the realm of grief and death, those who die will lose touch with God's love. Their physical death also becomes their spiritual death. Only if Jesus is present to his friends, the ones he lays down his life for, will they be sustained through the destruction of the body. Mary's recognition of this truth is what Jesus needs to galvanize him into action. From here on in, he will be establishing the second half of the sign that manifests God's glory and glorifies God's Son. God's Son will be glorified because he will bring divine love into a place where it was not. God will be glorified because this love will sustain those who receive it beyond the loss of the physical world. However, this spiritual communion needs a sign in the physical world in order to move people toward believing. The resuscitation of Lazarus will be the sign.

> **When Jesus saw her weeping, and the Jews who came with her also weeping, he was greatly disturbed in spirit and deeply moved.**
>
> **He said, "Where have you laid him?"**
>
> **They said to him, "Lord, come and see."**
>
> **Jesus began to weep.**
>
> **So the Jews said, "See how he loved him!"**
>
> **But some of them said, "Could not he who opened the eyes of the blind man have kept this man from dying?"**

So Jesus is about to enter the place of grief and death so he can bring God's life to this lifeless situation. First, he enters the world of grief. But he does not enter without cost. This world is not banished by a transcendent word. This world has to be inhabited. Seeing the weeping of Mary and the Jews, he begins the movement of divine consolation and compassion. He is troubled, even angered, at the anguish that death has caused. He wants to know where they have laid Lazarus, so he can raise him.

So they invite the Messiah, the Son of God, the One who is coming into the world into the human world of grief, death, and separation. They invite him as Lord, but he enters as the Son of Mary. He totally joins them in their tears for the only way beyond death and grief is through it. And in few words, the full truth of incarnation is revealed: "Jesus began to weep."

Some of the Jews saw the meaning of these tears. God's love in Jesus responds to all that threatens and terrorizes humans. The path of this response is compassionate sharing and the eventual transformation of grief and death. But others do not see this deeply. They want a miracle that forestalls death. They do not understand that opening the eyes of the blind man was not a onetime miracle on the physical level. It was an awakening to the spiritual truth of God in Jesus. If they had the eyes that Jesus gives to the blind, they would know these were the tears of love, just as the clay Jesus made for the blind man was the clay of love.

> **Then Jesus, again greatly disturbed, came to the tomb. It was a cave, and a stone was lying against it.**
>
> **Jesus said, "Take away the stone."**

It is Jesus' deep emotional response to the separating powers of death that moves him to the tomb. But he comes to it with a purpose. The stone separates the dead from the living and blocks people who love one another from communicating with each other. Therefore, it must go, for Jesus is about to talk to his friend whom he loves.

> **Martha, the sister of the dead man, said to him, "Lord, already there is a stench because he has been dead four days."**
>
> **Jesus said to her, "Did I not tell you that if you believed, you would see the glory of God?"**
>
> **So they took away the stone.**
>
> **And Jesus looked upward and said, "Father, I thank you for having heard me. I know that you always hear me, but I have said this for the sake of the crowd standing here, so that they may believe that you sent me."**

Martha, who is characterized as the sister of the dead man, speaks the truth about death. The fate of bodies is decay and stench. She thinks this reason enough not to open the tomb. But from Jesus' point of view it is *the* reason to open the tomb for it is the precondition for the glory of God to be seen. In their previous conversation Martha hoped Jesus would stop Lazarus from dying. Instead, Jesus said Lazarus would rise. Only this would show the glory of God, a loving care stronger than the ravages of death.

Moreover, Martha, along with the people standing by, will overhear Jesus praying. Martha thought Jesus could ask anything of God and God would hear him. She is right. But Jesus and the Father are so interwoven that they make a single reality. So it is not as though he asks the Father, and then the Father considers it and says yes. Rather, since Jesus only does what he hears from the Father, what he asks of the Father is what he has already heard. Therefore, the point of his praying is so that people may realize he comes from God and trace what he is doing to God's love.

> **When he had said this, he cried with a loud voice, "Lazarus, come out!"**
>
> **The dead man came out, his hands and feet bound with strips of cloth, and his face wrapped in a cloth.**
>
> **Jesus said to them, "Unbind him, and let him go."**
>
> **Many of the Jews therefore, who had come with Mary and had seen what Jesus did, believed in him.**

It is now time to enter into Lazarus' death, and Jesus does so with a voice that befits his identity as the Word. He is calling Lazarus in a loud voice. A loud voice symbolizes the presence of God. His voice penetrates into the open cave and reaches the ears of the dead. Lazarus comes out of darkness into light.

Death is imaged as an imprisoning reality, blocking the hands, nose, eyes, mouth, and ears of people. The feet are also bound so that people cannot walk. Jesus' command is to reverse this condition. God's glory is to free people and let them go. Centuries earlier Moses told Pharaoh that God commanded, "Let my people go"! (e.g., Exod 7:16, 20). Now, "Let my people go" is spoken to death by the one who calls himself "the resurrection and the life."

Teaching

It was a full five years after my father's death.

I was driving across Alligator Alley in southern Florida, traveling from Naples on the west coast to Boca Raton on the east coast. I was going to my parents' condominium. My mother was going to sell it the next day.

As I drove, I began to think of my father. Suddenly, I began to cry and I could not stop. I cried so effusively and unrelentingly that I had to stop at a rest station and change my shirt.

When I resumed driving, I thought it was over. Only it started again, and I was powerless in its grip. When I arrived at my mother's condo, I had to change my shirt a second time.

I told my mother what happened. She simply said, "Oh, you'll have days like that."

Grief is a wild ride. People may map its faces, predict its stages, and schedule its duration. But those are people who, for the moment, are not in grief. They have the luxury of observation. But when the loss of a loved one inhabits your soul, you are an occupied territory. Resistance is futile.

That is why I like this emotionally troubled, weeping Jesus being swept toward the tomb of the one he loves. It is his love that is causing him the grief, just as it is the love of Martha and Mary that is causing them their grief. If Jesus had not loved Lazarus and his sisters, he would have been unmoved but philosophically interested at best. We are all eager for love. But as a distraught young widow once said to me, "Someone should have told me that all marriages end either in divorce or death." The truth of eternally grounded people trafficking in time is: the deeper the love, the deeper the grief.

This is a truth we seldom think about when we give our heart away. In the temporary, perishing world we all inhabit, the advent of love is the seed of grief. Gabriel Marcel said, "To love someone is to say, 'Thou, thou shalt not die.'" Even if we do not say it aloud, even if we only whisper it in the cellar of the heart, love readies us for weeping. Our first kiss and our first tear are linked.

However, this same love that causes our grief can console us. But we must trust the love and follow it to its root. We must not see it as a futile rebellion against mortality but as a hint that there is more, more than meets the eye and more than conventional knowledge will admit. This love that makes us accompany the ill and even visit their graves after they die may be showing us something of God's love. Our reluctance to let people go may touch upon the truth of Lazarus' resuscitation. The love that troubles Jesus and makes him weep at the loss of Lazarus also makes him go after Lazarus and free him from the imprisonment of death. The love of God in Jesus will not let Lazarus go, and so death has to release him. The love that causes our grief is, at root, the love that consoles our grief.

Consolation ultimately comes from realizing love is stronger than death (cf. Song 8:6). This is not an easy realization to embrace. As Martha knew, the stench of death is strong. Sometimes our minds focus on the unyielding fact of physical death and we speculate about how some form of continued existence is possible. However, the story suggests another way to proceed.

Jesus is "the resurrection and the life," and those who can enter into him can participate in eternal life now. In this relationship with Jesus we find that the love of God that sustains and raises people is an intimate presence at the center of our own identity. The more we contemplate this presence (Mary) and integrate it into our lives (Martha), the more we realize its gentleness is an enduring strength. Sustained by this presence, we can grieve greatly the physical loss of our friends and hope greatly for their continued life in God. Love generates both grief and consolation. As St. Paul said, "do not grieve as others do who have no hope" (1 Thess 4:13). I assume he meant we should grieve as those who have hope. It is the weeping Jesus who cries out in a loud voice, "Lazarus, come out!"

Second Sunday of Easter

John 20:19-31

~~~~

Resurrecting with Questions

A Spiritual Commentary

When it was evening on that day, the first day of the week, and the doors of the house where the disciples had met were locked for fear of the Jews, Jesus came and stood among them and said, "Peace be with you."

It is still the first day of the week because the processes of the new creation are still unfolding. Earlier on this first day of the week the disciples, in the persons of the Beloved Disciple and Mary of Magdala, realize that Jesus is with God (John 20:1-18). Now on the evening of that same new day of creation, the disciples discover that he is simultaneously in their midst. Jesus is both with God (ascension) and with them (resurrection). This simultaneous presence emphasizes that he is a bridge, connecting the disciples with God and God with the disciples. He is the mediator between the divine and the human. That was what he was in his incarnate life, and that is what he is in his resurrected life. "And there was evening and there was morning, the first day" (Gen 1:5).

However, there is a major difference between the pre-Easter and post-Easter presences of Jesus. The post-Easter Jesus does not enter through doors, as people with physical bodies must do. The doors are locked, yet he was in their midst. This strongly suggests that the disciples have a spiritual realization of the presence of Jesus. He does not appear as an outer form as he previously did, but he manifests himself as a presence emerging from within and allaying their inner panic. His presence is known by the fact he brings peace in the midst of fear.

This peace is the fulfillment of his promise. "Peace I leave with you; my peace I give to you. I do not give to you as the world gives. Do not let your hearts be troubled, and do not let them be afraid" (John 14:27). Jesus leaves them peace, and this giving of peace is contrasted with how the world gives. The text does not go further with this contrast. But the overall sense is that the world gives and takes away. The security of one moment is replaced by the anxiety of the next moment. The world cannot sustain an abiding peaceful presence. Yet that is precisely how Jesus sees himself, an abiding presence that transcends the vagaries of the world. Jesus does not stop the chaos of the world. Rather he is present within it, calming and untroubling the heart, bringing peace.

After he said this, he showed them his hands and his side. Then the disciples rejoiced when they saw the Lord.

The showing of his hands and feet accompanies and makes real his word of peace. The disciples are able to read these signs of his wounded and opened body, and so they see the Lord. "Seeing the Lord" does not mean a physical sighting of the resuscitated body of Jesus. Rather it is a code phrase for knowing the revelation of Christ at such a depth that life is changed. This knowing happens when the disciples see the opened wounds.

But what is it they know? How do they read the signs in the hands and side?

Jesus is interiorly united to the Father. But this interior unity is not a private possession. It is meant to flow forth, bringing divine life to all who are disposed to receive it. This flowing forth is how Jesus glorifies the Father. The crucifixion is the supreme hour of this glorification. It is the time and place when divine life and love are most powerfully visible and available, present and transcendent in and through physical death. The throes of death reveal the greater flow of life.

The symbolic carrier of this spiritual truth is the lancing of the side of Jesus from which flows blood and water (John 19:34). Although this image triggers many interpretations, the gushing of blood and water is universally connected to the process of birth. And that this gushing comes from the side of Jesus recalls the birth of Eve from the side of Adam. Therefore, the opening in the side of Jesus is how his interior union with God becomes available as a life-giving birth for others. The openings in his hands perform the same symbolic function. They are channels that make available his interior life with God. This is what constitutes "seeing the Lord," receiving divine life through the symbols that mediate his "love that lays down its life for his friends." This is the truth of his death, and its realization leads them to rejoice.

They are living out the situation Jesus described earlier:

> [S]ome of his disciples said to one another, "What does he mean by saying to us, 'A little while, and you will no longer see me, and again a little

while, and you will see me'; and 'Because I am going to the Father'?"
. . . [Jesus said] 'Very truly, I tell you, you will weep and mourn, but the
world will rejoice; you will have pain, but your pain will turn into joy.
When a woman is in labor, she has pain, because her hour has come. But
when her child is born, she no longer remembers the anguish because of
the joy of having brought a human being into the world. So you have
pain now; but I will see you again, and your hearts will rejoice, and no
one will take your joy from you. (John 16:17, 20-22)

The sorrow they had at the loss of Jesus' physical presence is now replaced by a joy that cannot be taken away. The reason this joy cannot
be taken away is that it is grounded in a spiritual presence that is not
subject to loss the way physical presence is. In this sense, this new
situation is superior to the old situation. It is a never-ending presence.
Therefore, this joy "no one will take . . . from you" complements a
"peace the world cannot give" (see John 14:27).

**Jesus said to them again, "Peace be with you. As the Father has
sent me, so I send you."**

**When he had said this, he breathed on them and said to them,
"Receive the Holy Spirit. If you forgive the sins of any, they are
forgiven them; if you retain the sins of any, they are retained."**

Jesus offers them peace a second time. The beloved disciple had to
look twice into the tomb before he came to belief. Mary Magdalene
had to turn twice before she recognized the gardener as the teacher.
Now the disciples hear the word of peace twice. It brings them into the
fullness of revelation. The first time Jesus' word of peace expelled fear
because it was the reception of perfect love, the love of God for God's
children. "There is no fear in love, but perfect love casts out fear" (1
John 4:18).

Now that the disciples are grounded in the peace that perfect love
brings, Jesus confers peace a second time. This time peace is the power
of mission. The disciples have received the divine life that is stronger
than death mediated through the open wounds of Christ. However, divine life cannot be possessed. It can only be received and given away.
Therefore, they are immediately sent, commissioned by Jesus in the
same way the Father commissioned him. They have to give the life
they have received to others. The chain is established: from the Father
to Jesus, from Jesus to the disciples, and—by implication—from the
disciples to whomever the disciples will commission.

The key to this mission is the capacity to receive the Holy Spirit. Just as in the Genesis story God breathed into the clay of the earth and the human person became a living soul (see Gen 2:7), so now the Risen Lord breathes into his disciples and they become a new creation, a creature living by the breath of God. Living by the Spirit, they join the work of the Spirit. The work of the Spirit is to make things one.

The path to this oneness is through the forgiveness of sins. Sin is what separates God from the world and people from one another. Jesus has taken away the sin of the world, replaced the fundamental separation between God and the world with communion. The communion with God is the condition for the possibility of people forgiving one another and coming into unity. However, people must realize and engage this responsibility. If they hold onto the sins that separate, then separation will continue. If they let go of (forgive) those sins, unity will develop. The Holy Spirit enlivens people to co-create the human condition. This is the power of the resurrection, the freedom to overcome separation and bring unity.

> **But Thomas (who was called the Twin), one of the twelve, was not with them when Jesus came.**
>
> **So the other disciples told him, "We have seen the Lord."**
>
> **But he said to them, "Unless I see the mark of the nails in his hands, and put my finger in the mark of the nails and my hand in his side, I will not believe."**

The story line shifts. Thomas, who is called the Twin, was not present when the other disciples "saw the Lord." The other disciples bear witness to what they have seen, but it is not enough for Thomas. Taking the word of another does not suffice. He has his own criteria for believing, and community attestation is not among them. He wants to probe the flesh. In particular, he wants to probe the marks of Jesus' death. Presumably, this physical confirmation will convince him it is really Jesus. The one who was crucified and the one whom he once knew in the flesh will be confirmed as alive. This is sense knowledge, the type of knowledge most people rely on as an indication of reality.

This demand for physical verification is misplaced. Jesus is not a resuscitated corpse and resurrection is not a return to earthly life. However, there is irony in what he wants. The only way he will see the Lord is if he enters into the wounds. But these wounds are not available for his intrusive probing. These wounds are ones that Jesus shows to people so they may receive God's life and realize his true identity. The criteria for knowing the ultimate truth about Jesus are the same after his death as before his death. The person must go beyond the physical level and open himself or herself to the communication of divine life and recognize Jesus as God's incarnate presence. This is spiritual knowledge; the type of knowledge most people think is too subtle and evasive.

> **A week later his disciples were again in the house, and Thomas was with them. Although the doors were shut, Jesus came and stood among them and said, "Peace be with you."**

The coming of Christ into their midst is a regular happening. Every first day of the week Jesus is with them. When they gather, he gathers with them. Once again, he is not there physically because the doors were locked. He is in the midst of the disciples, emerging from within, as the communication of peace and the presence of joy. This time Thomas is present. More importantly, Thomas is with the other disciples. He is part of the community, and it is as part of the community that he will experience the risen Lord.

> **Then he said to Thomas, "Put your finger here and see my hands. Reach out your hand and put it in my side. Do not doubt but believe."**

> **Thomas answered him, "My Lord and my God!"**

Jesus invites Thomas into his wounds, into the correct understanding of his death and through that understanding into the reception of divine life. Although Jesus uses words similar to what Thomas said—which was essential for him to believe—he is not complying with Thomas' demands. The meaning is quite different. Jesus is encouraging Thomas to reach for the divine life that flows through him. It plays upon a line from the Adam and Eve story of Genesis: "See, the man [sic] has become like one of us, knowing good and evil; and now, he might reach out his hand and take also from the tree of life, and eat, and live forever" (Gen 3:22). Jesus is asking Thomas to reach out and live forever. Thomas must have obeyed Jesus' command for his cry, "My Lord and my God," signals both the reception of divine life and the recognition that Jesus and the Father are one. It might also signify that Thomas now knows he is not the twin of Jesus, not on the same level as the Son.

But there is a large omission in the story. What Thomas does not do is physically probe the wounds. He does not get his flesh and blood verification, but he does come to belief. The message, a consistent message in the Gospel of John, is that believing is not a matter of physical observation but of realizing spiritual truth. In fact, it is in the community of believers enlivened by the presence of the risen Christ that Thomas comes to know Jesus at a level that eluded him when he knew Jesus in the flesh.

In John's Gospel the character of Thomas has an ongoing difficulty in grasping the true meaning of Jesus' death. In the Lazarus story, when Jesus decides to go back to Judea where he will be in danger from the authorities, Thomas enthusiastically speaks to and for the other disciples, "Let us also go, that we may die with him" (John 11:16). It is a statement of bravado, perhaps even loyalty. But it is without understanding. They are not to die with Jesus; their task is to learn to receive the divine life that will come to them through Jesus' death. Jesus is not a reckless revolutionary courting death, and they are not kamikaze disciples.

Thomas' ignorance of the meaning of Jesus' death continues during the Last Supper conversations. Jesus is reflecting on his transition from this world to the Father. He insists that his upcoming separation from his disciples is only to prepare a place for them. Then he will come and take them to himself "so that where I am, there you may be also" (John 14:3). In other words, Jesus predicts a brief separation followed by a permanent, life-giving communion.

Then he tells them, "And you know the way to the place where I am going" (John 14:4). Although Jesus says they know, Thomas speaks for the group and says they do not know: "Lord, we do not know where you are going. How can we know the way?" (John 14:4). Jesus responds, "I am the way, and the truth, and the life. No one comes to the Father except through me. If you know me, you will know my Father also. From now on you do know him and have seen him" (John 14:5). We are not told whether Jesus' response to Thomas brought him from not knowing to knowing. But the whole context suggests that it did not. Although Thomas has seen Jesus in the flesh and talked to him, he does not know him in his theological identity as being both the path to God and the very presence of God. In particular, he does not know that the way to this simultaneous knowing of Jesus and the Father is through grasping the spiritual truth of Jesus' death.

Therefore Thomas' interactions with the incarnate Jesus, the Jesus available for physical probing, did not facilitate the deepest truth about him—namely his oneness with the Father and communication of divine life through his death. Thomas learns this truth through Jesus' spiritual presence within the gathered community. There is an important implication of this path of belief. The fact that Thomas knew Jesus in the flesh is not an extraordinary privilege to understanding the revelation of Christ. Common sense would seem to suggest that those who saw Jesus in the flesh have a great advantage over those who did not. But Thomas' experience suggests that the spiritual presence of Christ within the community is the way to come to a correct understanding of the pre-Easter Jesus. Thomas moves from darkness into light only on the evening of the first day of the week.

Jesus said to him, "Have you believed because you have seen me? Blessed are those who have not seen and yet have come to believe."

How would the literary character of Thomas answer Jesus' question, "Have you believed because you have seen me?" "Seeing the Lord" in the sense of probing his wounded flesh was how Thomas thought he would come to belief. That was his condition for believing, and that condition kept his consciousness on the level of the flesh. However, he never did probe the wounds, and yet he came to belief. So physically seeing Jesus is not how belief comes about. The answer to the question is no. Thomas did not come to faith through physical sight.

Thomas came to belief by spiritually grasping the meaning of Jesus' death and, through that understanding, he received the divine life that is stronger than death. He expressed and communicated this experience by exclaiming Jesus as *his* Lord and *his* God, the one who "took him to himself" (see John 12:32) and in the process took him into God. This experience is available within the community of disciples who gather each week and who find that Jesus is among them offering them the life that flows through his open wounds. It is not necessary to physically see him in the flesh. In fact, even those like Thomas who saw him in the flesh in his pre-Easter days only understood him and believed when they contacted his spiritual presence within the believing community. This experience of the risen Lord is not relegated to the past. It is present and available when the disciples gather "next week." The time and date of the gathering is "evening on that day, the first day of the week."

Now Jesus did many other signs in the presence of his disciples, which are not written in this book. But these are written so that you may come to believe that Jesus is the Messiah, the Son of God, and that through believing you may have life in his name.

The life of Jesus is a life of signs—words and deeds that were capable of pulling people into the mystery of Spirit. His disciples were present for these signs, only some of which have been written down. Therefore, the disciples know much more than is written in this book. The living Christ of the community supercedes any written material.

However, this writing is important. It is not only that these signs have been committed to written form and therefore can outlast the death of the disciples. It is also the way these signs were written. They were written in a way that reflects the signs in the actual historical dynamics of Jesus' life. In particular, the writing reflects the complex interplay between the physical and spiritual dimensions of life.

Therefore, this writing is itself a sign. It is meant to draw the reader into full belief that Jesus is God's Son and Messiah. This belief will open the reader to the flow of divine life that comes from Jesus. Readers, even though they have not met Jesus in the flesh, will experience the imparting of divine life through this written text within the community of disciples.

Teaching

Rainer Maria Rilke, the German poet, is often quoted as encouraging us not to excessively prize answers but to live questions. Behind this advice is a sense that we, as human beings, have not completely explored who we are and who we might become. One way this adventure in self-discovery could be pursued is by paying close attention to the questions that emerge in human consciousness. Sometimes these are questions about the adequacies of old ways of thinking and behaving. Sometimes these are questions that are tied to inklings in the present, or flashes of insight, or intuitions that challenge the dominance of rational logic.

Whenever I ponder St. John's Gospel in general and the stories of Christ's resurrection in particular, a number of questions enter my mind. I usually dismiss them because they threaten the comfortable boundaries of my confined consciousness. I sense that even asking them in a sustained way will take work, and living them will demand stepping off the edge of security-consciousness into a night of trust. Ordinary people may hold unexamined opinions about these questions or entertain them after a third beer. But they are seldom seriously pursued. However, once you accept that humans are only aware of a small fraction of what they are experiencing, the door is opened into a world where people can be present even though the doors are locked.

I wonder: what kind of a barrier is death? While people are alive, we often talk of a spiritual presence to one another. At least part of what that means is that we sense a reality deeper than body and mind that is crucial to the identity of a person. We presume that this deeper reality is mediated through body and mind. Therefore, when body and mind have fallen away, this deeper reality is inaccessible. Body and mind constitute "remains"; spirit goes into another world, the spirit world. The deceased is with God and at rest, i.e., inactive. However, in St. John's Gospel ascension and resurrection are distinguished. Ascension means Jesus is with God; resurrection means he is still present to the ones he loved. His love relationships are intact. The disciples do not have to go on without him. They have to go on with him in a new way.

Is Jesus a special case? Or is the disciples' experience of the death, ascension, and resurrection of Jesus a revelation of the spiritual structure of reality, a spiritual structure in which all participate? Do all who have given and received love in this incarnate life continue to do so after the death of the body? Is love really stronger than death?

Perhaps our advice to those grieving the loss of a loved one is too influenced by the powerful, yet limited, capacity of physical sight. We expect those left behind to grieve their loss and then get on with life, accepting the absence of the one they once loved. Is it crazy to think that they should assume a spiritual presence that cannot enter fully into most human consciousnesses and then get on with their life? If so, how should we think about this in such a way that consciousness may eventually open to it?

When we are impressed with the power of death to sever ties, we often seek signs that something of the person has survived. The person may not be with us in the way they once were, but we want some indication that they are somewhere and they are at peace. It seems that we will accept the loss if we know the person is happy in another reality. Separation is presupposed. But we would like a word from beyond that everything is all right. When it comes our time to die, this loved one is often imagined as someone who has gone ahead and prepared a place and will be waiting for us. We have all heard stories of people who are close to death seeing visions of deceased loved ones. It is assumed that they are a welcoming committee, guiding the about-to-die person to the other side. Death means reconnecting with those whom we have loved and lost.

This rendition is often the way Christian faith in life after death is characterized. However, it is not the spiritual consciousness of resurrection in John's Gospel. John's "Good News" is not impressed with the separation power of death. Jesus may be going to God, but that does not mean he is leaving his loved ones on earth—just the opposite. His death will bring about a condition in which the disciples will be able to see his abiding love clearly: "I will not leave you orphaned; I am coming to you. In a little while the world will no longer see me, but you will see me; because I live, you also will live. On that day you will know that I am in my Father, and you in me, and I in you" (John 14:18-20). The world that sees with physical eyes will no longer see Jesus after his death. But the disciples, the ones whom he loves, will see him because they will perceive him with spiritual eyes. This will happen "On that day," the day when he physically dies.

Why will the death day of Jesus be also his resurrection day, and the day the disciples will grasp the communion between God, Jesus, and themselves? The human person is a composite being. In classical language, we are body and soul, material and spiritual. When we appreciate ourselves as physical, we know what it means to say we are *with* someone or *beside* someone or *above* someone or *below* someone. Physical realities are separate from one another. When they come together, they do so only to break apart again. This sense of separation is so pervasive that even the moments of togetherness are haunted by thoughts of future separation. Most of us are very aware of this combination of together and separate. When we love someone very deeply, we instinctively fear they will die and leave us: the stronger the sense of togetherness, the stronger the fear of separation.

However, we can also appreciate ourselves as spiritual beings. When we do this, we know what it means to say we are *in* someone. Spiritual beings interdwell. They can be in one another without displacing anything of the other within which they dwell. "Interdwelling" is the essential spiritual condition—"I am in the Father, you in me, and I in you" (see John 14:10; 15:4; 17:21). In spiritual consciousness togetherness holds sway with such force that separation is inconceivable. When the physical falls away, this spiritual communion remains and takes "center stage." This is why Jesus says, "On that day," the day of his physical death, they will realize the truth of spiritual indwelling. When the physical is present, it monopolizes consciousness. When it is absent, the emptiness can be experienced not only as loss but also as possibility. There is a new form of presence. It is not waiting for us beyond death. Even though the doors are locked, he or she is "in our midst." On the spiritual level, we are never orphaned.

Can this be true?

How do we live this question of the resurrection?

Third Sunday of Easter

Luke 24:13-35

~~~~~

Sacrificing into Life

A Spiritual Commentary

Now on that same day two of them were going to a village called Emmaus, about seven miles from Jerusalem, and talking with each other about all these things that had happened.

In Luke's Gospel all the resurrection stories happen on the same day. The women and Peter going to the tomb, the two on the way to Emmaus, the appearance to the disciples in Jerusalem, and the ending of the Gospel with the disciples praying in the temple are a single flow of events. They are all part of the same spiritual experience. Each episode is integral to the whole revelation.

These two travelers are not out for an idle stroll. The fact that there are two of them probably indicates that they are Christian missionaries. Christian missionaries were sent out two by two. However, they are moving toward Emmaus. This is a strange destination for any follower of Jesus. Scholars are unsure about the exact location of Emmaus. Some think that it might have been the site of a Roman garrison, built around a pool of water. If this is the case, the symbolic goal of their journey is that they are moving toward Roman power. Roman power was displayed in the death of Jesus, and to the victor go the spoils. The spoils in this situation are the followers of Jesus.

The symbolic significance of this movement toward Emmaus is underlined by the geographic information that it is a movement away from Jerusalem. In Luke's Gospel avoiding Jerusalem is avoiding the true path of Christ. The whole Gospel is a journey toward Jerusalem, the revelation of the cross takes place in Jerusalem, and the story ends in Jerusalem. Walking away from Jerusalem and toward Emmaus means that they are abandoning the "unworldly" power of Christ displayed in his passion and death and embracing the "worldly" power of Rome that executed him. They are not travelers but deserters, not people on a mission but people walking away from a cause.

This story is sometimes called "The Road to Emmaus," but they never arrive at Emmaus. And it is just as well! If they walked through the gates of Emmaus, they would be within the walls of Rome and the way of life that Roman rule symbolizes. Then the real failure would not be the death of Jesus but their inability to comprehend the spiritual truth hidden in his social and political suffering and dying. The more appropriate title for this story is "The Road Back to Jerusalem." But the road back is also the road less traveled. Before they turn and return, something must happen.

They are remembering Jesus. At the Last Supper Jesus told them how to remember him: "he took the loaf of bread, and when he had given thanks, he broke it and gave it to them, saying, 'This is my body which is given for you'" (Luke 22:19). These were instructions to memory: "Do this in remembrance of me" (Luke 22:19). But these two disciples are remembering him in a different way.

> **While they were talking and discussing, Jesus himself came near and went with them, but their eyes were kept from recognizing him. (NAB: And it happened that while they were conversing and debating, Jesus himself drew near and walked with them, but their eyes were prevented from recognizing him [vv. 15-16].)**

"[I]t happened"—the unplanned accompaniment by Jesus who goes unrecognized. This unrecognized Jesus is the storyteller's mystical device that will be the catalyst for the conversion of the two disillusioned followers. There is always the temptation to interpret this "unrecognizability" as a physical limitation. Their eyes were cloudy and they could not quite make out who this sudden fellow traveler was. Perhaps even God caused this ocular fuzziness for a deeper purpose.

However, their inability to recognize Jesus is not a physical defect. There is no physical description of Jesus in the Gospels. Although the early Church thought Jesus was the most important person ever to live, they did not physically describe him in their writings. There is a spiritual reason for this failure to tell us his height, weight, bearing, and, of course, the color of his eyes. Physical descriptions apply to individuals but not to persons. Persons are not known by description but by action. The reason the two do not recognize Jesus is not because their eyes cannot pick up his physical characteristics. They do not recognize him because they have forgotten his characteristic gesture. The person of Jesus is summed up and symbolized by an action, an action he did with them and told them to do with one another, an action that is the key to the mystery of his suffering. They have forgotten this eucharistic action. Therefore, they do not recognize him.

And he said to them, "What are you discussing with each other while you walk along?"

They stood still, looking sad.

Then one of them, whose name was Cleopas, answered him, "Are you the only stranger in Jerusalem who does not know the things that have taken place there in these days?"

He asked them, "What things?"

The fellow traveler inquires about their conversation. So far in the story we have been told they are discussing what has happened, but we do not know the tone of the discussion. Jesus' question causes them to stop walking, and we are told they are sad. Whatever they are talking about, it is not causing them any happiness.

We are given the name of one traveler, but not the other. Is the reader-listener of this story asked to become the second traveler? Are we asked to journey from a conventional understanding of the death of Jesus that causes sadness to a deeper understanding of his death that causes joy? Is this a story about everyone's temptation in the face of what seems like senseless suffering and dying to escape to a more secure and more powerful space?

Cleopas' question is deeply ironic. Jesus is the only one who does know what has happened in Jerusalem. His two dialogue partners have no idea of the deeper meaning of the events. In a moment they will demonstrate their ignorance in a lengthy recitation of the facts culminating in a statement of complete community blindness.

Cleopas calls the unrecognized Jesus a "stranger in Jerusalem." This harkens back to his birth, when in the city of David (Bethlehem in the infancy narrative; Jerusalem in the crucifixion narrative) there was no room at the inn (see Luke 2:4-7). In one way Jesus is a true son of Jerusalem. He is the fulfillment of the Law and the prophets (cf. Luke 16:16; see the story of the Transfiguration, Luke 9:28-36 and parallels). He is most at home in the Temple where as a child of twelve he was "about my Father's interests" (Luke 2:49; NRSV alternative trans.). Yet in another way he is a stranger. The ruling elite do not recognize him, and they crucify him outside the walls. The conundrum of the story is embodied in the phrase, "stranger in Jerusalem."

Jesus simply responds, "What things?" He invites them to tell him what had happened to him in Jerusalem. They are now going to remember him. It is a rule of thumb to be leery when a spiritual teacher asks you a question. That person is going to see more in what you say than you had intended. These two sad people unload their grief at length.

They replied, "The things about Jesus of Nazareth, who was a prophet mighty in deed and word before God and all the people, and how our chief priests and leaders handed him over to be condemned to death and crucified him.

This is a true but partial appraisal of Jesus. He is a prophet, but more profoundly he is the Son of God. What happened to him is not just the murder of one more prophet. It is also true that he was held in high esteem by God and by many people. However, this description also runs the risk of reducing him to a reputation. Their memory is already askew.

They remembered him as a victim. The chief priests did something *to* him. He was not an active player in his own death. He was the passive recipient of the condemnation of others. Their lack of understanding is beginning to show.

But we had hoped that he was the one to redeem Israel.

They remembered him as an ethnocentric messiah. But Jesus was not sent only to Israel. He was sent through Israel to all people. We now know why they are sad. Their hopes have been dashed. However, what they hoped for was never what Jesus was sent for. His mission and their expectations are not in sync.

Yes, and besides all this, it is now the third day since these things took place.

They mention "the third day." The reader-listener gets the impression that for them it is a simple matter of counting. The number "three" is a factual statement. But the reader-listener knows that the number "three" is symbolic. This is the day of the revelation. This is the day they will understand.

Moreover, some women of our group astounded us.

Amazement is a first step in the process of spiritual perception. But it is only a first step. Eventually they must "see." Their predicament is that they cannot recognize Jesus. Amazement by itself does not bring sight, and sight is what is needed.

They were at the tomb early this morning, and when they did not find his body there, they came back and told us that they

had indeed seen a vision of angels who said that he was alive.
Some of those who were with us went to the tomb and found it
just as the women had said; but they did not see him."

They have all the facts and none of the meaning. Their memory of
Jesus culminates in this series of observations that encapsulates their
litany of misunderstandings. They have remembered him as a reputation, a victim, and a failure. Now they remember him as a dead man.
They go to the land of the dead to find the living. They gather at the
place where he is not, thinking his body (his reality) must be there
somewhere.

The storyteller has given these two sad followers a lot of "air time."
They have many lines, each one further contributing to the gathering
darkness of their minds. They needed this much rope to hang themselves so thoroughly. The last phrase, "they did not see him," is not another entry. It is the conclusion of their confusion. When you remember
Jesus as a reputation, a victim, a failure, and a dead man, "him you will
not see."

Then he said to them, "Oh, how foolish you are, and how slow
of heart to believe all that the prophets have declared! Was it
not necessary that the Messiah should suffer these things and
then enter into his glory?"

Jesus is not happy. It is hard to read these two sentences and not
conclude they are the words of a ticked-off resurrected Christ. He does
not appreciate how they have remembered him. He calls them foolish.
"Fools say in their hearts, 'There is no God'" (Psalms 14:1; 53:1). In
other words, the foolish person tries to interpret and establish life
without considering the spiritual dimension. These two have interpreted Jesus in strictly sociopolitical terms. They have neglected the
spiritual perspective that he tried to communicate to them at the supper. Therefore, they are foolish.

They are also slow of heart. In biblical spirituality the heart is connected to the eyes. When the heart burns, the fire pushes up the chest
and flows out the eyes. This allows the person to see. The eyes are like
the headlights of a car. They are lit from within in order to peer into the
darkness without. When the fire in the heart dies down, the person's
sight dims and eventually goes out. This may be poor physiology, but
it is good spirituality. When people are not in touch with their deepest
center (the heart), they cannot see the events of life from a spiritual

perspective. On the physical level they may have 20/20 vision, but on the spiritual level they are visually impaired. The path to spiritual sight is to stir the embers of the heart. This is precisely the strategy of Jesus.

Their foolishness and sluggish hearts are the result of their failure to penetrate into the deepest meaning of prophecy. The story does not elaborate on what the prophets spoke. It only suggests that the glory of Christ inevitably entails suffering. "Was it not necessary [?]" is a powerful phrase. It recalls what the prodigal father told the older son: "It was necessary to rejoice and be glad, for this your brother was dead, and is alive. He was lost, and now is found" (Luke 15:32; translation mine). We are at the center of the mystery. Jesus seems to be saying, "Don't you see? It had to be this way. This is the only way to bring God's love to a recalcitrant humanity. Any other way would betray God's love and compromise human freedom." However, at the moment they are not capable of comprehending this spiritual logic.

Then beginning with Moses and all the prophets, he interpreted to them the things about himself in all the scriptures.

These two are treated to a tour of Scripture by Christ himself. It is part of the storytelling teasing of St. Luke that he tells us *that* Jesus told them, but he does not tell us *what* Jesus told them. I have often thought this story could be profitably expanded at this point. But the principle is that the storyteller has given us everything we need to appropriate the spiritual perspective that is being developed. Although the content of what Jesus told them is crucial, the storyteller has other "fish to fry." The focus is not on what he is saying but on what is happening to them as he is talking to them and interpreting the Scripture. But we will not find out what is happening to them until a little later in the story.

As they came near the village to which they were going, he walked ahead as if he were going on.

But they urged him strongly, saying, "Stay with us, because it is almost evening and the day is now nearly over."

So he went in to stay with them.

The two are getting close to the destination of their original intent. They are not there, but they are drawing near. Jesus is not going there. He is journeying further. Why does he appear "as if he were going on"? It may be that he is still unhappy with their faulty memory of him. They have said nothing to show they have come to a better perspective. It may be that Jesus is on his way to the ends of the earth. His risen mission is universal. He will tell whomever he meets. Those who understand will follow along and those who do not will stop. Whatever the reason for the seeming separation, it is forestalled by one urgent, simple plea, "Stay with us."

This is a crucial move in becoming a disciple of Jesus. Jesus always walks further. He outdistances his followers. However, once you ask him to stay, he immediately replies. This is because the invitation to remain shows an openness to him. What he has already told you is fascinating enough to want more. Both Jesus and his Father never refuse an invitation. The reason the two have asked him to remain is "because it is almost evening and the day is now nearly over." In other words, it is time to eat, and this has always been a special moment for Jesus. He characterized himself as bread (John 6:48), so when people are hungry, he is eager to be with them. There is very little doubt about what he will do at supper.

When he was at the table with them, he took bread, blessed and broke it, and gave it to them. Then their eyes were opened, and they recognized him; and he vanished from their sight.

Jesus now repeats what he did at the supper before he suffered. He engages in his characteristic gesture, the action that reveals the truth about him and his sufferings. This action—repeated after his suffering, after their misinterpretation of his suffering, and after Jesus' reinterpretation of his suffering in the light of Moses and the prophets—is understood. Their eyes are opened and they understand. The next line is translated above as, "he vanished from their sight"; the NAB agrees with this NRSV translation. I translate the phrase as, "he became invisible from among them." The same Greek word is used as when he drew near to them. So his entrance into and exit from the story can be viewed as special moments of manifestation. At the beginning this manifestation is unrecognized. When it is recognized, it disappears. The risen Christ has "done his job." He has brought his community to a deeper realization and taught them, a second time, to remember him correctly. Exit Jesus.

Is there a spiritual meaning to Christ's disappearance? If the story is a literary form geared to promote a spiritual sensitivity, there is a reason for his sudden vanishing. Christ becomes invisible as a character in the story when the truth of his identity is seen. Christ always was and now is the ultimate source of wisdom and communion among his followers. He is present whenever and wherever he is remembered correctly. The correct remembrance has to do with performing the characteristic gesture within the community, the eucharist.

This is a gesture of taking your life in your hands, giving thanks for the life that has been given you, and giving that life to others so that they may grow strong on it—as a person who eats bread grows strong on bread. Whenever the divine life wells up in one person and is poured into another person so that that person is built up from within by that gift of life, then Jesus is present as the invisible power and energy of that relationship. He is no longer one more visible, physical entity among them. Nor is he in the tomb. Nor is he a ghost. He is the invisible spirit of their communion. The key to finding the risen Christ is knowing where to look.

> **They said to each other, "Were not our hearts burning within us while he was talking to us on the road, while he was opening the scriptures to us?"**

This is the reason they came to understand and could see him. Their hearts, their spiritual centers, were awakened. Previously, they were sluggish and therefore spiritually myopic. Now with the spiritual center awake they can see the world of spirit. The way this happened is that the Scriptures were opened up. The purpose of the Scriptures is to burn the heart. Once the heart burns, the eyes are opened to see the spiritual dimension of what is taking place. It is only on the level of spirit that the suffering, death, and resurrection of Jesus can be understood. This understanding takes place on the way. The way is the attempt to follow after Jesus, to apprentice ourselves to his life, to walk behind him, and to try not to be afraid.

> **That same hour they got up and returned to Jerusalem; and they found the eleven and their companions gathered together. They were saying, "The Lord has risen indeed, and he has appeared to Simon!" Then they told what had happened on the road, and how he had been made known to them in the breaking of the bread.**

This is the "hour" that was mentioned at the beginning of the Last Supper episode: "When the hour came . . . " (Luke 22:14). It is the "same hour" because the same revelation has taken place. Only this time the indication is that they understood it. "They got up" means they share in the resurrection of Jesus. Resurrection may be understood, in the first moment, as an event in the life of Jesus. But it is equally an event in the life of the early followers of Jesus. Their resurrection is that they participate in the fullness of Spirit that Jesus revealed and communicated. This participation turns them back to the sufferings and crucifixion that they had been walking away from. They never enter Emmaus and the worldly power of Rome because they finally understand the unworldly power of Jesus' suffering in Jerusalem.

What happened to the two on the road is confirmed by the community in Jerusalem. It is not an isolated experience or an offbeat interpretation. The Lord is risen. This designation of Jesus as Lord may carry the weight of his new form of presence. This presence manifests itself to people. Although we do not have the account of the Lord appearing to Peter, we have the proclamation. This spurs the two to tell their story. They started their journey by discussing the things that had happened in Jerusalem. This discussion is now superseded by what happened on the road and their sudden discovery of the essence of Christ that transcends death. His resurrected presence is known in the action of breaking the bread.

Teaching

The disciples come to understand that Jesus was always giving his life for others, as a person breaks bread and gives it to others as food. The Crucifixion was the ultimate example of this self-giving. To the last, he was forgiving those who were abusing him: "Father, forgive them; for they do not know what they are doing" (Luke 23:34) and offering salvation to the repentant criminal who was crucified with him: "Truly I tell you, today you will be with me in Paradise" (Luke 23:43). Therefore, on the social level, the Cross is the violent taking of Jesus' life. But the spiritual truth that suffuses this violence is that Jesus is giving his life to anyone who will accept the offer. He never strayed from his mission. He was food for the life of the world—from the feeding trough of his crib to the table fellowship with disciples to the invitations from the cross. Therefore, the Cross and the Eucharist mutually interpret one another. If you get the Eucharist, you will get the Cross. If you get the Cross, you will get the Eucharist.

But I have often wondered about the Cross and the Eucharist in our own lives. I have wondered about our giving, the endless secret acts of self-sacrifice, the countless pourings of life into life so that other life could grow strong.

Self-giving probably dominates our days, but it is often missing from our conversations. We have to be reminded that it is a major part of our comings and goings. We are quick to reach for our trophies, name our triumphs, cite our awards. We forget the times we have reached out. That was something we did in between the important events. It was decent, but not noteworthy, and certainly not the secret essence of who we are. It is sentimental to watch George Bailey in *It's a Wonderful Life* and to be reminded of his good deeds as an antidote to suicide. However, that's a movie, and a Christmas movie to boot.

What if we looked at breaking bread and breaking bodies as the primary human activity because it corresponds with divine activity? What if we were all a sacrifice into the world process? Max Scheler wrote about the sacrificial impulse (emphases mine):

> This sacrificial impulse is an *original* component of life and *precedes* all those particular "aims" and "goals" which calculation, intelligence, and reflection impose upon it later. We have *the urge to sacrifice* before we ever know why, for what and for whom! Jesus' view of nature and life, which sometimes shines through his speeches and parables in fragments and hidden allusions, shows quite clearly that he understood this fact. (*Ressentiment*, ed. Lewis A. Coser, trans. William W Holdheim [New York: Free Press of Glenco, 1961] 89)

Who we are is there before we know it, operating in a covert way throughout our ego-driven lives. We are undercover agents to ourselves—secret sacrificers masquerading as megalomaniacs

My grandfather used to play a dawn-of-time game with me. I was small, maybe four or five. He would take a cookie or biscuit or roll in his hand and show it to me. He would put both hands behind his back and then bring them back in front. Both hands were closed into fists.

"If you can guess what hand the cookie is in, you can have it," he would say.

I would walk around his hands trying to catch a glimpse of cookie between the cracks of his fingers. But his hands were large and the cookie was well tucked inside. Finally, I would venture a guess and tap a hand. Both hands would open and turn over, flat as plates. On each hand was half a cookie. The scoundrel had broken the cookie in half behind his back.

I would say, "Pop, you cheated!"

But by that time he had eaten one of the halves. He would say to me, "You had better hurry."

I think we break bread and life like that—half for us and half for others. I think Jesus ate the bread he broke and fed himself on his own life. Sacrificers are fed by their own sacrifice. That is the secret we seldom see. There is more love when it is given away than when it is kept, more love for those who give it and more love for those who receive it. In the world of Spirit there is no scarcity.

But there is another secret to sacrifice. It is captured in a single phrase of the eucharistic expression, "Jesus took bread and gave thanks" (see Luke 22:19; translation of expression mine). Jesus does what we are all capable of doing. He takes his life into his hands, as a person picks up bread and is about to break it. But before the breaking, before the sacrificial pouring out, there is gratitude. This life is not the property of Jesus. It is not his alone. This life is the free gift of God and so acknowledgement must be made.

The sacrificer is a person of secret gratitude. The giving is not from guilt or compulsion or the expectation of payback. Nor is it from scarcity, a giving that depletes the giver. This is a giving from fullness, from the realization of all that God has given and gives to the giver. We can take our life in our hands. But if we would give it easily and without strings, we must know that what we give away is given to us from beyond. Then we enter into the full picture of sacrifice: what is freely received is freely given.

Fourth Sunday of Easter

John 10:1-10

Entering through the Gate of Christ

A Spiritual Commentary

[Jesus said:] "Very truly, I tell you, anyone who does not enter the sheepfold by the gate but climbs in by another way is a thief and a bandit. The one who enters by the gate is the shepherd of the sheep.

The gatekeeper opens the gate for him, and the sheep hear his voice. He calls his own sheep by name and leads them out.

When he has brought out all his own, he goes ahead of them, and the sheep follow him because they know his voice. They will not follow a stranger, but they will run from him because they do not know the voice of strangers."

Jesus used this figure of speech with them, but they did not understand what he was saying to them.

So again Jesus said to them, "Very truly, I tell you, I am the gate for the sheep. All who came before me are thieves and bandits; but the sheep did not listen to them.

I am the gate. Whoever enters by me will be saved, and will come in and go out and find pasture. The thief comes only to steal and kill and destroy. I came that they may have life, and have it abundantly."

Shepherd is a symbol for both teachers and rulers, people who have influence in the lives of others. The way these teachers and rulers relate to people shows whether they are true shepherds or thieves and robbers. Thieves are people who steal by craft and deceit; robbers are people who steal with violence. But both steal. They take things away from people. They are rapacious, depriving people of whatever resources they have. St. John uses the strong trio of "steal and kill and destroy" to describe them. Thieves and robbers always leave people less than when they found them.

True shepherds are the opposite of thieves and robbers. They leave people more than when they found them. They are capable of this because they know people by name. This means they discern the inner potentiality of people and adjust their voice so that this inner possibility can hear them. In this way, the voice of the shepherd is not the voice of a stranger. It resonates with the inner world of the sheep. Also, in this way, these true shepherds walk ahead of people, bringing them to pasture, to places where they can find food to nourish them. Teachers and leaders who are true shepherds are artists of human development.

True shepherds come to the sheep through the gate of Jesus. Jesus is the one who knows how to spiritually develop people. He always characterizes himself as a flow of life into others. He is "the bread that comes down from heaven" (John 6:50), "living water" (John 4:10-11; cf. 7:38), "the resurrection and the life" (John 11:25), "the true vine" (John 15:1), etc. All of these are images of life flowing through him and entering others. In this text he states his mission and purpose clearly. He came so that people may have life and have it more abundantly. If anyone has ever been instrumental in awakening life in another, this has happened only because they have entered into that other through the gate that is Christ.

Teaching

I have always been intrigued by Jesus' statement, "I came that they may have life, and have it abundantly" (John 10:10), especially when this goal is connected to the roles of teacher and leader. It means that the art of leading and teaching entails providing life for people or releasing life within people; however, as far as job descriptions go, this is very vague. It is never going to replace lesson plans or strategic goal setting.

There is a need for greater precision in understanding "life." Although Jesus heals people of bodily ailments, I know "life" does not mean increased physical vitality. Nor does it mean greater length of days. If we can have it more abundantly, it must point to a reality that ebbs and flows, a reality to which we can open and close. Jesus' mission seems to be tied to maximizing the possibility of people participating in "life."

But what is "life?"

It was seven o'clock on a Sunday morning. The phone rang. The woman's voice on the other end was panicky. "Tom died," she said. "How am I going to get through?"

She was a woman whom I had been seeing for spiritual direction or, depending on how you define it, pastoral counseling. She had cancer and it had metastasized to the bone. She was to undergo a bone marrow transplant in about two weeks. I felt comfortable talking with her about "spiritual matters." She had excellent medical care, belonged to a cancer support group, and saw a psychologist on a regular basis—so I knew we would not have to wander into those areas. In fact, I suspected that I was the last of the people who had been recruited to help her through this serious illness. She had covered the medical, psychological, and social bases. Why not the spiritual? You never know.

I knew her, but I did not know who Tom was. Was he her husband, brother, friend?

"Tom?" I asked.

"My doctor, Tom," she said, with urgency and exasperation. "He was killed in a boating accident on Lake Michigan yesterday. How am I ever going to get through? I have to see you."

A half hour later she walked in and sat in her usual chair. She went through what she knew of Tom's death, punctuating it every so often with, "How am I going to get through?" I was not quite sure what she meant by that. Did she mean her own illness? Did she mean the upcoming bone marrow transplant? Did she mean that this loss, given everything else, would break her courage and resolve? I decided not to pursue it.

I said, "Do you want to try a text?" She nodded.

We had done texts before. I had taken her through a psalm, the fear of persecution texts in Matthew, and a few others. I would run through a text and together we would try to wrestle it into a blessing. She told me she liked this because it creatively engaged her and got her to see things differently. She was a Christian, but she had very little knowledge of the Bible.

So I tried to center myself, and I began to talk.

"When it was noon, darkness came over the whole land until three in the afternoon" (Mark 15:33). And I told her how darkness can come upon the earth when you least expect it, in the middle of the day.

"At three o'clock Jesus cried out with a loud voice, 'Eloi, Eloi, lema sabachthani?' which means, 'My God, my God, why have you forsaken me?'" (Mark 15:34). And I told her how in this darkness we can cry out the absence of God even as we assume the presence of God, and both can be held in the same mind, knowing and not knowing together. Darkness and light are pairs. The three o'clock cry of Jesus participates in both.

"When some of the bystanders heard it, they said, 'Listen, he is calling for Elijah.' And someone ran, filled a sponge with sour wine, put it on a stick, and gave it to him to drink, saying, 'Wait, let us see whether Elijah will come to take him down'" (Mark 15:35-36). And I told her how not all people are capable of living with both darkness and light. They can only hope for miraculous relief, and so they stay alive and keep others alive in the hope of a sky rescue from human exceptions like Elijah, who in legend did not die.

"Then Jesus gave a loud cry and breathed his last" (Mark 15:37). And I told her how this one who shows us our true potential enters into diminishment with a loud voice, engaging the darkness and not shrinking from it.

"And the curtain of the temple was torn in two, from top to bottom" (Mark 15:38). And I told her that this is the hidden truth of the God-grounded person, and the only way to see it is for the temple curtain to be ripped. What separates us from the Holy of Holies must be seen through.

"Now when the centurion, who stood facing him, saw that in this way he breathed his last, he said, 'Truly this man was God's Son!'" (Mark 15:39). And I told her that when someone swallows death with a loud voice, even soldiers, accustomed to worshiping physical force, acknowledge the spiritual revelation. He shows us not a way out but a way through, not an escape but an engagement.

That is what I told her. It took three to four minutes. During the telling, she never looked at me once. She had her head in her hands. After a good minute of silence, she looked up and said, "I'm going to the wake and funeral service."

"Good," I said. So that was it, I thought. That's what she meant, "How am I ever going to get through it?" She was not going to get through the wake and funeral of her doctor.

Then the biblical text that filled her mind for a moment faded, and the old tapes returned. She rehearsed all her feelings of vulnerability, loss, and helplessness. She pined for a sky rescue, but Elijah had sunk beneath the waves of Lake Michigan. Then suddenly her "loud voice" emerged, and, as it often does, it expressed itself as a small conquest.

"I don't care if I break down. I'm going to the funeral," she said.

"Good," I said.

She got up to go. As she walked out the door, she turned. "I'm sorry to have inconvenienced you. Calling and barging in at this hour," she shook her head in a "How could I?" gesture. "I apologize," she said.

I wanted to tell her there was no inconvenience, only feast. I wanted to tell her that I would rather be here than any place on earth. I wanted to tell her that when the hardened terrors of her mind relented and the subtle Spirit emerged with its meek unyielding strength, I shared her aliveness and drank from her well. I wanted to tell her that in the world of the Spirit, giving and receiving turn mutual and the "sower and reaper may rejoice together" (John 4:36). I wanted to tell her that when she opened to her soul, it was the Grand Canyon to me.

But I said, "No problem. I'm an early riser. I was up anyway."

This was one experience that taught me something of "life" and how opening to it can bring a sudden abundance and impel us into difficult situations with truth and courage. As for my own role as teacher, I felt neither pride nor usefulness. Instead, I was humbled in a way that was far more thrilling than any moment of inflated ego. On reflection, I became convinced that I had entered into her life through the gate of Christ.

Fifth Sunday of Easter

John 14:1-14

⸺⁕⸺

Calming Troubled Hearts

A Spiritual Commentary

[Jesus said to the disciples:] "Do not let your hearts be troubled. Believe in God, believe also in me. In my Father's house there are many dwelling places. If it were not so, would I have told you that I go to prepare a place for you? And if I go and prepare a place for you, I will come again and will take you to myself, so that where I am, there you may be also. And you know the way to the place where I am going."

The disciples' hearts are troubled by Jesus' upcoming departure. Jesus' remedy is faith in God and himself. But if faith is going to calm emotional distress, it needs to be deeply understood. Faith always seeks understanding, and if understanding is not present, faith has very little impact on feelings. Our feelings are cognitively dependent. They are trigged by mental frameworks. Jesus is trying to give the disciples, his friends, a different mental framework that will bring them peace. At the moment, all they can fathom is loss, and this sense of loss triggers sadness and fear.

Jesus envisions reality as his Father's house. This house of love has many dimensions. The earthly dimension that is available to the senses is only one of many. Jesus, in his physical reality, is going to depart this dimension. But, good housekeeper that he is, he is going into another dimension to prepare a place for them. Then he is coming back to take them to that place where he is. Love can endure temporary separation. But it cannot abide permanent loss. Jesus assures them that they know where he is going and the way he is taking.

Thomas said to him, "Lord, we do not know where you are going. How can we know the way?"

Jesus has told the disciples what they know, and Thomas has interrupted saying they know no such thing. Understanding does not calm his heart because he does not understand. He is ignorant both of the "where" (the Father) and the "way" (Jesus). However, confessing ignorance is a first step toward understanding, and it gives Jesus a chance to reveal the symbiotic relationship between the "where" and the "way."

> **Jesus said to him, "I am the way, and the truth, and the life. No one comes to the Father except through me. If you know me, you will know my Father also. From now on you do know him and have seen him."**

Jesus perceives that their problem with grasping the future possibility of reunion is that they do not comprehend who he is now. He is the way into the many dimensions of the house of love. He reveals the truth of this house of love and manifests its everlasting life. Jesus (the way) and the Father (the where) are so linked together that it is impossible to come to Father and not go through Jesus. Their relationship is so complete that if the disciples know Jesus, they will know the Father. They do not have to die to find heaven. Heaven permeates earth. The spiritual and physical interpenetrate one another. Jesus is the Word made flesh (see John 14:1). If they can grasp this present reality, they might come to believe in the future reunion.

> **Philip said to him, "Lord, show us the Father, and we will be satisfied."**

Jesus has just made the equation: see me, see the Father. But Philip cannot follow the math. Instead, he courts faith's fantasy. If only God would be a physical reality and we could see God with our physical eyes, then everything would be fine. Our hearts would be calmed, and we could go about our business. The vision Jesus is articulating is not the vision Philip wants. He knows what will calm his heart, and he is asking Jesus to supply it.

> **Jesus said to him, "Have I been with you all this time, Philip, and you still do not know me? Whoever has seen me has seen the Father. How can you say, "Show us the Father"? Do you not believe that I am in the Father and the Father is in me? The words that I say to you I do not speak on my own; but the Father who dwells in me does his works. Believe me that I am in the Father and the Father is in me; but if you do not, then believe me because of the works themselves. Very truly, I tell you, the one who believes in me will also do the works that I do and, in fact, will do greater works than these, because I am going to the**

**Father. I will do whatever you ask in my name, so that the
Father may be glorified in the Son. If in my name you ask me
for anything, I will do it.**

Jesus mildly upbraids Philip for not understanding. Philip has been
with Jesus a long time and he should have caught on by now. Ultimate
love does not make independent appearances. Rather it manifests itself
through the Word, the Word through whom all things were made (John
1:3), and the Word that is made flesh in Jesus (John 1:14). Said another
way, Jesus' relationship with the Father is his inner essence. This relationship is so completely a shared flow of life that Jesus' speech and
works are the Father's speech and works. They mutually indwell in one
another.

Jesus' explanation of his relationship with the Father should allow
the disciples to believe in him, to enter into a relationship with the
Father through him. However, this entails understanding, and understanding seems to be partial at best. So the disciples should look at the
works that Jesus does. These works, manifestations of God's love in
the physical and social worlds, will lead them into faith in Jesus and
faith in God. If this happens, the Father will work through these believers as the Father worked through Jesus. In fact, these believers will
do greater works because Jesus' time for earthly work is coming to an
end. But he will not be separate from them. If they ask Jesus for something, it will be given to them. In this way, the self-giving love of the
Father will continue to be manifested in the Son.

The disciples are facing the death and loss of Jesus and their hearts
are troubled. Jesus is seeking to calm their hearts by reinterpreting his
death as departure and their loss as temporary because they will be reunited in another dimension of the Father's house. Their ability to believe this and allow it to bring them peace will depend on their present
comprehension of who Jesus is. They must know now that the Father
and Jesus are interpenetrating realities; thus they can never be separated. They are connected to Jesus and through him to the Father to
such a degree that they do the works of Jesus and the Father. Therefore, they cannot be separated, even by death. They are bound in a
holy communion.

So why should their hearts be troubled?

Teaching

I think our hearts become troubled by death and loss because we believe in too small a God. We need an understanding of God that blows our mind.

I read that St. Anselm created the ontological argument for God to remedy the ennui of monks. Without going into detail, the ontological argument states God is that than which nothing greater can be thought. If you carry out this experiment in thinking, you will always be approaching God without ever arriving. It will only dawn on you in retrospect that it is the incomprehensibility of God that brings consolation. Despite what we may think, we are not calmed by knowing-for-sure. Our hearts relax through a process of profound not-knowing that leads to trust.

Another way of saying this is: we dwell in essential mystery. Accidental mystery is something we do not presently know but will know someday. Essential mystery is the experience of "the more we know, the more mysterious it is." Increased knowledge does not end essential mystery; increased knowledge increases mystery. Spiritual and theological traditions value this type of knowledgeable not-knowing because it safeguards both the transcendence of God and the human capacity to acknowledge the divine without fully comprehending it. When our minds dwell in this rarified atmosphere of knowing and not-knowing, the smaller fears that normally terrorize us lose some of their power. It is not that they go away, but that we see through their menacing masks. Better said, they are taken up into larger truths that provide a meaning more in accord with love.

The more our minds entertain larger truths about God, the more we are personally and existentially in a relationship of trust. When I think that every event of creation has been taken up and stored everlastingly in what followers of the philosopher Alfred North Whitehead call the consequent nature of God, or when I ponder the combination of divine immanence that suffuses all creation and divine transcendence that stretches beyond it, or when I contemplate the eternal now that is present in passing time, I sense that to surrender to this reality is to let the wind carry me. I also intuitively know that there is no other way to calm the heart.

Sixth Sunday of Easter

John 14:15-21

~~~~

Dancing Beyond Death

A Spiritual Commentary

[Jesus said to the disciples:] "If you love me, you will keep my commandments.

Jesus is not wagging his finger at the disciples and insisting that declarations of love must be backed up by action. "If you *really* love me, then you will do as I do." Rather this is a statement of the implications of spiritual communion. If the disciples love Jesus, stay in communion with him, then this communion will provide the inspiration and energy to live as Jesus lives. The ability to love one another is grounded in their love of Jesus who pours divine love into them. Therefore, loving Jesus, remaining united to him, is the key to faithful Christian action.

But how can they stay in touch with Jesus when he has told them he is returning to the Father?

And I will ask the Father, and he will give you another Advocate, to be with you forever. This is the Spirit of truth, whom the world cannot receive, because it neither sees him nor knows him. You know him, because he abides with you, and he will be in you.

At the request of Jesus the Father will send another companion to the disciples. Jesus is the first advocate, and the second advocate will continue his work. Jesus was the revelation of the truth, and this second advocate will be the Spirit of truth. Also, Jesus insisted that following him meant "remaining with him," interiorly entering into the structure of his selfhood. This Spirit will remain with the disciples and be within them. This sense of shared mission and internal dwelling makes the Spirit the continuing interior presence of Jesus.

However, the "world"—those who are outside the revelation of Jesus— cannot respond to this inner truth. They are both unable to perceive the reality of Spirit and to understand it. It is simply beyond their comprehension.

I will not leave you orphaned; I am coming to you. In a little while the world will no longer see me, but you will see me; because I live, you also will live. On that day you will know that I am in my Father, and you in me, and I in you.

Through the Spirit the disciples will always be connected to Jesus and through Jesus to the Father. Therefore, although Jesus is going to leave them, he is not going to leave them orphans. Perhaps better said, he is going to leave them in one way and remain with them in another way. His departure through death is not loss. It is a different form of presence. On the day of the resurrection, with Jesus' postdeath presence in the life of his disciples, the disciples will realize this mutual indwelling of the Father, Jesus, and themselves. This mutual indwelling will constitute an inner, unbreakable unity, a flow of life that is deeper than the disruptions and perishings of the physical world.

Once again, this realization is hidden from those who see only with the eyes of the world. For them Jesus' death will mean the loss of his physical presence and so the loss of him. Their physical eyes will no longer see him, and so he will be absent.

They who have my commandments and keep them are those who love me; and those who love me will be loved by my Father, and I will love them and reveal myself to them."

These words restate the interior unity of Jesus, the Father, and the disciples. But they uncover this unity in a detective-like way, beginning with what is observable and tracking it to its invisible, interior support. When the disciples live out Jesus' commandments, their behavior is available for all to see. However, this activity, observing Jesus' commandments and loving one another, shows they are interiorly connected to Jesus, for he is the living reality that empowers them to act in the way they do. But the essence of Jesus is to be loved by the Father, so the disciples who are connected to him inevitably experience this love of the Father. To enter into the love communion of the Father and Son is to enter more deeply into the revelation of the Son. The point seems to be: the more the disciples act out of the love of Christ, the more deeply they experience that love, a love that is simultaneously the love of the transcendent Father.

Teaching

William Shannon, a Thomas Merton scholar, wrote a very direct letter to a woman who had lost her sister.

I hope you have been able to come to grips a bit more with your feeling about your sister's death. I realize how very hard this is for you. You need to keep reflecting on the fact that, while in one sense death separates us from the loved ones, in another and more ultimate sense it deepens our spiritual union with them. When there is only *that*, then *that* becomes most important. And of course it should really be most important at all times. We are one with one another, because whatever of us there is that is really worthwhile is from God and in God. And that is something that death does not and cannot change—though it appears to do so, since we are so accustomed to think of a person solely in terms of her empirical ego. Death is the end of the empirical ego, but not of the person. We are all eternally one in the love of God. ("Thomas Merton and the Quest for Self-Identity," *Cistercian Studies* 22, no. 2 [1987] 172)

This seems to be very close to what Jesus is telling the disciples. The scenario is not: Jesus is going to God and when they die, they will go to God and be reunited to him. The scenario is: once he has died and is no longer physically among them, he will not be gone. He will be present to them in and through the Spirit in the depth of their own beings. They are not being encouraged to hope for life after death. They are being instructed in a consciousness change, to become aware of spiritual presence without physical manifestation.

The ongoing presence of Christ or any loved one is a truly consoling thought, but it is also a very difficult thought to accept. Part of the difficulty is that we are of "the world," and Jesus says the world does not know this level of reality. The world is alienated from the spiritual, partially because it is addicted to sense knowledge. When the physical sights and sounds of people are not present to us, we assume, as "worldly beings," they are gone. Both Jesus and William Shannon are questioning this assumption, and both acknowledge the difficulty of shedding this assumption and entertaining another possibility of presence. But both also insist that it has to be done.

Shannon thinks that "reflecting on the fact that, while in one sense death separates us from the loved ones, in another and more ultimate sense it deepens our spiritual union with them" will help. My guess is this type of reflection must be akin to T. S. Eliot's advice in *The Four Quartets*, "We must be still and still moving / Into another intensity / For a further union, a deeper communion . . ." But what should be the path of reflection? This strange possibility is outside the range of our everyday consciousness. When we try to ponder it, our mind blocks; how should we unblock it in order to go further?

The path of pondering should follow the clues of relationality. Human living is best appreciated from the perspective of relational flow rather than individual separateness. From Jesus' words I sense the deeper, inner world he reveals does not honor the boundaries of the surface world. God, Jesus, and the followers of Jesus are not separate realities. Certainly they can be distinguished, but they seem to mutually define one another. If this is so, our way into this dimension of spiritual communion is to ponder the centrality of relational flow. This pondering will not jeopardize our individuality, but it will bring into consciousness the relational ground out of which our individuality emerges.

On the physical level, we come into being in the meeting of a sperm and an egg. Then we live through our mother's blood for nine months, before we are born into a larger womb of air that our lungs breathe in and out. This symbiotic relationship with the universe deepens as we eat food and drink water. We may forget we are essentially connected to the material world, but upon reflection we must acknowledge that our bodies are established and sustained in relationship with all other material reality.

On the social-psychological level, we are cared for by others and internalize their influences. There are many theories of social-psychological development, but all of them stress the relational context of how we become ourselves. Most of the words we use to describe ourselves name relationships: son, daughter, mother, father, husband, wife, brother, sister. Although at times we conceive ourselves as "pulling ourselves up by our own boot straps," this self-reliant caricature cannot stand up to scrutiny. When the sense of "I" is pursued, we always find it grounded in an interdependent "we."

On the spiritual level, the relational flow is a wild ride. Spirit is that reality that can be present in another reality without displacing any of that reality in which it is present. Therefore, spirits can interpenetrate one another. And if the Creator Spirit is distinguished from created spirits, the picture is one of the Creator Spirit continuously present in the created spirits—sustaining them in existence and filling them with its life. The reality of this communion is eternal, and therefore it is not subject to losses associated with time. It is a dance that survives death.

Christian theologians have characterized the inner life of the Trinity as "perichoresis." Perichoresis is a dance, a life-giving movement that goes round and round without beginning or end. This is the love and the life of the Father, of the Son, and of the Spirit. Jesus, the Son, revealed that this Trinitarian dance is not for divine persons only. God invites human persons into this dance. This is the love and life that Jesus reveals and imparts to his disciples. This dance is going on right now, right beneath the surface of our worldly eyes. Music is playing just beyond the range of our worldly ears. But as we listen to Jesus console his disciples, our consciousness opens ever so slightly, and our feet begin to tap on the vibrant earth.

Seventh Sunday of Easter

John 17:1-11

Finishing Life

A Spiritual Commentary

This upcoming text is part of the last will and testament of Jesus and draws its emotional power from the shadow of Jesus' imminent death. However, the Johannine Jesus does not see his death as ending his influence or as a catastrophic loss for his disciples. Rather it is a departure to the Father and a new way of being with those who are still in the world. Therefore, his prayer is not desperate or permeated by pleading. Rather his words deepen his relationship with the Father and reinforce the mission that they share together. This prayerful reflection naturally expands to include all those who have known the Father and accepted Jesus. These people have grasped the intimate relationship between the Father and the Son and so received eternal life. Of course, the reception of eternal life is always a commission to communicate it to others. All of this, and more, enters into Jesus' prayer.

Although Jesus' prayer is cast as a conversation between the Son and the Father, it is not a private affair. The storyteller wants us to eavesdrop. Overhearing Jesus at prayer is a way we can grasp the essential truth of his identity, enter into his heart, and understand our participation in the divine plan.

After Jesus had spoken these words [to his disciples], he looked up to heaven and said,

Jesus' consciousness is focused on the divine presence. Although a spatial metaphor of "looked up to heaven" conveys this God-consciousness, so would the metaphor "eyes closed." If "the kingdom of heaven is within" (Luke 17:21; NRSV alternative trans.), then attention to it would be an interior journey. Jesus' interior communion with God is the place where prayer naturally arises.

The height image of heaven can give the impression that God is at a distance and needs to be contacted by "leaving the earth"; the depth image of soul can give the impression that God is present and is contacted by "plumbing the earth." Either way, prayer is the explicit attending to the divine that is always present. Prayer is more a response to God's presence than an attempt to contact that presence.

> **"Father, the hour has come; glorify your Son so that the Son may glorify you, since you have given him authority over all people, to give eternal life to all whom you have given him. And this is eternal life, that they may know you, the only true God, and Jesus Christ whom you have sent.**

The death of Jesus is near at hand. He envisions it as the context of his prayer. Although this death will be at the "hands of evil men," it is also part of a divine plan for the world. The phrase, "the hour has come," conveys the sense of a planned happening, a scheduled time of revelation.

A key feature of this "hour" is to understand the crucifixion of Jesus as a life-giving event for all who are able to come close and receive it. "And I, when I am lifted up from the earth, will draw all people to myself" (John 12:32). This is the glory that Jesus prays for. He wants to become a magnet drawing all people to himself. But this desire for centrality is not to extol himself or seek individual fame. People come to the Son only to receive the life of the Father. So the spiritual mutuality is in place: God glorifies the Son by attracting people to him, and, in turn, the Son glorifies the Father by communicating divine life to the people attracted to him. The Father brings people to the Son, and the Son brings people to the Father. Said in different language, the Father and the Son mutually indwell in one another, and the importance of one is the importance of the other.

This same spiritual mutuality is manifested in giving Jesus authority over all people (Matt 28:18). Why is authority over people given to Jesus? So he might impart eternal life to them. With Jesus' authority come honor and glory. But the only reason for this honor and glory is so that, through Jesus, God might pour life into all those whom God originally attracted to the Son.

The spiritual reasoning has come full circle. God initiates a process of bringing people to Jesus and completes that process by pouring divine life into them through Jesus. Therefore, the ultimate purpose for honoring and esteeming Jesus is that he is the Son and, as the Son, he is the way to the Father.

Realizing this reciprocal connection between the Father and the Son is more than a theological nicety. Personal realized knowledge of the one true God, the God who gives life rather than the false gods who demand life, coupled with the knowledge of Jesus Christ who fully reveals this God is, in itself, eternal life. In other words, in-depth understanding of the relationship of the Father and the Son releases eternal life. Therefore, Jesus' prayer is not concerned exclusively with himself. As he says in another context, "And what should I say—'Father, save me from this hour'? No, it is for this reason that I have come to this hour. Father, glorify your name'" (John 12:27-28). The Father glorifies the divine name by giving life through Jesus' death. Jesus' prayer is interwoven with his mission: "I came that they may have life, and have it abundantly" (John 10:10).

> **I glorified you on earth by finishing the work that you gave me to do. So now, Father, glorify me in your own presence with the glory that I had in your presence before the world existed.**

The theme of mutual glory continues. Jesus has glorified the Father by finishing the work he was sent to do. This work was to communicate divine life into creation and, in doing so, reconnect it to the creator. Now that the work is over, the Son will return to the Father and resume their eternal relationship. This glorification of Jesus is not a reward for work well done. The relationship of the Son to the Father was established "before the world existed." So this glory is not a new status for the Son. Rather the incarnate life of the Son was part of an eternal plan. This part of the plan is coming to a conclusion; another part of the plan is unfolding. Who will be left on earth when the one who glorified the Father on earth has returned to heaven?

> **I have made your name known to those whom you gave me from the world. They were yours, and you gave them to me, and they have kept your word. Now they know that everything you have given me is from you; for the words that you gave to me I have given to them, and they have received them and know in truth that I came from you; and they have believed that you sent me. I am asking on their behalf; I am not asking on behalf of the world, but on behalf of those whom you gave me, because they are yours. All mine are yours, and yours are mine; and I have been glorified in them.**
>
> **And now I am no longer in the world, but they are in the world, and I am coming to you. Holy Father, protect them in your name that you have given me, so that they may be one, as we are one."**

Later in John's Gospel, Jesus will tell Pilate, "For this I was born, and for this I came into the world, to testify to the truth. Everyone who belongs to the truth listens to my voice" (John 18:37). Jesus reveals the name of God and through that revelation allows divine life to flow into the world. All who are already in touch with the true God hear this Word and gravitate to Jesus. In this sense, the Father has given people who belong to him to Jesus. Their contact with the true God, however minimal, readies them for the revelation of Jesus. They have discerned the true God as the source of creation. Now when the Word "through whom all things were created" (John 1:3; trans. mine) enters the world, they have the capacity to respond to him. And once these people have entered the circle of Jesus' revelation, they grasp the mutual indwelling of the Son in the Father and the Father in the Son. This knowledge, as Jesus indicated earlier, is eternal life, making them children of God: "But to all who received him, who believed in his name, he gave power to become children of God" (John 1:12).

Now these people, who were the Father's and have become the Son's, enter into the process of mutual glorification. In other words, they share in the flow of life between the Father and the Son. As the Father has been glorified in Jesus, because Jesus made available divine life to creation, so Jesus is glorified by those who came to him and accepted and understood his words. More precisely, their acceptance and understanding enabled them to pass on to others the life that Jesus had passed on to them. This ability of the followers of Jesus is important. Jesus is going to the Father, and so will not be available in incarnate form. But those who belong to the Father and the Son are still in the world, continuing to carry out the mission of the Father and the Son's love. Since this is a mission to develop a new human community, they will witness to it when they are one as the Father and Son are one.

Teaching

When I read this calm and confident prayer, filled with "mission accomplished" language, I do not know how to "square it" with the random, anxious, unpredictable experiences of death and dying. In particular, Jesus' assertion, "I glorified you on earth by finishing the work that you gave me to do" (John 17:4), seems to set him apart from all who die without this assurance. In the face of death, most prayers go in a different direction—regret for missed opportunities, repentance for wrongdoing, apprehension in the face of darkness.

In the Gospel of Mark, we hear Jesus cry on the cross, "My God, my God, why have you forsaken me?" (Mark 15:34) and we know he is one of us. In the Gospel of John, we hear Jesus say on the cross, "It is finished" (John 19:30). This is not a neutral remark meaning his life is over. This is a statement that his work is completed. It is time to go because everything is done. He has fulfilled Nietzsche's exhortation, "Die at the right time!" However, this providentially guided death of Christ seems far from us.

Excepting suicide, death and dying are not within our control. We do not choose the time; the time chooses us. We do not choose the accident or the disease; they choose us. Death is no respecter of persons. It interrupts life. Even when we have our affairs in order—wills, funeral arrangements, letters to loved ones—there is a sense of disruption. There is so much that ties us to the earth. It is seldom that anyone is completely ready to depart. There is the story of an old man who surrendered his soul to God and was willing to die. Then he looked out the window, saw a rose, and decided to stay alive. In some circumstances, we say it is a blessing to go. But more often, we feel death is a premature wrenching. Unless we are in debilitating pain, there is always more to do and experience.

Recently, a friend of mine, forty-five years old, died suddenly. He was playing basketball. He left his feet for a jump shot and was dead by the time his feet returned to the court. At the wake, it was remarked, "Tom loved the game. It was the perfect way for him to go, only he should have been eighty when he took the final shot." He did not die at the right time. His children were young, and his considerable potential for contributing to the world only partially realized.

How can we say, "It is finished"? How can we say we have accomplished what we were sent to do?

It is helpful to remember that from a social point of view Jesus' life was unsuccessful and brutally interrupted. As pious Christian literature has tediously pointed out, Jesus was a failure. The religious elite did not accept his message. One of his disciples betrayed him; one denied him; the rest fled. He was executed with criminals, mocked by both soldiers and priests. From this perspective, he did not die at the right time. His life was taken from him. As the two travelers on the road away from Jerusalem say, "our chief priests and leaders handed him over to be condemned to death and crucified him" (Luke 24:20). This is the social truth of Jesus' life, and it is not a picture of accomplishment.

I believe the social truth of everyone's life is failure. Even if we die, pain free, in the fullness of years, a mantle lined with trophies, applauded by contemporaries, with family and friends around us, and leaving abundant inheritance, we die incomplete. Our deepest identity is not a social construction, and so social circumstances cannot fulfill us. On the social level, there is no perfect death and there is no right time. Although we should expend all our efforts at helping each other die well, we should also realize that "completion" must recognize the full, complex reality of the human person; completion is not achieved only by maximizing social conditions.

However, we might be able to talk about an accomplished life in spiritual terms. But it will entail some radical rethinking about life and what counts as success. Life is not about length of days or the magnitude of accomplishments. The mission of life is to release divine love into the world. Every person is a child of God who mutually indwells with the Father (Parent God) and reveals the Father's name. The adventures of life are invitations to actualize this spiritual identity. This identity may be actualized once or it may be actualized many times. The "child of God" may emerge at the "hour" of death or at any "hour." Whenever the child of God emerges, whenever the Son and Father "co-glorify" one another, it is the "hour" of revelation—and the work we were sent to do is accomplished.

As strange as the words of Jesus' prayer initially sound, they are words our hearts wait eagerly to hear. They do not articulate only Jesus' relationship to the Father and his relationship to the group he calls "friends." The words are exceptional, but not because they are devoid of the common emotions we associate with contemplating death. They are exceptional because they evaluate life from a consistent, theological perspective. It is a steadfastly spiritual appreciation of the human person. The prayer shows us the hidden spiritual reality that is difficult to see amid the tumult and noise of our social lives. Each person is a mission of love meant to stir love in others. When this happens, God is glorified, the work is accomplished, and life is complete.

Can we believe this?

Tenth Sunday in Ordinary Time

Proper 5

Matthew 9:9-13; 18-26

~~~~~~~

Learning the Meaning of Mercy

A Spiritual Commentary

As Jesus was walking along, he saw a man called Matthew sitting at the tax booth; and he said to him, "Follow me." And he got up and followed him.

Jesus, whose name means the one who saves people from their sins (see Matt 1:21), naturally notices Matthew who needs saving from his sins. Matthew is a tax collector. From the point of view of the scribes and Pharisees, he is a collaborator with the Romans and, most probably, an extortioner. His profession and his behavior put him outside the Law, and therefore outside those who obey the Law. Righteousness demands he be ostracized. But the one who said to his disciples that their righteousness must surpass that of the scribes and Pharisees (Matt 5:20) makes contact. Jesus seeks out the one whom others avoid.

It appears Matthew has been waiting. Jesus' command is met by an obedient response. He rises out of where he has been and follows Jesus. Although this brief exchange leaves much unsaid, the overall direction is clear. Jesus has initiated contact with a man known as a sinner and a process of salvation is under way,

And as he sat at dinner in the house, many tax collectors and sinners came and were sitting with him and his disciples.

Jesus not only seeks out tax collectors and sinners, they seek him out. "Tax collectors and sinners" is a social category of undesirable people, those who had unclean professions and who were morally and religiously lax. But they manage to find the house of the "church," of which Jesus is the center, and participate in its table fellowship. Once again, so much is left unsaid. Why did they come? What did they talk about? Did Jesus condone their lifestyles? The story does not answer these curiosities. But the event of table fellowship makes one thing clear: Jesus and these people belong together.

197

But why? What is the deeper meaning of their appropriate togetherness?

When the Pharisees saw this, they said to his disciples, "Why does your teacher eat with tax collectors and sinners?"

But when he heard this, he said, "Those who are well have no need of a physician, but those who are sick. Go and learn what this means, 'I desire mercy, not sacrifice.' For I have come to call not the righteous but sinners."

The question the Pharisees ask the disciples of Jesus emerges out of their assumptive world. In their world there are two separate groups—the pure and the impure, the clean and the unclean, the righteous and the sinners. The righteous who heed the many prescriptions of the law avoid the sinners who ignore those prescriptions.

However, Jesus freely associates with sinners. So this association needs an explanation, and the Pharisees ask the disciples for one. The emphasis is on what "your teacher" (not ours) is doing. But the disciples do not get to respond. The teacher himself has overheard this question, and he has something to say.

"I am with these people because a physician naturally gravitates to the sick and the sick naturally seek out a physician. These people know they are spiritually sick and that is the first step on the way to health. They also sense that I am the cure and care for their souls. They are right, for I have pondered the text that you do not understand. 'I desire mercy, not sacrifice.' God is a mercy that finds people who have lost their way, mends people who are broken, heals people who are afflicted. Since I am the presence of this God, I can be found among the lost, the broken, and the afflicted. This offer of mercy is the primary way people come back into relationship with God. It supersedes liturgical reconciliation and ritual sacrifices of atonement. This path of mercy is only available to those who recognize their waywardness. Those who make themselves righteous do not know this path. So I cannot call them. Since I have come from the merciful God, I can only call those who are ripe for mercy, those whose lack of perfection has opened them. Given who my Father is, I am eating with the right people."

While he was saying these things to them,

The background question to the following story, as it is with the exchange with the Pharisees above is: what is the ultimate power of human life about? Is it a reality that demands costly sacrifice from people? Or is it a reality that shows mercy to its children? This is not an intellectual question that is answered by rational argument. It is answered by hearing and watching Jesus in this episode that could be called, "A Tale of Two Daughters."

> **suddenly a leader of the synagogue came in and knelt before him, saying, "My daughter has just died; but come and lay your hand on her, and she will live."**
>
> **And Jesus got up and followed him, with his disciples.**

A leader of the synagogue interrupts Jesus' discourse because sorrow cannot wait. He respectfully kneels and requests what Jesus has revealed: God's life-giving power is in service to the suffering of the world. This leader of the synagogue even knows the gesture that will produce life: "with a strong hand and an outstretched arm" (Psalm 136:12) God rescues people. The warm hands of Jesus on the cold body of his daughter will start the flow of blood in her. Blood belongs to God and Jesus belongs to God. Therefore, Jesus can make blood flow.

This faithful request is so close to the heart of Jesus that he immediately rises and follows him. His disciples tag along. Perhaps they will learn something. In the Gospels many people follow Jesus, but Jesus follows divine desire. And he has just heard divine desire in the voice of this leader of the synagogue.

> **Then suddenly a woman who had been suffering from hemorrhages for twelve years came up behind him and touched the fringe of his cloak, for she said to herself, "If I only touch his cloak, I will be made well."**
>
> **Jesus turned, and seeing her he said, "Take heart, daughter; your faith has made you well."**
>
> **And instantly the woman was made well.**

Hiding from sight, playing invisible, so long shamed by her ailment, ritually impure, life-giving blood exiting, God leaking out of her body, abandoned, unworthy to be noticed, excluded. But she was planning a secret touch, harboring a hope, reaching out in anonymity, stealing salvation from a famous man in a hurry.

Jesus turns and sees; she is suddenly seen, discovered, addressed, praised for courageous faith, called daughter, included. And, oh yes, she is healed, made whole, saved.

The blood stops. The life-giving power of God that can start blood can also stop it. Not only by the touch of Jesus' hands, but by the word of his mouth. God is in Jesus and God's power is attending to pain, healing it.

> **When Jesus came to the leader's house and saw the flute players and the crowd making a commotion, he said, "Go away; for the girl is not dead but sleeping."**
>
> **And they laughed at him.**
>
> **But when the crowd had been put outside, he went in and took her by the hand, and the girl got up. And the report of this spread throughout that district.**

Is faith only born out of incredible pain? The pain of a father who can no longer hold his daughter and the pain of a hemorrhaging daughter who can no longer be held? Is it suffering that drives out cynicism and derision? Is it suffering that makes us move beyond a stubborn allegiance to the senses? Are there secrets that are hidden from health?

The crowds are consumed with the flute playing of death and their own wailing. All they can do is laugh at the thought of waking the dead. They must be put outside for they have blocked themselves off from life. Now the warm hand of God's Son takes the cold hand of the girl, and blood flows. When people spread the news throughout the district, they simply said, "We have learned how to desire mercy."

Teaching

In an article on aging and life review, there was a story about an older man who stood in front of a full-length mirror and beat himself with both his fists, pummeling his face and torso. He did this steadily and unemotionally, without screaming or comment. The nursing staff could not get him to stop, and eventually they had to put him in restraints.

The explanation for this self-flagellating behavior was simple and terrifying. In the process of his life review, the man remembered and fixated on his many mistakes. In his eyes his choices and actions were always wrong, and he could find no forgiveness for what he had done. His judgment on himself was negative, and so he carried out his own punishment. C.S. Lewis once remarked, "The gates of hell are locked from the inside." This man was in hell, and he had lost the key. He could not release himself from his own prison.

Although this man is an extreme example, many people have faced this same negative examination of conscience, especially in later life. When we look back at the decisions we made and the actions we performed, we are not satisfied. We do not accept our "one and only life." Rather we feel that we have "blown it." Add to this the fact that time is running out, and we begin to feel the quiet desperation of a life lived the wrong way.

Our attempts to modify this self-evaluation are unconvincing. We cannot justify what we have done. Although we may fabricate many excuses, none completely exonerates us. We realize the only righteousness we can manage will be bought at the price of self-deception. So we give up justifying ourselves "before the eyes of others" (see Luke 16:15) and enter the category of "tax collectors and sinners." What we do not know is that this recognition of failure has turned us into the people whom Jesus seeks out, the people ready to hear about the mercy of God.

We seriously entertain the mercy of God when we come to the place the First Letter of John articulates: "by this we will know that we are from the truth and will reassure our hearts before him whenever our hearts condemn us; for God is greater than our hearts, and he knows everything" (1 John 3:19-20). When our hearts condemn us, we open to God who is greater than our hearts and who has more comprehensive knowledge. This more comprehensive knowledge is sometimes characterized as a steadfast love that sustains the person even though the thoughts and actions of the person are unacceptable. In our negative evaluation of ourselves, we have confused who we are with what we have done.

However, God's mercy is clear sighted. It reestablishes the person anew in each moment. Although we will have to bear the negative consequences of our past actions, we are not defined by those actions or consequences. The mercy of God reminds us that we are not irredeemable sinners but temporarily lost sons and daughters. We can rest and be renewed in this greater knowledge of God, a mercy that softens our fierce and narrow condemnations.

As consoling as this "greater than our condemning hearts" thought may be, there is another version of the mercy of God. This version does not focus on our sinfulness: evil actions, their consequences, and the rehabilitation of the person. It focuses on our finitude, the choices we have made, and the paths we have taken. In the film classic, *Babette's Feast*, Babette makes a magnificent meal for a small, aging religious

community. Many of them are reviewing their life choices and wondering if they have chosen rightly. At the table is General Lowenhielm
who has never married. The woman whom he loves is also at the table.
He offers a toast that begins with a verse from Psalm 85, "Mercy and
truth have met together. Righteousness and bliss shall kiss one another" (cf. v. 10: NRSV; v. 11 NAB). Then he continues,

> Man in his weakness and shortsightedness believes he must make
> choices in this life. He trembles at the risk he takes. We do know fear. But
> no. Our choice is of no importance. There comes a time when our eyes
> are opened. And we come to realize that mercy is infinite. We need only
> await it with confidence and receive it with gratitude. Mercy imposes no
> conditions. And, lo! Everything we have chosen has been granted to us.
> And everything we rejected has also been granted. Yes, we get back even
> what we rejected. For mercy and truth have met together. Righteousness
> and bliss shall kiss one another.

Mercy is the realization that our lives are redeemed by ever higher appreciations, ever higher perspectives. Our task is to await mercy with
confidence and receive it with gratitude.

Jesus suggests that the scribes and Pharisees go and learn the meaning of mercy. Mercy is not a single act, but the sea in which we swim.
It gives hope to both our sinfulness and our finitude.

Eleventh Sunday in Ordinary Time

Proper 6

Matthew 9:35–10:8

(The *Revised Common Lectionary* offers the possibility of including
Matthew 10:9-23, not considered here.)

Protesting the Way Things Are

A Spiritual Commentary

**Jesus went about all the cities and villages, teaching in their
synagogues, and proclaiming the good news of the kingdom,
and curing every disease and every sickness. When he saw the
crowds, he had compassion for them, because they were harassed and helpless, like sheep without a shepherd**

Jesus is on the move, teaching, preaching, and healing. He is bringing his way of life to all who will hear him. His energy comes from
compassion. The storyteller gives us a peek into the interior of Jesus
and discloses what moves him to action. When he sees people troubled
and abandoned, he identifies with them. His heart goes out to them.
This is the prophetic "sigh," the profound grief at the suffering condition of God's good creation, a gut wrenching sense that what Jesus is
seeing shouldn't be.

The shepherds (leadership) who should be tending to these sheep
do not notice them. In fact, it is usually the leadership who is causing
the trouble and producing the sense of abandonment. But these people
do not escape Jesus' notice or concern. In fact, his compassion for them
triggers the expansion of his mission.

> **Then he said to his disciples, "The harvest is plentiful, but the
> laborers are few; therefore ask the Lord of the harvest to send
> out laborers into his harvest."**

The prophetic protest at the way things are leads to a prophetic vision
of how things should be. The images move from troubled and abandoned sheep to ripe grapes and bursting wheat. There is a possibility in
this distress, a harvest ready to be gathered in. But who will do it?

The work that needs to be done is more than Jesus' personal predilection and mission. It is God's mission to God's people. Therefore, Jesus tells his disciples to ask the master of the harvest for more laborers. This is a sly instruction to his disciples. If they pray for laborers, it will slowly dawn on them that they are the laborers they are praying for. This prayer of the disciples prepares them for Jesus' next step.

> **Then Jesus summoned his twelve disciples and gave them authority over unclean spirits, to cast them out, and to cure every disease and every sickness. These are the names of the twelve apostles: first, Simon, also known as Peter, and his brother Andrew; James son of Zebedee, and his brother John; Philip and Bartholomew; Thomas and Matthew the tax collector; James son of Alphaeus, and Thaddaeus; Simon the Cananaean, and Judas Iscariot, the one who betrayed him.**

The twelve become laborers and continue the work of Jesus. If they continue the work of Jesus, it is presupposed they are impelled by the same compassion that drives Jesus. Their names are made explicit. They are specific, concrete, identifiable men. The mission is enfleshed.

> **These twelve Jesus sent out with the following instructions: "Go nowhere among the Gentiles, and enter no town of the Samaritans, but go rather to the lost sheep of the house of Israel. As you go, proclaim the good news, 'The kingdom of heaven has come near.' Cure the sick, raise the dead, cleanse the lepers, cast out demons. You received without payment; give without payment."**

Jesus delimits the target population. The pagans and the Samaritans will wait for another day. The twelve are to focus on the crowds that caused Jesus to be moved with compassion: the sheep without shepherds, the lost sheep of the house of Israel.

The disciples are to tell them the days of their distress and lostness are over: "The kingdom of heaven has come near"; then they are to manifest that kingdom through actions that address the "trouble and abandonment." Although these actions appear spectacular, their underlying concern is to lavish love and life on people who have never experienced it. Since this love and life is what the twelve have freely experienced from God in Jesus, they should freely pass it along to others. They are giving to others what they have already received. The preparation for carrying out the work of the kingdom is to experience the kingdom in yourself.

Teaching

So much begins when the heart cries, "This shouldn't be!"

"The way this education is being conducted shouldn't be." "The way this health care is being delivered shouldn't be." "The way this neighborhood lives in fear shouldn't be." "The way this city is run shouldn't be." "These banking policies shouldn't be." "These governmental rules shouldn't be." "These church procedures shouldn't be."

It took me a long time to value prophetic grievers, the people who felt the underlying pain of situations and gave it a voice. I always felt: "Enough already; let's get on with it." Prophetic grieving was the first step, and I was always leery it would be the last step. We would complain and do nothing.

What I valued was the analyst who could size up situations and the strategist who could lay out an action plan and implement it. For me this text begins to move when Jesus delegates and commissions his disciples, turning them into apostles, "ones sent." I imagine intensive training in driving out unclean spirits and curing diseases. Then when the twelve are named, I am reminded of a classic scene in Howard Hawks' film, *Red River*. When the cattle drive is about to begin, the camera focuses on each cowboy who screams out, "Yiha!" Then the drive begins. I see the naming of twelve as focusing on each individual agent, singling him out as a significant player. If they could, Simon called Peter, and his brother Andrew, James, the son of Zebedee, and his brother John, Philip and Bartholomew, Thomas and Matthew, the tax collector; James, the son of Alphaeus, and Thaddeus; Simon from Cana, and even Judas Iscariot would leap out of the pages and cry, "Yiha!"

I also appreciated Jesus the strategist. When he advised beginning with the house of Israel and steering clear of Gentiles and Samaritans, I understood him to be working his home turf first. Pilot it in Israel before taking it on the road. Also, concrete instructions about what to do are always important. Proclaim and cure, raise, heal, and drive. All that was needed was to put these commands into bullet points. We have here the beginnings of organizational structure and leadership development.

However, we are also a long way from that bursting heart that energized the training, sending, and action plans. But the truth is the heart has to accompany the analyst and the strategist. It is the movement of the heart that creates the desire for change. The analysis that follows, however expert, will always need to be redone. The strategy that is implemented, however effective, will always need to be complemented and evaluated. Since all attempts to change the world are long-haul projects of success and failure, the heart that created the desire will also have to sustain the desire. As obstacles multiply and people betray and diseases win out over cures and driven-out demons return to stay, apostles will have to return to the heart with its primordial sigh, "This shouldn't be!" It begins with a movement of Jesus' heart when he sees the trouble and abandonment of the crowd. When this movement goes away, the analysis becomes sterile and the strategy unworkable.

The pressing problem may be what the pragmatist takes it to be: we can't make things work. But the foundational problem may be what the prophet has always suspected. We have become numb. We have anesthetized ourselves to the pain of the world. Our heart no longer moves, and we no longer cry out.

Twelfth Sunday in Ordinary Time

Proper 7

Matthew 10:24-33 *LM* • **Matthew 10:24-39** *RCL*

Choosing to Speak the Truth Despite Suffering

A Spiritual Commentary

[Jesus said to the twelve:] "A disciple is not above the teacher, nor a slave above the master; it is enough for the disciple to be like the teacher, and the slave like the master. If they have called the master of the house Beelzebul, how much more will they malign those of his household!

There is no attempt to soft sell the consequences of following Jesus. Jesus has just predicted that his disciples will be flogged, dragged before governors, delivered up to councils, made to flee from town to town, ostracized, and hated—all this because they are associated with Jesus. But this terrible treatment should not surprise them because "they" have done the same to Jesus. The servants will go the way of their master; the disciples will go the way of their teacher; those in the house will go the way of the master of the house. The cross of Christ will be the cross of his followers. Persecution is inevitable

So have no fear of them; for nothing is covered up that will not be uncovered, and nothing secret that will not become known. What I say to you in the dark, tell in the light; and what you hear whispered, proclaim from the housetops.

Of course, this prospect of impending suffering causes the disciples to tremble. They are afraid for their physical and social lives. This fear can grow in them and cause them to "fall away in times of persecution." They can become examples of the seed that falls upon rock and, because it does not develop roots, is scorched and withered by the sun (see Matt 13:5-6, 20-21). Jesus interprets the fate of this seed as symbolic of people who receive his teaching immediately and with joy, but they abandon it in times of persecution. Fear makes them wither.

The way seed withstands sun is by developing roots. Developing roots means knowing and holding onto the deeper realities of faith.

These deeper realities of faith always have to do with the spiritual identity of the human person, the nature of God, and God's purposes for creation. It is only people who are in touch with their own souls and their grounding in God who will have the courage and resolve to persevere in the face of persecution.

Therefore, Jesus will try to plant ideas in the minds of his disciples, ideas that will connect them to their deepest selves and the persistent purposes of God. If these ideas are persuasive and the disciples realize their truthfulness, they will be able to deal with the fear of persecution.

The theological root is to remember, as Leonard Bernstein pointed out in *Mass*, "You cannot imprison the Word of the Lord" (see 2 Tim 2:9). The point of the persecution is to silence the disciples. "They" want the revelation of Jesus' words and deeds concealed and kept a secret. Everything he is about must be stopped.

But this is not what is going to happen. Human resistance may impede God's activity in Jesus, but it cannot crush it: "From the days of John the Baptist until now the kingdom of heaven has suffered violence, and the violent take it by force" (Matt 11:12). This is Jesus' great assurance—God wins out.

Therefore, this knowledge of the inevitability of the kingdom will help the disciples overcome their fear. They are not to shrink away under threats, but they are to join in God's work. They are to bring the revelation from darkness to light, from whispering to proclamation. What Jesus has told them, they must tell to others. They have been entrusted with ultimate truth, and they must bear it into the future.

In fact, persecution, which is the violent effort to silence the truth, will have the opposite effect. It will be an opportunity to proclaim the revelation. In times of trial, God will speak through the disciples: "When they hand you over, do not worry about how you are to speak or what you are to say; for what you are to say will be given to you at that time; for it is not you who speak, but the Spirit of your Father speaking through you" (Matt 10:19-20). The Spirit of God will always be present and working through them. No matter how much harm is done to them, they are part of the future of the earth. If the disciples can incorporate into themselves this deeper truth, they will be able to manage their fear of persecution.

Do not fear those who kill the body but cannot kill the soul; rather fear him who can destroy both soul and body in hell.

The second theological truth is to remember Ultimate Muscle. Fear has a hierarchy. The hierarchy is arranged around how much damage can be done to the person. The persecutors can attack and kill the body. However, they cannot go further. The soul is beyond their reach. So, while fear of them is real and debilitating, it is not ultimate. Fear of what they can do must be placed in the context of what a more comprehensive power can do.

Ultimate fear is reserved for that which can destroy the total human person, both body and soul in hell. Therefore, it would make sense to fear this greater power rather than the more limited power that can only inflict bodily harm. In conventional theological thinking, this greater power belongs to God. Therefore, fear of God is the beginning of wisdom for it acknowledges the *fact* of superior divine power and the *fact* of limited human power. This fear of God is often called salutary for it correctly focuses human fear and puts the person on the path of salvation. It acknowledges God as the most important reality, and therefore the reality that must be taken into account. Simply said, more is at stake with God, and so God should be the one who is feared.

However, taken by itself, this line of reasoning is seriously inadequate. It makes divine power into a burlesque of human aggression, a bigger stick with which to hit people. It is not the modification of fear in the light of God's love. It is the escalation of fear in the light of God's punishment. If you confess Jesus, Herod will kill your body. If you abandon Jesus, God will destroy both body and soul in hell. Sheer self-interest dictates loyalty to Jesus in order to keep on God's good side. This theological root so emphasizes the destructive power of God that the destructive power of human persecutors seems the lesser of two evils. It is not an elegant argument and it presents a lopsided view of God, but it has been known to be persuasive. We are still a far cry from 1 John 4:18, "perfect love casts out fear."

> **Are not two sparrows sold for a penny? Yet not one of them will fall to the ground apart from your Father. And even the hairs of your head are all counted. So do not be afraid; you are of more value than many sparrows.**

The third theological root is to remember and realize Ultimate Love. The path to this realization begins with Jesus asking a question with which the disciples will certainly agree. It is common knowledge that two sparrows are sold for a small coin. Sparrows are not expensive and prized; they are cheap and dispensable. In the human world, money determines worth. Sparrows do not command money, and therefore they are not valuable.

Yet the Father of the disciples knows about the perishing of each sparrow. All living and dying are within this Father's knowing and, by implication, within the Father's care. It is not said that the Father stops the fall of sparrow, but that the falling of the sparrow does not go unnoticed. What is not valuable to the world is the object of divine knowledge and divine care. What humans consider insignificant, God prizes. The ways of God are not the ways of people.

This knowing and caring on the level of sparrows extends to the disciples. But they are not cheap. The world may count money, but the Father counts the hairs on the heads of his children. This is a symbol of intimate and infinite knowledge and care. Therefore, the falling of a disciple is not a lonely experience of being forgotten and neglected. It takes place within the deeper context of a Father's love. If the Father knows and cares about the passing of sparrows which are not valuable, how much more will this Father know and care for the passing of his children who are so valuable that even their hairs are numbered and recorded. Therefore, do not be afraid, even of God. The all-powerful God is a loving Parent.

> **Everyone therefore who acknowledges me before others, I also will acknowledge before my Father in heaven; but whoever denies me before others, I also will deny before my Father in heaven.**

This theological truth is to remember Ultimate Judgment. Jesus' special status is as a mediator. He intercedes between his followers and the heavenly Father. If on earth people acknowledge Jesus before human tribunals, then Jesus will return the favor and acknowledge them before God's tribunal. The reverse is also true. If they deny Jesus before earthly tribunals, Jesus will deny them before the heavenly tribunal. The disciples may fear persecution but their freedom is still intact. How they exercise this freedom will determine their ultimate destiny. If they hold on to the deeper truth and do not waver, they will overcome their fear and choose correctly.

Therefore, the fear of persecution that leads to "falling away" can be countered if the disciples remember that Jesus' revelation is destined to be made known and they are its proclaimers, that God's destructive powers are greater than human destructive powers, that the Father's love for his children means he does not abandon them when they fall, and that their loyalty to Jesus determines their eternal future with God.

For *Revised Common Lectionary* users:

"Do not think that I have come to bring peace to the earth; I have not come to bring peace, but a sword. For I have come to set a man against his father, and a daughter against her mother, and a daughter-in-law against her mother-in-law; and one's foes will be members of one's own household. Whoever loves father or mother more than me is not worthy of me; and whoever loves son or daughter more than me is not worthy of me; and whoever does not take up the cross and follow me is not worthy of me. Those who find their life will lose it, and those who lose their life for my sake will find it."

See the Thirteenth Sunday in Ordinary Time / Proper 8.

Teaching

When we see something with clarity, there is a strong urge to speak. When the "something we see" is the real truth about ourselves and potentially the real truth about others, not to speak is to lose this truth. If we do not embody illumination, it recedes into darkness. If we have discovered a new self, it needs to breathe and grow in a genuinely earthly way. We may rejoice at what we have found but, as the poet Anne Sexton has said, "The joy that isn't shared dies young." It may have begun in darkness, but it yearns for light. It may have begun as a whisper, but it builds into a shout. Secrecy and silence mean the death of what is struggling to be born. The Gospel of Thomas says, "If you bring forth what is within you, what you have will save you. If you do not have that within you, what you do not have within you [will] kill you" (GT 70).

At the same time, we realize that if we speak, many people will be disturbed. Some will abandon us; some will criticize us; some will move to silence us. We will become the object of gossip and ridicule. We will lose status, family and friends, property, wealth, profession, and perhaps even our lives. At this prospect we shake with fear. Surely it would be better to deny this truth about ourselves. Why put ourselves and everyone else through this ordeal?

Yet if we do not speak, can we live with the cowardice? Can we live with the sham the rest of our life will become? We will become one of T. S. Eliot's people, "living and partly living." The choice is between the life we have always led and the new life that will have to embrace suffering.

When Jesus told his disciples to move out into the open with what they knew, he was not urging them to share information. It was not a matter of facts, social critiques, or theological formulations. It was a matter of their new identity as followers of Jesus, as sons and daughters of the Father in heaven, as children of God, as images of God, as burning hearts. This identity might have been conceived in the whispering darkness of their inner lives, but that was only an incubation period. The revelation of the truth was not given to them for themselves. What they found for themselves was the potential identity of all who would hear them. They were meant to invite others into this truth. To let fear silence them meant they had to return to their old selves and allow others to "cling to their false gods." On one level, this may have been denying Jesus. But, on another level, they were denying themselves and generations to come. They were depriving the earth.

Ken Wilber has talked about this inner passion to speak the spiritual truth that has been revealed to us.

> And therefore, all of those for whom authentic transformation has deeply unseated their souls must, I believe, wrestle with the profound moral obligation to shout from the heart—perhaps quietly and gently with tears of reluctance; perhaps with fierce fire and angry wisdom; perhaps with slow and careful analysis; perhaps by unshakeable public example—but authenticity always and absolutely carries a demand and duty: you must speak out, to the best of your ability, and shake the spiritual tree, and shine your headlights into the eyes of the complacent . . . Those who are allowed to see are simultaneously saddled with the obligation to communicate that vision in no uncertain terms: that is the bargain . . . And this is a terrible burden, a horrible burden, because in any case there is no room for timidity. (*One Taste: Daily Reflections on Integral Spirituality* [Boston: Shambhala, 1999] 35)

The disciples of Jesus are blessed and burdened with a revelation. It has "unseated their soul," and the housetop, from which their voice can be heard, is their only authentic standing place.

What I like about Wilber's words is that he makes room for many ways in which the shout from the heart can be manifested. It flows through each of us differently: quiet tears, angry wisdom, careful analysis, unwavering example. The shout from the heart is neither monolithic nor overbearing. There are many ways to move from darkness to light, from whispering to housetops. However, he does not make room for timidity. As far as I am concerned, there is always room for timidity, as long as timidity itself is not the room.

Before we speak the truth we know, fear is the room we live in and freedom is curled up, its arms tightly wrapped around itself. Once we speak, freedom is the room we live in and fear is confined to a chair. It does not go away, and attempts to completely expel it are usually futile. We must love and respect our fears because they are our life companions. I think this is part of what the Buddhists mean when they say, "Serve your dragons tea." If eventually freedom grows so large that it can house fear without capitulating to it, laughter may spontaneously flow from this previously unimagined integration. For the poet is correct:

> Erect on Freedom's highest peak
> Laughter leaps.

> (Nikos Kazantzakis, *The Odyssey: A Modern Sequel*
> [New York: Simon and Schuster, 1958])

The laughter recognizes something we thought impossible. We love God more than we fear suffering. We finally "get" Jesus' prayer in the garden. He wants the cup to pass; he has no love affair with suffering. Our natural path, as Thomas More in *A Man for All Seasons* (London: William Heinemann, 1960) reminds us, lies in escaping. But more than the desire to escape is the desire to do the will of the Father. The Father's will is to offer love and reconciliation, to reveal God's intentions for the wayward creation. If this means suffering, then let the suffering itself be the revelation of God. Jesus cannot be silent. He must honor the "bargain of illumination." The word of the sky that told him he was the Son must be told to every son and daughter. The more he prays and realizes this unshakeable priority, the more his fear falls from him, like drops of blood watering the earth.

Thirteenth Sunday in Ordinary Time

Proper 8

Matthew 10:37-42 LM • **Matthew 10:40-42** RCL

≻≋≽

Prioritizing Love

A Spiritual Commentary

[Jesus said to the twelve:]

This first Scripture quotation (from the NRSV translation) and its commentary are given for users of the *Lectionary for Mass:*

> **"Whoever loves father or mother more than me is not worthy of me; and whoever loves son or daughter more than me is not worthy of me; and whoever does not take up the cross and follow me is not worthy of me. Those who find their life will lose it, and those who lose their life for my sake will find it.**

Since Jesus represents God and God is Spirit, it is possible to love father, mother, son, and daughter (to say nothing about spouse) in Christ. This means to cherish them as mediations of divine love. In principle, there is no need to set up a competition between Jesus and family.

However, the rhetoric of this text is comparative. It insists that the disciples of Jesus have proper priorities. There is a hierarchy of values, and it must be respected. Loyalty to the revelation of God in Christ is absolute. Ultimate commitment is reserved for ultimate reality. Therefore, if you value what is not ultimate as ultimate, you are not worthy of Jesus who is a Jew of the first commandment: "I am the LORD your God . . . you shall have no other gods before me" (Exod 20:2-3).

The same prioritization is true of life in society. The cross of Christ represents both Jesus' commitment to God's purposes and the religious-political rejection of those purposes. Jesus' cross is erected in the spiritual tension between divine love and human refusal. The disciples whose ultimate commitment is also to God will necessarily have to face this same societal rejection. In this sense, they will have to take up their cross because they are worthy of Jesus.

If the disciples find their life within the present roles and positions of society, roles and positions that do not acknowledge the revelation of God in Jesus, they will lose the deeper life of communion with God. However, if they lose that socially approved but spiritually vacant way of life because they are committed to the revelation of God in Jesus, then they will find the deeper life of truth, grace, and justice that Jesus makes available by following him. When societal life is lost because of following Jesus, spiritual life is gained. Once again, there is a need to choose where you will place your ultimate loyalty.

The predicted scenario is that ultimate commitment to God in Jesus will mean rejection by some members of your family and some segments of society. This rejection happens simply by the disciples' refusal to make family and society ultimate, to give them the allegiance they owe only to God. But the future holds more than rejection.

For users of the *Revised Common Lectionary* and the *Lectionary for Mass:*

> **Whoever welcomes you welcomes me, and whoever welcomes me welcomes the one who sent me. Whoever welcomes a prophet in the name of a prophet will receive a prophet's reward; and whoever welcomes a righteous person in the name of a righteous person will receive the reward of the righteous; and whoever gives even a cup of cold water to one of these little ones in the name of a disciple—truly I tell you, none of these will lose their reward.**

As surely as there will be rejection, there will be welcoming. To receive persons is to embrace them in terms of what they most truly are. Since the disciples are intimately related to Jesus, and Jesus is intimately related to God, a chain of receiving goes on. The embrace of the disciple includes embracing Jesus, which includes opening to God's grace. The experience of God in Jesus is not going to be lost in the flow of history. All that the disciples have experienced with Jesus, and through Jesus with God, will be available to others. If people are able to receive the disciples in terms of their prophecy, righteousness, and openness to God (their quality as "little ones"), then they will receive precisely that. They will enter into the prophet's passion, the righteous person's justice, and the little one's humility, and they will participate in those spiritual blessings. The movement that begins with Jesus is continuous and contagious, embracing both actors and receivers.

Teaching

In current parlance, it is quipped that the human person is "hard-wired" for God. This phrase is often spoken as if it were an act of daring. It is a way of denying secular assumptions that humanity can be reduced to physical, social, and psychological aspects. There is more, a spiritual dimension that is ultimately grounded in God. Believing this is a step beyond secularity. But it is a step that leads to other steps, steps that are more complex and dangerous.

In the biblical tradition, the fact that people are "hardwired" for God means there is a "God drive" that has to be respected in each person. However, there are also other drives in the hybrid reality of what people are. We have physical drives for food, drink, air, and sex. We have social drives to be respected, to have excellent clothes and shelter, to be in control rather than to be controlled, etc. Both our physical and social drives swirl about in our unique mental constellations. Our minds, on unconscious and conscious levels, sort out these drives and prioritize them. The problem is not that we are hardwired for God. The problem is that we are hardwired everywhere, and it is difficult to find a right ordering.

This basic human condition is the raw material for a wrong ordering called idolatry. We do not reserve the God drive for God. We attach it to money or family or social position or even food or sex. We then ask these finite realities to do for us what only God can do for us. We ask that that they give us ultimate worth, meaning, and life.

The key word is "ultimate." The goods of physical and social life are capable of giving us proximate worth, meaning, and life. That is their allure, and they work well on that level. The problem is that we are more than that level. We are oriented toward God. If we do not consciously attend to this truth, we will attach that God drive onto things that are not God. The moment we do that, and we do it consistently, these things begin to disappoint. They are proper for proximate allegiances, but they cannot bear the weight of ultimate commitment. As St. Matthew writes, "Do not store up for yourselves treasures on earth, where moth and rust consume and where thieves break in and steal" (Matt 6:19). The perishing world does not fill our hunger for the imperishable.

In this text, Jesus insists that life will only flow properly if ultimate allegiance is given to him and the revelation of God that is emerging in his life. This is the true home of the God drive, the anchoring that puts everything else in perspective. The path to this grounding in God necessarily includes relativizing two of the most powerful usurpers of the God drive: family relationships and societal standing. We value family and social position so much we are tempted to give them ultimate status. We must see through this temptation to make them gods and, at the same time, give them their due importance. On their own level they are fine. But when they compete for the God drive, they have to be put in their place.

However, this secondary and subordinate place is not a put down. When family and society are not distorted by the imposition of the God drive, they can be what they are. They are the arenas where the spiritual identity of the human person is played out in love and justice. The father, mother, son, daughter, and spouse are not pulled into an ultimate void and asked to fill it. Rather they are the relationships where the one loved by God loves others. The many mechanisms of society are not desired and grasped as attempts to secure enduring importance and worth. Rather they are the places where the one rooted in God expresses this relationship in compassionate and just actions. Things fall into place, and life, the life of God in us, flows rightly.

When the life of God flows rightly in us, it also flows through us. We join those transparent people known as prophets, the righteous, and the little ones. People welcome us, but they are not attracted because we share a related genetic package or because we hold a position of power and prestige. They receive us precisely because prophecy, righteousness, and humility are God-grounded activities. This is what they seek and this is their reward: the right ordering of spiritual, physical, psychological, and social life.

Fourteenth Sunday in Ordinary Time

Proper 9

Matthew 11:16-19; 25-30

Experiencing Rest

A Spiritual Commentary

[Jesus spoke to the crowd saying:] "But to what will I compare this generation?

This generation refers to a recalcitrant group of people, those who refuse to respond to what God is doing.

> **It is like children sitting in the marketplaces and calling to one another, 'We played the flute for you, and you did not dance; we wailed, and you did not mourn.' For John came neither eating nor drinking, and they say, 'He has a demon'; the Son of Man came eating and drinking, and they say, 'Look, a glutton and a drunkard, a friend of tax collectors and sinners!' Yet wisdom is vindicated by her deeds."**

Nothing can please these people. They respond negatively to every invitation. If the game is funeral, they will not join in the wailing. If the game is wedding, they will not dance to the sound of the flute. What they do best is sit in the marketplace and make judgments, fabricating reasons that justify their paralysis.

John the Baptist invited them to repent. But his strong words and desert abode gave them their "out"—"He has a demon." Jesus invited them to feast. But his table fellowship with those they deemed undesirable gave them their "out"—"a glutton and a drunkard."

None of these are their real reasons. These are the fabrications, the smoke screens, the camouflages. These are the reasons that make them look good, respectable, aboveboard. The real reason they refuse invitations to change is that they are the privileged. The way the system is set up sets them up. They are protecting their status, holding on tightly to what they have.

But wisdom, God's truth, is not vindicated by the reception it receives from people who will neither wail nor dance. Wisdom is justified by the things it does. So do not gauge Jesus by how this generation avoids his invitation and judges his actions. Look at the deeds themselves.

At that time Jesus said, "I thank you, Father, Lord of heaven and earth, because you have hidden these things from the wise and the intelligent and have revealed them to infants; yes, Father, for such was your gracious will.

Although Jesus' teaching is being rejected by "this generation" (the religious elite), it is being accepted by those who are not as sophisticated or as learned. Jesus and his teachings do not appeal to important people. Instead of lamenting this situation, Jesus praises the Father who is at work in these situations. Jesus' mission is from his Father who is also the guiding force of all creation ("Lord of heaven and earth"). If the Father both hides and reveals in this way, the one who does the will of his Father acknowledges this turn of events. Obviously, this is how his mission should unfold.

However, from the human side there is something about the wise and the learned that can block receiving the revelation of "these things." "These things" refer to the mysteries of the kingdom, how the revelation of divine love enters the human heart and transforms persons and society. The wise and the learned do not perceive things this deeply. They are wise and learned about the 613 dictates of the law. They "tithe mint, dill, and cummin, and have neglected the weightier matters of the law" (Matt 23:23) and "strain out a gnat but swallow a camel!" (Matt 23:24). They like everything that can be seen: salutations in the marketplace, first places at table, the outside of the cup, long robes, and widened phylacteries (e.g., see Matt 23:5-7, 26; Mark 12:38). They are masters of minutiae, obsessing over the surface without any sense of the depths, examining the trees without any sense of the forest.

Also, they use this trivial knowledge as a cookie cutter on any new experience. What does not fit with what they already know is dismissed. Their knowledge is expert at categorizing people as sinners and excluding them from community. But most of all, their knowledge is marshaled to support their privilege and position. The type of knowledge they possess leads to debate and theological jousting. All the people the Gospels say come to test Jesus belong to the wise and the learned. They are never seeking the truth. They are competitively seeking their own glory and trying to trap Jesus in mental mazes of their own making (e.g., Mark 12:13; Luke 20:20, 26). This surface,

defensive, and egotistical mindset does not have the equipment to receive "these things," the love of God revealed in the person and work
of Jesus.

However, little ones can receive the revelation. A child mind is contrasted with this type of wise and learned mind. The child mind is
eager and open. It is not defensive, or cluttered with many thoughts
and opinions, or inordinately attached to what it thinks. The child
mind is always learning from experience and testing things to see if
they are of benefit. This flexibility initially allows it to give a hearing to
the new teaching of Jesus.

But most importantly, the child mind is essentially relational. It is explicitly defined by its interchanges with a parent. It does not think it is
something in itself, and so it does not spend its energies in protection
and isolation. Even as a mature adult, a person can have a child mind.
This means the mind is in service to the deeper dimensions of the person, prizing the knowledge that opens the soul to God. It is not resistant but ripe for revelation. This mind is ready to enter into the mind of
Jesus and to know what he knows. The invitation is about to arrive.

This readiness for revelation of the child mind gives God pleasure.
It is God's gracious will to pour divine love into his children. When the
children are so eager for it, the Father is profoundly affirmed. "[Y]es,
Father"! God may want people to be good and just. But the real work
of the Father is not exhortations to virtue. The thrilling essence of the
Father is to pour life and love into his children. If they receive this
pleasure, they will walk in goodness and justice.

> **All things have been handed over to me by my Father; and no
> one knows the Son except the Father, and no one knows the
> Father except the Son and anyone to whom the Son chooses to
> reveal him.**

Jesus exemplifies the child mind. He lives by what the Father has
handed over to him. What he has been given is all things—the wisdom
to understand God's love as the permeating force of all creation and
the will to enact this love in ever creative ways. This wisdom and will
come about because Jesus and the Father know one another, and this
knowing is so mutual and complete that one cannot be fully known
without the other. This is not surface knowledge, but profound interpersonal sharing. It is knowledge of persons and not information
about laws, infractions, and punishments. What Jesus and his Father
know is quite different from what the wise and learned know.

But this intimate knowledge between the Father and the Son is not the private preserve of Jesus. Jesus, the Son, can invite anyone he pleases into his relationship to the Father. He can reveal the Father and join in the divine pleasure as it communicates its life to people.

But whom will he invite?

> **Come to me, all you that are weary and are carrying heavy burdens, and I will give you rest.**

He invites the ones whose labor weighs them down. These are those who struggle to be righteous by conforming to multiple religious laws. The laws are endless and petty; they defeat the human spirit rather than nurture it. But those who labor and are burdened also include people oppressed by taxation, discrimination, and injustice. In fact, this invitation goes out to all who are world weary, who can no longer find zest and pleasure in life, whose backs are bent with the burdens of each day. This is an invitation to all of suffering humanity, especially those whose suffering has caused them to lose heart.

Jesus promises them rest. But this does not mean less work and more sleep. Jesus is not proposing a social change for shorter hours and more pay. This is the rest of the seventh day of creation when God saw that it was good and rested. Rest happens when our true nature is realized. If St. Augustine was right and our hearts are restless until they rest in God, then Jesus promises to introduce them to the God who will fulfill them and restore to them the goodness of creation. This inner realization of rest happens when we live in harmony with our selves, our neighbor, nature, and God.

> **Take my yoke upon you, and learn from me; for I am gentle and humble in heart, and you will find rest for your souls. For my yoke is easy, and my burden is light."**

The way to this rest is to yoke yourself to Jesus. This means you must undertake Jesus' disciplines and learn from him. This rest will be granted only through a process of serious discipleship. What must be learned are the heart energies of meekness and humility. As heart energies, they are inner qualities that are grounded in God and radiate outward.

Meekness is the steady flow of gentleness. Meekness does not break the bruised reed or quench the smoldering wick. Yet it is unrelenting and courageous. It never resorts to the stick and the sword to get its way, exerting its will independent of the divine will. It watches God's grace unfold and participates in its mission.

Humility is the partner of meekness. Humble people know their place in the order of things. They do not arrogate to themselves divine powers. They remember at all times they are creatures, dependent on God and meant to serve God's purposes.

The meek and the humble live at peace, and their actions flow easily and effortlessly from a deep center. They live in inner communion with God and creation, and so their labor and their burdens are shared. Their polar opposites are the violent and the arrogant.

This yoke of humility and meekness is easy because it is the true nature of people, a nature that is supported by divine grace. The labor and burdens Jesus imposes are light because they are not struggles of the will but expressions of the true being of people. The invitation of Jesus is to experience rest, the realization of a completed, good creation of which they are a part.

Teaching

I came home after a five-day road trip, giving twelve talks in three cities. As I took the elevator up to my apartment, I envisioned drink, food, television, and sleep. When the door closed behind me, I heard myself sigh. I put down my bags, took off my coat, and said aloud, "I'll sit for a moment before I make dinner." When you live alone, you learn to talk to yourself. It is the best conversation you can get.

I woke two hours later, stumbled into the bedroom, and sprawled on the bed. Eight hours later I took off the clothes I had slept in, showered, made some coffee, sat in a chair, and looked out the window. I had slept, but I still needed more rest. I knew that if I sat there, which I did, I would revive sometime later in the afternoon.

We all know this scenario of exhaustion. We can work for only so long, even if we push ourselves and fight off sleep. Eventually the body needs rest, and it will have its way. We "fall" asleep. Sleeping is not so much a conscious act as coming to the end of waking consciousness. We have no choice but to be obedient to the body, to the physical rhythms of exertion and rest.

But there is also a weariness that afflicts the mind. This weariness—a labor and a burden—becomes too much for it. Although physical sleep may help the tired mind, its fatigue is not solely caused by the limited energies of the body. Some ways of thinking cut the mind off from its natural source in the soul, depriving it of spiritual energy. Ideas capture the mind, and they whip it night and day, making it work against its better instincts.

Many years ago a young woman came to see me. I had known her as a teenager. She was intelligent and vivacious and had been admitted to one of the top colleges in the country. When she walked in the door, I was shocked. She was unkempt and seemingly exhausted. She had dark semicircles under her eyes.

I asked her immediately if she was sleeping enough. She avoided the question and began a long, rambling, and confusing story. I set her up with a psychologist who had her tested. With her permission he told me the results of the testing.

After he had shared the diagnosis, I asked him, "What about the obvious fatigue, the rings under her eyes?"

He said, "Oh, as a theologian you should know the answer to that." I didn't say anything. He continued, "God doesn't sleep."

"I don't get it," I said.

"She has to control everything. She can't trust enough to sleep. If she rests, everything might come tumbling down. Her body is exhausted because her mind is ever vigilant."

Responsible people know their decisions count. They carefully weigh what they do. In fact, controlling the future through planning is a large part of adult waking life. "Trusting things will come out all right" is an abdication of our duty to make things come out all right. This firm emphasis on human freedom and decision making may be true, but from a spiritual point of view it is a half-truth. Life, at the deepest level, is not only a conscious project but an unsolicited gift. If all we are aware of is the demand, it may take us over and turn us into control freaks. As the body flourishes in the rhythms of exertion and rest, so the mind also flourishes when it oscillates between exertion and rest.

Jesus suggests that the mind rests by disengaging from its wise and learned status and by embracing its child status. Its child status is to recognize its relationship to higher realities of which it is a part and on which it can rely. The mind can rest in the soul and the soul (the son or daughter) can rest in God (the Parent). Jesus knows how this happens, and he invites all those who feel labored and burdened with an excessive sense of responsibility and control to put on his easier yoke and pick up his lighter burden.

Poets have expressed this experience of inner rest. Rilke pictures it as a swan in water. He first describes the awkward "laboring steps" of the swan on land. Then he portrays the swan as he

> . . . lets himself down
>
> into the water, which receives him gaily
> and which flows joyfully under
> and after him, wave after wave,
> while the swan, unmoving and marvelously calm,
> is pleased to be carried, each moment more fully grown,
>
> . . . .

(trans. by Robert Bly in *Selected Poems of Rainer Maria Rilke*
[New York: Harper & Row, 1981], 141)

Spiritual rest is allowing ourselves to be carried by life energies without strain or effort on our part. Even more than that, we are invited "to be pleased to be carried."

D. H. Lawrence pictures spiritual rest as

> . . . a cat asleep on a chair
> at peace, in peace
>
> . . . .
>
> Sleeping on the hearth of the living world
> yawning at home before the fire of life
> feeling the presence of the living God
> like a great reassurance
> a deep calm in the heart . . .

(from "Pax" in *The Complete Poems of D. H. Lawrence,*
ed. Vivian de Sola Pinto and Warren Roberts
[New York: Viking Press, 1964] 700)

Spiritual rest is trusting in the life that has been given, realizing that "All that matters is to be at one with the living God / to be a creature in the house of the God of Life." To be a creature is not only to bump into limits and be subjected to death. It also means receiving life at every instant from the Creator and, therefore, to have the "experience of being" as well as the "experience" of doing.

Accepting Jesus' invitation means learning the lessons of the swan and the cat.

Fifteenth Sunday in Ordinary Time

Proper 10

Matthew 13:1-23 *LM* • Matthew 13:1-9, 18-23 *RCL*

Loving the Listener

A Spiritual Commentary

That same day Jesus went out of the house and sat beside the sea. Such great crowds gathered around him that he got into a boat and sat there, while the whole crowd stood on the beach.

Jesus leaves the house church where the "already converted" have been gathered and goes to the sea. He is looking for fish, and they arrive in large numbers. So Jesus, the fisher of people, appropriately sits and teaches from a boat.

And he told them many things in parables, saying: "Listen! A sower went out to sow. And as he sowed, some seeds fell on the path, and the birds came and ate them up. Other seeds fell on rocky ground, where they did not have much soil, and they sprang up quickly, since they had no depth of soil. But when the sun rose, they were scorched; and since they had no root, they withered away. Other seeds fell among thorns, and the thorns grew up and choked them. Other seeds fell on good soil and brought forth grain, some a hundredfold, some sixty, some thirty. Let anyone with ears listen!"

There are two elements in parabolic and allegorical teaching: conventional situations and spiritual wisdom. Conventional situations focus on some aspects of physical and social life. Spiritual wisdom deals with the laws and operations of the spiritual dimension. Knowledge about conventional situations is more easily accessible than spiritual wisdom. People know about the physical and social reality through the five senses and available cultural information. Therefore, one path to spiritual wisdom is to use the knowledge about conventional situations to communicate spiritual wisdom. This is the purpose of parables. They are also Jesus' preferred mode of teaching for he teaches the crowds "many things in parables."

225

However, parables are not pablum. They make demands on the listener. They may tell stories about conventional situations (legal tangles, agricultural problems, medical procedures, weather predictions, etc.), but they always include a little strangeness. In this case, a sower scatters seed in a reckless fashion, indicating that this is not a tract on productive farming. Also, the yield is extremely abundant, indicating that this is not a normal harvest. The strangeness in the parable is a tipoff that the story should lead the listeners to the spiritual level.

Ultimately, each individual listener is responsible for this journey of understanding from conventional situations to spiritual depth. This journey is undoubtedly helped by close attention to the parable. But the guidance of a spiritual teacher, who is often the teller of the parable, is also needed. The parable is not an end in itself. It initiates a process of consciousness change. "Let anyone with ears listen!" means that the parable is over and the struggle to understand has begun.

This first part of this Scripture quotation (from the NRSV translation) and its commentary are given for users of the *Lectionary for Mass:*

> **Then the disciples came and asked him, "Why do you speak to them in parables?" He answered, "To you it has been given to know the secrets of the kingdom of heaven, but to them it has not been given. For to those who have, more will be given, and they will have an abundance; but from those who have nothing, even what they have will be taken away. The reason I speak to them in parables is that 'seeing they do not perceive, and hearing they do not listen, nor do they understand.' With them indeed is fulfilled the prophecy of Isaiah that says: 'You will indeed listen, but never understand, and you will indeed look, but never perceive. For this people's heart has grown dull, and their ears are hard of hearing, and they have shut their eyes; so that they might not look with their eyes, and listen with their ears, and understand with their heart and turn—and I would heal them.' But blessed are your eyes, for they see, and your ears, for they hear. Truly I tell you, many prophets and righteous people longed to see what you see, but did not see it, and to hear what you hear, but did not hear it.**

Some people "get" parables; some people don't. Some people follow the conventional situation into spiritual wisdom. Some are confused. Parables are not plain speech, and so they leave some behind.

Jesus suggests that the disciples "get" the parable of the sower, seed, and soils. Although their "getting it" can be attributed to many factors, Jesus signals out their inner receptivity to divine grace. The "secrets of the kingdom of heaven" have "been given" to them. God has revealed the meaning of the parable to their open and ready hearts. As they listen to the parable with their physical ears, God is working in their hearts to give them spiritual ears. Parable reception is both an outer word and inner word. On the outside Jesus is speaking, on the inside God is speaking.

There is also growth in understanding. As the disciples grasp the meaning of the parable, they will realize more and more the spiritual significance of the story. "[T]o those who have, more will be given" (Matt 13:12). In fact, as the revelation deepens, they enter into a realm that the prophets and the righteous have desired to enter. Their growth in the revelatory knowledge the parable conveys develops their spiritual perception. They are sharpening their spiritual eyes and ears.

However, the hearts of others are not as receptive as the disciples.' They are "gross," hardened against following the conventional situation into spiritual wisdom. So they hear the parable and see events, but they do not come to spiritual wisdom. They have experienced the outer event of the parable, but no revelation has occurred because the requisite inner receptivity to divine grace is lacking. Therefore, no conversion goes on, and the healing powers of the spiritual are denied them.

This is the answer to the disciples' question, "Why do you speak to them in parables?" Jesus speaks in parables because the outer symbolic language of the story gives God a chance to work in the hearts of those who hear it in order to bring them to understand "the secrets of the kingdom of heaven."

For users of the *Revised Common Lectionary* and the *Lectionary for Mass*:

Hear then the parable of the sower. When anyone hears the word of the kingdom and does not understand it, the evil one comes and snatches away what is sown in the heart; this is what was sown on the path. As for what was sown on rocky ground, this is the one who hears the word and immediately receives it with joy; yet such a person has no root, but endures only for a while, and when trouble or persecution arises on account of the word, that person immediately falls away. As for what was sown among thorns, this is the one who hears the word, but the cares of the world and the lure of wealth choke

the word, and it yields nothing. But as for what was sown on good soil, this is the one who hears the word and understands it, who indeed bears fruit and yields, in one case a hundred-fold, in another sixty, and in another thirty."

The spiritual teacher helps the disciples move into greater understanding of this parable. He interprets the parable in terms of the obstacles to hearing the word. In this sense it is a parable about how to hear Jesus' teaching in general and the parables in particular.

In the Matthean Jesus' interpretation the seed is always sown, but its ongoing life is in continual peril. The evil one may immediately steal it away. Or the word will be received enthusiastically, but it will not be pondered and acted upon. Therefore it will not develop roots, and so this person will not be able to withstand trouble and persecution. Or the spiritual word will find itself in unfavorable competition with the cares and wealth of the world. This person will not bear fruit. However, when the word and soil come together completely and effectively, the result is an abundance and an excellence beyond imagination. Although four possible persons are envisioned, it is more realistic to understand each seed as belonging to every person. At one time or another every person loses the word to the evil one, is enthusiastic but not persevering, pursues riches at the expense of soul, and also bears abundant fruit.

Teaching

Spiritual teachers are a highly individual lot. There is no one type or one teaching style or one way of accepting and refusing students. However, a prejudicial, and perhaps unfair, distinction is often made between teachers. There are those who love the students and those who love the teaching.

Those who love the teaching spell it out in full detail. They are spiritually brilliant, and there is no shortage of words to explain and elaborate. They make connections to other traditions, raise objections and answer them, present the teaching with wit, and are often charming. In general, they overwhelm the student. But they always take questions. It gives them a chance to talk more.

The spiritual teachers who love the students talk a little and then listen to the student. They are listening for the level of understanding, for the blocks to advancement, for the pathways the mind takes and the ones it avoids. They are expert at sizing up the mental maze before them.

What happens next is why they love the student more than the teaching. They see what is needed, but they do not explicitly state it. They do not instruct the student, explaining and clarifying. Rather they say and do things that give the student the opportunity to discover the next step. They provide the outer stimulus for an inner revelation. In this way the students are not dependent on the insight of the teacher. If they can follow the clues, they will know for themselves. Loving the student, therefore, is a disciplined approach. It withholds personal knowledge while creatively finding ways to prod the student into illumination.

In a sense, every parent has faced this situation. When parents help children with homework they are always tempted to supply the answers. (This temptation applies to all subjects except the "much hated science project.") But soon they develop a Socratic style that helps children find the answers for themselves. In a metaphor that would apply well to Jesus in the boat on the sea, they are not giving the children a fish. They are teaching them how to fish. This option applies to any teacher and any educational process.

When Jesus tells parables, he is a spiritual teacher who loves the listener. The parables are enigmatic. As such they invite participation and response. They are not merely information. They necessarily involve engagement. This engagement is helped by a number of human abilities, primarily what Robinson Davies called "the ability to hack metaphor."

But St. Matthew sees something else at work. Since the parable is ultimately about spiritual wisdom, the Holy Spirit is interiorly at work facilitating the understanding. When Peter recognizes Jesus as "the Messiah, the Son of the living God" (Matt 16:16), Jesus comments that "flesh and blood has not revealed this to you, but my Father in heaven" (Matt 16:17). When people "get" the parable, the interior Holy Spirit is revealing it to them. In the last analysis, this is how Jesus loves the listeners. He introduces them to the presence of God in the depths of their own being.

Sixteenth Sunday in Ordinary Time

Proper 11

Matthew 13:24-43 *LM* • **Matthew 13:24-30, 36-43** *RCL*

Progressing Humiliation by Humiliation

A Spiritual Commentary

[Jesus] put before them another parable: "The kingdom of heaven

The kingdom of heaven is always a combination of divine initiative and human freedom. Divine initiative is encountered in creation itself, the history of Israel, and supremely in the life, death, and resurrection of Jesus Christ. This initiative has many aspects, but one of its overriding qualities is relentlessness. It will not be put off, and so eventually it will succeed.

No matter how small the beginning or how threatened the middle, the end is never in doubt. Both in life after death and at the end of history, the kingdom *will* come and the will of God *will* be done. In Christian faith that is a given. It is called the Second Coming of Christ, and it brings to completion the work of the First Coming of Christ. It has also been called the Great Assurance.

However, human understanding and freedom are essential components of the kingdom of heaven, and they cannot be coerced. People embrace, resist, and reject the divine invitation. Therefore, there is a tendency to divide people into good and evil, those who hear the word and integrate it into their lives and those who turn a deaf ear and go on as usual. But neat divisions do not reflect the complexities of the interaction between God and people. The struggle to hear and embrace the invitation is internal to each person and each group.

The disciples are a case in point. At one moment they understand and at the next moment they are benighted. At one moment they follow Jesus closely, then suddenly they are following him at a distance, and finally, when they flee, they follow him not at all. As is well documented, humans not only do not go along with God, they go along for awhile and then they go off on their own. So tension develops between the Great Assurance and the Great Vacillation.

230

may be compared to someone who sowed good seed in his field; but while everybody was asleep, an enemy came and sowed weeds among the wheat, and then went away.

So when the plants came up and bore grain, then the weeds appeared as well. And the slaves of the householder came and said to him, 'Master, did you not sow good seed in your field? Where, then, did these weeds come from?'

He answered, 'An enemy has done this.'

The slaves said to him, 'Then do you want us to go and gather them?'

But he replied, 'No; for in gathering the weeds you would uproot the wheat along with them. Let both of them grow together until the harvest; and at harvest time I will tell the reapers, 'Collect the weeds first and bind them in bundles to be burned, but gather the wheat into my barn.'"

In Jesus' preaching and teaching, divine initiative sows the seeds of good wheat. However, Jesus is not the only one sowing in the field. When people are asleep, unresponsive to his revelation, an enemy sows the seeds of weeds. The story stresses that the preaching and the teaching of Jesus are not responsible for the weeds. He and his disciples sowed only good seed. Evil can never be attributed to divine initiative. But when divine initiative demands a response, an evil side of people may emerge.

The origin of the weeds is a nameless enemy who seizes opportunities when people are asleep and in the dark. "Enemy" signals someone with the opposite intention of the sower of the good seed. Theologically, it cannot insinuate a dual origin of creation by both good and evil forces. But it does emphasize a primordial condition. Although the wheat was sown first, the weeds join them immediately, and they are sown all through the wheat. The wheat seed and the weed seed do not lie side by side. From the beginning they are interwoven. The enemy, having done his work, leaves. The work of the householder, the true owner of the field who wants to bring the wheat to harvest, has just begun.

When growth begins and the seeds break soil and become visible, the wheat seed and the weed seed are revealed. They are growing together. They are so intertwined that to uproot one is to endanger and uproot the other. Therefore, for the present time, the householder, who knows how to take out from his storehouse the new person and the old person (see Matt 13:52), decides they will be allowed to grow together. It is often pointed out that this is dubious agricultural wisdom. The sooner the wheat and weeds are separated the better. But it is profound spiritual wisdom.

The kingdom of heaven in time and history will always be a struggle of responding to divine initiative and resisting it. Good and evil in individuals and in humanity as a whole will always coexist. The work of the kingdom of heaven on earth is unending repentance, as the preaching of Jesus and the preaching of John the Baptist have proclaimed. Repentance is not a prerequisite of the kingdom. Repentance is the kingdom of heaven as it moves into the soil of the earth. When the wheat and the weeds have ceased growing and have attained a fullness, then there will be a separation. But that time is not now.

In the meantime, how goes the struggle between divine invitation and human response?

The next Scripture quotation (continuing the NRSV translation) and its commentary are given for users of the *Lectionary for Mass:*

> He put before them another parable: "The kingdom of heaven is like a mustard seed that someone took and sowed in his field; it is the smallest of all the seeds, but when it has grown it is the greatest of shrubs and becomes a tree, so that the birds of the air come and make nests in its branches."
>
> He told them another parable: "The kingdom of heaven is like yeast that a woman took and mixed in with three measures of flour until all of it was leavened."
>
> Jesus told the crowds all these things in parables; without a parable he told them nothing. This was to fulfill what had been spoken through the prophet: "I will open my mouth to speak in parables; I will proclaim what has been hidden from the foundation of the world."

The struggle goes well. The same reality that sowed the wheat seed sows a mustard seed in a field and sows yeast into wheat flour. This reality is a catalytic agent for growth. It starts a process, and the law of relentless inevitability sets in. The mustard seed becomes a tree with room for everyone. The yeast raises the dead wheat flour to a life of bread for the feast.

The divine initiative will see the process through. With time and freedom, more and more people will respond and certain individual people will progress on their spiritual path. The Jews took unleavened bread out of Egypt because they did not have time to allow the leaven to work on the wheat flour (see Exod 12:33-34). Now there is time, and the leaven can work. Also, it takes time for the smallest of seeds to become the largest of bushes. And it takes time for all the birds of the air to find their way to its shade. But this can happen. There is hope for the kingdom of heaven to be planted on earth. This hope is grounded in the relentlessness of God who will not stop sowing seed and the unfolding of time in which human freedom can respond.

This process of growth has been going on from the beginning. In fact, it is how the world is established, maintained, and transformed. The foundational structure of creation is the adventure of divine initiative and human response. But it has worked in secret. Now the parable teller is revealing it to those who have ears to hear and eyes to see.

For users of the *Revised Common Lectionary* and the *Lectionary for Mass:*

> **Then he left the crowds and went into the house. And his disciples approached him, saying, "Explain to us the parable of the weeds of the field."**
>
> **He answered, "The one who sows the good seed is the Son of Man; the field is the world, and the good seed are the children of the kingdom; the weeds are the children of the evil one, and the enemy who sowed them is the devil; the harvest is the end of the age, and the reapers are angels.**
>
> **Just as the weeds are collected and burned up with fire, so will it be at the end of the age. The Son of Man will send his angels, and they will collect out of his kingdom all causes of sin and all evildoers, and they will throw them into the furnace of fire, where there will be weeping and gnashing of teeth. Then the righteous will shine like the sun in the kingdom of their Father.**
>
> **Let anyone with ears listen!"**

But make no mistake about it. God will not be mocked forever. Good will be rewarded and evil will be punished. The kingdom of heaven is growing in time, but time is not infinite. It is obviously not infinite for individuals, and neither is it infinite for humanity as a whole. Human freedom has consequences. Deeds repay the people who do them.

Teaching

The wife of a man who takes seriously the spiritual life and struggles to become spiritually mature remarked, "My husband went on a prolonged retreat and when he came back, he was loving, considerate, and compassionate. That is, until his mother came to visit." The indication is he "lost" it. Whatever the combination of inner awareness and outer behavior is, the presence of this man's mother was enough to seriously disturb that connection. The high of his retreat gave way to the low of old tapes that dragged him along unresolved childhood conflicts.

Of course, he is not alone.

People leave church on Sunday buoyed by the liturgy. They feel centered, and they are confident they can face the tests of the world with steady justice and compassion. The parking lot traffic is their first undoing. Leaning on the horn, they sing a hymn not in the worship book.

We all move from moments of realization and centeredness into scattered and fractured behavior. We think we are in charge, able to bring love into the situations of our life. Then we get our buttons pushed. In the Gospel of John, Peter says to Jesus, "I will lay down my life for you" (John 13:37). This is the love that Jesus says is the greatest: "No one has greater love than this, to lay down one's life for one's friends" (John 15:13). Peter can comprehend and feel that love and envision his fidelity to it.

However, Jesus does not have the same confidence in Peter that Peter has in himself: "Will you lay down your life for me? Very truly, I tell you, before the cock crows, you will have denied me three times" (John 13:38). Peter's inflated sense of his fidelity will not weather the difficulties of the upcoming events. The man who realizes in his head that he will lay down his life for Jesus will not be able to pull it off.

But "the cock crowing" is more than the moment of betrayal. It symbolizes the advent of morning, the moment of illumination. Peter will be chastened, but he will also understand and return to the following of Jesus (see Luke 22:31-32). A part of what he will understand is that we can dream more than we can enact. We can have experiences of intense realizations when we love God and our neighbor, but we can lose those realizations and fail to let them influence our behavior.

In the symbols of the Gospel, wheat and weed grow together. In fact, they are so intertwined that they make an inseparable unit. Wheat grows on the earth when we successfully embody our deeper realizations of love. Weeds grow on the earth when we fail to embody those realizations. We are a wheat-weed reality.

Also, it takes time for a small seed to become a major tree and for leaven to raise the dough into bread. Time is the opportunity for repentance, the chance to change our minds and try again. We are repeat offenders, and so we become "repeat repenters." This is not a situation that is remedied in this life. We may be confident that eventually the field will be all wheat and the dough will be bread and the tree will be the home of all. But that does not relieve us of the here-and-now struggle.

> The struggle is the goal
> the path is what we know
> all the rest is heaven.

When we fail, we feel humiliated, brought back to the truth that we have not progressed as far as we thought. But these humiliations are their own forms of progress. We learn that the movement from realization to integration, from the inner feeling of love to embodying love, is a never-ending process. We must not become discouraged. There is another way to see it. In a moment of truth we can acknowledge how we have been lost, and we can make amends. Out of our errors and frailty come some of our most profound lessons. In a heartfelt conversation, in a quiet moment when we take stock—even on our deathbed— freedom awaits. The "freedom that awaits" is to simply return to the spiritual project, carrying luminous inner spaces into the darkness of the next moment in which we live.

Seventeenth Sunday in Ordinary Time

Proper 12

Matthew 13:44-52 *LM* • **Matthew 13:31-33, 44-52** *RCL*

~~~~~~~~~~

Selling with Joy

A Spiritual Commentary

Users of the *Revised Common Lectionary:* see comments on Matthew 13:31-33 in the previous chapter.

[(Matt 13:31) **Jesus put before the crowds another parable:] "The kingdom of heaven is like treasure hidden in a field, which someone found and hid; then in his joy he goes and sells all that he has and buys that field.**

Our spiritual core is most valuable because it relates us to God and centers us correctly in the world. It is the one, true treasure. But it cannot be found on the surface of life, in the tangle of physical and social interactions. It is hidden, buried in the field of ourselves.

Therefore, it can go undiscovered. It can be as the Gospel of Thomas suggests: "the Father's kingdom is spread out upon the earth, and people don't see it" (GT 113).

Not finding this treasure is akin to Meister Eckhart's remark that each person has a vintage wine cellar, but they seldom drink from it.

So when we come upon this spiritual depth, this kingdom of heaven within us (see Luke 17:21; NRSV alternative trans.), it surprises us. We see it, and then we don't see it. Our mind flickers, finding it and hiding it simultaneously. But we see enough to experience how valuable it is and we desire more. Therefore, we are not reluctant to realign our energies, to sell everything in order to pursue what we have found. In fact, we do it joyously because of the actuality of what we have found and the promise of what will happen when we buy. Entry into the kingdom is a full process of finding, selling, and buying.

Again, the kingdom of heaven is like a merchant in search of fine pearls; on finding one pearl of great value, he went and sold all that he had and bought it.

236

We are merchants on the make, always searching, always looking to connect with the source of who we are. This is the pearl of great price, the life-giving relationship with God. When we find this relationship we undergo a process of purification, ridding ourselves of everything that would block the love of God from working in our lives. We are buying into God, hoping that God will buy more completely into us. The finding, selling, and buying of the treasure and the pearl symbolize the journey of spiritual consciousness.

> **Again, the kingdom of heaven is like a net that was thrown into the sea and caught fish of every kind; when it was full, they drew it ashore, sat down, and put the good into baskets but threw out the bad. So it will be at the end of the age. The angels will come out and separate the evil from the righteous and throw them into the furnace of fire, where there will be weeping and gnashing of teeth.**

Once again, finding is not enough. The full experience of the kingdom includes selling and buying. Just being caught by the net of Christ is a first step but not the last condition. Each fish will be examined on shore. People are expected to develop spiritually. This means greater understanding of Jesus' teachings and greater integration of those teachings into creative ethical behavior. People are judged by their use of the gifts they have been given. If they have found the treasure and the pearl and have been caught by Jesus the fisher of people (see Matt 4:19), they will be judged by how they have continued this initial moment of revelation. The contrast between good and bad, righteous and wicked highlights the seriousness of the spiritual project and the inevitability of evaluation.

> **Have you understood all this?"**

> **They answered, "Yes."**

This admission of understanding is truly the hook of Jesus, the fisher of people, for "If you know these things, you are blessed if you do them" (John 13:17). Understanding is the first step of integration, but integration is an ongoing process of further understanding, purification, and action. In the light of the whole Gospel, the disciples' "Yes" has to be qualified. They have just heard these parables and Jesus has not helped them interpret them, as he did with the sower, seed, and soil (Matt 13:3-9, 18-23). They may have an initial grasp, but at this stage they lack the thorough comprehension that leads to transformation. Their understanding needs to mature and become more complex. Jesus will now point out the path of this development.

And he said to them, "Therefore every scribe who has been trained for the kingdom of heaven is like the master of a household who brings out of his treasure what is new and what is old."

The student of the kingdom of heaven must become wise in putting together the new and the old. This is the way understanding increases and moves toward integration. In this interaction between the new and the old, pride of place is given to the new. The new experience of the kingdom, unraveled in the preceding parables, must be honored, understood, and pursued. What was found has to be bought. But in order to buy, there is a need to sell. This will mean evaluating what went before. Some of the old beliefs, choices, and behaviors will be allies of the new experience and assist greater understanding and action. Other past beliefs, choices, and behaviors will be detrimental, obstructing progress in the new way. It will take wisdom to know how to work the storeroom for both the new and the old.

Teaching

Cultural commentators point out that Americans are spiritually hungry. This may mean many things, but it often includes a quest for spiritual experience. People want a firsthand experience of soul and God. They dream of walking in the woods, or strolling along the ocean shore, or holding the hand of someone they love, or passionately pursuing a course of justice—and suddenly there will be a breakthrough. They will realize the presence of God underlying all things and be completely identified with this unitive consciousness. Their doubts will give way, and they will live with the assurance of ultimate meaning.

This spiritual awakening will have immediate benefits for personal and professional life. They will become more wise and loving in their intimate relationships, and they will become more excellent in their work. In all the externals, life will go on as it did before their spiritual awakening. Only now there will be a heightened consciousness that will add passion, pleasure, and purpose to who they are and what they do. This is the daydream of many people who are spiritually interested.

However, this cultural understanding of spiritual experience does not take into account the disruptive character of spiritual experience and the reevaluation it encourages. Spiritual experiences have after-maths. Initially, they may introduce people in a firsthand way into the spiritual realm. But what is realized during spiritual experience can be both exhilarating and discomforting. We may find a treasure and a pearl and exclaim enthusiastically, "Yes!" But it will soon dawn on us that if we want to buy the treasure and the pearl, we may have to sell all the trinkets we have ardently collected. Or we may only have to sell some of the trinkets. In another metaphor, we may have to leave a lot of "stuff" we previously trotted out in the storehouse and dust off "stuff" we had forgotten was in there. If spiritual experience is taken seriously, the finding unfolds into a selling, and the selling means reevaluating this new realization in the light of old commitments. The price of the treasure and the pearl may be all we have.

Put less metaphorically, spiritual experience initiates transition. What previously we valued and pursued may not be as attractive as it once was. We may reconsider well-paid work in the light of meaning-ful work. The people we once sought out as companions may no longer appear to be soulmates. On the other hand, people we once thought were "out of it" may seem to be "with it" in a way we never suspected. In other words, spiritual experience is dangerous and dis-ruptive, as the lives of mystics and prophets attest.

Although the parables stress three moments in the process of spirit-ual development, it is the middle activity of letting go that is crucial. As we let go of habits of mind and behaviors that have preoccupied us, we discover more space and freedom to pursue the new find. At first, the cost of letting go seems enormous. We realize we have given over our identity and security to so many ideas, people, and activities that are no longer serving us. When we take back our identity and reassess our security, we feel dispossessed. Psychologically and socially, we have brought about our own undoing. The emptiness is both frighten-ing and fascinating.

My father had an expression, "He [or she] has sold the farm." It prob-ably came from his Irish parents with their farming background. He used it in situations where persons had taken a great risk and were re-arranging their lives. It might have been a change in occupations or re-lationships or geography. Another expression my father used with the same intent was, "She [or he] has rolled the dice." It meant that some-one had taken a chance. A person's very self had been put on the line. That person had risked the unknown. With this background it should not have come as a surprise that my sister during the grace before meals on Thanksgiving Day gave thanks to God and immediately followed it with a word of praise for all people who reinvent themselves.

I believe this is what the kingdom of heaven entails. It is an ongoing process of putting together the new and old, of finding, selling, buying our lives, of reinventing ourselves in the light of the ongoing revelation of God. The cost may be considerable, but it is cheap at any price.

Eighteenth Sunday in Ordinary Time

Proper 13

Matthew 14:13-21

Maximizing Assets

A Spiritual Commentary

Now when Jesus heard this, he withdrew from there in a boat to a deserted place by himself.

Herod has killed John. Now he is panicked by superstition and thinks Jesus is John come back from the dead. Jesus is in danger. He withdraws into the desert, a place useless to the political and religious elite but a place where scarce human resources open people to the possibilities of divine abundance.

But when the crowds heard it, they followed him on foot from the towns. When he went ashore, he saw a great crowd; and he had compassion for them and cured their sick.

Jesus may be rejected by some, but he is pursued by many. He may have wanted solitude, but he is met by a crowd. However, his response is not to get back into the boat and escape. Rather his heart goes out to them. They do not have to come all the way to him and beg a reluctant and harried man. As they move toward him, he moves toward them. It is the meeting of misery and mercy that goes by the name of compassion.

And the compassion unfolds into healing. The healing entails physical cure, but goes beyond that. It calms anxious minds and restores relationships. But it also goes beyond the psychological and social. It symbolizes God's presence and care. They came out of their towns, the narrow boundaries of their separate identities, to follow the sailor on foot. They wanted what he knew how to do: they wanted to be bound to one another and to God. Jesus does not disappoint.

When it was evening, the disciples came to him and said, "This is a deserted place, and the hour is now late; send the crowds away so that they may go into the villages and buy food for themselves."

It is evening, and the need that arises every evening arises—the need for food at the end of the day. The disciples have a way of meeting that need. They note that they are in the desert where food supplies are not available. So the people will have to go elsewhere to be fed, namely to the village markets. But it is already late and the markets might be closing. So Jesus should abruptly dismiss them so they can go away from him and buy food.

This seems a sane proposal. It recognizes scarcity and thinks that the remedying resources are not with them in the desert. So they must go someplace else and buy it from others. Going and buying is the solution for their situation.

> **Jesus said to them, "They need not go away; you give them something to eat."**
>
> **They replied, "We have nothing here but five loaves and two fish."**

Jesus has another solution: instead of the crowds going and buying for themselves, the disciples should supply food. However, their understanding is that they do not have enough. What they focus on is their lack of resources. They have "five loaves and two fish," perhaps enough for themselves but not enough for all. But five plus two equals seven, a sacred number symbolizing that what they have is a gift from God. There are two choices: look at the food as God's gift or look at it as not enough. How you see it will determine what is possible.

> **And he said, "Bring them here to me." Then he ordered the crowds to sit down on the grass. Taking the five loaves and the two fish, he looked up to heaven, and blessed and broke the loaves, and gave them to the disciples, and the disciples gave them to the crowds.**

Jesus sees whatever they have as God's gift. When this spiritual consciousness emerges, the desert becomes a garden. People sit down on green grass. Jesus takes the available food and recognizes it as God's gift by looking to heaven, the mythological abode of God, and he praises and thanks God. Gratitude for what is given fills Jesus completely, fills him to overflowing. With this abundance of Spirit he breaks the too few loaves and gives them to the disciples. He has freely received and now he freely gives. The disciples have learned from their teacher. What they have received, they give to the crowds.

And all ate and were filled; and they took up what was left over of the broken pieces, twelve baskets full. And those who ate were about five thousand men, besides women and children.

Satisfaction ensues. The physical satiety symbolizes the spiritual fullness: "Blessed are those who hunger and thirst for righteousness, for they will be filled" (Matt 5:6). Two sets of numbers bring home this revelation of spiritual abundance for hungry people. The sacred number of twelve baskets of fragments left over reinforces the truth that there is no scarcity in the Spirit. Spiritual reality does not work in the same way as physical reality.

But just how many people were there? How many is a vast crowd? The storyteller saves the actual number of people until the end and then drives home the point with understatement. There were "five thousand men." Pause. "Not counting women and children." Mathematical numbers are daunting for physical scarcity but not for spiritual abundance.

Teaching

As the faculty of an educational institution, we were working in accord with standard organizational wisdom. Through surveys and interviews, we had done a needs analysis of a prospective student population. We figured out what they wanted.

Then we designed a program to meet those needs. It was an impressive projection, meeting the requirements of accrediting agencies and embodying sound pedagogical principles.

Then a few of the designers paused and puzzled, "Who is going to run this program?" We had created a program that was needed, but we did not have the personnel to pull it off. We looked around the table at ourselves. That was all we had, and it was not enough.

Someone suggested we hire new faculty. We should "go and buy" some good people. But that would require money we didn't have. The program, as they say, never came to fruition.

As I look back at that experience, I see that we began with needs and then discovered that we could not meet them. In fact, the more we explored the needs and what type of programming was required, the more helpless we began to feel.

This way of thinking that leads to inaction is analogous to how the disciples construe the situation in this Gospel episode. Beginning with need is beginning with what we lack. People have needs that cannot be met in the present situation with the present resources. So they have to "go and buy" what they need from some outside resource before it is too late. When we work this way, we are conscious of what we do not have and what other people do have. In the Gospel story, the disciples think the crowds do not have food and the markets in the village do have food. The strategy is to get the crowds to the markets—before they close.

Jesus, the teacher of the kingdom of heaven, redirects the attention of the disciples to what they have. He tells them the crowds do not have to go away. They should feed the people. However, in their minds they do not have enough. They are locked into the enormity of need and paucity of resource. They have "five loaves and two fish." But they characterize it as, "We have nothing here but . . . " meaning it is not enough.

But for Jesus a crucial shift has gone on. They have moved from the preoccupation with lack to the awareness of assets. They now know what they have. They are no longer looking outside themselves for an answer. They have turned their gaze within. This is the first step in learning about spiritual resources. Going and buying may work in the physical world, but what works in the spiritual world is standing still and becoming aware. Knowing what you have is the first step of spiritual transformation.

Jesus asks that they bring him what they have. Then he performs the second step in the process of spiritual transformation. He gives thanks for what they have. This is an enormous step. They move from seeing it as too little and cursing it to seeing it as a gift and becoming grateful. The third step is to give away the gift to people (the disciples) who in turn give it away to others.

No one takes and holds; everyone receives and gives. The result is participation in divine abundance, an experience that is completely satisfying for it is the fulfillment of the created potential of people. This is a process of wholeness and completion, an experience that begins with the sacredness of seven and ends with the sacredness of twelve. This process will bring to satisfaction as many individual people as are present.

What is this story trying to tell us?

The way to proceed is to be leery of the mind's tendency to focus on lack and to continuously think going and buying from others is the solution. We should know what we have, give thanks for it as God's gift, and give it to others who in turn will give it to others. This process of self-knowledge, gratitude, and communal love produces not only satisfaction but abundance.

But does it?

I don't know. The bean counter in me wants a physical miracle and not a spiritual lesson. I want God in Jesus to make abundant food whenever people are hungry. But there are problems with physically multiplying loaves and fishes. A man once told me he was no longer a Christian because if Jesus could produce food for hungry people and only did it once, he did not want anything to do with him. He should have done it many times and left the recipe for his followers.

But I wonder: when people of faith find themselves in the desert, as many today do, how should they proceed? I wonder what would have happened at the educational planning meeting if we had looked around the table and asked what we had rather than what we did not have. I wonder what would have happened if we became grateful to God for having what our practical minds construed as too little. And I wonder what would have happened if we ceased to look at prospective students as consumers of educational goods but as the first receivers of what they would learn to give away. I wonder what would have happened if we had let the spiritual "in" on our physical and social plans.

Nineteenth Sunday in Ordinary Time

Proper 14

Matthew 14:22-33

⸺✦⸺

Sinking with Courage

A Spiritual Commentary

[Jesus] made the disciples get into the boat and go on ahead to the other side, while he dismissed the crowds. And after he had dismissed the crowds, he went up the mountain by himself to pray. When evening came, he was there alone, but by this time the boat, battered by the waves, was far from the land, for the wind was against them.

This description sets the scene for what is to follow. Jesus physically separates himself from both the crowds and the disciples. The disciples suggested that Jesus dismiss the crowds so they could feed themselves. But Jesus dismisses the crowds only *after he* has fed them. He also forces the disciples into a boat. He may be pushing them off into missionary activity, but he is staying behind. He will be distant from his followers.

Then Jesus ascends the mountain, a symbol of closeness to God, and opens himself in prayer. Although the mountain top may be close to God, geographically it is the point farthest away from the lake where the disciples are struggling. The disciples in the boat of "the church" are experiencing tumult, resistance, and danger. The cosmic images of wind and waves symbolize the social forces that are both resisting the teachings of Jesus and openly persecuting the disciples. They are in trouble, and Jesus is not physically with them.

But he is at prayer, and through prayer he is in the presence of God, and through the presence of God he is able to be with his disciples. This situation parallels the conditions of the early Church. After the death and resurrection of Jesus, he was not with them physically but, through the power of God, he was present to them spiritually. This spiritual presence of the risen Christ was especially important in times of crisis. The boat of the Church, tossed by waves and resisted by winds, is in crisis. What follows is a training lesson for the disciples in faith and fearlessness.

246

And early in the morning he came walking toward them on the sea. But when the disciples saw him walking on the sea, they were terrified, saying, "It is a ghost!" And they cried out in fear.

Unbidden, Jesus comes. His spiritual presence is described in symbols that express and communicate his intimate relationship with God. Jesus comes to his disciples walking upon the sea, a prerogative reserved for God who made the seas. Therefore, the tumult of the seas does not have power over him. He strides over the waves rather than sinks beneath them. Also, the winds that are against the disciples in the boat of the Church do not appear to hinder Jesus. All this happens between 3:00 A.M. and 6:00 A.M., the time when God rescued Israel by dividing and then closing the waters of the Red Sea. It is the resurrected Jesus coming to the aid of his disciples through the power of God.

However, the disciples mistake "Jesus coming to the rescue" for a ghost who has come to threaten them. The fact they see Jesus but apprehend a ghost conveys the difficulty in discerning the resurrected presence of Jesus. Obviously, the usual way of identifying Jesus by physical description is not available. His presence is disembodied, and so their minds respond to what they see with a "knee jerk" reaction, and they categorize him as a "ghost." Ghosts are considered the shades of the once living who linger on the earth and whose appearance terrifies people. In particular, ghosts have haunted the seas and allegedly been seen in late night mists. However, resurrection is a different reality. It is not the appearance of the surviving weakened remnants of earthly life.

But immediately Jesus spoke to them and said, "Take heart, it is I; do not be afraid."

Jesus immediately corrects their mistake and instructs their fear. It is not a ghost they are encountering and so their fear is misplaced. Jesus identifies himself as "I am" (a literal translation of the Greek), the name of God. This "I am" is translated "it is I." So it functions to ground Jesus in the reality of God and to assure the disciples it is not a specter. They are dealing with the real Jesus, albeit Jesus in a new form. This full and real presence of Jesus is functionally equivalent to God's presence. Therefore, courage should replace fear, for the presence of God is greater than all the forces that threaten the life of the disciples.

Peter answered him, "Lord, if it is you, command me to come to you on the water."

He said, "Come."

Peter hears both the correction and the command. He takes courage and acknowledges Jesus as Lord, one in intimate relationship with God. But he requests further confirmation. If it is not a ghost, if it is the empowering presence of God in Jesus, then Jesus will do what Jesus always does. He will communicate his abilities to his disciples. He will show them how to deal with fear the way he deals with fear. But Peter cannot presume this ability or arrogantly try to appropriate it. It has to be done according to the way of Jesus.

Jesus must issue a command and Peter must obey it. In obeying it, Peter will enter into the mystery of the reality and ability of Jesus. He will make the power of Jesus his own, but he will never replace the power of Jesus with his own power. The master-disciple relationship remains forever, even as the disciple grows in the powers of the master.

Therefore, Peter does not ask to walk on the water. Rather he requests that Jesus command him to come to him on the water. It is always a journey ever deeper into Christ, a journey that entails the overcoming of fear. This is the proper positioning of "the courage not to be afraid." Therefore, Jesus grants Peter's request and responds with one unvarnished word of command, "Come."

> So Peter got out of the boat, started walking on the water, and came toward Jesus.
>
> But when he noticed the strong wind, he became frightened, and beginning to sink, he cried out, "Lord, save me!"
>
> Jesus immediately reached out his hand and caught him, saying to him, "You of little faith, why did you doubt?"

Peter courageously obeys the command of Jesus, and initially, with his eyes on Jesus, he is a fearless walker of the waves. But then his consciousness shifts from Jesus to the strong winds. As the strength of the resisting winds fills his mind, it also captures his emotions and he becomes frightened. The growing fear threatens to engulf him. So he cries out to the Lord. Immediately, the Lord stretches out his hand, as YHWH often does, to save him.

Jesus' comment and question to Peter, "You of little faith, why did you doubt?" help Peter understand why he sank and, therefore, they show him the path of advance. Peter has faith. He has discerned the spiritual presence of Jesus and taken courage to enter into it, to try to live out of it. But he has not yet learned the path of perseverance. In the language of the sower, seed, and soil parable, he is still the enthusiastic receiver of the seed of the word who has not yet developed roots (see Matt 13:4, 21). His doubting came when he allowed what threatened him to capture his mind and heart more completely than what calmed him. His inner focus on the reality of Jesus was replaced by an outer preoccupation with the wind. As the saying goes, whatever you identify with dominates you. So he sank.

The actual sinking shows his faith to be still immature and, in that sense, "little." But *knowing why* he sank is a step toward greater faith, a greater ability to learn from Jesus the way of fearlessness. As always, when Peter's failure is understood, it is a path of progress.

When they got into the boat, the wind ceased. And those in the boat worshiped him, saying, "Truly you are the Son of God."

Once Jesus joins his disciples in the boat of the Church, the forces of resistance do not have their previous powers. The winds die, not the disciples. The disciples realize that Jesus mediates God's ultimate power, and they are safe as long as he is with them. At the end of the Gospel, he will promise to be with them until the end of time. Their faith in what Jesus can do is strong and they recognize the source of his power: "Truly, you are the Son of God."

However, in the light of the whole episode, this faith in Jesus must translate into participating in his powers. The point is not to rely on Jesus but to learn and develop the spiritual powers he offers. Faith cannot be content with worship and homage, no matter how important that is. It must push on into understanding and action. Peter may be back in the safety of the boat with his Savior, but he awaits another chance at the resistant winds.

Teaching

Pastors often complain that for many people God is a fallback belief.

When people are imperiled, they pray. When they get sick, or they lose their jobs, or their relationships are in trouble, or their life is threatened by forces outside their control, they cry out to God. If they get well, or they find work, or their relationships are reconciled, or the forces that threatened them subside, then God has reached the divine hand toward them and lifted them out of the raging seas. They are thankful. Then they go their way until the next crisis.

But sometimes the crisis is chronic. People are forced to face their limits and mortality, to stare into and eventually to walk into death. In this case, there is still a place for God in their reckoning. They are invited to consider a spiritual stability in the midst of physical, psychological, and social storms.

So fallback belief has two positions. The first is renewed safety in this world after a dangerous episode. The second is personal safety even though life in this world is perishing. This common way of believing perceives God as a safety net, and it is true as far as it goes.

The last scene of this Gospel episode seems to embody the first position of fallback belief. When Jesus, the "I am" of God, joins the disciples in the boat, the danger withdraws. The all-consuming fear turns to relief, and the recognition of the power that brought this safety is immediate and glorious: "Truly you are the Son of God"! Life was threatened; then the threat was removed. Who among us does not know the sweep of relief and the gratitude when we have been given a second chance?

However, in the Gospels the ultimate safety of the follower of Christ is not a fallback belief. Rather it is a launching pad for pushing into what endangers life. Cowering in the boat and then rejoicing in Christ the Savior is only part of the story. The real adventure is Peter who does not want to rely on Christ the Savior. He wants to learn his master's courage and ability. Peter will welcome Christ into the boat, but he really wants to lean into the wind. His failure is not because he desired the wrong thing but that he was reaching for a higher level of consciousness and action in his life. Peter does not walk on the water then sink because he is impetuous and does not know his place. He walks on the water and then sinks because he is learning the path of confronting what threatens life while working with his own fear.

Therefore, Jesus, the "I am" of God, is a savior for Peter in a different way than he is for those completely paralyzed by fear. In another place in Matthew's Gospel, Jesus says, "Not everyone who says to me, 'Lord, Lord,' will enter the kingdom of heaven" (Matt 7:21). But it seems that if you are in the kingdom of heaven, struggling to learn how to encounter and calm the terrible, and you cry, "Lord, save me," divine support is available. The one who says, "Come!" does not abandon those who respond.

But the reward for Peter's courage is not only Jesus' outstretched hand. It is the question the master asks, "You of little faith, why did you doubt?" This is the adventure in faith, trying to stay so focused on

God's enabling presence that the resistant winds do not defeat us. The way the wind works is to create fear. Fear captures the mind and pulls it out of God's presence. This shift in the mind's attention is what it means to doubt.

However, it may be in the nature of a grand task to doubt. Whenever we align ourselves with the divinely guided evolutionary course the world is on, we may become afraid and lose focus. We are not making a chair or concocting a soup. We are struggling for peace-seeking leaders, for more educational opportunities and academic excellence, for more comprehensive and respectful health care, for less crime, for just business practices, for humane organizational life, for less hypocritical religion, etc. In St. Matthew's language, we are trying to bring heaven to earth (see Matt 6:10).

In this process we become afraid. This fear may be for our physical lives. But it may also be the fear of failure, of having dreamed too large. We notice the winds are stronger than we thought. Violence, ignorance, greed, injustice, and inhumanity will overcome the better efforts of ourselves and other people. We doubt that things are better, that what we have done has mattered. Our efforts to calm the waves have been ineffectual. Our minds are taking us down a despairing path. Before the outstretched hand of Christ reaches us, let the thought console us that there is no finer way to sink.

Twentieth Sunday in Ordinary Time

Proper 15

Matthew 15:21-28

(The *Revised Common Lectionary* offers the possibility of including
Matthew 15:10-20, not considered here.)

Doing What It Takes

A Spiritual Commentary

**Jesus left that place and went away to the district of Tyre and
Sidon. Just then [behold] a Canaanite woman from that region
came out and started shouting, "Have mercy on me, Lord, Son
of David; my daughter is tormented by a demon."**

Jesus is in Gentile territory and a Gentile woman seeks him out. The
woman is portrayed as assertive, coming forward to Jesus. She ignores
any cultural taboos about Gentile women talking to Jewish males. She
is also noisy, crying out as she is coming forward. We are told to "behold" her for she will be the catalyst of the revelation the story wants
to communicate.

She may be both assertive and noisy, but she is also insightful. She
knows who Jesus is. She calls him "Lord, Son of David," a comprehensive set of titles. Jesus is Lord, intimately connected to God, and therefore meant for all people. But he is also Son of David, coming from a
definite people with a particular heritage and distinctive traditions.
Jesus is universal yet particular. She acknowledges this dual lineage.

The one who knows who Jesus is also knows what he has to give.
She asks for mercy. This is what the combination of divine and human,
of Lord and Son of David, is supposed to mediate. When the human is
properly related to the divine, the divine—whose core is mercy—flows
through the human. Since Jesus is the divine-human relationship in its
most heightened form, she is only asking for the truth of him to come
forth.

The reason for this assertive, noisy, and bold begging for mercy is
that her daughter is in agony with a demon. However, she is in such
solidarity with her daughter that if Jesus has mercy on her, it will flow
through her to her daughter. She does not want something for herself.

What will be given to her will immediately be given to her daughter. She gives as she receives and she is a conduit to her child. Overall, this is Jesus' type of woman.

But he did not answer her at all.

So why does he not talk to her? This woman knows both his identity and mission. She is only asking the Messiah to fulfill his calling and expel the demon who torments God's good creation. But Jesus refuses to recognize both her presence and request.

And his disciples came and urged him, saying, "Send her away, for she keeps shouting after us."

He answered, "I was sent only to the lost sheep of the house of Israel."

The disciples, the storyteller's foil, are on hand to suggest a reason why Jesus is silent. They think the woman is the problem. More specifically, the fact that she is making a scene is what is bothering Jesus. It is the eternal dilemma: crying women and embarrassed men. So, being experienced sycophants, they suggest to Jesus what they think he is thinking. In this way they hope they will ingratiate themselves and win favor.

However, they are wrong. The problem is not with the woman. Jesus' lack of response has nothing to do with her pleading and crying. The problem lies elsewhere. It lies in Jesus' mind. He has construed his identity and mission within the boundaries of Israel and this is a Canaanite woman from the regions of Tyre and Sidon. He belongs to Israel and the gathering in of the strayed members of that house. This woman is outside that house, and so she is of no concern to the savior of the Jews.

But she came and knelt before him, saying, "Lord, help me."

She is reminiscent of other Gentiles in Matthew's Gospel who knew who Christ was and did him homage: the Magi (Matt 2:1-12). But most importantly, she is not put off. Even Jesus' declaration of his exclusive Jewish identity and mission did not keep her from coming forward. When she addresses him, it is with a simple and unvarnished need. There is no flattery, no bargaining, and no argumentation. There is only vulnerability: "Lord, help me."

In this plea there is a very important omission. When she addressed Jesus the first time, she called him, "Lord, Son of David." These titles acknowledged both his particular origins as a Jew and his universal outreach as Lord. Now she knows that he is stressing his Jewishness at the expense of his wider humanity. He is coming down on his particularity and slighting his universality. The result is that she is outside him and her pleas go unheard. In this situation she is certainly not going to remind him that he is a Jew. So she drops the title "Son of David," leaving only "Lord" to linger in his ears. Women with sick children are remarkably resourceful.

> **He answered, "It is not fair to take the children's food and throw it to the dogs."**

> **She said, "Yes, Lord, yet even the dogs eat the crumbs that fall from their masters' table."**

This is a quick and remarkable bit of word play on the part of Jesus and the woman. Its dense symbolism is the key to the unblocking of the Son of David and the emergence of the Lord. I once read a scholarly article that reconstructed the roles of animals and, in particular, dogs in the time of Jesus.

Dogs were not allowed in a Jewish house. In order to feed dogs with the "bread of the children," a Jew would have to take the bread off the table, walk to the door, open it, and throw it outside. The dogs were always outside the house. But in Gentile houses the dogs were allowed inside. If they wanted to feed the dogs with the "bread of the children," Gentiles did not have to go outside the house. All they had to do was reach down with the leftovers. The dogs were avidly waiting.

Jesus told the woman that in order to feed her he had to take the bread that was inside the house and throw it outside the house. She was an outsider and what he has belongs to the insiders. She says, "Yes, Lord." She agrees that the food belongs to the children or, in more theological language, "salvation is from the Jews" (John 4:22). But she continues her emphasis on Jesus' universal outreach by calling him "Lord," the one meant for everyone. When Jesus lives within that identity, she is not outside the house. She is inside his house. She may not be a child at the table, but she is one who is eager for any food that Jesus has to offer. "I am already in the house, Lord," she effectively says, "just notice me."

> **Then Jesus answered her, "Woman, great is your faith! Let it be done for you as you wish."**

The title "woman" that Jesus uses is not simply a description of her gender. And it is certainly a far cry from dog. I suspect that it means the one who gives life. And the one she gave life to is the one who calls her woman. The NAB reads, "O woman, great is your faith" (Matt 15:28), and I take the "O" to suggest a shock of recognition, a sudden revelation. The pestering one becomes the bearer of a deeper truth. This is her great faith. Through persistence and cleverness she reminded Jesus of his true identity. He is a Jew. But, more importantly, he is Lord.

As a consequence of this powerful exercise of faith on her part, Jesus says something quite remarkable to her. Jesus is not usually swayed by the wishes of other people, either Pharisees, disciples, or individual seekers. He is driven only by the will of his Father; that is his food and drink (see John 4:34). He says and does only what he hears from his Father.

Therefore, it is remarkable to hear him say he will do the will of this woman. Could it be that in this woman's words he hears the voice of his Father? His Father's voice may come from the sky (see Matt 3:17, e.g.), but it also speaks from the earth, through the people who search for mercy in a demon-ridden world. Whenever and wherever Jesus hears his Father's voice, he is alert, ready, in touch, flowing. And that is what happened.

And her daughter was healed instantly.

Once the block is removed, mercy flows freely. The flow of mercy was momentarily dammed by too narrow an identification. Once identity expands, mercy flows, immediately and with full effect.

Teaching

I once did a workshop on theological reflection at Mill Hill outside London. At one point the group decided to work with this story from St. Matthew. The discussion was wide ranging. People shared many ideas about how to interpret this story and how to apply it to contemporary situations, especially to issues about women in the Church.

There was a quiet, older woman who did not participate very much. But she was very attentive and seemed avidly interested. Finally, after everyone else had their say, she quietly contributed, "It's her daughter. She wants her daughter better, and she'll do what it takes."

It rang true.

The character of the Canaanite woman changes throughout the story. She is noisy and assertive, then pleading and compliant, then clever and confrontative. Her consistency does not lie in her attitudes and behaviors. She is unified by her mission. She has a demon-afflicted child, and if this Jewish Messiah can help, he is going to. Little things—such as ethnic diversity and hatred—will not stand in the way.

Jesus characterizes this woman as having great faith. We often think of faith as belief in God. "Great" faith is often construed as believing in God even in situations of suffering. In suffering situations there is the temptation to feel we have been abandoned by God. Great faith asserts God is present even when obvious signs of that presence are missing. Holy people always acknowledge and pray to God.

However, this is not the great faith of the Canaanite woman. Her faith is that she is a tiger. There is a situation that needs healing, and she is the single-minded servant of that possibility. If she has to twist the arm of a Jewish Messiah and remind him that although there may be many ethnic groups and religions there is only one God, then so be it.

I once saw a contemporary mother tell her son about her commitment to ridding him of the particular demon that had taken up residence in his attitudes. "I want you to know I am never going to stop. You think you can sulk and avoid me, and I will go away. I am never going away. I want you to know that. And you can never run far enough to get away from me. This stuff is going to change." If you heard her voice, the tone and timbre, you would know that you had encountered an absolute, an unshakeable presence in a world of swaying reeds.

However, faith is not only a relentless commitment to the betterment of people and situations. It is also the creative ability to find a way to that betterment. The thing about creativity is that it does not have a preset agenda. It has an ultimate mission, but it does not have a canonized strategy. Creativity does not know what it is up against. It does know that there will be resistance, but it does not know the exact nature of that resistance. So it is ready, alert, poised, marshaled for whatever it takes. Does it take argument? Then there will be argument. Does it take obeisance? Then there will be obeisance. Does it take confrontation? Then there will be confrontation. Of course, there are limits. The end does not justify the means. But the point is: the full range of human creativity is exercised in pursuit of healing.

When we understand great faith as the persistent creativity to bring about the good, the ranks of the saints swell with a different crowd of people. There is a research doctor with his eyeball glued to the microscope, a community organizer in the back of the hall urging voices not used to talking, a teacher finding a way into a closed mind, a banker figuring out how to get a loan to a woman on the edge of qualification, a salesperson dedicated to the customer, etc. In fact, great faith belongs to all of us when we remind each other of the deeper truth of who we are, and compassion flows from us into situations where it is deeply needed.

Twenty-First Sunday in Ordinary Time

Proper 16

Matthew 16:13-20

~~~

Getting It Right

A Spiritual Commentary

Now when Jesus came into the district of Caesarea Philippi, he asked his disciples, "Who do people say that the Son of Man is?"

And they said, "Some say John the Baptist, but others Elijah, and still others Jeremiah or one of the prophets."

Jesus calls himself the "Son of the Human" (my translation). This is more than a self-designation. He is referring to the human possibility that is emerging through him. Through him, the Son of the Human, human beings are called to a new identity and mission. Jesus asks how people are reading this emerging human possibility. He is proclaiming it and offering it, but how are people understanding and receiving it? He asks this question of his disciples in the region of Caesarea Philippi, a place where the human paradigm proposed by Rome is enshrined.

His disciples give him their impression of what "people" are saying. Some think Jesus is a revival of past prophetic activity. He is continuing the work of different dead prophets, and so these prophets are living again through him. There is some justification for this interpretation, for Jesus speaks and acts like a prophet. However, it is not deep enough. It is a social discernment that emphasizes judgment and change, but it does not explicitly take into account the possibilities of a new spiritual identity.

He said to them, "But who do you say that I am?"

Simon Peter answered, "You are the Messiah, the Son of the living God."

Jesus' second question contrasts this prophetic understanding of what *people* are saying with what his *disciples* are saying. Peter, in a moment of lightning insight but not complete comprehension, speaks for the disciples. The human possibility that is emerging in Jesus is to become God's representative on earth (the Christ), living out of the reality of God at every moment (son and daughter of the living God). This identity of the human is not about the revival of a dead past, even a grand prophetic tradition. It is about conscious participation in the divine life and the way that participation expresses itself in human living. This is what is coming to birth in the "Son of Man."

> **And Jesus answered him, "Blessed are you, Simon son of Jonah! For flesh and blood has not revealed this to you, but my Father in heaven. And I tell you, you are Peter, and on this rock I will build my church, and the gates of Hades will not prevail against it. I will give you the keys of the kingdom of heaven, and whatever you bind on earth will be bound in heaven, and whatever you loose on earth will be loosed in heaven."**

Peter got it right, and this correct perception constitutes his blessedness. However, Jesus takes this confession of Peter and develops it in startling ways. The impression is that Peter has said more than he knows, and Jesus is instructing him in the implications of what he has said. In doing so, Jesus shifts the focus from himself to Peter. Peter has seen and acknowledged the identity and mission of Jesus, and now Jesus is unfolding the identity and mission of Peter. The two are intimately linked together.

From Jesus' point of view, Peter's capacity to recognize the ultimate truth of who Jesus is and what he is offering is rooted in the truth about himself. He is a human being *(Simon bar Jonah)*. This is the earthly dimension, the level of flesh and blood. However, this level has not given him the eyes to see the spiritual truth of Jesus. Rather it is his own connection and openness to the heavenly Father that has allowed him to receive the revelation of Jesus' special relationship to the Father. Therefore, the consciousness of the confessing Peter has penetrated through to the spiritual dimension. In symbolic code, he is "in heaven." The heavenly Father of Jesus who dwells within Peter has allowed Peter to acknowledge the heavenly identity and mission of Jesus.

This "heaven consciousness" is the rock that survives storm: "Everyone then who hears these words of mine and acts on them will be like a wise man who built his house on rock. The rain fell, the floods came, and the winds blew and beat on that house, but it did not fall, because it had been founded on rock" (Matt 7:24-25). The rock comes about when hearing the words of Jesus moves through understanding to action. The words of Jesus are the Word of God. When they are understood and enacted, they become an unassailable foundation. This is bringing heaven to earth, forming the rock upon which Jesus can build his Church.

This is how Jesus understands what Peter has just uttered. When the inner revelation of the heavenly Father burst forth in earthly recognition of Jesus, heaven and earth came together. Peter heard the interior word of God and spoke it on the earth. Immediately a rock was formed, and Jesus, who always knows when and where God is at work, named it. It is this process of aligning heaven and earth that will be the foundation of the people who gather together to confess Jesus and, in doing so, receive the new human identity he is proposing. He will call these people his Church.

This rock that is formed by aligning heaven and earth through confessing the God-grounded identity and mission of Jesus is the ultimate and lasting truth. Even when the gates of the netherworld are opened and all its negative fury is unleashed, it cannot prevail against the Church built on this rock. The gates of the netherworld are powerless because Peter and the disciples have the key to another set of gates. They have the key to the gates of the kingdom of heaven. In other words, they can open heaven so its power and energy flow into earth. They have learned how to pray: "Our Father in heaven, hallowed be your name. Your kingdom come. Your will be done, *on earth as it is in heaven*" (Matt 6:9-10). This ability to keep the gates between heaven and earth open is what will make the forces that flow through the gates of the netherworld ineffective.

As later Christian legend and lore will elaborate, Peter is the gatekeeper. However, his role is not the afterlife security officer who hears and judges our pleas for entrance. Rather the gates for which he has the keys are the gates of human consciousness, how we can open to the influences of heaven and incarnate them on earth. This is the supreme act of the new humanity that is being revealed in Jesus. It is an act of consciousness and freedom. Whatever the followers of Jesus tie themselves to on earth, they bind themselves to it with the spiritual force of the heavenly reality they are in touch with. Whatever the followers of Jesus loose themselves from on earth, they free themselves from it with the spiritual force of the heavenly reality they are in touch with. In other words, they are free to engage and disengage, to engage in situations that make for life and to disengage from situations that contribute to death. This is the freedom of the new human paradigm that is emerging in the "Son of Man."

Then he sternly ordered the disciples not to tell anyone that he was the Messiah.

Jesus told Peter and the disciples a complex and difficult teaching. They do not have the capacity to fully grasp it. So Jesus tells them not to tell anyone that they have recognized him as the Messiah (or Christ). False ideas about the Christ abound, and people might wrongly apply them to Jesus. But also the true understanding of the Son of Man is not a disinterested observation. It entails a revolution in consciousness for those who would see it rightly. It is as much about them as it is about Jesus. Therefore, at this stage any announcement would be premature and certainly be misunderstood.

Teaching

With regard to the spiritual dimension of life, getting it right is not an ego accomplishment of which we can be proud. Nor does it mean "mission accomplished" and we can now move on to other things. Rather it means we have momentarily allowed the Spirit to have influence. But this is a beginning, not an ending. Getting it right initiates a process.

Peter's confession that "gets it right" does not solve the riddle of Jesus' identity. It opens him to the essential mystery that unites Jesus and himself, an essential mystery that now beckons him further. Therefore, another phrase for "getting it right" might be "in over your head." Or, put in another more enigmatic way, "getting it right" lays a firm foundation for a life of "getting it wrong."

The disciples in the Gospels are eloquent testimony to the rhythms of getting it right and getting it wrong. Jesus compliments them and criticizes them in equal measure. In this story he names Peter the rock upon which he will build his Church. In the next episode Peter will be called Satan and told to get back into Jesus' following (Matt 16:21-23). "Getting it right," having a spiritual insight, begins a process that requires ongoing correction and adjustment. We know the bedrock truth of what we have perceived, but we do not know the full scope of what we have said or all of its implications.

Spiritual teachers often make a distinction between realization and integration. Realization is "getting it right." We grasp, for a moment, the necessity of Jesus' death on the cross or the meaning of grace or our grounding in eternal life. A man who had a powerful religious experience exclaimed, "So that's what it is!" When he was asked, "What?" he said, "God, that's what God is!" He had always heard about God, but he had no idea what the word referred to. This religious experience filled the word with meaning. He realized the truth of a theological concept he had inherited. He got it.

But what will he do with it? How will he integrate the God realization into his life?

Strange to say, the sage advice is to ponder and not to rush. Jesus does not want Peter and the disciples talking to others about the Messiah because they will get it wrong. They do not know the full reach of their initial insight. They have inherited ideas about the Messiah and the Son of God. What they see in Jesus challenges those ideas. But it will take time before they are completely rejected or modified. They need to understand more fully before they act.

I think this is true for most of us. Spiritual insight seldom comes with a clear path of action attached. We need to ponder, to take more inner time to comprehend and see implications. Any rush to action might be premature. As a friend of mine is fond of saying, a year of bold action is usually followed by a year of apology. In spiritual teaching action is ripe fruit that falls from the tree. We have to wait for the harvest. When we fully realize our initial spiritual insight, we will see paths of integration.

When the appropriate actions flow, "getting it right" turns into "getting it complete." The problem is we cannot envision the action ahead of time. We can give broad categories like compassion, love, justice, mercy, etc. But this does not disclose the concrete way these values will be enacted. But, if my experience is any indicator, when it happens, it will come as a surprise. Denise Levertov, the poet, once described the fig tree that Jesus cursed (Matt 21:18-22) as telling the disciples that they were withholding "gifts unimaginable." We know we are in the full reaches of "getting it right" when gifts unimaginable are flowing from us.

Twenty-Second Sunday in Ordinary Time

Proper 17

Matthew 16:21-28

———

Finding and Losing Life

A Spiritual Commentary

From that time on [after Peter's confession], Jesus began to show his disciples that he must go to Jerusalem and undergo great suffering at the hands of the elders and chief priests and scribes, and be killed, and on the third day be raised.

We are not told exactly how Jesus explained this upcoming scenario of suffering, death, and resurrection. It seems his suffering and his death would be the work of the religious leadership who are situated in Jerusalem. It is assumed that his resurrection on the third day would be the work of God.

Yet the prediction is not presented as a divided series of events, suffering and death under the control of elders, chief priests, and scribes, with resurrection under the control of God. Rather the whole plan is enacted under a "must"—must go, must suffer, must be killed, and must be raised. Rejection and resurrection are interlocking parts in a bigger picture that provides the ultimate meaning of Jesus' identity and mission.

However, this bigger picture is not spelled out. Its inner logic is not unfolded. Jesus may have explained it further. But if he did, it was unpersuasive to the leader of the disciples who had just confessed him as "the Messiah, the Son of the living God" (Matt 16:16).

> **And Peter took him aside and began to rebuke him, saying, "God forbid it, Lord! This must never happen to you."**
>
> **But he turned and said to Peter, "Get behind me, Satan! You are a stumbling block to me; for you are setting your mind not on divine things but on human things."**

Whatever Jesus said, it seems that Peter heard nothing but to suffer and die. This is so outside his way of thinking that he is compelled to take on the role of the master, taking Jesus aside and setting him straight. He speaks the sentiments of conventional religiosity. He wants God to forbid the suffering and death of Jesus. Ironically, even as he rebukes Jesus with this thought, he calls him "Lord."

The turning of Jesus to Peter symbolizes a completely different way of thinking. Jesus thinks that the rock that is the foundation of his Church has become a rock that is a stumbling block, an obstacle. He must get back into a proper following of Jesus. He must submit himself to Jesus' leadership and struggle to understand what Jesus has predicted. The way he thinks is an ordinary way of thinking. It is how humans put things together. But it is not how humans in touch with God put things together. This is what Peter must learn.

> **Then Jesus told his disciples, "If any want to become my followers, let them deny themselves and take up their cross and follow me. For those who want to save their life will lose it, and those who lose their life for my sake will find it. For what will it profit them if they gain the whole world but forfeit their life? Or what will they give in return for their life?**

Following Jesus demands a new way of thinking, a way of thinking that goes against conventional, culturally approved thought forms. People who have internalized these thought forms and identified with them will have to deny themselves. These thought forms have to do with the avoidance of suffering and death at all costs, and the imploring of God to help in this enterprise of preserving physical life in its present form. These dominant thought forms have to be replaced by an alternate way of thinking.

This new way of thinking emphasizes the doing of God's will no matter what the consequences are. In a world diametrically opposed to God's will, those consequences include suffering and death but also resurrection. The disciples are not to grudgingly endure this situation; they are to lean into it. This means taking up their cross (see also Matt 10:38, besides 16:24), not having it put on them. If they understand and do this, it will be a path of transformation for others and the path of resurrection for themselves.

Jesus tries to help them understand that this following of him that looks like loss is really gain. If they try to hold onto their present life in its temporary security and social position, they will do this by not opening to and enacting a deeper life. In particular, they will bend to the oppression of the civil and religious authorities because they fear reprisals. They will save the present way they are living at the expense of God's life that is coming to birth in them. If they let go of this present way of life, they will find this deeper, divine life.

Since this deeper, divine life is what is most valuable, it would do them little good to gain the whole world. The whole earthly world is still on a lesser level than the kingdom of heaven that Jesus is offering. There can be no tradeoff. The following of Jesus will entail sacrifice, but it is a rational sacrifice based on a hierarchy of values.

> **For the Son of Man is to come with his angels in the glory of his Father, and then he will repay everyone for what has been done. Truly I tell you, there are some standing here who will not taste death before they see the Son of Man coming in his kingdom."**

There is always the ultimate context to consider. When all is said and done, the Son of Man will come and repay everyone in accordance with how they have responded to Jesus' offer of a new humanity. This scene of the Son of Man, angels, the Father's glory, and repayment symbolizes the theological insight that the appropriateness of any action is only known in the light of the whole. The ongoing events of history do not judge themselves. Their value is only known in the light of the culmination of history. The end of history judges history, and the end of history belongs to the Son of Man and the new humanity who follows him.

Teaching

It is a sad but predictable fact that those who stand up get knocked down. Whistle blowers are a prime example. A cop reports that other cops are abusing suspects. He is shunned and punished in very clever—and often violent—ways. A woman reports accounting abuses in a large corporation. Her boss thanks her and comments on her courage. Within a week she is downsized for no apparent reason. A priest reports another priest for sexual abuse. The bishop tells him it will be taken care of. Instead, he is taken care of and sent to a remote assignment. Criticism and cover-up go together, and part of the cover-up is to eliminate the criticism.

Jesus was a fierce critic. He pointed out the thoroughgoing hypocrisy of religious leadership. They were taken up with their own importance, loving the trappings of their position rather than its substance (see Matt

23:1-31): They loved money, elaborate robes, the first places at table, salutations in the marketplace, and being called teacher. Image was everything. They polished the outside of the cup and were concerned about weighing the mint and the herb. They kept people from the knowledge that would help them, laid burdens on them, and watched them falter. Jesus saw clearly the organizational abuse and, prophet that he was, he blew the whistle.

Therefore, Jesus' prediction of his suffering and death was not a supernatural vision of the future. It was rooted in the amply documented tendency of those in power to eliminate those who question it. Today also those who stand against organizations, governments, and institutions—and call into question their unethical practices—know that reprisal is their fate. The rhetoric may be that criticism is welcomed. But the reality is that anyone who questions the status quo will be treated harshly by those benefiting from the status quo.

Often this comes down to being attacked with the very practices they are criticizing. If they are pointing to financial abuse, they will be stripped of work and money. If they are pointing to physical abuse, they will be beaten. When leadership does not know what to do, it does what it knows best. What it knows best is punishing dissent and covering up.

Why do people do it then?

There are as many reasons as there are people and groups who have walked this lonely path of confrontation. Some say, "I just couldn't let it go on" or "I couldn't live with myself if I didn't do something" or "This was once a great company [or church or organization or government] and it means something to me."

The reason given in the Gospel is that the deeper life of God depends on it. There is a deeper life of God in us, and this life is nurtured by expressing it in the face of the myriad situations we encounter. If this life is silenced, especially if it is silenced because we are afraid that its expression will mean we will lose our surface life, then this most valuable life is lost. The paradox is that by our silence we have gained some significant footing in the world, but we have lost our soul. As in the Esau and Jacob story (Gen 25:29-34), we have sold our birthright for a pot of stew. In Robert Bolt's play, *A Man for All Seasons* (London: William Heinemann, 1960), Thomas More sees that the man who has perjured himself is wearing a chain of office for Wales. It is his reward for lying. Thomas More says to him, "Richard, it does not profit a man to lose his soul for the whole world, but for Wales?"

It is difficult to grasp how spiritually momentous not speaking out is. Ordinary consciousness thinks it is an ethical option. After all, it is not something we are doing. It is something we are not doing. At best, it is a sin of omission. Some may think it is important to confront what is happening. If it is "their thing," fine. Others may have different business to conduct. In *A Man for All Seasons,* Thomas More also says, "Our natural path lies in escaping." This is a piece of advice well worth heeding.

However, the Gospels are not that blasé. They think our soul is at stake. So they encourage freely shouldering the cross. "The Cross" is merely what happens to those who persist in righteousness in an unrighteous world. Every time "the Cross" happens, and it happens daily, a double revelation unfolds. Divine love in some finite human person shines forth and human resistance in some hardened persons is seen for what it is. "The Cross" is the symbol of the standoff between divine love and human recalcitrance.

This dangerous possibility of discipleship so terrifies us that we immediately plead for a reprieve. Jesus must take us aside as he took aside Peter. He must explain to us once again how this is necessary, how this is a "must." Given who God is and who we are, it cannot be any other way. And it is only a seeming terror, for this is the path of finding the deeper life that sustains us. But Jesus the teacher must continue and slowly get us back into his following. He must tell us about the word we cannot hear, the word at the end that was lost because our hearts were pounding at suffering and death, the mysterious word: resurrection.

Twenty-Third Sunday in Ordinary Time

Proper 18

Matthew 18:15-20

Reconciling with Spirit and Skill

A Spiritual Commentary

[Jesus said to the disciples:] "If another member of the church sins against you, go and point out the fault when the two of you are alone. If the member listens to you, you have regained that one. But if you are not listened to, take one or two others along with you, so that every word may be confirmed by the evidence of two or three witnesses. If the member refuses to listen to them, tell it to the church, and if the offender refuses to listen even to the church, let such a one be to you as a Gentile and a tax collector.

Jesus teaches and exemplifies a relentless drive for reconciliation. Within the Church this moral imperative spawns a set of procedures to be applied to breakdowns of community relationships. Follow these steps and there is a good chance that Humpty-Dumpty will get put back together again. If reconciliation does not happen after the first step, the procedures escalate.

Begin with a one-to-one sit-down and get it out and on the table. The onus is on the one offended to seek out the offender. The outcome is successful if the relationship is restored. "Winning your brother or sister over" does not mean being proved right (Matt 18:15; NAB: "you have won over your brother"; NRSV: "you have regained that one"). It connotes coming to an understanding that effects reconciliation. If it can be handled on this level, it goes no further.

If this does not work, witnesses are brought in to mediate the dispute. Their role is to sort out what really happened and to suggest what has to be done to bring things back together.

If this does not work, the larger community is brought in to bring the two people together. I imagine procedures at this level are more formal and authoritative.

If this does not work, the offending person is considered as someone in need of missionary work in order to be brought back into the

267

community. They are like a tax collector or Gentile, a special object of the community's relentless care.

These procedures may seem sketchy, but like all guidelines they are fleshed out and built up through the experiences of community living. They are psycho-social expressions of the deeper, theologically grounded drive for reconciliation. What these procedures reflect is the underlying passion for reconciliation, a passion that God puts into people. This spiritually informed passion continually constructs a next step, a next possibility for the hardened heart to open.

> **Truly I tell you, whatever you bind on earth will be bound in heaven, and whatever you loose on earth will be loosed in heaven.**

The theological and spiritual grounding for the social-psychological dynamics of reconciliation is introduced by the solemn "Truly I tell you" (NAB: "Amen, I say to you" [Matt 18:18]). The disciples are reminded that they are the mediators of the flow between heaven and earth. They are not to collapse into the easy, earthly ways of alienation and exclusion. What they have to let go of on earth and what they have to bind themselves to on earth is dictated by their allegiance to heaven. The new humanity they are part of has the freedom and the capacity to establish new ways of being together. This spiritual identity must inform their step-by-step protocols.

> **Again, truly I tell you, if two of you agree on earth about anything you ask, it will be done for you by my Father in heaven.**

Heaven's agenda is for two disciples on earth, previously alienated, to come together in agreement. This is how heaven comes to earth. If the two involved pray for that, the heavenly power of the Father's love will energize them in order to bring it about. Prayer opens the heart to the Father, and the will of the Father is that the children live in peace. When the children will that too, there is a readiness to receive the Father's love. Once again, the procedures need to be followed. But the inner attitudes of the disagreeing people need to be informed by their spiritual citizenship in the kingdom of heaven and by praying for the Father's reconciling love to be present among them.

> **For where two or three are gathered in my name, I am there among them."**

This love is present when two or three are gathered not only around their own injuries but also in the name of Jesus. When this gathering is an intensified search for "togetherness," then Jesus is not with one or with the other. He is "there among them." He is doing what he always does. He is breaking down the barriers between people and encouraging the restoration of relationships. He is manifesting the love of God that Paul Tillich once described as the "power that drives everything there is toward everything else that is."

Teaching

The counselor told me, "They don't have the background to make it." He was referring to a couple I had sent to him for marriage counseling. "They have never learned to work through conflicts. Walking away is what they know best."

Reconciliation becomes possible when people possess the skills to accomplish it. If the reconciling efforts are on the interpersonal level, the offended person has to have a self-reflexive grasp of what the problem is. One cannot just be inarticulately hurt. One must be able to say what is really the cause of rankling, be able to state it in clear terms, and not be wedded to a particular way of seeing things. One also must refrain from predicting what the offender will say. Having the conversation in one's head before having it in person can undercut the possibilities of true dialogue.

There is also a question of courage. Confronting another person's behavior is never easy. In fact, often the first step the Gospel suggests is skipped: the one-to-one encounter. We immediately move to "higher-ups" in the hope of having the offender chastised. Often we seek punishment first because reconciliation demands mental and emotional abilities we do not have.

The ones accused of offending must also have certain skills. The Gospel thinks that disciples must be able to listen. Listening demands concentration, and in many conversations we tune in and out. But when we are listening to personal criticism, it is especially difficult to stay focused and attentive. We are too busy formulating a devastating response. Our defenses are in full fury.

In general, we are more skilled in justification than in self-examination. Sometimes we swing between rigid defense and flippant apology. We say we are sorry just to get the whole thing over with. What is often helpful in the reconciliation process is for both parties to have a history of repentance. If confession and change are part of our self-image, we engage conflictual situations with more flexibility. Our egos bend more easily.

When reconciliation moves off the interpersonal level and involves third parties and social implications, it becomes more complex and demands more skills. Instead of litigation, we seek mediation. Instead of war, we engage in peace talks. Instead of division, we seek negotiation. Instead of hostilities, we seek peace. Professionals are brought in who have a history of mending what is broken. They have fashioned procedures out of their past experience. These procedures are more detailed than the broad brush of the Gospel. A contemporary expert in reconciliation might read St. Matthew's advice to people in conflict and say, "Pretty sketchy."

However, the Gospels view reconciliation as ultimately a spiritual activity. This does not mean organizational procedures and individual skills can be bypassed. They are always needed. It means a deeper dimension of Spirit is present and bringing that dimension into the process increases the chances of success. This can be done in two ways.

In the first way, a psycho-social skill becomes spiritual when it is done from the spiritual center of the person and serves the well-being of others. The skills of listening, confrontation, negotiation, can be self-serving tools of manipulation. They can be practiced from an aggrandizing ego with the goal of manipulating the process for our own advantage. Our abilities become ego assets to get our own way. In ecclesiological language, our gifts are not put at the service of the community.

However, when psycho-social skills are exercised from the spiritual center of the person, the skills are perfected and put at the service of communal well-being. It is the nature of the spiritual to go into "things" and to make them all they can be. In some Christian theologies, grace perfects and elevates nature. When Spirit enters listening skills, the listening becomes deeper and more inclusive. When Spirit enters mediation skills, the skills become more respectful. When Spirit enters negotiation skills, the skills become more direct without causing anger. This presence of the Spirit within the skill signals that the skills are being used for the purposes of reconciliation.

Prayer is the way we inform skill with Spirit. However, prayer in this context is not petitioning an outside God for help. Prayer is staying in touch with the inner spiritual center and its drive for reconciliation. This may mean being silent, decluttering the mind, and recommitting to the goal of a peaceful restoration of relationship.

When this refocusing in Spirit returns to skill, it may result in the skill becoming an art. All skills are in danger of becoming wooden and predictable. When this happens, they are so busy doing what they always do that they miss the potential that is present in the situation. Reconciliation becomes an art when the potential in the situation is discerned and maximized. Then the skills weave the many threads of the emerging conversation into a single tapestry.

The second way Spirit informs skills is by becoming sensitive to the lure of peace that is present among the disagreeing people. Spiritual teaching assumes that on the metaphysical level all things are in communion with God and through God with one another. However, the psycho-social level is often not in sync with this deeper level of communion. On the visible and more easily observed level, there is alienation and separation. But this alienation and separation is always being pressured by the underlying communion to conform, to reflect this deeper spiritual truth. Spiritually informed skills await this lure from the spiritual depths, and help people open to its influence. As one married couple told me, "It is like we have a rubber band around us. We can run from each other only so far before the rubber band begins to pull us back." God is this rubber band, this lure of peace. The spiritual skill is to sense its pull and surrender to its pressure.

Processes and skills are necessary for reconciliation. But they work best when they are informed by Spirit and sensitive to the promised presence and power of Christ. Where two or three are gathered to seek agreement, Christ is an active presence drawing them together.

Twenty-Fourth Sunday in Ordinary Time

Proper 19

Matthew 18:21-35

Bestowing the Future

A Spiritual Commentary

Peter came and said to him, "Lord, if another member of the church sins against me, how often should I forgive? As many as seven times?"

Jesus said to him, "Not seven times, but, I tell you, seventy-seven times.

Peter appears to be asking a practical question. He envisions repeated offenses against him by a member of the Christian community. At the beginning he forgives the offender, as a follower of Jesus is enjoined to do. But this forgiveness is not met by effective repentance. The offender continues.

At this point, we might want to know more. Is the offender malicious? Is he taking advantage of Peter's commitment to forgiveness? Or is he simply weak, unable to change? And what is the offense? Is it minor or is it major? Is this hurt deeply wounding to Peter or is it an irritant? However, this type of information, which common sense thinks is important, is not given. Peter may be asking a practical question, but the storyteller wants to make a theological point.

The emphasis is on the limits of forgiveness. No matter what the offense is or who the person is, when can retaliation begin? At what number can Peter strike back? Peter seems to think seven might be the outside number. This is a quite generous estimate. Most people stop forgiving and start getting even at two. But the number seven is also a symbolic set-up. It allows Jesus to use another number.

Jesus responds with the word play of "seventy-seven times." This recalls the boast of Lamech in Genesis: "I have killed a man for wounding me, a young man for striking me. If Cain is avenged sevenfold, truly Lamech seventy-sevenfold" (Gen 4:23-24). The opposite of forgiveness is not a measured response in kind. It is escalated revenge.

This is not "eye for eye" (Lev 24:20) but an eye for a fingernail, a murder for a slap. Without forgiveness there is only increasing violence. In the following parable of the unforgiving forgiven servant, violence will only stop when forgiveness is present.

Therefore, Jesus, who always speaks to the heart, is not into the number game. Rather he targets the foundational attitude of Peter. Peter is ready to retaliate. He just wants to know when. With this attitude, forgiveness is a temporary, stalling strategy. If it works, fine. If it does not, there are other ways. This half commitment to forgiveness keeps people from investing their full creative potential into it. When the fallback is revenge, we may fall back too quickly. Jesus wants a full commitment to forgiveness as the only way—and with it a full use of our creative powers in the service of reconciliation. But with "paying back in kind" so normal a response, why should we be so unrelentingly committed to forgiveness?

> **For this reason the kingdom of heaven may be compared to a king who wished to settle accounts with his slaves. When he began the reckoning, one who owed him ten thousand talents was brought to him; and, as he could not pay, his lord ordered him to be sold, together with his wife and children and all his possessions, and payment to be made.**
>
> **So the slave fell on his knees before him, saying, 'Have patience with me, and I will pay you everything.'**
>
> **And out of pity for him, the lord of that slave released him and forgave him the debt.**

This is a symbolic story in its basic structure but not in all its details. It begins by portraying the relationship between God (the king) and a sinner (the servant) who is mercifully forgiven. The story opens with an accounting, a revelation of debt, and a judgment that destroys the life of the servant and his family. He has made a "huge" mistake, a mistake that is found out and cannot be repaid. This mistake will put him and his family in bondage forever.

Since the sinful servant is about to lose everything, he will promise anything. He pleads with the king in the only categories available to him, the conditions of strict justice. He wants more time in order to repay. However, even if this is granted, his life continues to be dominated by his mistake. The amount is so huge he will be eternally in debt. Any way the king decides, the rest of his life will be equated with his mistake and burdened by it. There is no way justice can save him. He may be on his knees before the king, but his back is against the wall.

Suddenly compassion appears, and it releases a flow of mercy in the king. This flow of mercy is what some Christian theologies consider the essence of the divine. The human condition of being mired in sin and not being able to get out occasions the mercy. But it does not cause it. The energy of mercy comes from the heart of God. It is grace, a free response of God arising out of divine compassion for the servant beneath the sinner, for the person beneath his impossible debt.

Therefore, in the story, the mercy comes as a shock. Nothing the king or the man has previously done prepares us for it. It comes out of the future, not as a logical extension of the past. When it arrives, it changes everything. The man is both released from bondage and forgiven his debt. What previously dominated and threatened his life is no longer there. In his case, the slogan is accurate: this is the first day of the rest of his life. He is a characterization of the classic Christian category: a forgiven sinner.

I believe this story wants every Christian, especially Peter, to see themselves in this servant. This is the basic Christian perception. Our own attitudes and actions have put us in bondage to sin. We have sold ourselves into slavery, and there is no way we can get ourselves out. This is a huge mistake. Although we may pretend that all we need is more time, the truth is that no amount of time is sufficient. We cannot do this by ourselves. Our cleverness has come to an end. We need a whole new start. We have to be released from the eternal consequences of our mistake, but we cannot make it happen.

Then we experience the mercy of God, a mercy beyond our bargaining and our pleading. This mercy severs the ropes that tie us to our sins and lets us go free. We have a second chance. We no longer live indebted to sin; we now live indebted to God. However, just as there are consequences in living in debt to our huge mistakes, there are also consequences in living in debt to divine mercy.

> **But that same slave, as he went out, came upon one of his fellow slaves who owed him a hundred denarii; and seizing him by the throat, he said, 'Pay what you owe.'**
>
> **Then his fellow slave fell down and pleaded with him, 'Have patience with me, and I will pay you.'**
>
> **But he refused; then he went and threw him into prison until he would pay the debt.**

The servant has been forgiven, but he has learned little. He may no longer be a debtor, but he is still a creditor. He may plead for himself, but he is demanding and violent with his fellow servant. He wants his money, and he wants it now. Although the amount is smaller (symbolizing the interaction between humans) and not "huge" (symbolizing the interaction between God and humans), the debt is still not payable. This debtor pleads within the categories of strict justice as his creditor had done only moments before, categories that only deepen his predicament. But the creditor does not see himself in this desperate entreaty. He does not hear himself when his exact words are spoken by another: "Have patience with me, and I will pay you." Therefore, he cannot love his neighbor as himself (see Matt 19:19; Lev 19:18).

So without forgiveness, violence emerges. Not only does he throttle the man, he consigns him to bondage, imprisoning him until he pays. But, of course, in prison he cannot pay. So this second debtor is doomed to the consequences of his sin. Symbolically, the one who has been forgiven by God does not forgive his neighbor. The forgiven sinner does not forgive in turn.

> **When his fellow slaves saw what had happened, they were greatly distressed, and they went and reported to their lord all that had taken place.**
>
> **Then his lord summoned him and said to him, 'You wicked slave! I forgave you all that debt because you pleaded with me. Should you not have had mercy on your fellow slave, as I had mercy on you?'**
>
> **And in anger his lord handed him over to be tortured until he would pay his entire debt.**
>
> **So my heavenly Father will also do to every one of you, if you do not forgive your brother or sister from your heart.'"**

The unforgiving forgiven one is summoned before the king and addressed as "wicked slave!" His wickedness consists in his failure to pass on to others the mercy he received from God. This failure is subtly tied to the servant's consciousness. The king forgave him because he pleaded. It was the pleading that moved the king, not his impossible repayment plan. The consciousness of the king identified with his desperation, and this identification moved him to mercy.

But this wicked servant did not remember either his own desperation or the unwarranted mercy of the king. His short memory did not allow him to say, "This fellow servant is me before I was forgiven" or "I am a forgiven person who is ready to forgive." Rather he focused on the debt he was owed. His mind was only on his missing money, and so no mercy flowed.

Then a startling thing happens. The king's mercy dries up. It recedes back into him, so to speak. This leaves the man to the consequences of his original mistakes. Divine mercy may be freely given, but if it is not imitated and given away, it ceases to be effective in the lives of those who have received it. Divine forgiveness and human forgiveness constitute a tightly linked dynamic. They are connected through the heart, the spiritual center of the person.

The heart is the symbolic place that opens to both God and neighbor. It receives mercy from God and extends that mercy to others. If it fails to extend mercy to others, it loses the mercy it has received from God. The dangerous phrase from the Lord's Prayer has been his undoing: "forgive us our debts, as we also have forgiven our debtors" (Matt 6:12). That is exactly what is happening. His lack of forgiveness rescinds God's forgiveness. This is not because divine reality has changed its mind but because another spiritual law has become operative. The measure he measures is measured unto him (see Matt 7:2).

So this is what Jesus is saying to Peter who wants to know when he can strike back. "You live by the forgiveness of God. You must never forget that. That is your identity-forming experience. It is *this* experience, and not the experience of being wronged, that you always 'repay in kind' or 'pay . . . back in full' (Matt 18:26; NAB). The more you extend that experience to others, the more you grow in its mercy. However, the failure to do this means that the mercy recedes. You are returned to a life of bondage to the consequences of your huge sin. If you understand this truth, you will not ask, 'How many times?'"

Teaching

The dynamics of forgiveness are so particular to each situation and so woven into the psychology of the people involved that any generalization can be refuted by a specific instance. But still, the path the Matthean Jesus maps out is powerful and provocative. I believe it is supposed to convince Christians who think deeply about their life.

But does it?

The spiritual wisdom can be stated: "We all live by the forgiveness of God and if we do not forgive one another in turn, this divine forgiveness is withdrawn."

Is it persuasive? How can we understand it as a reflection of common Christian experience? What inner work do we have to do to make this spiritual wisdom our own?

We must realize we are all living through the power of divine forgiveness. This perception is difficult because we do not clearly see our entrenched sinfulness. We are too mediocre to owe a huge amount. There are some people—murderers, rapists, etc.—who are in bondage to sin and cannot extricate themselves. But most of us see our indebtedness in more manageable amounts. "Have patience with me, and I will pay you" is not last ditch desperation but a decent proposal.

Therefore, to realize how essential divine forgiveness is, we must realize our sinfulness. That is why Luther exhorted people to sin boldly. It is the forerunner to the realization of grace. However, this theological strategy of convicting people of sin in order to open them to divine forgiveness has been strongly criticized.

Another approach, and one that resonates with me, is to realize how sinful experiences claim us. The experiences of both being sinned against and sinning are seldom over and done with. They continue to extend their influence long after the actual offense has ended. The "huge amount" may be their power to dominate us and bring our future under their control. Negative experiences infiltrate our mind and heart and constrict our freedom. They become the bondage and prison the servants in the story experience, a bondage and a prison from which they cannot free themselves.

Therefore, the focus of forgiveness shifts. It is not primarily overlooking past sinfulness or, in the metaphor of the story, canceling past debt. Rather "for-giveness" is an intense giving of life and energy into the freedom of a person on the edge of newness. This giving must be intense because the weight of negative experiences of the past is great.

In fact, this weight is so overwhelming it reduces us to pleading. The pleading is an admission of our helplessness. It opens us, and we receive what we ask for. We are given time. However, the time is not to repay the past. It is to break the hold of our mistakes and find a new future. This type of time is not the "march of time," the mindless tomorrows that inevitably come. This is the advent of the new, the arrival of possibility into an impossible situation. This is how God gives time, not endless minutes but endless opportunities.

It is here, in the freshness of a new life we did not create, that our consciousness must rest. We must not bolt out of our prison and go on with life exactly as before—without understanding or appreciation.

We must allow what has happened to form and influence us. If we do not deeply grasp both the bondage to our mistakes and the unmerited forgiveness, we will not persist in the freedom and the future we have been given.

The open future we walk into is not the result of anything we did. So we cannot claim it. The usual way we differentiate ourselves from others is not operative. It is not our merit that has forced the forgiveness, or even our potential for more service that has made forgiveness a reasonable choice. We might try to attribute the forgiveness to dumb luck. We got the king on a good day. But the depth of what we have experienced will finally penetrate. A future, free from the consequences of our mistakes, was bestowed upon us.

The implications of this graceful experience come into view when we meet our former self in another. We gradually realize *our* situation is *the* situation. Everyone is tied to their past failures until a future is bestowed upon them. These failures may be small, but they hamper freedom. They imprison people. Since we were given a way out, we know the way out. Only now we are on the other side. Our hope is to remember clearly the conditions of our liberation. If we forget them, we will return to bondage. This will happen long before we are reported to the king. It happens the moment we put our hands around the throat of our debtor. We are once again sold into the slavery of revenge, retaliation, and reprisal.

Twenty-Fifth Sunday in Ordinary Time

Proper 20

Matthew 20:1-16

~~~

Comparing Salaries

A Spiritual Commentary

[Jesus said to the disciples:]

In this context disciples are those who, by following Jesus, are doing God's work. In the metaphor of the parable to follow, they are laboring in the vineyard. The disciples are represented by Peter who has just asked Jesus a question that is never far from the human heart: "Look, we have left everything and followed you. What then will we have?" (Matt 19:27)

This juxtaposition of sacrifice and reward was prompted by the exchange between Jesus and the "young man" with "many possessions" (Matt 19:16-22). He left nothing and followed the lure of his possessions rather than the call of Jesus. But Peter and the disciples have left everything to follow Jesus. Quite frankly, what is the payoff?

In extravagant apocalyptic language Jesus assures Peter and the disciples that doing God's work will bring them to the pinnacle of human fulfillment. Every sacrifice will be restored to them a hundredfold with eternal life flowing into them. If Peter is worrying about a poor payoff, Jesus overwhelms him with a vision of gratuitous abundance. Yet there is something in Peter's comparative attitude and his need for the assurance of reward that does not fit well with laboring in the Lord's vineyard. The story tries to point out the problem and correct it.

> "For the kingdom of heaven is like a landowner who went out early in the morning to hire laborers for his vineyard. After agreeing with the laborers for the usual daily wage, he sent them into his vineyard.

This unrealistic social story attempts to express and communicate a basic spiritual truth about each person's relationship to God. God is like a landowner seeking people to work on the home estate. People are like day laborers. Socially, day laborers are a vulnerable group.

They do not have a permanent standing with a single employer but are dependent everyday on a call. This reflects the spiritual condition of people before God. They have no claims on God but each day God calls people to work in the world.

The agreement is: if people work for God day by day, God sustains their life day by day. This is symbolized by the fact that the compensation is "the usual daily wage," what is necessary to sustain life in the present. The workers are not given enough for the next day. If we were, we might envision a life outside of continual divine support.

This reflects one of the phrases of the Lord's Prayer. Disciples are encouraged to pray for *"daily* bread" (Matt 6:11). God does not give more and God does not give less. The economic acts of saving and hoarding are used to symbolically convey the delusion that we are self-sufficient, capable of living outside God's love. We cannot save and hoard—and in the process become independent and move outside God's sustaining life. God invites and sustains all people who do God's work.

> **When he went out about nine o'clock, he saw others standing idle in the marketplace; and he said to them, 'You also go into the vineyard, and I will pay you whatever is right.' So they went.**
>
> **When he went out again about noon and about three o'clock, he did the same.**

The tension in the story begins with the landowner going out and calling people at nine, noon, and three. He tells them he will give them what is just. But what is "just" to this landowner? How will they be distinguished from the first group? Also, what he notices about the day laborers is that they are idle. It is this observation that spurs him to send them into the vineyard.

> **And about five o'clock he went out and found others standing around; and he said to them, 'Why are you standing here idle all day?'**
>
> **They said to him, 'Because no one has hired us.' He said to them, 'You also go into the vineyard.'**

The idleness theme is developed and deepened with the hiring that takes place one hour before the end of the day. The landowner may be concerned about grapes rotting on the vine, and so he may be desperate for more workers. But the story does not talk about the need for harvesting.

Instead, it pictures the landowner as concerned with unproductive people who are unproductive precisely because they have not been called to work. They do not answer the landowner's question about their idleness by saying they are lazy, indifferent, or unable to work. The problem is they have not been hired, and that situation is quickly remedied. "You also go into the vineyard." No mention is made of wages.

This first part of the story suggests that the Divine Source is continually recruiting people into the work. Some (the first hired) have a detailed understanding of the contract. Others (those hired at nine, noon, and three) have a promise of justice. Still others (those hired at five) are not told the reward of their labors. The workers do not represent three different groups but three levels of understanding.

> **When evening came, the owner [*kyrios*, "lord"] of the vineyard said to his manager, 'Call the laborers and give them their pay, beginning with the last and then going to the first.'**

> **When those hired about five o'clock came, each of them received the usual daily wage. Now when the first came, they thought they would receive more; but each of them also received the usual daily wage.**

This movement from last to first is the literary device that will highlight the way the owner of the vineyard works. The last-hired laborers received the "usual daily wage" that the first-hired laborers agreed to. Something immediately strikes us as wrong. Conventional social dealings would dictate the eleventh-hour hires would receive one-twelfth of what the first laborers agreed to. What could be the reason they received "the usual daily wage"?

> **And when they received it, they grumbled against the landowner, saying, 'These last worked only one hour, and you have made them equal to us who have borne the burden of the day and the scorching heat.'**

The first-hired laborers are thinking in terms of standard social conventions and expect more. Although they received what they agreed on, this causes them to grumble at the perceived inequality. But the way they state it is significant. What the landowner has done is make all people who work in his vineyard equal, regardless of how long they have worked. The landowner gives to all the same. Can the landowner explain these actions?

> **But he replied to one of them, 'Friend, I am doing you no wrong; did you not agree with me for the usual daily wage? Take what belongs to you and go; I choose to give to this last the same as I give to you. Am I not allowed to do what I choose with what belongs to me? Or are you envious because I am generous?'**

The landowner speaks to one in particular and by calling him friend signifies that the upcoming confrontation is meant for his benefit. Given the larger context of this parable, the friend is Peter whose comparative attitude about rewards occasioned the parable.

Peter and the disciples will get the usual daily wage because this is what they agreed on. In other words, it is assumed they have grasped the truth about God that Jesus has struggled to communicate to them. When people "seek first the kingdom" (Matt 6:33; NAB) and pray to follow God's will (Matt 6:10), there is no need to ask for what you need. Your Father already knows and gives what is needed (Matt 6:8, 32-33) to those who work in the vineyard.

However, this bestowal of "daily bread" (Matt 6:11) is not correlated to the amount of work done. It flows out of the nature of God as good and gracious. The landowner told them that he would pay them what is just. What is just for the landowner is always "the usual daily wage." This is what people need in order to work in the vineyard, and this is what is always given.

But when the first-hired laborers see the last-hired laborers receiving the same as themselves without putting in the same time and effort, the comparative mind of social convention takes them over. They have done more so they should receive more. The outcome is grumbling. They are not happy with what they agreed on.

It is this unhappiness that the landowner will use to force them into self-examination. They cannot argue with what the landowner says. They have not been treated unjustly, and the landowner is free to act according to personal choice. Therefore, the last question, "[A]re you envious because I am generous?" (literally, "Is your eye evil because I am good?") has to be answered positively. The goodness of God causes them to be envious.

> **So the last will be first, and the first will be last."**

A word-by-word reading of this code phrase denotes reversal. But as a conclusion to the story, it signifies the inadequacy of comparative thinking when dealing with spiritual reality. First and last are social categories. When we deal with the heavenly Father of Jesus, the good God, another way of thinking and acting has to be considered.

Teaching

In some corporations comparing salaries is forbidden. Usually the reasons for this prohibition are not spelled out. But the company, always eager to help, gives workers a comeback in case a fellow worker might indiscreetly ask, "By the way, what do you make?" The loyal employee is to respond, "That's for me, the boss, and the tax collector to know."

Comparing salaries is considered volatile activity. Chances are it will lead to charges of unfairness, a sense of being discriminated against, a decline in employee morale, and, as the Gospel indicates, an epidemic of grumbling. Even if the employer comes clean and discloses the reasons for the discrepancy in wages, the grumbling will persist. No reason is good enough when we sense someone got away with something and we did not.

That is why this parable of the workers in the vineyard is arguably the most disliked parable of the Gospels. Its unfairness is so overwhelming it edges out that other egregious Gospel conundrum: a welcome and a feast for the son who squandered the inheritance (Luke 15:11–32). Although the argument of the owner of the vineyard is beyond refutation ("Am I not allowed to do what I choose with what belongs to me?"), it makes no headway against our outrage. We instinctively feel a mistake has been made. There is a deep sense of unfairness when the last are paid the same as the first. And we, who are always quick to feel offended, identify with the weary, heat-beaten first laborers.

This feeling of unfairness springs from a well-constructed mental tape. Its basic message is: "If someone gets what I am getting but hasn't put in as much work as I have, I am being cheated. Is there any other way to see this?" Most of us have this tape running continually. This makes us, in the language of the parable, grumble-ready.

The truth of this tape seems obvious because it confirms our fundamental stance. We are the center of the universe, and we evaluate everything that happens from the point of view of our own comparative well-being. If it protects or promotes us, we praise it. If it makes us vulnerable or demotes us, we, not to put too fine of an edge on it, piss and moan. "You have made them equal to us who have borne the burden of the day and the scorching heat." Outrageous!

To grasp the pervasiveness of this ego-centered attitude, we could play at midrash and extend this parable imaginatively. We might picture the last and first workers in a heated exchange. The first would continue to insist on the unfairness of it all, and the last would praise the generosity of the lord of the vineyard. Although first and last would appear to be at odds, they would actually be working out of the same self-obsessed standpoint. The first would be lamenting salary difference because it did not benefit them. The last would be praising salary difference because it did benefit them.

To see these two in the same position, we would have to create a third group: "The owner of the vineyard went out at 5:30, and found even more strays still without work. 'Get going,' he said. And they went. At the end of the day the 5:30 group got the same as the 5:00 group. The 5:00 group grumbled and joined ranks with the first-hired laborers. They insisted on more equitable contracts. They wanted the daily wage to be broken down into an hourly wage and the hourly wage to be broken down into half-hour increments." Ah, justice at last.

"It depends," as the discerning person said, "on whose ox is being gored."

But if the story knows our egocentricity, it also knows another possibility. It suggests seeing things from God's point of view. But this is a real stretch. In fact, it is difficult to even entertain this possibility because our egocentric point of view is so entrenched. When we move outside of it, we are in such a strange world that we immediately reject it. But let's venture out of our identification with the first-hired laborers and try to see it as the landowner (God, the Lord of the Vineyard) sees it.

From the Lord of the Vineyard's point of view, what really matters is not what you get but that you work in the vineyard. The real problem is idleness in the marketplace. You do not know or comprehend that a larger reality permeates your physical, mental, and social life and calls you to join with it in harvesting a new human reality. Therefore, you stand around waiting. But this Lord of the Vineyard will have none of it. The owner visits the marketplace often and sends everyone off to the vineyard. The owner is shameless in the diversity of the ways the calls are sent to people. What is paramount is the work.

Once in the vineyard you are in the owner's domain, and the rules change because of who the owner is and what the owner is about. The work itself is the reward. The joy is in the contribution, in the ecstasy of joining with the Lord of the Vineyard in the creation of the world. Remember, you are now in a consciousness called the kingdom of heaven and not in a consciousness that could be called "Comparative Status" or "Fear of Not Getting What You Deserve." You do not need to worry and look out for yourself for the One for whom you work knows what you need and is only too willing to supply it (Matt 6:8, 32-33).

You begin to value the full heat of the day because, as Gerard Manley Hopkins intimated, you "burnish in use." You no longer live in the envious world of comparison but in the abundant world of God's goodness. In this world God's goodness gives you a good eye. This eye connects your soul to the expansive world of Divine Spirit. The soul, in turn, works and flows like liquid light, each effort a response to grace, each effort releasing grace.

The Lord of the Vineyard has no choice. God has to give you all that God has. Which, of course, is one day's wages.

Twenty-Sixth Sunday in Ordinary Time

Proper 21

Matthew 21:23-32

~~~~~

Changing Our Minds

A Spiritual Commentary

When [Jesus] entered the temple, the chief priests and the elders of the people came to him as he was teaching, and said, "By what authority are you doing these things, and who gave you this authority?"

Authorities always have questions about authority, especially when they are in the temple, the symbol of their own authority. They are more concerned about who authorized Jesus than they are about the "things he is doing." Once Jesus healed a man's withered arm on the Sabbath (see Matt 12:9-14). The religious leadership who witnessed it asked, "Who gave you the right to do this on the Sabbath?" They could have said, "Nice arm." But they never really saw the arm. They only see what they are conditioned to see. If all you have is a hammer, everything is a nail.

Of course, their question about authority is a trap. If Jesus says he does these things on his own authority, he appears to be a maverick, without any legitimation from his faith tradition. If he says he does them on God's authority, he has infringed on their turf, for they are the guardians of the law and the official interpreters of what comes authentically from God. Jesus' best strategy is to turn the tables with a question of his own. If they can construct a trap, so can Jesus.

Jesus said to them, "I will also ask you one question; if you tell me the answer, then I will also tell you by what authority I do these things. Did the baptism of John come from heaven, or was it of human origin?"

And they argued with one another, "If we say, 'From heaven,' he will say to us, 'Why then did you not believe him?' But if we say, 'Of human origin,' we are afraid of the crowd; for all regard John as a prophet."

So they answered Jesus, "We do not know."

And he said to them, "Neither will I tell you by what authority I am doing these things.

Jesus avoids the horns of their dilemma by putting them on the horns of his dilemma. And we, the readers, get to watch them squirm. Instead of honestly addressing the question of the authority of John the Baptist, they gauge how whatever they say will be received. Their real concern is not John's authority but their own; and they cannot answer Jesus' question without weakening it.

If they say John's authority was from heaven, they have to account for the fact they did not credit it. If they say John's authority was of human origin, the crowds will turn against them because they believe John was sent by God. In either case, they do not look good, and looking good is essential.

Even the answer they do give jeopardizes their standing. "We do not know." But they are religious authorities who should know, who should be able to discern whether or not John was an authentic prophet. The fact they cannot make this decision throws doubt on their own fitness. Where is *their* authority from? Jesus has unmasked them, and he is about to reveal the depths of their deceit and intransigency.

> **What do you think? A man had two sons; he went to the first and said, 'Son, go and work in the vineyard today.'**
>
> **He answered, 'I will not'; but later he changed his mind and went.**
>
> **The father went to the second and said the same; and he answered, 'I go, sir'; but he did not go.**
>
> **Which of the two did the will of his father?"**
>
> **They said, "The first."**

This is a classic ploy of the prophet. He tells a story and asks his listeners to make a judgment, to evaluate the characters in the story. They are usually quick to respond for they are people with firm opinions and unyielding judgments. What they do not know is that by judging the people in the story they are judging themselves. They are more involved than they think.

The religious leaders value action over words. Mere lip service to the Father is not following his will. Actually doing what the Father commands is obedience to his will. Therefore, it is the first son who did the will of the father.

But this son also changed his mind. If they endorse *doing* over *saying*, they also have to endorse the change of mind that brought the first son to obedient action. It is this ability to change one's mind that Jesus wants to emphasize. Both John the Baptist and Jesus have stressed that *metanoia*—a change of mind—is needed to enter the kingdom of God.

> **Jesus said to them, "Truly I tell you, the tax collectors and the prostitutes are going into the kingdom of God ahead of you. For John came to you in the way of righteousness and you did not believe him, but the tax collectors and the prostitutes believed him; and even after you saw it, you did not change your minds and believe him."**

By profession the chief priests and elders of the people are expected to be close to God and, by profession, tax collectors and prostitutes are thought to be far from God. But what is thought to be far from God is "going into the kingdom of God ahead of" what is thought to be close to God. The reason is: when tax collectors and sinners heard John, they repented. They changed their minds and began to live in a new way. But the chief priests and elders did not change their minds, even though they knew that John was righteous. Something kept them from believing in John, possibly John's insistence that they had to think in a new way.

The problem is profound; their recalcitrance is deep. They might have been against John at the beginning. But when they saw that John's preaching had the power to convert sinners, to lead them into the ways of righteousness, they should have rethought their position. They are supposed to urge repentance. But when they would not support John in his important work, they abdicated their responsibilities as religious leaders.

Yet there is no doubt that repenting and leading a life of righteousness is doing God's will. This is what the first son does and what they themselves commended. However, they are the second son. They say that they will do God's will, but they do not actually do it. They are known to be righteous because of what they say with their lips, "Yes, Father." But they are not actually righteous because they do not carry out what they say. Their endorsement of the first son is a judgment on themselves. They are the second son, and their real failure is that they cannot change their mind.

Teaching

Einstein once said, "Everything has changed but our thinking." The mind is always the last to know. Life is always movement and flow, but the mind always lags behind. It holds onto past moments, and so it cannot ride the new that is happening. Therefore to enter into life—the kingdom of God—the mind has to continually change.

A story from the Sufis goes like this:

> There was a case against Mulla Nasruddin in the court, and the judge asked him, "How old are you, Nasruddin?"
>
> And he said, "Of course, you know and everybody knows I am forty years old."
>
> The judge was surprised, "But five years ago, you were also in this court. When I asked you then how old you were you said forty. How is this possible? After five years you are still forty."
>
> Nasruddin said, "I am a consistent man, sir. Once I say I am forty, I will remain forty forever. You can rely on me."

Loyalty to the mind is foolish. Consistent thinking, holding the same position now as we did earlier, has a high price tag. It often entails denying our participation in the river of life. The spiritual adage is: the mind makes a good servant but a poor master. Too often we cling to what we think. When we do this and it keeps us from attuning ourselves to the deep rhythms of life that are bringing us to redemption, the mind is the master.

Another story-joke tells of a student and teacher:

> The student asked the teacher, "Professor, do fish think?"
>
> "Do fish think?" The professor repeated the question. "Let me see. There is a fish pond in the back of my house. Every evening for three weeks, I threw fish food in the water near the left bank. The fish came and ate. Then one evening I threw fish food into the pond near the right bank. I noticed the fish were still going to the left bank. For nearly three weeks I threw fish food near the right bank, but the fish were still going to the left bank. Then one evening the fish noticed the food was over at the right bank. They swam across the pond. But they were so starved from not eating, they died right before they came to the food. Do fish think? Yes, but not fast enough."

If the mind is always a day late and a dollar short, where does that leave us? If we do not think fast enough, are we destined to miss what is presently happening?

There is another story:

> The foremost teacher of the certain musical instrument was giving lessons to a small class of eight. First he instructed them as a group. Then he would move from student to student to give them individual counsel. One of the students noticed that the great teacher was mumbling to himself as he moved from student to student. The student wanted to know what the teacher was saying, but she did not want to ask. So, as the teacher approached her, she stopped playing and listened intently. She caught what the teacher was saying.
>
> Under his breath to himself, barely audible, the teacher was saying, "Allah knows. I don't." (Elizabeth Lesser, *The New American Spirituality: A Seeker's Guide* [New York: Random House, 1999] paraphrased)

Here is the foremost teacher of this musical instrument relativizing his considerable knowledge. He is afraid that his mind will keep him from seeing what is new in the students before him. So he holds his knowledge lightly, always countering it with "not-knowing." This makes his mind flexible, able to use what he knows at the same time as he is able to see beyond it.

When it comes to knowledge of God and God's actions, theological traditions have tried to balance knowing and not knowing. The human mind can discern divine activity but it cannot exhaustively capture it. Some theologians go so far as to say we can only *acknowledge* God. We cannot know God.

So the mind has its models of divine activity that help us discern the presence of the Spirit. But the model is limited. If we totally attach ourselves to it, we may miss the divine activity that the model is not made to discern. The religious leaders of Jesus' time did not heed John the Baptist because their minds were made up. They could not unmake them, so they did not do the will of the Father.

I wonder if the same predicament plagues us today.

Twenty-Seventh Sunday in Ordinary Time

Proper 22

Matthew 21:33-46

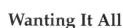

Wanting It All

A Spiritual Commentary

[Jesus said to the people:] "Listen to another parable.

The target of this parable is religious leadership. Religious leadership is prone to many temptations, and the Gospel spells them out in detail. However, at the core of leadership's failures is a subtle switch from being guardians of the tradition to being its owners, from being humble servants of God to being proud possessors of authority. They claim position and privilege and are immune to criticism. They silence any voice that calls them to accountability. They reject anyone who reminds them that God is the ultimate authority and they will be judged by their obedience or disobedience to that authority. They want it all, and the prophet reminds them that it is not theirs and never will be theirs.

There was a landowner who planted a vineyard, put a fence around it, dug a wine press in it, and built a watchtower. Then he leased it to tenants and went to another country.

The landowner supplies the fundamental structure of the vineyard. He plants so all that remains is to harvest; he puts up a hedge so wild animals cannot attack the grapes; he digs a wine press so that all the tenants will have to do is bring the grapes; he builds a tower as a watch post and a place of shelter. These actions establish his priority, ownership, and care for those to whom he will lease the vineyard. He has done everything he can. In the book of Isaiah that inspired this image, the owner asks, "What more was there to do for my vineyard that I have not done in it?" (Isa 5:4).

The allegorical pieces are in place. God is the owner of the vineyard. Israel, as the bearer of God's revelation, is the vineyard. The tenants are the religious leaders. The owner is on a journey, signaling God is not present in the same way as at the beginning. But everything is set for productivity. What could go wrong?

> **When the harvest time had come, he sent his slaves to the tenants to collect his produce. But the tenants seized his slaves and beat one, killed another, and stoned another. Again he sent other slaves, more than the first; and they treated them in the same way.**

What goes wrong are the tenants. They refuse to produce wine in accord with the original planting. Instead, they beat, kill, and stone the landowner's servant-representatives. These servant-representatives are the prophets who throughout the history of Israel continually remind the religious leaders to bear fruit consistent with the original covenant agreement.

The landowner does not give up easily. Although his servants are treated badly, he sends others. In fact, he sends more and more. Perhaps he is thinking more will get the hearing that the few did not. But he is mistaken. The "more than the first" are treated the same way. The religious leaders do not repent and listen. Instead they perpetuate the persecution of prophets. They refuse to produce the wine from the grapes the landowner planted.

> **Finally he sent his son to them, saying, 'They will respect my son.' But when the tenants saw the son, they said to themselves, 'This is the heir; come, let us kill him and get his inheritance.' So they seized him, threw him out of the vineyard, and killed him.**

The landowner's concern is to persuade the tenants to be faithful to what was given them. He sent some servants, then he sent more servants, and now he decides to send his son. His thinking is that the increased prestige of the son will persuade them. After all, the son is not only a messenger from the owner but represents the very being of the owner. They will respect the son in a way they did not respect the servants.

But the tenants see the presence of the son as the opportunity they have been waiting for. The story has not previously revealed their motives. But now we see what drives them. They want the vineyard for themselves. They are not happy with the status of tenants; they want to be the owner.

Of course, Jesus is the son the religious leaders do not listen to or respect. They do not respect him because they want nothing to do with God. They want to be autonomous. They do not want to live in a covenant agreement. They want to live by their own dictates and pursue power and privilege. Only the death of the son will allow them to do that. There will be no heir, and so the tenants can take over. All connections with the owner will be severed. So they seize him, throw him outside the vineyard (give him over to Rome), and kill him.

> **Now when the owner of the vineyard comes, what will he do to those tenants?"**
>
> **They said to him, "He will put those wretches to a miserable death, and lease the vineyard to other tenants who will give him the produce at the harvest time."**

The religious leaders unwittingly judge themselves. Since they have consistently persecuted the prophets of God and conspired to kill the son, they have forfeited their place in the vineyard. Their own wickedness will destroy them. Wretched men will undergo a wretched death. But the landowner will continue to look for other tenants. Who will make wine from the grapes the landowner planted?

> **Jesus said to them, "Have you never read in the scriptures: 'The stone that the builders rejected has become the cornerstone; this was the Lord's doing, and it is amazing in our eyes'? Therefore I tell you, the kingdom of God will be taken away from you and given to a people that produces the fruits of the kingdom. The one who falls on this stone will be broken to pieces; and it will crush anyone on whom it falls."**
>
> **When the chief priests and the Pharisees heard his parables, they realized that he was speaking about them. They wanted to arrest him, but they feared the crowds, because they regarded him as a prophet.**

Jesus quotes scripture, and the very fact that scripture is introduced indicates that God's plan has taken into account both the failure of the tenants and the rejection of the prophets and the son. Although these were pernicious attempts to wrest the vineyard from the owner's control, they will not be successful. The One whom the original tenants rejected will become the resurrected leader of new tenants. The Lord has turned the rejected stone into the cornerstone of a new building. This is a truly wondrous event for human eyes because what seemed like the end of the son is really the beginning of the son. The heir has received the inheritance, and the vineyard will bear fruit. This reversal bears witness to God's creative and persistent intention to have this vineyard produce wine in accord with the original planting. The crucified-resurrected Jesus and his followers will make exquisite wine.

Teaching

Excluding is a well-documented human habit. On every level of our being we push things away. It seems the right thing to do. It is a purifying process. If we have thoughts that disturb us, we do our best not to think them. If there are people who are undesirable, we make sure they are not welcomed into our homes, schools, clubs, and churches. We clear a space where we think we can breathe pure air.

Rigorous reasoning accompanies our hard work of exclusion. These reasons are impeccable, acceptable to our friends. In fact, they are acceptable to all clear-thinking people because they are based on unalterable facts. They reflect "the way the world is." The inner and outer processes of excluding and reasoning make us feel safer, saner, more in charge, and more ourselves.

Zealous exclusions provide us with a well-defined identity. We not only know our boundaries, we guard them. We count ourselves among the elite, the chosen, the elect. Every time we see the mob, we recoil into our superior status. We know who we are by knowing who we are not.

But there are those who say exclusions can get out of hand. When they become a way of life, they narrow us down. We "circle the wagons," but we may circle them too tightly. In our desire not to be infringed upon, we may be pushing away the very thing, person, situation, feeling, thought, and experience we need. A friend of mine is fond of saying, "We avoid with a passion the very thing that will *save* us."

Jesus' name means "he will *save* his people from their sins" (Matt 1:21). In classical theology sin is considered to be a process of separation. Through the use of their freedom, people separate themselves from God and from other people. In doing this, they also separate themselves from their own souls. This exclusionary process results in a false and isolated sense of themselves. Sin-defined people are, as St. Augustine and Martin Luther pointed out, *"incurvatus a se,"* wrapped up in themselves.

Therefore, to save people from their sins is to bring them out of separation into communion, to connect them with God, neighbor, and self. This is the offer of Jesus to the religious leadership of his day. His liberating consciousness and inclusive behavior are what they need. Jesus is asking them to relate to the God of all people by including all people. He is asking them to join the party, but they cannot tolerate so motley a collection of characters. They choose to remain in their isolation. They are better at shunning than welcoming.

But why?

Although philosophy, psychology, and sociology have explored exclusionary processes at great length, the story of the murderous tenants suggests a simple reason. They only share this simple reason among themselves, telling it to each other in order to take energy from it. This is the reason beneath the reasons, the dark desire lurking behind the rational explanations: "come, let us kill him and get his inheritance."

They want the inheritance. They want it all. They want it all for themselves. They do not want to be accountable to God or other people. Their isolation has turned them greedy. They grab for everything they can get. For them, "including" only means there will not be enough for me—enough righteousness, enough money, enough prestige, enough land, enough everything. They live in a world of scarcity, and they are making sure that "they get theirs." When more are included, they instinctively feel that they will have less. They exclude because they want it all.

Wanting it all is a crazy desire, born of isolation and fear. Its social face is acquisition and greed. Its psychological face is accusation and defensiveness. Its theological face is the preaching of a God I own rather than a God who owns me. But the real God has gone elsewhere.

> The water of life, wishing to make itself known on the face of the earth, bubbled up in an artesian well and flowed without effort or limit. People came to drink of this refreshing water and were nourished by it, since it was so clean and pure and invigorating. But humankind was not content to leave things in this Edenic state. Gradually they began to fence the well, charge admission, claim ownership of the property around it, make elaborate laws as to who could come to the well, and put locks on the gates. Soon the well was the property of the powerful and the elite. The water was angry and offended; it stopped flowing and began to bubble up in another place. The people who owned the property around the first well were so engrossed in their power systems and ownership

that they did not notice that the water had vanished. They continued selling the nonexistent water, and few people noticed that the true power was gone. But some dissatisfied people searched with great courage and found the new artesian well. Soon that well was under the control of the property owners, and the same fate overtook it. The spring took itself to yet another place—and this has been going on throughout history.

We do not own the vineyard; we work in it. When we want it all, we inherit nothing.

Twenty-Eighth Sunday in Ordinary Time

Proper 23

Matthew 22:1-14

❦

Marrying the Son

A Spiritual Commentary

Once more Jesus spoke to them [chief priests and Pharisees] in parables, saying:

Religious leadership is prone to protect the received traditions against infringement. They wager that past revelations are more reliable than present experience. Any talk that God is revising the ancient covenant agreements is rejected. Guardians of truth are always suspicious of new claims. The major events were back then; now is the aftermath of glory. With this mindset, announcements of symbolic wedding feasts that suggest God is doing something new do not stir a desire to participate.

> **"The kingdom of heaven may be compared to a king who gave a wedding banquet for his son. He sent his slaves to call those who had been invited to the wedding banquet, but they would not come.**
>
> **Again he sent other slaves, saying, 'Tell those who have been invited: Look, I have prepared my dinner, my oxen and my fat calves have been slaughtered, and everything is ready; come to the wedding banquet.'**
>
> **But they made light of it and went away, one to his farm, another to his business, while the rest seized his slaves, mistreated them, and killed them. The king was enraged. He sent his troops, destroyed those murderers, and burned their city.**

The kingdom of heaven is a state of consciousness and action. It begins with the realization that a special moment has arrived. An unparalleled event in the history of the religious tradition of Israel is unfolding. God is inviting people to partake in the fullness of joy, the time when his son, Jesus, will marry. But in this surrealistic story the bride is not mentioned. Whom the son will marry is still a mystery.

Of course, the religious leadership of Israel, representing past special moments, are invited. However, they refuse. Even when God reaffirms that this is a special time and a special feast—with all in readiness—they go about as if nothing important is happening. Their farming and their businesses demand their attention. Ordinary time consumes them as the special time eludes them. Some go beyond ignoring the invitation. They attempt to murder it. Of course, their violence rebounds back on them. Their destructiveness becomes, in turn, their experience of being destroyed. They are out of the way. However, the feast is ready and it will happen.

> **Then he said to his slaves, 'The wedding is ready, but those invited were not worthy. Go therefore into the main streets, and invite everyone you find to the wedding banquet.'**

> **Those slaves went out into the streets and gathered all whom they found, both good and bad; so the wedding hall was filled with guests.**

What began as a select guest list becomes an indiscriminate one. The main roads bear universal traffic, and it is there that servants are sent. Whomever they find is invited. There is no ethnic, gender, age, or health requirement. There is not even a moral requirement. The wedding of the son has become a beggar's feast, a gathering of those who hear and accept the invitation.

> **But when the king came in to see the guests, he noticed a man there who was not wearing a wedding robe, and he said to him, 'Friend, how did you get in here without a wedding robe?'**

> **And he was speechless.**

However, the selection that did not occur at the time of invitation occurs at the wedding feast. It seems that the guests are the bride. They were not invited to witness a wedding; they were invited to be married to the son. They were not invited to observe; they were invited to participate. The requirement is a wedding garment, an eagerness to be united to the son.

This wedding garment signals a readiness to understand and act on Jesus' teachings. They must make them their own. They must marry the revelation and bear children, acts of justice, compassion, and love in the world. If they do not do this and are reduced to silence, a silence of incomprehension, they cannot remain at the feast. This is a wedding only for those who want to be married.

Then the king said to the attendants, 'Bind him hand and foot, and throw him into the outer darkness, where there will be weeping and gnashing of teeth.'

For many are called, but few are chosen."

If a guest comes to the wedding without the intention of marrying, he or she experiences the opposite. Instead of being within the wedding feast of light, they are outside in the darkness. Instead of eating with their hands and dancing with their feet, they are bound hand and foot. Instead of laughing and singing, they weep and gnash their teeth. They not only are excluded from the community, they live in bitter regret. Their own failures torment them.

A story that began as a judgment against the leadership of Israel ends as a cautionary tale to Christians. Just belonging to the Church is not enough. Hearing the call is a first step, but it is not the final condition. Each Christian is chosen as a bride for Christ, chosen to have intercourse with the revelation of God and be filled by God's grace. That means going beyond silent attendance. Hearing the call is easy; marrying the son is difficult.

Teaching

"Marrying the son" is a symbol for the Christian adventure of spiritual development. The Church carries the mystery of Jesus Christ. When one enters the Church through baptism, one enters into the mystery of Jesus Christ. But to enter into the mystery is not the same as marrying it, as being in full communion with it.

In the baptismal rite for children, the parents of the child are asked if they understand "the responsibility of training him (her) in the practice of the faith . . . to keep God's commandments as Christ taught us, by loving God and our neighbor"; the godparents are questioned about their readiness "to help the parents . . . in their duty" (Collegeville, Minn.: Liturgical Press, 2003). Thus entry into the Church implies growing into the teachings of Christ. The often timid "yes" of godparents is an indication that this growth process might not be central to their experience. After the ceremony they might be at a loss about what their "yes" entails. As important as baptism is, even adult baptism, it is only a first step.

This same emphasis on spiritual development can be approached from the idea of inherited faith. Within Christian religious traditions faith is presented as the gift of someone else. It comes from past generations, going all the way back to the apostles and Christ. It is given to each new generation in codified forms: Scripture, creeds, liturgies, dogmas, spiritual practices, etc. But, if the maxim "faith seeks understanding" is correct, the gift comes wrapped, and it must be opened by each new Christian. This act of reception—seeking understanding—entails mindfulness, a struggle to understand and live what this faith is all about. Faith may belong to the community and the tradition, but it is always appropriated or ignored by individuals.

Matthew points this out with his usual blunt options of destruction and salvation. Jesus concludes the Sermon on the Mount:

> Everyone then who hears these words of mine and acts on them will be like a wise man who built his house on rock. The rain fell, the floods came, and the winds blew and beat on that house, but it did not fall, because it had been founded on rock. And everyone who hears these words of mine and does not act on them will be like a foolish man who built his house on sand. The rain fell, and the floods came, and the winds blew and beat against that house, and it fell—and great was its fall! (Matt 7:24-27)

Hearing may be a beginning, but just hearing is a fatal end. Hearing must be followed by understanding, and understanding must lead to action. As Jesus states in John's Gospel: "If you know these things, you are blessed if you do them" (John 13:17).

Where does this leave us? What does this mean for people who call themselves Christian? Is the Church a two-tier system: those who take the teaching seriously and struggle with it and those who hear the words and glaze over? And if so, can these two types of Christians be institutionalized so clergy and religious are the serious ones and laity the mere hearers? Or does the division cut across all the organizational groups? There are clergy, religious, and laity who take it seriously and clergy, religious, and laity who do not let it into their conventional minds and their predictable behaviors. Church analysis has often separated sheep and goats, the serious and the lax, the seekers and the sitters, the good and the fallen away, the *cognoscendi* and the ignorant, etc.

However, I believe that the imperative of Christian revelation to "marry the son" should not lead to a division of people but to a respect for timing. People go deeper into their inherited faith at different times. Some are attracted in their youth, some in the middle years, still others in old age. Some come looking for succor after failure; some come in gratitude after success. Many come after death has knocked on their door and taken someone who ate at their table.

It is too facile to say that eventually all will put on the wedding garment. But it is too cynical to say that some certainly will not. We are all Christians, but the timetables of our lives are quite distinct and individual. If home is a place that when you have to go there they have to take you in, the Christian community is a place that when you are ready for more you are always welcomed.

For me the open invitation in the story is more crucial pastorally than the wedding garment. I am sure Matthew, great lover of dual outcomes that he is, would not agree. All are invited, good and bad alike. But good and bad are not final states; they are temporary designations. Once inside, you might come to learn that the Son finds you desirable. Even though you did not come with a wedding garment, the groom has one for you. He has chosen it with great love

Twenty-Ninth Sunday in Ordinary Time

Proper 24

Matthew 22:15-22

⁓

Avoiding Traps

A Spiritual Commentary

[T]he Pharisees went and plotted to entrap him in what he said. So they sent their disciples to him, along with the Herodians, saying, "Teacher, we know that you are sincere, and teach the way of God in accordance with truth, and show deference to no one; for you do not regard people with partiality. Tell us, then, what you think. Is it lawful to pay taxes to the emperor, or not?"

The Pharisees are insincere. They converse with Jesus only so they can trick him into saying something incriminating. They have constructed a plot that will bring Jesus down. That is why they have brought along the Herodians. The Herodians want to keep Herod in power, and Herod stays in power at the behest of the Romans. The Romans keep him there to collect the taxes. If Jesus speaks out against taxes, it will be sedition against Rome. The Herodians will witness this sedition, and Jesus will be subject to prosecution.

If, on the other hand, Jesus submits to the Roman tax, he will discredit himself as a prophet and lose his following. The people who follow Jesus hate Roman taxes for theological as well as economic reasons. If the land belongs to God, what right do Romans have to collect taxes on everything from the fruits of the earth and animals to the fishes in the sea? Also, this taxation was crushing, not a reasonable percentage but an intolerable burden that included bribery and cheating. If Jesus sanctioned the taxation laws, it would contradict much of his preaching and teaching.

This is the plot the Pharisees have hatched, the two-edged sword they hope will slice Jesus on either side. But the first move is to grease the skids. They excessively flatter Jesus as part of their strategy to get him to "speak plainly" and reveal himself. They comment on his truthfulness and his refusal to say what people want to hear, especially those in authority. Therefore he will not try to evade the question or pander to those in power. They want Jesus to talk in a vacuum, to completely disregard those to whom he is talking. After all, truth is independent of its audience, is it not?

> **But Jesus, aware of their malice, said, "Why are you putting me to the test, you hypocrites? Show me the coin used for the tax."**
>
> **And they brought him a denarius.**
>
> **Then he said to them, "Whose head is this, and whose title?"**
>
> **They answered, "The emperor's."**
>
> **Then he said to them, "Give therefore to the emperor the things that are the emperor's, and to God the things that are God's."**
>
> **When they heard this, they were amazed; and they left him and went away.**

The flattery may be right. Jesus may not gear his speech to a person's status. But he does gear his speech to a person's moral state, and the moral state of these Pharisees is malicious. They are hypocrites. What they say on the outside does not match the inside (see Matt 23:25-26). The thoughts of the heart and the words in the mouth are completely different. They are not interested in taxes and God. They are interested in undercutting the influence of Jesus.

Jesus does not have a Roman coin, so he asks for one. This alone is an indication of where he is coming from. The Pharisees have asked a duplicitous question, so now Jesus includes them in the answer. He makes them say that the coin belongs to the emperor. And then the text ends with the enigmatic injunction: "Give therefore to the emperor the things that are the emperor's, and to God the things that are God's."

However this saying is interpreted, it does not directly answer the question: "Is it lawful to pay taxes to the emperor, or not?" It may mean: since everything belongs to God, pay nothing to the emperor. It may mean that the emperor has a certain domain and God has a certain domain, and they should not be confused. It may mean: taxes to the emperor are permitted as long as they do not infringe on the laws of God. Whatever it means, it is not the end of a conversation but a catalyst for further dialogue. The talk in the text may end, but the talk among those who read the text continues.

Teaching

Although the social situation has changed radically since the time of Jesus and Matthew, there is still theological discussion over taxes. There are also still traps, and traps could arguably be added to that permanent pair of certitudes: death and taxes.

The first trap of this story is to sucker Jesus into an ego debate. If these Pharisees could manage this it would mean a duel of minds rather than a search for truth. The real question would be: did Jesus win?

A hundred years ago when I was a student studying theology, I was involved in a theological debate. The debate day was the feast of St. Thomas Aquinas. I do not remember what piece of traditional theological knowledge the debate revolved around, but I do remember the outcome. The team I was on won. Afterward, a friend of mine said to me, "You really got them."

I was both flattered and a little taken aback. I was glad we won, but I didn't see it as "getting" them. In the evaluation of my friend, the debate was not about the subject matter but about gaining or losing stature. It made me think, and eventually it led me to avoid theological argumentation. There had to be another way to think and talk theology. Making it the raw material of ego contests seemed to do it a disservice.

Although theological debating continued to be the way I was trained in school, I saw the downside of this style in pastoral settings. Once at a parish staff meeting at the end of the school year a director of religious education was so enthused with what happened to both teachers and students during the year that she gushed, "I think we should make becoming a catechist an eighth sacrament." The pastor, who was trained as I was, quickly spotted an adversary with an unorthodox position. "There are only seven sacraments. There can't be an eighth." His teeth showed. The enthusiasm of the director faded.

There had to be another way of talking about faith and theology.

I came across a Taoist story about a man in one boat who sees another boat coming at him through the fog. He yells at the man in the other boat to steer aside. But the boat continues to come at him. He then curses and swears and rages at the approaching boat. When the boat is close enough so he can see it clearly in the fog, he sees the boat is empty. There is no one in the boat. Immediately his anger calms, and he easily steers his boat away, avoiding collision.

To avoid the trap of theological exploration becoming an ego test, I tried to become an empty boat. From years of practice, I know one thing for sure. It is easier to fight to be right than it is to be empty to be true.

The second trap Jesus avoids is to be caught between false alternatives. These Pharisees wanted a yes or no. In some areas yes or no seems the right way to phrase things. "Is the light red?" "Is it raining?" "Are there fifty-two people here?" But other areas do not admit to either-or, yes-or-no thinking.

Most theological and spiritual matters are best approached by careful exploration and balanced evaluation. This is especially true when the interaction between the spiritual and social realms is being considered. This is more complex than a factual yes or no. Avoiding the trap of false alternatives is the first step toward more adequate discernment.

Jesus avoids the traps of ego baiting and false alternatives. So he does not best his opponents; he names their malicious and ego-driven game and refuses to play it. He also does not fall into the rules of "yes or no" they have constructed; instead he names the terms of discernment, the everlasting tension between God and the emperor. This has to be a better map for how to reflect on the complexities of faith and society.

Thirtieth Sunday in Ordinary Time

Proper 25

Matthew 22:34-46

━━◆◆◆━━

Returning to Love

A Spiritual Commentary

When the Pharisees heard that he had silenced the Sadducees, they gathered together, and one of them, a lawyer, asked him a question to test him. "Teacher, which commandment in the law is the greatest?"

Religious debates have a reputation for being acrimonious. The pursuit of truth is quickly abandoned and dueling egos are on display. Jesus had silenced the Sadducees, and so it is the turn of the next contenders, the Pharisees. One of them, a scholar of the law, decides to drag Jesus into the labyrinth of the law. He hopes to lose him there.

Scholars tell us that there were over six hundred laws. To choose one as the greatest was an immediate challenge to people who had chosen another as the greatest. And, after all, are not all the laws from God and so are not all of them of equal importance? A vigorous debate is in the offing, but it is a debate that never happens.

He said to him, "'You shall love the Lord your God with all your heart, and with all your soul, and with all your mind.' This is the greatest and first commandment.

And a second is like it: 'You shall love your neighbor as yourself.'

On these two commandments hang all the law and the prophets."

Jesus does not choose one commandment. And, in a sense, he does not choose two commandments. He articulates the underlying structure of love that all law and prophecy is built on. Living in relationships of love to God and neighbor is the essence. Love is also an interior reality, and so there is a stress on the inner space from which an action comes. If you can structure your awareness around love of God and neighbor, you will be able to make your way through the labyrinth of laws and the demands of the prophets.

Now while the Pharisees were gathered together, Jesus asked them this question: "What do you think of the Messiah? Whose son is he?"

They said to him, "The son of David."

He said to them, "How is it then that David by the Spirit calls him Lord, saying, 'The Lord said to my Lord, "Sit at my right hand, until I put your enemies under your feet?"' If David thus calls him Lord, how can he be his son?" No one was able to give him an answer, nor from that day did anyone dare to ask him any more questions.

They had asked Jesus a question and he responded, twisting their question to what he wanted to say. Now he asks them a question and they are unable to respond. It is a theological question, and it could appear to be a very fine point about scriptural exegesis. But it is a question with teeth.

A question about parentage is not idle. It is trying to locate a person in terms of power and influence. In the Gospel of Luke, when the people of Nazareth say about Jesus, "Is not this Joseph's son?" (4:22), they are looking for special treatment. He belongs to their village, and so he should do miracles there (see Luke 4:16-30, esp. v. 23). When in Mark they say, "Is not this the carpenter, the son of Mary and brother of James and Joses and Judas and Simon, and are not his sisters here with us?" (6:3), it is a put-down: "Who does this Jesus think he is? He is just an ordinary man like the rest of us in this village." Origins determine who you are, how you fit, and how much honor has to be given to you.

The Messiah is not David's son. In fact, David calls him Lord. Therefore, the Messiah is greater than David and is not completely bound to David's house. Jesus, the Messiah, will "rule over the house of David." He will not be one of the household. He will also reach outside the house of David and welcome Gentiles into the kingdom. The Jewish tradition does not test the Messiah; the Messiah tests the tradition. They will not weigh Jesus in the balance; he will weigh them.

Teaching

Whenever people look for guidance, commandments are sure to follow. Some will be of a general nature, like the Ten Commandments, outlining the obligations and responsibilities to God and neighbor.

These general norms will give birth to a thousand detailed behaviors. There will be regulations about how to pray in the morning and how to pray in the evening, how to bless food, how to give thanks for the first flower of the season, how to visit the sick, what to say to an unrepentant sinner, a proper prayer for every situation, etc. And these laws are everywhere, surrounding every human activity: worship, loans, gift giving, parenting, violence, theft, food, sexual intercourse, Sabbath rest, etc. Soon the human person is continually consulting a book of right actions to determine if he or she is following the law.

In this atmosphere, what becomes important is the behavior. Was the law meticulously and literally followed? Was the right thing done? If it was, then that is enough. *Doing* the law is what counts. However, is not what is lost in this exclusive emphasis on action the space within the human person where action comes from?

There is a story about a busy man:

> One day a certain man hurriedly headed out the door for work. In his path was his three-year-old son playing with blocks. The man patted the boy on the head, stepped over him, opened the door, and went outside. Halfway down the walk a guilt bomb exploded within him.
>
> "What am I doing?" he thought to himself. "I am ignoring my son. I never play with him. He'll be old before I know it." In the background of his thoughts he heard the pounding rhythms of "Cat's in the Cradle," Harry Chapin's ballad to lost fatherhood. He returned to the house and sat down with his son and began to build blocks.
>
> After two minutes, the boy said, "Daddy, why are you mad at me?"

It is not only what we do that counts but from where we do it. Our actions come from different places inside us. These different places affect the quality and effectiveness of what we do. We may think the inside is of little consequence as we push into the outer world, but it can change the impact of our actions. "Steeling ourselves" and doing something is not the same as "opening ourselves" and doing the same thing. Playing blocks out of guilt is not the same as playing blocks out of love, and the difference is quickly spotted, even by three-year-olds, especially by three-year-olds. Doing something because it is expected and doing something from the heart are two different experiences. Perhaps that is why Jesus, in Matthew's Gospel, insists that we forgive our brothers and sisters *from our heart* (see Matt 18:21-35, esp. v. 35).

There is another story about a woman who took her aging mother into her home. The mother had had a stroke and needed time to recover. The daughter was very solicitous and painstakingly attentive to her mother's every need. Nevertheless, a terrible fight broke out—over a hard-boiled egg. In the middle of the war of words, the mother stopped short and asked, "Why are you doing all this for me anyway?" (It was a question of "from what inner space" is all this care coming.) The daughter began to list reasons:

> I was afraid for her; I wanted to get her well; I felt maybe I'd ignored her when I was younger; I needed to show her I was strong; I needed to get her ready for going home alone; old age; and on and on. I was amazed myself. I could have gone on giving reasons all night. Even she was impressed.
>
> "Junk," she said when I was done.
>
> "Junk?" I yelled. Like, boy, she'd made a real mistake with that remark. I could really get her.
>
> "Yes, junk," she said again, but a little more quietly. And that little-more-quietly tone got me. And she went on: "You don't have to have all those reasons. We love each other. That's enough."
>
> I felt like a child again. Having your parents show you something that's true, but you don't feel put down—you feel better, because it *is* true, and you know it, even though you are a child. I said, "You're right. You're really right. I'm sorry." She said, "Don't be sorry. Junk is fine. It's what you don't need anymore. I love you." (Ram Dass and Paul Gorman, *How Can I Help?* [New York: Alfred A. Knopf, 1985] 191–92)

Her actions were coming from every possible place inside her except from the one place her mother needed to have them come from: the place of love.

Jesus is concerned about the inner state of the acting person. Mindless compliance with the dictates of multiple laws makes one an outer person—conforming but not understanding. For the outer person following the biblical law, "You shall not . . . put a stumbling block before the blind" (Lev 19:14) means not putting a rock in front of a blind person. But when the love of God and love of neighbor center you and inform your consciousness, you know that the law means not to take advantage of anyone's vulnerability or weakness. In touch with the inner configuration of divine and human love, you move among the laws knowing their ultimate purpose. So you know when to heed them, when to modify them, and when to dismiss them. You might even heal cripples against explicit Sabbath commandments (see Matt 12:1-13).

Thirty-First Sunday in Ordinary Time

Proper 26

Matthew 23:1-12

Practicing and Repenting

A Spiritual Commentary

Jesus said to the crowds and to his disciples,

Jesus has confronted the religious leaders directly. Now he is talking to the crowds and the disciples about the problems of the religious leaders and how they should relate to them. When the crowds and the disciples understand the gross failures of the religious authorities, they will glimpse the new community to which Jesus is calling them.

> **The scribes and the Pharisees sit on Moses' seat; therefore, do whatever they teach you and follow it; but do not do as they do, for they do not practice what they teach.**

Jesus recognizes that these authorities are formally the guardians of the Mosaic Law. Although Jesus has problems with how they interpret Scripture and how they apply it to contemporary experience, they hold the office that allows them to do it. Out of respect for the office, the crowds and the disciples should listen to them and observe what they say. Given Jesus' ongoing disagreements with religious authorities, this is a generous acquiescence.

But the crowds should not follow their example, for they have not integrated the Law into their behavior. What they preach is one thing, what they do is another. What follows is a list of actions that contradict what they know from the Law and tell people to do.

> **They tie up heavy burdens, hard to bear, and lay them on the shoulders of others; but they themselves are unwilling to lift a finger to move them.**

Doing the Law, even the sacrifices of the Law, is meant to be joyous. But they do not know the yoke that is "easy" (see Matt 11:30). In Hinduism there is a saying, "Some carry Scripture the way a donkey carries sandalwood. They know the burden but not the fragrance." These authorities know only the burden, impose it on people, and do not help them with it. But, of course, when it comes to themselves, there are always exceptions. The hardness of the Law is for other people; the exceptions are for them. Jesus once told them, "If one of you has a child or an ox that has fallen into a well, will you not immediately pull it out on a sabbath day?" (Luke 14:6). In other words, "If it was *your* ox or *your* daughter or son that fell into a pit on a 'no-work day of rest,' you'd take it out, wouldn't you?" These administrators of the Law think they are above it.

> **They do all their deeds to be seen by others; for they make their phylacteries broad and their fringes long. They love to have the place of honor at banquets and the best seats in the synagogues, and to be greeted with respect in the marketplaces, and to have people call them rabbi.**

The goal of all their works is increased social status. They parade their pieties to promote themselves. Phylacteries are long boxes containing Scripture. Although Scripture is meant to be internalized, meant to become the eyes of the heart, they wear Scripture on their clothing, on the fringes of themselves. This is because they live completely in the outer world of externals. The inner world where the love of God and neighbor (see Matt 22:37-39) originates and develops is completely ignored. In place of the love of God and neighbor, they love themselves and the honor they are able to manipulate others into giving them.

> **But you are not to be called rabbi, for you have one teacher, and you are all students. And call no one your father on earth, for you have one Father—the one in heaven. Nor are you to be called instructors, for you have one instructor, the Messiah.**

The community Jesus envisions will not work in this oppressive hierarchical way. The fact that they all have one Father in heaven and one Master, the Messiah (Christ), will mean that they will not use the honorific titles of Father and Master for one another. They will be an egalitarian community, all brothers and sisters under one Father and one Instructor.

> **The greatest among you will be your servant. All who exalt themselves will be humbled, and all who humble themselves will be exalted.**

This paradoxical language of reversal where the greatest are servants, the exalted are humbled, and the humble are exalted shows that the Christian community is the polar opposite of the community led by these authorities. But playing these categories off against one another indicates more than simple reversal. It undercuts any use of these categories. Greatest/servant and humbled/exalted might not be the best way to think about the community Jesus has in mind. This Christian community can live off a flow of grace where all are receiving from God and giving to one another. In this flow of abundance the striving for status, recognition, and exemption will not entice the imagination and tempt people as much.

Teaching

Pir Vilayat Khan, a Sufi teacher, once remarked: "Of so many great teachers I've met in India and Asia, if you were to bring them to America, get a house, two cars, a spouse, three kids, a job, insurance, and taxes . . . They would all have a hard time."

Sri Aurobindo confirms this in a different way: "Realization [of spiritual truth] by itself does not necessarily transform the being as a whole . . . One may have some light of realization at the spiritual summit of consciousness but the parts below remain what they were. I have seen a number of instances of that."

Finally, listen to a person who is in the aftermath of a great spiritual awakening. This was an awakening where all the spiritual truths of life were clear to him:

> Some months after all this ecstasy came a depression, along with some significant betrayals in my work. I had continuing trouble with my children and family, too. Oh, my teaching was fine. I could give inspired lectures, but if you talk to my wife, she'll tell you that as the time passed I became grouchy and as impatient as ever. I knew that this great spiritual vision was the truth, and it was there underneath, but I also recognized how many things didn't change at all. To be honest, my mind and personality were pretty much the same, and my neuroses too. Perhaps, it's worse, because now I see them more clearly. Here were these cosmic revelations and I still needed therapy just to sort through the day-to-day mistakes and lessons of living a human life.

Jesus generously acknowledged that the Pharisees could preach, but they could not practice. Then after detailing how corrupt their practice was, he preached the vision of the Christian community. But the text stops before Jesus tells us if his disciples and the crowds can practice the preached egalitarian community of love. Given the history of Christianity and our own contemporary experience, I believe that Christians might fall under the same sentence as the authorities who opposed Jesus.

Actually, no one can practice everything they preach. It seems that we can envision future human possibilities with great clarity. We can even have inner revelations and illuminations that powerfully show us a new way of being alive. But when we try to live it out, we bump into our conditioned personalities, our lifelong habits, and our history of succumbing to social pressures. As Khan points out, a holy teacher may fall from grace when dealing with family and taxes. And Aurobindo knows many illumined people whose illumination stays in the rare air of the upper brain. And who would think that you could still be grouchy after visiting the seventh heaven?

Therefore, practicing what you preach means repenting of your practice. We do not do it right. Therefore, we either give up the project of being transformed by our vision of what could be or go back to the drawing board. Going back to the drawing board entails purifying ourselves of the material that keeps us from living the truth we know and the vision we see. This repentance should not be a stigma, branding us as failures. It comes with the territory of following something large enough for you to betray. When you preach an egalitarian community of love under one God and one Master, keep the sackcloth and ashes handy.

Thirty-Second Sunday in Ordinary Time

Proper 27

Matthew 25:1-13

Lighting Your Own Lamp

A Spiritual Commentary

[Jesus said to the disciples:] "Then the kingdom of heaven will be like this. Ten bridesmaids took their lamps and went to meet the bridegroom. Five of them were foolish, and five were wise. When the foolish took their lamps, they took no oil with them; but the wise took flasks of oil with their lamps. As the bridegroom was delayed, all of them became drowsy and slept.

The kingdom of heaven is a state of inner consciousness and outer action that Jesus embodies and offers to his disciples. However, receiving this offering entails strenuous work. The disciples must transform their own conventional consciousness into the consciousness of Jesus and have the courage and creativity to act in accord with this new knowledge. If this happens, they become a new person: "if anyone is in Christ, there is a new creation" (2 Cor 5:17). This parable highlights a prominent ability of the "new person in Christ." But more prominently, it shows the failure to develop this ability.

From the very beginning the story is symbolic and surrealistic. Usually only one virgin, the wife to be, comes out to greet the bridegroom. Here there are ten, the number of fulfillment. But this will not be a story of fulfillment because we are immediately told five are wise and five are foolish. Of course, the bridegroom is Christ. But who will be the ones worthy to walk with him in union as his wife? Obviously, the wise virgins will be the ones the bridegroom will recognize and with whom he will walk arm-in-arm into the wedding feast. The five foolish will not be worthy to be wives. But what makes the wise wise and the foolish foolish?

But at midnight there was a shout, 'Look! Here is the bridegroom! Come out to meet him.'

At the darkest moment the Bridegroom Jesus arrives. All are asked to come out and meet him.

314

Then all those bridesmaids got up and trimmed their lamps. The foolish said to the wise, 'Give us some of your oil, for our lamps are going out.'

But the wise replied, 'No! there will not be enough for you and for us; you had better go to the dealers and buy some for your-selves.'

It is time for the lamps to give light so the virgins can see the bride-groom and the bridegroom can see the virgins. In the mutual seeing they will recognize one another. However, the lamps can only shine if they have oil. The foolish have no oil and ask to borrow some. The wise refuse for seemingly foolish reasons. They appear to be looking out for themselves rather than sharing with those in need. Instead, they suggest to the foolish that they "go . . . and buy" some oil. In this brief and enigmatic exchange the foolish display their foolishness and the wise their wisdom.

The truth of oil is: you have to have your own. Although everyone has a lamp of consciousness, each person must supply oil from their own living out of the teachings of Christ. One cannot develop spiritu-ally by taking the consciousness and action of another as your own. Each person has enough for himself or herself. Each person's path is singular, and each person's lamp (to update the metaphor) produces its own wattage. Or to change the metaphor as Isaac of Nineveh did, "There is a love like a small lamp, fed by oil, which goes out when the oil is ended; or like a rain-fed stream which goes dry, when rain no longer feeds it. But there is a love, like a spring gushing from the earth, never to be exhausted" (E. Kadloubovsky and G.E.H. Palmer, *Early Fa-thers from the Philokalia* [London: Faber and Faber, 1981]). The wise vir-gins are in touch with the inexhaustible river. So the oil is continuously replenished rather than consumed.

The foolish do not know the way of individually maturing into a new person in Christ. They only know the way of "going and buying," looking outside themselves for what they need. "Going and buying" is an image for an outer-directed consciousness. In the first feeding nar-rative in the Gospel of Mark (6:30-44), the disciples tell Jesus to send the crowds away so they can "go . . . and buy" (v. 36) food them-selves. When Jesus tells them to provide the food, the disciples say, "Are we *to go and buy* two hundred denarii worth of bread, and give it to [all these people] to eat?" (v. 37). Jesus directs them to their own inner resources, but they insist that the only place they can get food is outside themselves. While Jesus is giving the Samaritan woman a drink, the author of the Gospel of John tells the readers that "His disciples had *gone* to the city to *buy* food" (John 4:8). The foolish do not have their own resources and so are addicted to going elsewhere for sustenance. They cannot envision another way.

> **And while they went to buy it, the bridegroom came, and those who were ready went with him into the wedding banquet; and the door was shut.**
>
> **Later the other bridesmaids came also, saying, 'Lord, lord, open to us.'**
>
> **But he replied, 'Truly I tell you, I do not know you.' Keep awake therefore, for you know neither the day nor the hour."**

Right to the end the foolish think that it is Jesus, implored as Lord, who will open the door for them. They do not understand that the kingdom of heaven has been passed on to them, and the door only opens when they have the ability to open it for themselves. It is the lamp of their consciousness burning from the oil of their own dedicated lives that will open the door.

Earlier in the Gospel, Matthew has Jesus say:

> Not everyone who says to me, "Lord, Lord," will enter the kingdom of heaven, but only the one who does the will of my Father in heaven. On that day many will say to me, "Lord, Lord, did we not prophesy in your name, and cast out demons in your name, and do many deeds of power in your name?" Then I will declare to them, "I never knew you. (Matt 7:21-23)

It seems that they must learn to do the will of the Father for themselves. Prophesying, casting out demons, and doing many deeds (NAB: "mighty deeds"; Matt 7:22) *in Jesus' name* are not enough. Paradoxically, Jesus does not know these disciples who know so much about him. They value him so greatly and are so dependent on him that they have not learned to value themselves as the new bearers of his inner consciousness and outer action.

Matthew's concluding comment is a caution. We must stay awake to this truth of personally appropriating the teachings of Jesus and enacting them in our lives. The fact that the day and hour of the bridegroom's coming are unknown means that every day and every hour are the time of realization and integration. Others cannot do this for us.

Teaching

When they asked Gandhi what his message was, he said, "My life is my message."

St. Francis of Assisi is reputed to have said, "Preach the Gospel. Use words if necessary."

The last words of the Buddha to his followers were, "Be a light unto yourself."

Martin Luther cautioned, "You are going to die alone. You had better believe alone."

Angelus Silesius asked, "What good if Gabriel hails the Virgin and does not hail me?"

Anyone alive in the 1960s said, "Walk the talk."

In the Gospel of Thomas, Jesus says, "Whoever drinks from my mouth will become like me; I myself shall become that person, and the hidden things will be revealed to him" (GT 108).

There is a brief but hard-hitting story:

> A man knocks on a door. The voice from inside says, "Who is it?" The man says, "It is your countryman." The voice behind the door says, "There is no one here."
>
> The man wanders for a year, returns to the door, and knocks a second time. The voice from inside says, "Who is it?" The man says, "It is your brother." The voice behind the door says, "There is no one here."
>
> The man wanders for a year, returns to the door, and knocks a third time. The voice from inside says, "Who is it?" The man says, "It is you." The door opens.

How does Christ know us? He knows us when he looks into our face and sees himself.

There is a delicate balance in the following of Jesus. On the one hand, Jesus is the Lord and Master and remains so. Although his disciples may do greater things than he has, as the Gospel of John (14:12) predicts, they will do them in communion with his Spirit. No one will take the place of Jesus, and at the end of time it will be he who judges the living and the dead. The revelation of God in Jesus Christ is the fullness in which everything else will either fit or be cast aside. Quite simply, as the Book of Revelation says, Jesus is the "the Alpha and the Omega, the first and the last, the beginning and the end" (22:13).

Yet worshiping Jesus from afar with extravagant praise and petition is inappropriate. You cannot ride on his coattails. You must receive Christ into your self as a person would receive bread, put it into the mouth, and swallow it. Then Christ will be within you, building you up from the inside. Or you must receive Christ so thoroughly that he will awaken you to your identity as a child of God. Then as a child of God you would be on God's mission and the divine pleasure would flow through you. This integration of Christ into your life means transformation. When it is occurring, you will understand Paul's cry: "it is no longer I who live, but it is Christ who lives in me" (Gal 2:20).

This balance is difficult to maintain. We simultaneously say, "There is only one Lord and Master" (see commentary on the previous Sunday and Matt 23:9-10, NRSV and NAB) and "You are another Christ." But the parable of the ten virgins is very clear about where a prevalent danger lies. We know everything about him except the one thing necessary (see Luke 10:42): we are called to be him. But if we take into ourselves his truth so that it becomes our truth, then the door opens.

Thirty-Third Sunday in Ordinary Time

Proper 28

Matthew 25:14-30

~❦~

Fearing God

A Spiritual Commentary

[Jesus said to the disciples:] For it is as if a man, going on a journey, summoned his slaves and entrusted his property to them; to one he gave five talents, to another two, to another one, to each according to his ability. Then he went away.

This story has a basic literary structure that reflects a traditional theological framework. A superior character has servants. He gives the servants gifts and/or responsibilities and/or directions before he goes on a journey. When he returns, there will be an accounting. The servants will be evaluated in terms of how they performed.

God creates people, and gives them gifts and/or responsibilities and/or directions. After creation God departs to heaven, and people live on earth. But God "will return" at the death of the person, or through a special historical event, or at the end of time. Then there will be a judgment. Did the creature act in accord with the will of the Creator?

But this story develops this classic literary-theological structure in a special way. The usual format is that after the master has given instructions and departed, the first two will do it wrong, and the third will do it right. When it is done this way, the story ends on a comedic note, with the last servant in the ascendancy. However, in this parable the first two do it right and the third does it wrong. So the story ends on a tragic note, with the last servant losing everything and consigned to outer darkness.

In addition, usually those who have "a lot going for them" manage to do it wrong, and those who "have little going for them" get it right. The underdog comes out on top. However, in this parable those who have "a lot going for them" get it right and have more, and the one who "has little going for him" gets it wrong and loses even that.

So this is not a "feel good" story. It is a tragedy for the little guy. But the way the story is set up, the "one talent" character is not in competition with the "five talent" and "two talent" characters. Rather all three

319

servants are in competition with themselves. What will they do with what has been given them?

> The one who had received the five talents went off at once and traded with them, and made five more talents. In the same way, the one who had the two talents made two more talents.
>
> But the one who had received the one talent went off and dug a hole in the ground and hid his master's money.
>
> After a long time the master of those slaves came and settled accounts with them. Then the one who had received the five talents came forward, bringing five more talents, saying, 'Master, you handed over to me five talents; see, I have made five more talents.' His master said to him, 'Well done, good and trustworthy slave; you have been trustworthy in a few things, I will put you in charge of many things; enter into the joy of your master.'
>
> And the one with the two talents also came forward, saying, 'Master, you handed over to me two talents; see, I have made two more talents.' His master said to him, 'Well done, good and trustworthy slave; you have been trustworthy in a few things, I will put you in charge of many things; enter into the joy of your master.'
>
> Then the one who had received the one talent also came forward, saying, 'Master, I knew that you were a harsh man, reaping where you did not sow, and gathering where you did not scatter seed; so I was afraid, and I went and hid your talent in the ground. Here you have what is yours.'
>
> But his master replied, 'You wicked and lazy slave! You knew, did you, that I reap where I did not sow, and gather where I did not scatter? Then you ought to have invested my money with the bankers, and on my return I would have received what was my own with interest. So take the talent from him, and give it to the one with the ten talents.
>
> For to all those who have, more will be given, and they will have an abundance; but from those who have nothing, even what they have will be taken away. As for this worthless slave, throw him into the outer darkness, where there will be weeping and gnashing of teeth.'"

There are spiritual laws, predictable ways the Divine Spirit and the human spirit work together. These spiritual laws are not inexorable juggernauts, rolling along and crushing everything in their way. Nor are they as easily discerned as the laws governing physical reality, or the certainties we can count on in the psychological and social realms. Rather they are unfolding processes, mosaics that come together again and again in the same way, sequences that string inner states together in a peculiar logic. If people contradict these laws, they suffer negative consequences. If people conform to these laws, they are positively supported. Cooperate and grow; refuse and stagnate. This is just the way it is. This parable is about the unfolding of a spiritual law to the benefit of two servants and the detriment of a third.

One of these spiritual laws concerns how we cooperate with our initial gift of Spirit that is given from God. God gives Spirit to human creatures because God is, in essence, self-donation. It is God's nature to give. So when humans receive the Divine Spirit into their human spirits, they are encouraged to cooperate with it by giving it away. What has been freely received is freely given. As soon as this happens, the human creature is conscious of more Spirit. When Spirit is given away, it doubles. With the increase in Spirit comes the consciousness of how Spirit grows and a greater responsibility to make that happen. This is a process of spiritual enjoyment and this parable calls it, "entering into the joy of your master."

Spiritual enjoyment is what unfolds in the first two slaves (NAB: "servants" for "slaves"; Matt 25:14). They cooperate with the five and two talents by trading them, giving them to others as they had been given to them. This immediately, according to the spiritual law, increases Spirit. According to physical laws, when a person gives something away, they no longer have it. But according to spiritual laws, when Spirit is given away, there is more of it. There is more both for the one who receives Spirit and for the one who gives it. And this increase is not a fraction but a perfect double. Whole generates whole. In this way spiritual growth is not incremental but exponential. It doubles with each giving. Two talents become two more; five talents become five more. This is just the way it is.

The returned master knows this spiritual law and tells the two servants that this has happened because they have been "good and trustworthy" (NAB: "good and faithful" [25:21, 23]). Earlier in the Gospel, Matthew says, "In the same way, let your light shine before others, so that they may see your good works and give glory to your Father in heaven" (Matt 5:16). The reason people will be able to do this is because it is God's goodness working through his cooperating servants. The servants have been faithful to this goodness by imitating it. It was given to them, and they gave it to others. They have learned to cooperate with Spirit, and so greater responsibilities naturally follow. They are now sharing in the joy of the Master who originally gave Spirit to them and now has watched it grow and unfold.

The last servant does not discover the joy of giving Spirit. In fact, he does the one thing that is not permitted by spiritual laws. He tries to possess Spirit, burying it rather than giving it away. He has the mistaken idea that one talent can remain one talent if it is carefully hoarded. He tries to return it just as he was given it.

But according to the laws of the Spirit, it is a "use-it-or-lose-it" proposition, an all-or-nothing enterprise. If Spirit is given away, it increases proportionately. If it is buried, it decreases proportionately. One talent buried is not one talent saved. It is one talent lost. The master, who knew the law of spiritual enjoyment, also knows the flip side of that law. So he has the one talent taken from the "wicked and lazy slave." He gives it to the servant who has ten talents because Spirit lives only by growing. It cannot stand alone. The spiritual law is unfolding and some are rising and some are falling. This is just how it is.

The master calls the third servant "wicked and lazy" which is the exact opposite of "good and faithful." But the servant himself names his motivation as "fear." His perception is that the master is so demanding that he wants increase without any contribution; the slave says to him that he is "a harsh man, reaping where you did not sow, and gathering where you did not scatter." In terms of the story this picture is not correct. The Master has initially given the talents, so he has planted and scattered. Has the third servant fantasized a master and then quaked at the product of his own imagination?

But the master does not argue with the picture of him that the third servant paints. Rather, he repeats it, emphasizing that this is what the servant knew. But then he draws a different conclusion. Knowledge of the harsh and demanding rules should have spurred him into effective action and not paralyzed him with ineffective fear. Here is what goes on, and there are no exceptions. Those who have and make more get rich. Those who have little and are not entrepreneurial have that little taken from them. They are so useless they are out of the game completely. Their failure to "get it" puts them in outer darkness where they weep over their fate and gnash their teeth in regret.

The master in this story has no compassion. But we all know the social world in which he is wheeling and dealing. It is the brutal and no-excuse world of finance. What is shocking and, at first, difficult to understand is that the spiritual realm may be structured according to the same no-nonsense principles.

Teaching

The Gospel of Matthew is filled with dire consequences. If people do not respond to Jesus and his teachings correctly, they are in for a considerable amount of trouble. They can be tied hand and foot and cast outside into exterior darkness where they weep and gnash their teeth (see Matt 22:13; 25:30). They can be handed over to torturers until their entire debt is paid, a debt they will never be able to pay (see Matt 18:21-35). They can be put to the sword and their cities burned (see Matt 22:7). Finally, they can fry in eternal fire (see Matt 13:24-30).

Certainly these images fuel our fantasies of hell. All people know physical pain and, from the pain we know, we can imagine what the pain must be like in chronic situations, chronic to the extreme of eternal. Also all people know social rejection and, from the exclusion we know, we can imagine the loneliness of being completely ostracized. Flannery O'Connor once said she created grotesque caricatures to catch the attention of the blind and deaf. She might have learned from Matthew. A lake of everlasting fire definitely makes you sit up and take notice.

Of course, these catastrophes happen to people in the stories. But for those reading the stories they are meant as salutary warnings. If self-interest motivates you at all, you should avoid the attitudes and behaviors that lead to these terrible punishments. Although this is the manifest objective of the story, I suspect it has the latent function of paralyzing people with fear.

Instead of being galvanized to imitate the first two servants, we find ourselves quaking and wondering if we have dug the hole deep enough to bury the single talent we have. The startling end of the narrative exacerbates the one-talent timidity that lurks in every person. When the image of God as a demanding master "who gathers but did not scatter and reaps but did not sow" is taken seriously, it plays into too much psychological and social "hardness." We know this type of master: the boss or banker from hell.

There are many ways to approach the psychological and spiritual state of fearing God. Some say that "[t]he fear of the LORD is the beginning of wisdom" (Prov 9:10); fear of the Lord is the "beginning of wisdom" but not the end. Fearing God gets God on the radar screen. Once there—and we explore the transcendent more and more—we realize that the "Almighty" (e.g., Gen 17:1) is a Father (e.g., Mal 2:10, Matt 5:16), the terror of divine immensity and power gives way to the deeper revelation of love.

Others point out the contradictions in the Gospels between gentleness and violence. Matthew uses Isaiah to describe Jesus as one who "will not break a bruised reed or quench a smoldering wick" (Matt 12:20; cf. Isa 42:3). If a candle was almost out, Jesus would not snuff it. If a reed was so badly damaged it was almost separated, Jesus would not deliver the final blow and break it. Jesus never contributed to death, even when death was imminent. He always gave life. Is this the same Son of God who told stories of divine violent retributions? If we have to choose between the punishing God who, like it or not, generates fear and the gentle God who encourages love, roll the dice and choose love.

Still others see the images of punishment and destruction as writ-large pictures of human freedom. They are not the result of literal actions of a separate Divine Being. They are imaginative portraits of the blessings and burdens of human freedom. If people respond to the divine invitation, all goes well, even better than expected. If people do not respond, all goes badly, even worse than expected. The slogan is: "Avoid God as creator: meet God as judge."

But these pictures of punishments should not be seen as fulminating threats from a personal Divine Being. Rather the pictures of loss are simple predictions. As the Bible stresses repeatedly in anthropomorphic images, God is faithful to God's self. There is a nature to spiritual reality. It works according to certain patterns, sequences, and operations. Correspond with them and grow. Contradict them and flounder.

What we really fear, however, may not be the demands and harshness of inevitable spiritual dynamics. What we may really fear is the edge of our own freedom. And what we must learn is what Odysseus learned in Nikos Kazantzakis' *The Odyssey: A Modern Sequel* (New York: Simon and Schuster, 1958):

> Erect on Freedom's highest peak
>   Laughter leaps.

Christ the King

Proper 29

Matthew 25:31-46

⁓❦⁓

Caring Without Calculation

A Spiritual Commentary

[Jesus said to the disciples:] "When the Son of Man comes in his glory, and all the angels with him, then he will sit on the throne of his glory. All the nations will be gathered before him, and he will separate people one from another as a shepherd separates the sheep from the goats, and he will put the sheep at his right hand and the goats at the left.

This is a picture of the judgment at the end of the world. It is taking place in a royal heavenly court, complete with angels and glorious throne. There is a certain amount of suspense in it. Ingrained in human thinking is the connection between finishing and evaluating. When things are over, we have to judge them. Although the tender ego in us fears evaluations, we know they must happen. The fact of judgment is a given.

What are not clear are the criteria of judgment. What principles and norms govern the evaluation? The Son of Man begins, in true Matthean form, by dividing the assembled nations in two. The sheep are on the right, the favored side. The goats are on the left (they should begin to worry now). But what is the principle of division? According to the Son of Man, what makes life a success and what makes life a failure?

Then the king will say to those at his right hand, 'Come, you that are blessed by my Father, inherit the kingdom prepared for you from the foundation of the world; for I was hungry and you gave me food, I was thirsty and you gave me something to drink, I was a stranger and you welcomed me, I was naked and you gave me clothing, I was sick and you took care of me, I was in prison and you visited me.'

Then the righteous will answer him, 'Lord, when was it that we saw you hungry and gave you food, or thirsty and gave you

> something to drink? And when was it that we saw you a stranger and welcomed you, or naked and gave you clothing? And when was it that we saw you sick or in prison and visited you?'

> And the king will answer them, 'Truly I tell you, just as you did it to one of the least of these who are members of my family, you did it to me.'

These criteria of judgment may come as a shock, but they have not been recently formulated. These sheep are entering a kingdom that was envisioned at the foundation of the world. The Father of the Son of Man-King is blessing them with this inheritance. The reason is: they were good to his Son.

The Son of Man-King lived among them and was often in need or in trouble. These "sheep" ministered to him, providing food, drink, shelter, clothing, medicine, and companionship. This is the "open Sesame" into the kingdom of the Father. The reader may be surprised by these criteria. What about keeping the Law? Or making great art? Or being a peacemaker? Is all that counts how you treated the Son of Man-King?

Even the righteous sheep are confused. They cannot remember seeing the Son of Man-King in these distressful conditions. They are being rewarded for actions they are not sure they did. But the Son of Man-King reassures them that he is so connected to his followers, even the least of the brothers and sisters, that when they performed those services for them, they performed them for him.

> Then he will say to those at his left hand, 'You that are accursed, depart from me into the eternal fire prepared for the devil and his angels; for I was hungry and you gave me no food, I was thirsty and you gave me nothing to drink, I was a stranger and you did not welcome me, naked and you did not give me clothing, sick and in prison and you did not visit me.'

> Then they also will answer, 'Lord, when was it that we saw you hungry or thirsty or a stranger or naked or sick or in prison, and did not take care of you?'

> Then he will answer them, 'Truly I tell you, just as you did not do it to one of the least of these, you did not do it to me.'

> And these will go away into eternal punishment, but the righteous into eternal life."

An eternal Kingdom is matched by an eternal fire. This too has been prepared from the foundation of the world for the devil and his angels. But it will also accommodate the accursed goats. They warrant this final home because the Lord was in all these dire circumstances and they did not help. They did nothing.

As the sheep before them, the goats are confused by this judgment. In fact, they ask the same kind of question as the sheep: "Lord, when was it that we saw you hungry or thirsty or a stranger or naked or sick or in prison, and did not take care of you?" And the King replies with the same kind of answer—with a significantly inserted "not." The King replies, "Truly I tell you, just as you did not do it to one of the least of these, you did not do it to me." "Least of these" (NAB: "least ones"; [v. 45]) is emphasized because the goats are very accustomed to helping the great ones.

Although the confusion of the sheep and goats is the same, and the Son of Man-King's answers are the flip sides of the same criterion, quite different dynamics are at work. The sheep did not see the King or the "Judge of All Things," the Son of Man. They just attended to the physical and social needs of hurting people without considering their status or their capacity to repay them, either with money or with favors. The goats did not see the Son of Man-King. But if they had known it was he, you can be assured that they would have helped. The Son of Man-King has the resources, both money and influence, to repay. This would have been a good deed that would eventually do them well. "If we had known it was you, O King, and not some miserable nobody, of course we would have helped." The sheep care without calculation and the goats care with calculation.

Teaching

The Christian ideal is for spirituality and ethics to form a unified whole. Followers of Jesus love their neighbor from their soul, which is filled with the Spirit of God. The more they cultivate their relationship with God, the more they care for their neighbor. And the more they care for their neighbor, the more they open to the presence and influence of the Spirit. This intertwined, reciprocal, mutual relationship is never to be broken.

But when we look at it from the side of ethics, how do we discern the presence of Spirit? Although Christian ethics may have philosophic rationales, the right actions are ultimately driven by the spiritual communion of the acting person with God. This gives the actions certain qualities. If these qualities are present in the caring action, we make a theological surmise that the Spirit is the ultimate author. So, from the point of view of ethics, we look at the qualities of the actions and discern the presence or absence of Spirit.

When we compile the gifts of the Spirit (based on Isa 11:2-3) and the fruits of the Spirit (based on Gal 5:22-23), we have spiritual qualities for ethical actions that are myriad. But recently I have focused on three qualities I think betray the influence of Spirit: proactive, uncalculating, and unobtrusive.

When actions are proactive, the Spirit is active. The golden rule begins, "Do unto others . . ." (traditional wording; cf. Matt 7:12). The idea is to be the first. Do not wait. Act. Often if we wait, we find a million reasons not to do the one thing that certainly needs doing. We engage in an internal monologue about the merits of our actions and speculate about their effectiveness. Of course, we must consider at length how much risk there is to us and our status. By the time we have sorted it all out, the moment and opportunity have passed.

I think some cautions are necessary to consider. But by far most of our interior weighing and worrying function only to delay the right action. When the Spirit is present we override the mental tapes of hesitancy to say the words of care and extend the hands of care. In the Gospels, the Spirit is often associated with the word, "immediately."

When actions are uncalculating, the Spirit is also exerting influence. As the Matthean judgment scene suggests, there is a tendency to help those who can help us. In the movie *As Good As It Gets,* a writer who is neurotically attached to a waitress at his favorite restaurant does her son a favor so she won't quit her job and leave him in other hands. Then he asks her for a favor, to accompany him and a friend on a trip. She says to him, "You think I owe you." He responds, "Is there any other way to see it?"

The Gospels know this aspect of our intentions. If we give to those who will give back, and lend to those who will repay us, and do good to those who will do good to us, what grace (Spirit) is there in that? (e.g., see Matt 5:42-46). This type of reciprocity is predictable and ungraced. As the Gospel says, even sinners do this (Luke 6:32).

However, there is a universal type of caring action. It does not regard the status of the person cared for or their potential to return in kind either now, in the near future, or in the far future. It is, if you will, a 360-degree, steady caring. It cares for those who are above the caring person, those on the same level as the caring person, and those below the caring person.

A friend of mine, known for her care and advocacy for poor and vulnerable people, once confided in me that she sent a letter of care and support to a high-ranking clergyman, a clergyman who had been active in persecuting her. Entrenched in the quid-pro-quo mentality, I asked her, "Do you think he will change his mind about you?" She smiled, "I didn't do it for that reason. But you're right. He will probably project that motivation on it." Her care was uncalculated, as universal as Spirit.

Finally, Spirit gets things done without calling attention to itself. It is unobtrusive. Some religious hypocrites blow trumpets, stand on street corners (Matt 6:5) and look glum (see Matt 6:16) so all will know serious material is "coming down." We may avoid this extreme ostentation, but we know the mental tape that drives them. There is a deep need to have our right actions applauded, even publicized. And we cannot resist talking about what some efforts cost us—in terms of time, money, and irritation. It is hard to imagine not taking advantage of every opportunity to promote ourselves.

But when Spirit is suffusing an action, the ultimate energy is coming from God and we are riding it into the world. The need to talk about the struggles of cooperation is not as strong as the need to be thankful to the enabling presence. Another friend of mine once visited an ashram of a famous spiritual teacher. Upon returning, she called to tell me that she had met the "real thing." She meant a genuine spiritual community with a genuine spiritual leader. When I asked her why she thought this, she told me of the following brief exchange.

She told the teacher that the community he had gathered around himself was truly remarkable. Without missing a beat, he said, "Everything you see here is because of the grace of my grandmother."

After telling me of this she paused and then said, "You see, Jack, he had no need to promote himself, no need to call attention to his abilities. He knew that they were supported and directed from elsewhere." When caring just happens and no one is claiming the care, the Spirit is active.

So if I could interview the sheep lounging around in their recently inherited kingdom and ask them how they managed to find themselves in these excellent digs, I imagine them saying, "We just cared for every person we met, immediately, without calculation, and it was no big deal."

Scripture Index